RAMBLES IN EIRINN

WILLIAM BULFIN

When I behold your mountains bold–
    Your noble lakes and streams–
A mingled tide of grief and pride
    Within my bosom teems.
I think of all your long dark thrall–
    Your martyrs brave and true;
And dash apart the tears that start–
        We must not *weep* for you
            Dear land–
        We must not weep for you.
            – *Ó'Hagan.*

ROBERTS WHOLESALE BOOKS LTD

Published by Roberts Wholesale Books Ltd
Unit 12
Benson Street Enterprise Centre
Hanover Quay
Dublin 2

First published in 1907

186079 010 0

Printed by ColourBooks Ltd, Dublin

TO THE READER.

These pages are the outcome of about three thousand miles of touring within the four seas of Ireland. They were written more or less hurriedly, as opportunity offered, here and there on the road, at irregular intervals, generally out of reach of books of reference; and with the sole object of sharing the writer's thoughts and feelings with certain Irish exiles on the other side of the world.

It never occurred to me at first that Irish people at home would take any special interest in my efforts to describe the things I saw and express the things I felt : and even when some of the literary men of Irish Ireland urged me to publish the "Rambles" in an Irish newspaper, I imagined that their judgment had been obscured by their friendship. Nevertheless I acted on their suggestion, and it would be more than churlish on my part not to acknowledge the keen gratification I have felt over the reception given to the articles as they appeared in "The United Irishman," and afterwards in "Sinn Fein." When they appeared in "The New York Daily News" their reception was also most cordial, and from many parts of the United States I received kindly greetings from people I had never met, suggesting that the series should be published in book form. Like suggestions came from Ireland and from the Argentine Republic. The present publishers came forward, and this volume is the result.

I do not offer it to the public without diffidence, for I am conscious of its defects. Yet I desire not to apologise for its philosophy nor for the spirit in which it was produced. All I care to say for it is that it was written after seventeen crowded years of exile, and that the heart of the writer was in the writing.

And even if the pleasure of writing it was at times not unclouded, there is nothing but gladness and pride in the thought of the friendships it has won for me at home and abroad amongst men and women who are thinking and working for Ireland.

W. B.

Derrinlough, March, 1907.

CONTENTS.

CHAPTER I.

Returned from over seas—Trial spin on my Wexford
  wheel—The Summer Glory of Ireland—Across the
  Brosna River—Skirting North Tipperary—Roscrea and Mount St. Joseph—Interviewing a
  Beggar-man—Hay-making.   1

CHAPTER II.

Around Lough Gill—Knocknarea—Sligo—The Lake
  —The Valley of O'Rourke—Drumahaire—
  O'Rourke's Table.   18

CHAPTER III.

On the Connacht Plains—A Land Laid Desolate—
  Rath Croghan of Meave and Dathi—Two Men
  Raving on a Wall—The Sheep-crooks—The
  Gentry and the People—Sketches of a certain Re-
  gatta   45

CHAPTER IV.

Through Royal Meath—From Uisnach to Tara—
  Poundeth Westmeath Caulcannon—Rochfort-
  bridge and the Rochforts—Lough Ennel—Lonely
  Dun-na-Sciath—The Irish Rain—The Drovers—
  Trim—A Stranger by the Fire—A Few Remarks
  on Grazierdom—Tara Rises into View—The Ap-
  proach—Up the Storied Hill at Last—Beside the
  Stone of Destiny.   73

CONTENTS.

CHAPTER V.

Tara of the Kings—The Croppies' Grave—The Lia Fail—The Traces of Vanished Greatness—Cormac Mac Art—The Flight of Diarmuid and Grania—The Cursing of Tara—The Royal City as it was. 96

CHAPTER VI.

Into Ulster—The Eastern and Western Routes—The Irish Railways—Belfast—Nationalism and Unionism—Religious Intolerance—The Forum at the Custom House Steps—The Orange Drum and the Drummers—Belfast's Claim to be the Capital of Ireland—An Inheritance of Spite. 113

CHAPTER VII.

Derry—A Lumpy City—A City of Contrasts—Politico-Religious War—Industrial Derry—Derry of the Sieges—The Walls—Derry of Columcille—The Saint—The Exile—His Return—Royal Aileach—The old Fortress of Niall the Great—A Superb Picture—The Sleeping Heroes. 133

CHAPTER VIII.

Through Tir-Owen—Dungannon—The Kinel-Conail—Mountcharles—Donegal—The Four Masters—The Clan Conail—The Humour of Donegal—A Woman who was able to Take Care of Herself—Ballyshannon—The Royal Irish Constabulary in Action—Belleek—By the Shores of Lough Erne to Enniskillen—Back into Leinster. 153

CHAPTER IX.

From Dublin to the Slieveblooms—A Glance at "Conciliated"—Rathcoole—The Humours of "Conciliation"—Newbridge College—Irish Cattle

CONTENTS.

PAGE

—A Motor Cyclist comes to Grief—Irish Ireland
Marching—The Curragh of Kildare—Knockallen,
Finn and the Fianna—The Gibbet Rath—Bridgid
the Great and the Neglected—A Pleasant
Country Side—" More Conciliation "—Monastere-
van—An Irish Irelander. 17ʃ

CHAPTER X.

Monasterevan—Transit in Ireland—Afforestation—
The Motor Cyclist Again—Mountmellick—The
Smiling Midlands—Clonaslee—The Motor Cyclist
Comes to Grief and Comments on Irish Road-
Making—The Armed Garrison—Kinnitty.   ...   201

CHAPTER XI.

The Valley of the Lower Shannon—From Aughrim
to Limerick—Mountain and Lowland Children—
The Rim of the World—Nenagh Town—Dairy
Farming—The Unharnessed, Idle, Beautiful
Shannon—An Exclusive Bodach—Upholding
First Principles—Killaloe—Ancient Kincora—
Brian and Mahon—Castleconnell Rapids—Lime-
rick in the Gloaming.   216

CHAPTER XII.

Limerick the Heroic—The City that Takes Life as it
Comes—Industrial Limerick—A Queerly Placed
Monument on Sarsfield Bridge—The Siege—
Sarsfield's Raid to Ballyneety—The Old Walls—
" The Black Gate "—Sarsfield's Fatal Ingenuous-
ness—The O'Connell Monument—George's St.—
St. John's—St. Mary's—The Founder of Limerick
—The Limerick Dogs—Garryowen and " Johnny
Collins "—Gerald Griffin—Lord Dunraven and
the Game of Poker.   234

CONTENTS.

CHAPTER XIII.

PAGE

Through Wexford—The Gael and the Gall—Wexford
History as Told in the Surnames—Enniscorthy—
Vinegar Hill—Forgetful Ireland—Wexford's
Gaelic Earnestness—A Distinguished Irishman's
Position in his own Country if he Happens to be
a Patriot—Labour and Education—The Slaney's
Sylvan Beauty—On to Ferry Carrick—Two Land-
marks of our History—Into Wexford Town. ... 258

CHAPTER XIV.

Wexford Town—No Commercial Shoneenism Worth
Noticing in Wexford—The Main Street—Father
Kavanagh, the Historian of '98—Industrial Wexford—Doyle's—Pierce's—Back to Enniscorthy
and Away.   281

CHAPTER XV.

In the Valley of the Inny—A Country which Drops
into Poetry—The Idle Rivers of Ireland—Barons-
town—Abbeyshrule—The Tinker Tribe—A Not-
able Discussion upon the Dramatic Work of Mr.
W. B. Yeats—The Country of the " Rising of the
Moon "—" Leo " Casey's Singing River—" Leo's
Songs."—By " Derry Heather " and " Leafy
Tang."   290

CHAPTER XVI.

A Beautiful District—A Tower of Mystery—A Jewish
Pedlar—A Descendant of the Impenitent Thief—
Into Goldsmith's Country—" Sweet Auburn "—A
Goldsmithian Stone Breaker—A Discussion by
the Roadside about Goldsmith and " Leo " Casey
—The Three Jolly Pigeons—On Baskin Hill ...   305

CONTENTS.

CHAPTER XVII.

Through Dublin and Wicklow—A Ride to Luggala— Killiney—The Vale of Shanganagh—The Self-Glorification of John Maupas, deceased—The Scalp — Enniskerry — Glencree -- A Mountain Herdsman—A Large Inheritance—Lough Bray—The Sources of the Liffey—The Sally Gap—The Glens—Wild Luggala—Back Through the Night. 322

CHAPTER XVIII.

Through Ossory to the County of Kickham—Beside the Infant Nore—The Motor Cyclist Once More Appears—An Excursion into Polemics—A Historic District—Aghaboe of Virgilius—Dunamase of Rory O'Moore—Durrow—In the District of "Knocknagow"—Kickham in Poetry and Prose —One of the Homes of Tipperary.   338

CHAPTER XIX.

Cork—The Valley of the Lee—A Tolerably Old City —Its Patron Saint—Finn Barr the Holy—Gougane Barra—Mediæval Cork—Patrick Street— The Covered Car—On Patrick's Bridge—The Irish Dress—Father Mathew—Industry and Education—" The Bells of Shandon "—Father Prout —" Paddy's Market "—The Cove of Cork   ...   359

CHAPTER XX.

Over the Galtees—From Tipperary to Mitchelstown— A Select Driver—Up the Hills—The Golden Vale —Cashel of Cormac—A Mountain Ravine—The Glen of Aherlow—The Select Driver's Authority is set at Naught—Through Aherlow—A Climb to the Top of Galtymore—An Intoxicating Moment—Mitchelstown—Fermoy—Mallow of Davis.   384

CONTENTS.

CHAPTER XXI.

PAGE

North-Western Leinster—By Cloghan and Ballina-
houn to Athlone—On the Bridge of Athlone—
Moate—The Stranger Stops the Work of a whole
District—The Rural Beauty of Westmeath—Uis-
nach Hill—Horseleap—Ballymore—The Inny
River—Into Annaly—The Delirium of Speed—
Back Through Offaly—A Post Car Ride.   ...   402

CHAPTER XXII.

Clonmacnoise—"Pattern" Day—The Ancient Home
of St. Ciaran—The Whispering Arch—The Cross
of Clonmacnoise—Spanning the Cross—St. Ciaran's Oratory—Other Ruins—The Round Towers
far Older than the Churches—Story of St. Ciaran
—King Diarmuid and the Saint—Love-making
Amidst the Ruins—The Blind Piper—Home
Through the Evening Glory.   425

CHAPTER XXIII.

L'ENVOI.

The Winter—A Farewell Ride Over Frozen Roads—
The Silences of Erin—The Mountain Sheep—
Sliding—An Affair of a Lasso—Coursing—"Come
Back Again."   440

PREFACE

THE man whom Bulfin loved, the man whom he
reverenced, the man whose life and work formed an
ever-fresh topic in intimate letter and delightful speech,
wrote a characteristic letter some years ago : " Bulfin
is on his way to Ireland. Come. Make arrangements
to be in readiness. Let nothing stand in the way.
Come." A week later the telegraph flashed : " Che
Buono is here. Wishes to meet you. Come at once."
With a mind full of joyous anticipations I trained for
Dublin. Within twenty-four hours my heart was given
into the keeping of one of the greatest and noblest men
of our generation : a surrender that was dight with the
richest joys my life has known. I went with a foretaste
of pleasure ; I left him feeling and knowing that the
race of Gaelic heroes was not extinct, that a truer Gentleman, a more manly Man, did not breathe. Little respect
for sentimentality have I ; still smaller store did I set
upon that polite reticence which fears to give vent to
its inmost feelings. Hence I rejoice in saying that I
loved William Bulfin.

We were not many minutes in the smokeroom of
that Dublin hotel when I caught my first glimpse of that
man, whose last letter, received so short a time before
his departure to a Better World, was so full of hope
and of cheerfulness as to make me doubt the terrible
and poignant truth of his death. In a flashing glance
my measure was taken by those keen kindly eyes. As
he strode across the room his magnificent stature and
masculine beauty were accentuated by his free, graceful

gait. My first impression was summed up : " A
cavalry officer." But the thoughtfulness of his face
and the total absence of the rigidity and swagger of that
military unit banished the thought. Withal I was convinced that he spent many a long hour on horseback,
for the easy swing of his legs could have come from no
other source. There was not the faintest suggestion of
that peculiar cast of features, that subtle nuance in
speech and in bearing, which are comprised in the word
" horsey." As he stood erect to the extent of some
six feet and more, with his hands clasped behind his
back, the slant of his shoulders, the clean-cut figure,
brought to your mind the long straight, strong spar of
a Norwegian pine. He looked like a lance in rest. As
he coursed from subject to subject, in vivid picturesque
talk, he brought a breeze of fresh air into the smoke-
coloured room. His illustrations were as vivid and as
pat as his vocabulary was choice and copious. It has
been my good fortune to have known courtly men and
refined gentlewomen, but none possessed a more beautiful urbanity, a more flattering deference, than William
Bulfin. He was a Chesterfield, with soul and heart
added. In any crowd he was a conspicuous figure ; in
Court he might have taken his place with the most
polished. One of the most distinguished of Irish gentlewomen, a graft of a long-rooted aristocratic tree, wrote
me of her first meeting with my true friend : " We were
seated in the open discoursing of what is nearest all
our hearts—Ireland, her rights and wrongs—when Mr.
Bulfin arrived in our midst on his bicycle. He is all
you say and more. A more charming man I never met.
To Mr. Bigger he addressed most of his speech, for he
seemed shy ! Strange that in a heroic frame ! He
brought with him the largeness, the freshness, and the
laughter of Nature. In such a presence nothing seemed
to matter, nothing seemed little, everything was possible
to Ireland, nothing could come amiss to the Gael. His
optimism is contagious. In the fight for Gaeldom he

must prove a tower of strength. His stay was short, too short. When he departed the landscape seemed bereft of interest." Mr. Bigger epitomised his delight on a post-card in words equally laudatory. William Bulfin's letter was couched in terms of boyish delight. There must be a veil drawn over these intimate confidences, for the living worthies might not care to see them in cold print. Che Buono gloried in meeting every man, every woman, every child who worked for Ireland. He never tired of hymning the praises of every sprig, of every stone, of every bank, of every wall which deflected or impeded the onrushing tide of Anglicisation.

I had noticed a certain restlessness, an ill-concealed nervousness and anxiety, during our first meeting. When on the homeward way, our mutual friend conveyed an apology for the " seeming hurry and discourtesy," as Mrs. Bulfin's illness made him a bundle of feverish anxieties. Two days later in O'Connell Street, a firm hand was laid on my shoulder and a cheery voice greeted me : " I'm delighted to meet you again, Sean Ghall. Forgive my late churlishness." Then we fronted His radiant face was good to look upon. The naked truth I uttered in declaring that the evening had been fraught with pleasure. " As for the alleged churlishness you were cordiality personified. From your voice I realise now that all is well with your lady and I rejoice thereat. I am not married ; but I have a mother, so I understood." He wheeled round, gripped my hand until I winced, saying : " Thank you sincerely, my friend. I knew you would." We walked through the Dublin streets chatting gaily and seriously, by turns. At last he invited me to lunch in an hotel. Loudly I laughed. " You don't seem to realise this is my holiday time, Che Buono. I have had breakfast but an hour ago." Heartily enjoying our mutual banter I entered and had a cup of coffee. I narrate this little incident because it gave me an insight into other compartments of Bulfin's mind. Long and lovingly he spoke of the nobility of his wife's character. " Whatever I am or hope to be, Sean Ghall, I owe to her ; she has been my support, my comforter, my sunshine, my guide, and my pride. Years ago I should have been submerged but for her stout heart and her prayerful soul." Suddenly he became silent. " You will forgive me, my friend, for speaking thus. I never breathed such sacred confidences to mortal before. Your manner made me open my heart unknowingly. Don't utter a word of what I have said whilst I live." That confidence I have respected. In the memorable years spanned by our correspondence no single letter reached me without some golden word anent that lady His very last epistle proved that he remained the proud, fond, and reverential Lover. Assuredly he was a man of deep and tender feeling.

Suddenly he shunted the conversation to another siding. In a moment we were on the moonlit Pampas. My sides ached and my eyes felt sore from laughing. Some of the ablest professional story-tellers I have listened to. He spoke loudly so that I should not miss a syllable. A delighted hush fell upon the room as the tale unfolded. Every ear was strained, every eye rested on him. As his face was to the wall he could not see the auditors. Grimly he smiled as laughter and applause greeted the denouement. " Sean Ghall, this is no place for us." But I vetoed the remark. The waiter, with empty tray, was entranced ; so he forgot business, for the nonce. William Bulfin lifted his head. " Waiter ! Where is the coffee ? " That mere action proved him a man born to command. The tone was polite and quiet, but in terror the man dropped the tray : " Oh, I beg your pardon, sir. Sure it was the story, sir." He got a plenary pardon and a liberal tip.

The circle of his intimate friends knew no sweeter words than those : " Bulfin has arrived." The information was hailed with the same joy as the cry : " Water ! water !" to a parched caravan in the desert. He had a

wondrous power of inspiring love. Although his immense stock of stories ranged from Cork to Peru we
were so insatiable that many had to be re-told time and
again. He was a social as well as a national tonic.
Had Che Buono gone on the stage he would have made
considerable reputation as a seanachie. Purity, kindliness, acute observation, insight into human nature, a
keen sense of the ludicrous, and rich humour were the
staple of his tales.

As the ruling ambition of the last year of his noble
life was quenched by Death I must tell Irish-Ireland
about it. Like Wolfe Tone, Davis, Rooney, indeed like
every well-balanced mind, every noble heart, that laboured to give back her own again to beloved Eire, Bulfin
was the sworn foe of provincialism. He loved Leinster
and Munster, he loved Connaught and Ulster. How
any sane-minded person could have reached the conclusion that a part is greater than the whole baffled him
as it must baffle Euclid's youngest disciple. If actions
speak louder than words this absurd belief is held by
many otherwise sensible men. Ireland is greater than
Munster or Leinster ; she is more precious than Ulster
or Connacht. In the unique " Rambles in Eirinn,"
Senor Bulfin did less than justice to Nationalist Belfast.
The pulsating heart of Northern Gaeldom did not
obtain a sympathetic sound-board from this patriot.
So the men of Uladh told me when I had the happiness
of being in their midst. I answered that he described
only what he saw. " Now I must tell you that when I
stood in your principal streets I thought I was in Leeds
or Manchester. Everything reminded me of England ;
Ireland seemed to find no resting place, save in the geniality of manner of the newsboys and on the tongues of
the jarveys Were I not brought into actual touch with
the sanctuaries of national endeavour I, too, should have
departed with the view that you were all seoinini."

Mr. Bigger acted as my host and cicerone. It was an
education in national feeling. " Dark and true and

tender is the North." True and tender and patriotic it
proved. In no other part of old Eirinn did I find more
loyal hearts, nowhere more courteous or large-hearted
hospitality. Hearts beat quick, and, what is nobler,
heads and hands move quickly in the sacred cause. If
you do not know the North you do not know one of
the most delightful and strenuous haunts of Irish-Ireland.
Its heart is deepened because its body stands in alien
corn. If there is not that softness of manners, that
exquisite deference of the South, there is a strength of
character that invigorates like a mountain breeze. I
have not yet tired of voicing my admiration for the simple
if rugged independence of bearing which characterised
the Presbyterian farmers and labourers I met. No
servile cringing, no bowing and scraping to a new coat,
or to a gold chain, which causes my gorge to rise in
Yorkshire, and in the east and south of Ireland. Laconic
in speech, manly in bearing, and zealous in toil—such
I found them. "The rank is but the guinea stamp, the
Man's the gowd for a' that." In the delectable tour
in Mr. Bigger's motor-car I searched in vain for the
"Black North." I saw the Green North, I saw the
Golden North ear-heavy in corn, I saw the clean
White-Wash North, the North of trim cottages, tidy
children, and as lovely a race of cailini as ever graced
God's earth. I saw the North of manly men, of resourceful Gaels, the land of the O'Donnells, O'Neills,
O'Cathains, MacDonnells, O'Hanlons, MacQuillans, the
land of John Mitchel, Henry Joy MacCracken, the
Neilsons, the Russells, the land of Ethna Carbery. No, I
could not see the Black North. The Northern Gaels feel
what they call "the patronage" of the other provinces.
They told me so. Jealous, and rightly too, of their
historic land, they are hungry for the praise which
work well done everywhere merits. Personally, I never
was conscious of the existence of such an asinine feeling.
If such flourished I should advise the Ultonians to
bring the men of other provinces among their nine Glynns

—exquisite haunts of loveliness—into Tir Eoghan, into
Tir Chonaill, into Lecale, anywhere, everywhere that
Heaven's smile rests on that glorious land. As I gazed
over Lough Neagh, as I panted on Dungannon's heights,
I understood why Uladh was the nurse of heroes, why
it had been the Home of the Strong Hand, the Champion
Heart. Truly such a country was worth the letting
of seas of the richest and purest blood to have and to
hold. Uladh won my enthusiastic admiration. Ulster,
Leinster, Munster, and Connacht, you are all noble
children of the noblest of mothers. Prove that you are
worthy of your birthright by praising what is lovely
and of good report in one another.

I wrote to Buenos Aires from Mr. Bigger's Home of
Hospitality concerning what the Ultonians said, and
of my vain quest for the Black North. I narrated
my guide's badinage. " That's a corn-field, Sean Ghall.
Did you even imagine we had yellow corn ! Yon is an
apple tree ; mind ye, we have some apples here too.
There is a wee duck, but it has only two legs in the black
North." And so on through a whole litany of delicious
sallies. The Senor replied, in a repentant mood, determined to see and describe the North as it deserves to
be viewed and limned. I gave him a bibliography of
the works pertaining to the province. His last letter
expressed the eagerness with which he was looking
forward to a cycling tour through the eastern part
of the province, from Newry to Dunluce. All are
familiar with the altered impressions of his final
visit to Belfast ; all do not know that he ended by
falling in love, as I told him he would, with the men and
women and ideals of Irish Ulster. After his final
acquaintance with the North his letters were palpitating
with desire to do justice to the Gaels there. Writing
on the 16th October last he said :—" Yours of the
13th, gave me a good half-hour and a fresh start. I was
just considering where and how to tackle Ulster when
your letter came to quicken my desire of writing the

Uladh chapters well and with my whole strength, such
as it is, in the writing.

" Now, I have decided to write the following on
Uladh this winter, please God :

(1) Cave Hill.

(2) A fruitless search for the Black North—Temple-
patrick, Carnmoney, etc—Orr, Neilson, Russell, Jemmy
Hope.

(3) A flight around Lough Neagh.

(4) Behind the Gates of the North—the country over
Newry to Portadown, etc.

The eastern part from Newry, through the Glens to
Dunluce next year. Looking down on Belfast from
Cave Hill—from Mac Art's Fort, I can say what I like
about Belfast (but only the truth)—say some true and
stirring things of its men who loved Ireland in the past
and love it now." But work, too much other work,
crowded out these plans. Death called him ere his ideas
took shape on paper.

Bulfin regarded every sod of turf, every blade of grass,
from Malin Head to Cape Clear as sanctified. Patriotism
was a religion to him, and Religion patriotic. In the
" Southern Cross " of Buenos Aires an English gentleman
says, with perfect truth, that Ireland was holy ground
to William Bulfin. Those to whom he has given laughter
and tears, joy and hope, national pride and self-reverence,
in the inimitable pages of " Rambles in Eirinn," know
but a part of his spirit. His heart, mind, and soul were
suffused with as passionate a love of our peerless country
as ever warmed the heart, quickened the brain, or made
active the hand of patriot. It is with him sleeping and
waking. All other feelings were absorbed by it. On the
Pampas, in the streets of New York, under the torrid
sun of West Africa, on the sheep ranches of New Zealand,
along the Karroos, beneath the Southern Cross, in the
cosmopolitan crowds of Singapore, in the European
quarter of Hong Kong, in the towns of Great Britain,
and in our own isle. Irishmen stiffened their backs

because of Bulfin's words in that wonderful evangel, " Rambles in Eirinn." I know this fact from the exiles I met, from the letters I received. " Ireland first " was always his motto. Reading his articles in the *Southern Cross* I felt proud of the land that gave me the privilege of calling him fellow-countryman, proud of the unconquerable spirit of the lion whelps of Gaeldom, proud of the journal that sent his opinions broadcast. In his inspired moments he beat out his sentences in such a heat, with such an intensity of feeling, as to make the reader involuntarily shout with joy: " John Mitchel, your spirit moves and breathes in Bulfin." He was passionately jealous of the reputation of his journal for Nationality and Catholicism. " It would make me turn in my grave, Sean Ghall, if it proved traitor to the Green or to the God of our Fathers," he wrote. As we chatted for the last time in O'Connell Street his eyes glowed and his whole frame was animated in detailing its possibilities for good. " I shall die in peace when I know it will keep a straight keel."

Through all Bulfin's writings there is a breeze of fresh air ever blowing. He gives you the sky, the Wind, the Rain, and the Brown Earth as companions. His National Gospel is breezy, his deeply critical mind kept a tight rein on his soaring imaginative powers, his magnetic love of the motherland never dimmed his eyes to the rocks and boulders which strew the road to freedom. He etches a character in a phrase, photographs a mood— if I may say so—in a sentence, and limns a scene, a character, in a paragraph. Never did his inventive powers, in the " Rambles," come to his aid : with almost literal exactitude he set down just what he saw and no more. But the alembic of his mind mellowed and illuminated the commonplaces to such a degree as to make his fellow-traveller marvel at his intuition, at his picturesque grip of seemingly unimportant details, at his graphic pen. The sedate book-worm now, then the polished much-travelled man of the world; in the

morning as happy-hearted as a child, in the evening as
grave as a philosopher ; now his grasp of business details
surprised you ; again he gave his Pegasus rein and no
Puck himself could be more fanciful. Always a simple,
joyous, great-hearted man emerged from his multi-
farious characters. " I send you, Sean Ghall, a photo
of ' Che Buono,' the man of lassoing and stock classi-
fication and all that—the half-tamed gaucho who likes
to go back to the tall grass from his books, and who
likes to come back to his books out of the tall grass."

After recovery from illness he wrote : " Thank God I
am all right now, and only I had my hair cut I would
write a poem about the longing to go back into the thick
of things and ride like fury in the ruck where the pace of
thought is made." Again : " it is God's will and wish,
I think, that the service of Ireland should be one of
sacrifice. The guerdon is not in gold ; it is in the
pride of service given for love, and the thought of what
weight a man's word may carry because it is out of
reach of a price. In Ireland you know such men, Sean
Ghall, to whom you would go down on your knees in
reverence of their worship of truth and unselfishness
in our loved land's service." As we strolled along the
banks of the Slaney discoursing on Wexford in '98 he
reverted to his favourite topic—the unconquerable
spirit of Erin's hope in her great future. Eloquently
he dilated on the past. " What though an earthquake
swallowed all Irish Irelanders this hour, what though
every heroic young worker, every hoary toiler, were
struck down by the sword of the Lord, the fight would
go on, the march would not be impeded. The fight
would go on, it must go on, until Irishmen rule Ireland
for Ireland's weal. Bah ! the weeping figure of Eire !
It causes my gorge to rise. Turn her face to the sun !
Cowards snivel and whine about sad Fate ; leave tears
to women ; men—real men—must fight cheerfully,
must step sturdily, must toil terribly though every
inch of ground were covering our best and noblest and

dearest ; " in some such words he poured out his heart.

The gospel of Davis and of Rooney had no abler transmitter, Ireland no more passionate lover or more strenuous labourer, Friend a more lofty-souled Friend, child more tender a Father, Wife a more reverential and loving husband, Nature no more finished a man.   Were I to fill columns I could but falter a part of his worth. His inner life, his relationship to his Creed, his drawn encomiums from his relatives and friends.

> " The world external knew thee but in part ;
>   It saw and honoured what was least in thee ;
>   The loyal trust, the inborn courtesy ;
>   The ways so winning, yet so pure from art ;
>   The cordial reverence, keen to all desert,
>   All save thine own ; the accost so frank and free,
>   And shunned alike base praise and hireling's mart.
>
>   These things men saw ; but, deeper far than these,
>   The under-current of thy soul worked on,
>   Unvexed by surface-ripple, beam, or breeze,
>   And, unbeheld, its way to ocean won.
>   Life of thy life was still that Christian Faith
>   The sophist scorns.   It fails thee not in death." *

Lordship to thy spirit, William Bulfin !   Praise, Honour, and Renown to thee. Great Heart, Peerless Soul. Lordship to Ireland who bore thee !

                    seán ȝall

                * Aubrey de Vere.

RAMBLES IN EIRINN.

❖

Returned from over seas.—Trial spin on my Wex-
ford wheel.—The Summer glory of Ireland.—
Across the Brosna River.—Skirting North
Tipperary.—Roscrea and Mount St. Joseph.—
Interviewing a Beggarman.—Haymaking.

I was hungry for a feast of the summer glory,
and I was filled with a desire to dim the workshop
lustre of my brand new Wexford wheel. It was the
last day of June, and the weather was perfect. The
people along the road said it was " shocking warm,"
and " scorching," and " terrible hot, glory be to
God," but after seventeen sweltering years of the
sunny South I found it just charming. The first
few miles of my trial spin took me down the valley
of the middle Shannon, and I laid my seven blessings on the Irish sunshine which never blisters, and
on the perfumed winds of the Irish summer which
are never laden with flame. How often during the
cloudless dog days of the Pampas had I yearned for
a cycling tour through Ireland! And how often
the thought would come to me that if ever my hopes
were realised the fruition would prove flat and stale
compared with the pleasures of anticipation. But
it was just the reverse.

And I knew that—knew that it was going to be
like a visit to fairy-land—before we reached Dublin
at all; for like most returning exiles, we were up long
before sunrise, watching from the spar-deck of the
steamer for the first glimpse of Ireland.   There
was a faint bluish something at first, on the
horizon, which might be a flake of cloud; but little
by little it rose into the sky and changed from blue
to purple, and we knew that we were looking
at the hills over Dublin.   It was a splendid dawn.
We seemed to have brought with us some of the sunshine of the South, for earth and sea and air were
flooded with morning gold. It flamed in the soft
clouds which dotted the sky   It flushed the blue.
It lay on the hills   It rippled on the water.   Soon
the headlands began to stand out along the coast.
The fields on the mountain sides threw their green
into our faces, as one might say—threw it, in soft
playfulness and welcome.   The woods and groves
which at first were only blotches of shadow now
caught the light which danced gaily on the masses
of foliage.   You could see where the feathery larches
lay against the deeper verdure of the elms; where the
chestnuts and sycamores flung broad shadows on the
lawns; where ash and spruce and poplar and copper
beech alternated along the slopes, or in the
valleys.   And you could see the hawthorn, all white
and gay in its mantle of summer blossom.   There
was a ribbon-like streak of country road over which
swelled a heathery mountain, and below it was the
glint of a river.   As the sun climbed higher the sky
softened in tone, and a haze of golden grey spread
itself over everything.   It hung over the city smoke,

it capped the summits of the hills, it veiled the
broad fields of tender blue between the fleecy clouds;
it even lay over the woodland shadows.

Oh, it was beautiful, beautiful! And then the
three hours' homeward run by train from Dublin to
the midlands! Every mile of it was a new delight.
It took us by Lucan, where the sheep and cattle were
deep in flower-strewn grass on the meadows that knew
the Sarsfields before the Wild Geese flew from Ireland. Across the Liffey it whirled us, between thick
hedges, by some of the Geraldine lands, and under
the tree-clad hills where there were Rapparees of the
O'Dempseys once upon a time; and on and on,
through valleys that had re-echoed to the hoof-
thunder of the riders of O'Connor of Offally, in the
olden days. On still, to brave old Dunamase, and
down and through the hills where O'Moore drew
steel upon the Saxon; past Maryborough, called
after the Tudor wife of Spanish Philip; through
northern Ossory, where there were the *duns* of the
MacCashins and the castles of the Fitzpatricks;
and then, over a bend of the Slieve Blooms, into
ferny hollows below Knockshigowna of the fairies,
and down through the woods of Sharavogue into the
chieftainry of Ely O'Carroll. Beautiful and ever
beautiful. And, above all, it was Ireland—the
homeland at last.

Maybe you remember the melodious lines in which
Mary Elizabeth Blake tells of the loveliness which
she dreamed of and found under Irish skies. I am
thinking of them now, and I cannot deny myself
the pleasure of writing them down:

Many and many a day have I longed for thy green-
    robed splendour
Thine eyes of the deep sea gray and thy soft love
    patient and tender—
For the croon of thy welcoming voice, and thy
    smiles, half joy and half sadness,
Soul of my soul rejoice, for this is the hour of thy
    gladness!

> Sure if I never had heard
>   What land had given me birth,
> And cradled the spirit's bird
>   On its first weak flight to earth;

If I never had heard the name of thy sorrow and
    strength divine,
Or felt in my pulses the flame of fire they had
    caught from thine;
I would know by this rapture alone which sweeps
    through me now like a flood,
That the Irish skies were my own, and my blood
    was the Irish blood.

Proud did I hold thy race,
    Yet knew not what pride might dare;
Fair did I deem thy face,
    Yet never once half so fair;
Like a dream with rich happiness fraught
    That some happier dawn makes true,
Nothing was glad in my thought
    But gladness still more in you—

Other lands look lovelier from far away. But
Ireland never is so beautiful as when the eye rests

upon her face. You need never be afraid that you
are flattering her while painting her from even your
fondest memory.

That was all in my thoughts as I crossed the
Brosna River into Munster, a few miles above its
confluence with the Shannon, and left Leinster
behind me, on my first ramble in Eirinn. I was in
the valley of the Shannon for an hour, and it was
like living in the past to wander leisurely along the
Summer roads. The tall grass was waving in the
South wind on the Annagh Callows, and the corn
was of the softest green on all the slopes of the hills
from Ballylea to Rathcabban   Out of the flaggers,
beside the water, on the verge of the moor, a wild
duck and three " flappers " rushed with frightened
" quacking," and dived into the cool security of the
pool under the leaves of the water lillies. Further
away from the road, a water hen and her chickens
were feeding in the sedge along the margin of the
little lough, and when they caught sight of the
intruder they took refuge in the deep shadows cast
by a mountain ash.   It brought back the stolen
pleasures of the long-gone Summer days when more
attention was given to bird-nesting, and the general
study of bird life, and the life habits of every wild
thing that moved on Irish ground, than parents and
school teachers deemed proper.

Rathcabban was basking drowsily in the sun as I
cycled past the schoolhouse. The village was quiet,
and a policeman and a goose had the street all to
themselves. I went to the shop and inquired for
the homes of some old friends and found them out.
But not all the friends were to the good in dear

Tipperary. Some of them were far away and some of them were dead. The survivors were clamorous for the suspension of my journey and a stay of a week. But I told them I was under vows to visit Lorrha Abbey that morning, and made other excuses for tearing myself away from them.

Soon after leaving them I crossed the track of what had once been the railway from Birr, on the border of Leinster, to Portumna, on the border of Connacht. This railway has been defunct for years. It passed through a fertile district. It tapped the Shannon Valley, linking it up with the central railway system. It could have been worked at a minimum of expense. Even if it did not give a dividend, mile by mile, its value as a feeder to the main line could not have been small. And yet the Great Southern and Western Railway of Ireland stopped work on this road. The tracks were left there to rust. The sleepers are rotted. The bridges and culverts are neglected. The line is utterly wrecked.

And all this happened in Ireland in the end of the nineteenth century! While other countries were building hundreds of miles of new roads, Ireland, under the blessings of a maternal English rule, saw a railway to die. While other countries were making laws to protect the people against the aggressions of railway companies, the English Government in Ireland allowed a band of capitalists to abandon a line which was necessary to the progress and prosperity of an important district. Why? Just because the company had failed to insert a clause regarding a guarantee fund from public taxation in its charter. The Clara and Banagher Railroad, in another section of the Shannon Valley, does not pay a mile-by-mile dividend, but the same company which abandoned the Portumna road, condescends to keep this line open. Why? Just because in the charter there is a clause—an iniquitous clause, too—which guarantees that the mile-by-mile loss shall be made good out of a cess levied on the overtaxed people of the district. This cess is levied, I believe, upon the barony of Garry-castle, and amounts to over 6d. in the pound. In presenting their yearly bill to the taxpayers for the loss on the working of the Banagher and Clara Railway, the company never calculate the benefits received by the main line from this branch, which acts as a feeder to the trunk road.

A run of almost an hour took me to Lorrha, where the ancient Abbey of St. Ruadhan stood—a place fateful in the history of Ireland. It was here Aodh Guaire of Hy-Many took refuge after slaying the steward of Diarmid Mac Cerbhaill, Ard Righ of Tara. St. Ruadhan was the uncle of the fugitive, and when the officers of Diarmid arrested him, despite his claim of sanctuary, and when his uncle protested against the taking away by force of one who had been granted the protection of the abbey, war was virtually declared between the civil and ecclesiastical powers in Ireland. The cursing and the desertion and ruin of Tara followed. Lorrha was famous as a great monastic establishment long after the fall of Tara, but for centuries it has been, like Clonard and Clonfert, and many another great ecclesiastical foundation of the early days of the

Irish Church, silent and deserted. Gone are the cloisters and schools. There is nothing left but crumbling stones and grass-grown mounds and the graves of the dead.

After passing Lorrha you strike a lovely stretch of Munster—long, winding, shallow vales, fine tracts of tilled land, green pastures, too, and shady groves and woods; and all along the eastern and southern horizon stand the blue peaks of the guardian mountains—Ard-na-h-Eireann, the Keepers, Devil's Bit and Slieve Phelim. I covered mile after mile through this beautiful district until I found myself in ancient Ossory. The road was rising, rising, under the first swell of the hills, and the south wind had freshened to a stiff breeze, against which cycling had ceased to be a mild form of exercise. The sun was low, too, so I called a halt and shaped my course homeward by Roscrea.

It was in the old Monastery of Roscrea (Ross or wood of Crea) that the Book of Dimma, at present in the library of Trinity College, Dublin, was written. The monastery was founded by St. Cronan somewhere about the beginning of the seventh century. There is a legend in connection with the writing of the Book of Dimma which still lives around Roscrea. Dimma was a very skilful scribe, and St. Cronan employed him to produce a copy of the Gospels.

"I can only give you one day for the transcription," said Dimma, "as I have other work to do; so you need not expect me to produce a very beautiful copy in so short a time."

" It is morning now," said the saint, " so begin at once and write until sunset."

Dimma began to write, and the legend says that the light of the sun did not cease to shine around him for forty days and forty nights. By that time the Book of Dimma was finished. One of the Chieftains of Ely O'Carroll had a costly shrine made, in which to guard this beautiful manuscript. When the monastery was suppressed the Book of Dimma and its shrine were taken away by the monks. Some boys who were out rabbit-hunting found the book in 1789 in one of the crevices of Devil's Bit Mountain. It passed into the possession of a gentleman in Nenagh, and from him it went to Dr. Todd, who presented it to Trinity College. The old monastery in which it was written is a ruin, but close to Roscrea is a splendid new monastery of the Trappists, whose house at Mount Melleray is world-famous.

Mount St. Joseph, the monastery near Roscrea, is a most picturesquely situated place. It stands in a noble park, which was once known as Mount Heaton. The park and mansion came into the possession of the Trappists through the princely generosity of Count Moore, who purchased the estate after the death of its eccentric owner, Mr. Heaton. This Mr. Heaton seems to have been a recluse, a misanthrope, and a worldling of the most selfish type.

" He was a bit of a rhymer, too," said a stalwart youth, who chatted with me about the last of the Heatons, as I cycled past the monastery.

"I never read any verse of his," I remarked, "nor do I remember to have heard his name in connection with poetry."

"Oh, I don't suppose he ever published any," said my informant, "but he made it, right enough. Mostly all the verses he used to make were about eating. I don't remember any of them very well, but one was something like this:

> Bacon is bacon
> And mutton is mutton,
>   Not bad to eat.
>
> Bacon is bacon
> And mutton is mutton,
>   But only beef is meat.

"I only remember one more—the one he made when he was dying. He made his servant lift him up in the bed, so that he could look out into the park and see the trees and everything. And says he:

> Farewell beef,
> And the cabbage leaf,
> Farewell mutton.
> And farewell bacon,
> Oh! sweet Mount Heaton,
>   Must I leave you?

"I don't think I have it off rightly, but that is more or less the run of it, like. He made dozens of others—all about eating and drinking ,and his money. But he had to go away, heels foremost, at last, and leave it all behind him."

The Trappists have turned the mansion into a monastery, and have added a magnificent church and other buildings, including an Irish-Ireland College. There is a guest house, the same as at Mount Melleray, and the hospitality of the Fathers is boundless Mount St. Joseph is much frequented by men who go thither to make retreats. The monastery of Mount Melleray is also a haven for such penitents. People are to be met in both houses from all parts of the world—the United States, Australia, Africa, the Continent, South America, and from England and Scotland as well as Ireland. There is absolutely no charge. Guests may come and go in scores, and stay while there is room for them. The guest table is most hospitably served, although the Fathers themselves never eat meat except on Christmas Day. Every modern comfort is provided for visitors; and if they do not make voluntary contributions on leaving, no one asks them for a penny. The lay brothers of the order and some of the Fathers spend certain hours of the day in working in the fields. They have a model farm, and, in a material as well as in a spiritual sense, the monastery is a helpful, uplifting influence in the locality. It is also an Irish influence, for the Irish Trappists are intensely national, and many of them are Irish speakers.

"And are you a Gaelic Leaguer?" I asked of the fine young athlete, whose company I was enjoying along the shady road by the monastery demesne.

"Of course I am," he replied, laughingly; "why shouldn't I? Roscrea is in Ireland. We didn't think of that fact until lately, but now we see it

clearly enough. Do you know that in the convent
the children are learning Irish, and Irish history,
too? Oh, yes, we are Irish here! "

I asked him if he could tell me where the Battle
of Roscrea was fought, and he told me that it was
near the old abbey, where the great fair used to be
held. It was in the days of the Danish invasions
that the battle took place, between the years 943
and 950. Oilfinn, Chief of the Danes of Connacht,
marched his hosts to Roscrea to plunder the rich
merchants who were wont to assemble there from
all parts of Ireland, and also from foreign countries,
at the great fair held every year, according to the
Abbe Mac Geoghegan, on the 29th of June, St.
Peter and Paul's day. The news of the march of
the Norsemen soon spread, and every man who
attended the fair went armed. Instead of engaging
in buying and selling they went out to meet the
enemy in their thousands, and a terrible fight
ensued. Oilfinn and 4,000 of his men were slain,
and the Danes were utterly defeated.

Down the pleasant sloping country from Mount
St. Joseph I cycled towards Knockshigowna. I was
thinking of leaving my wheel by the wayside and
climbing the storied hill to see the sun going down
into the Shannon, when I rounded a bend in a shady
hollow and came upon a cross-roads. There was a
hospitable cross-roads house, and I halted in the
" bawn" thereof. I got the loan of a stool from
mine hostess and sat by the roadside and smoked
and entered into conversation with a man who
was seated on the grass eating watercress off a
cabbage-leaf. It was difficult to draw him into

conversation at first, so preoccupied was he with his salad. Beside the cabbage-leaf, on the grass, lay a piece of brown paper containing a little salt, and he was paying the nicest attention to the quantities which he took with each bunch of cress.

"Is this the Birr Road?" I asked, by way of establishing social relations. He merely shook his head while he dipped a few sprigs of the watercress into the salt and turned the morsel round and round, shaking it daintily, and eyeing it with the air of an epicure before conveying it to his mouth. He wore a tall silk hat, bottle green with age and the stress of travel. He showed a frayed and yellow collar and the remnant of a black tie. His frock coat was tightly buttoned across his chest. His trousers were patched at the knees and frayed at the feet. His boots were in the last stages of decay, and were clamouring for the restfulness of the grave. At first I thought he might be a broken-down landlord. But I was mistaken. He was simply a tramp. He was not a tramp in the American sense, but he belonged to the consuming class all the same, and disclaimed all affiliation, fraternity and solidarity with the producers. He belonged apparently to the class known as beggarmen. He appeared a beggarman from his protruding toes to the crown of his sixteenth century hat. Such was evidently his rating in the economy of the universe. I felt easy in my mind once I had thus placed him, and my road to his confidence seemed clearer.

"Have you walked far to-day?" I asked.

He nodded, munching a bunch of salted cress, with every outward sign of enjoyment.

"You look like a man that has seen better days," I remarked, not that I believed he had, but merely to get him to talk.

"Do I now?" he asked with a sour grin, as he helped himself to another morsel of his repast.

"Yes," I said. "You do. Have you come down far in the world?"

"Would you think, now, that I ever followed a hunt?" he asked by way of reply.

"Certainly."

"Then, bedad, you're right, sir. So I did—many a one, too. But I went on foot, you understand, not on horseback."

"Oh, indeed!"

"A fact, and as for seein' better days, well, I don't know but I have. I was always a beggarman, anyhow, and my father and grandfather before me were the same, so I never fell in the world at all— unless maybe now and then of a fair night, when times was good and refreshments were flowin' about plentiful."

"And how do you find the times?" I enquired.

"Bad, bad, bad!" and he shook his head sadly. He said that a beggarman in Ireland now has a "poor" occupation in every sense of the word. It was once far better—one lived at his ease, and could support a large family, and have a full skin, from year's end to year's end. Now, unless, as in his own case, one had an old-established connection, it was difficult for a beggarman to make ends meet. And even with a good connection it was no easy matter. He supposed that, if things continued to go on as they were going now, he would, sooner or later, be obliged to work or go to the poorhouse.

He was the only beggarman I met during the whole of a month. When I was a lad, the country was infested with them. I was glad to note the change that had taken place in this respect.

" It is not that the country is poorer nor it used to be," he exclaimed. " It's just that there isn't any feelin' in the people for a beggarman."

A run of a mile or so through the lengthening shadows brought me to a sharp hill, which I was obliged to negotiate on foot. As I gained the crest a whiff of the unpurchasable fragrance of new mown hay greeted me, and over the hedge to my right lay a big rye grass meadow in windrows. Four men were rolling the windrows into cocks, and the rustle and perfume of the yellowing hay came to the road, through the hush and calm of the sunset.

" God bless the work," I said.

" You, too," they answered cheerily.

" Have you a spare fork there ? "

" Aye, have we," said one of them, using a quaint idiomatic affirmative of Northern Munster.

" Then here goes," I said, leaving my wheel on the roadside and leaping over the hedge.

It was for the sake of old times. I longed to renew my friendship with the ancient art of hay-making, and the four smiling haymakers were nothing loath. They regarded me in the light of a harmless patient, and when I tackled a windrow all by myself they said, encouragingly :

" 'Deed it isn't the first time for you to take a fork in your hands, God bless you! "

Be it known unto all nations that during the Summer I took part in haymaking in nine different counties in the four provinces. I lent a hand at the saving of " new " and " old " meadow, blistered my hands, broke fork handles, made tramp cocks, and grass cocks and fork cocks, drank oatmeal water, and buttermilk; and, in a word, made myself thoroughly acquainted with the present aspects of Irish haymaking.

It has changed, and changed in some ways for the better. The romance of it has gone. That part of it went down into the past with the scythes and the advent of the hay rakes and tedders. The growing scarcity of labourers made machinery necessary. In the old days the hay was dried almost to a cinder—dried until it crackled when you took up a handful of it. It was as dry, in fact, as if it had been placed for hours on a kiln. When the ropes were made for the tramp cocks, the hay had to be wetted first in order to make the twisting of it possible. Now the hay is put into tramp cocks quite heavy.

We sat on the golden-tinted cocks near the road when the work was finished, and they told me about the harvest prospects, and about hares and foxes and many other things while the west grew rosy and shook out purple swathings to welcome the homing sun. They were fine hearty fellows, strong-limbed, clear-complexioned, bright-eyed, and as for their health, it seemed to come to them out of every stubble and grass-blade in all the magnificent country-side. They were hurlers, they told me, forwards in the local team, and were proud of the fact. They were splendid children of the soil, and they were worthy of it. Their native sod could scarcely have been fairer. Green acres of rich pasture, hedged with white-thorn, woodbine, and wild rose, stretched out below us, brightened by greener cornfields and the luscious promise of root crops. Along the valley and half way up the opposite ridges ran heavy foliaged woods; and around the woods, and by the banks of a gleaming river, were fringes of soft moorland, heather-grown and fern-scented. Thrown against the olive shadows of the trees, and against the blending shade of sunlit verdure were thin wreaths of turf smoke, spread by many a white-washed homestead where the supper pots were boiling. The hush of evening fell around us, and through it, pulsing up along the slope bathed in the crimson glory of the hour, came the ringing laughter of some girls who were driving home their cows to the milking.

It was after sunset when I left the meadow and took my way along the wooded slopes to Ballybrit. It was the mystic gloaming—the dewy close of the lingering twilight—as I cycled along the road which led through tall rushes and luxuriant heather. It was night as I passed through Birr, and I shared the starlit country with the sleepless corncrakes as I made my way through the north of Ely O'Carroll, home to bed.

CHAPTER II.

Around Lough Gill—Knocknarea—Sligo—The Lake
—The Hills—The Valley of O'Rourke—Drum-
ahaire—O'Rourke's Table.

I had decided on a tour into northern Connacht,
so with a mixture of " the white wind from the South
and the brown wind from the West" on my shoulder.
I pulled out on one of the main roads leading
through Ely O'Carroll and faced for the Shannon.
Lough Gill was my destination, and I shaped my
course as follows:—Athlone, Roscommon, Boyle,
Sligo, Drumahaire.

Had I hearkened to the oracular guidance of a
road book, edited by a West Briton, which had cost
me a shilling, I would have gone to Sligo by train,
for, according to the book, the road from Dublin
to Sligo is " an uninteresting route and road indifferent." But a month's experience had taught me
that the most I could expect from this book was an
occasional piece of unconscious humour.

The " uninteresting route " alluded to above is
really one of the most interesting in all Ireland.
It crosses the magnificent plain of Meath, passing
close to Tara. It takes you past scores of historic
and beautiful places in fair Westmeath of the lakes.
It leads you over the most picturesque of the Longford uplands; and whether you decide to cross the
Shannon at Lanesborough or at Carrick, it shows
you the hills of Annaly of the O'Ferralls, and gives
you the choice of a look at beautiful Lough Ree, or
a ramble through the delightful country between
Newtownforbes and Drumsna.

When you cross the Shannon the Sligo road takes you over the Connacht plains and brings you within sight of royal Cruachain. It leads you into Boyle, and thence through the Pass of the Curlews, or you have an alternative road to Sligo round the northern spur of the Curlews by the rock of Doon, and the shore of Lough Key and to Sligo by Knocknarea.

" An uninteresting route ? " Not if you are Irish and know some of the history of your land, and feel some pleasure in standing beside the graves of heroes and on ground made sacred by their heroism. Not if you delight to see the hay-making, and the turf cutting, and in observing the simple, beautiful life of rural Ireland. Not if you feel at home among the boys and girls at the cross-roads in the evening time, or if you know how to enjoy a drink of milk and a chat with the old people across the half door, or on a stool beside the hearth. Not if you love the woods and the mantling glory of waving corn ripening in the sun, and the white, winding roads made cool on the hottest day by the shade of flower-laden hedges.

But if you are one of those tired and tiresome souls desirous only of treading in the footsteps of the cheap trippers who follow one another like sheep, if you have no eye of your own for the beautiful, and if you think it your duty to go out of your way to put money into the pockets of vampire rail-ways, then in the name of all the Philistines and seoinini take the train, or stay away out of the country altogether, or go to some peepshow and surfeit your narrow photographic soul on " views."

The road over the Curlew Mountains from Boyle is a grand one. If you are an average roadster you can pedal up the greater part of the gradient. They tell a story in Boyle of a man who negotiated the mountains in night time without becoming aware of it. He said, when asked how he had found the roads, that they were all right, but that he thought he had met a sort of a long hill somewhere. He was either a champion rider or a humorist.

Anyhow the ordinary tourist will have to get off his machine for a few steep zigzags. The rest is nothing more formidable than a good tough climb. You can rest now and then and admire the spreading plains behind you to the eastward. You can see into Mayo and Galway to your right, and Boyle is just below you, the old abbey lifting its twelfth century gables over the trees. To your left is beautiful Lough Key.

A little higher up you come to the verge of the battlefield of the Curlews. They call it Deerpark or some such history-concealing name now. Ballaghboy is what the annalists call it. You can see the stone erected on the spot where Clifford, the English general, fell. You can see where the uncaged Eagle of the North prepared for his swoop, and the heart within you leaps as your eye follows adown the slope the line of his victorious onset. God's rest and peace be with your soul, Red Hugh! You were a sensible, practical patriot, although there is no big tower one hundred and goodness knows how many feet high erected to your memory on Ireland's ground. And although you had no blatant press to give you high-sounding names and sing your praises to the world, you believed that liberty was worth the best blood in your veins, and you did not waste breath on windy resolutions. And when you raised your hand, a bouchal, it was not the ever-lasting hat that you held out in it to the gaze of the nations, for it had that in it which was worthy of Ireland and of you. 'Twas something that gleamed and reddened and blazed and that flashed the light of wisdom and duty into the souls of manly men.

After passing Ballaghboy the road leads upward into the fastnesses of the Curlews, where for a while the world is shut off. The heath-clad summits of the peaks hem you in. For about a mile you ride in this solitude and then suddenly there is a turn and the world comes back again. Below you the valleys and woods are alternating in the near distance. In front of you is a green hillside dotted with farm houses. There, too, is Lough Arrough, and beyond it, away in the hazy distance, is the purple bulk of Slieveanierin and the gray masses of Knocknarea and Benbulben. Ten minutes will bring you to the town of Ballinafad. The road from here to Sligo is a grand one for the cyclist. It is smooth and level nearly all the way.

After a few miles of this pleasant road you come to an ancient-looking demesne. The timber is old and lofty, the wall along the roadside is moss-grown, the undergrowth beneath the oaks and pines is thick and tangled. This is the Folliat or Folliard estate. It is where the scene of "Willie Reilly" is laid. Here lived the "great Squire Folliard" and his lovely daughter—the heroine of one of the most

popular of Anglo-Irish love tales, and the subject of
a ballad that has been sung in many lands :

Oh ! rise up, Willie Reilly, and come along with me !

The suggestion of the metre must have come to the
balladist in the lilt of some old traditional air of
Connacht. I have nearly always heard it sung in
the Irish traditional style—the style which lived on
even after the Irish language had fallen into disuse.
I have heard it sung in two hemispheres—by the
Winter firesides of Leinster and under the *paraiso*
trees around the homes of the Pampas. I had followed it around the world, through the turf smoke
and bone smoke—through the midges and mosquitoes
and fire-flies. I was glad to find that I had run it
to earth at last, so to speak.

There is a gloom over the Folliat demesne now.
The shadow of a great sorrow is on it. A few years
ago a daughter of the house went out on the lake in
a boat to gather water lilies for her affianced lover,
who was returning that evening to her after a long
absence. She was drowned. They were to have
been married in a day or two. The place has never
been the same since then.

Collooney was meant by nature for great things.
The river flowing by the town supplies it with immense water power. Under the rule of a free people,
Collooney would be an important manufacturing
centre. At present it is a mere village, struggling to
keep the rooftrees standing. There are various mills
beside the river, some of them, I fear, silenced forever. There is a woollen factory which is evidently
trying conclusions with the shoddy from foreign

mills. It is engaged in an uphill fight, but I hope it is winning. After passing the woollen factory, you cross the bridge, and, skirting a big hill, you drop down on the Sligo road, which takes you through one of the battlefields of '98.

The battle was fought close to the town. On the 5th of September, 1798, the advance guard of Humbert's little army arrived at Collooney from Castlebar. Colonel Vereker, of the Limerick militia, was there from Sligo with some infantry, cavalry and artillery. He was beaten back to Sligo, and he lost his artillery. Humbert then marched to Drumahaire and thence towards Manorhamilton, but suddenly wheeling he made for Longford to join the Granard men. Ballinamuck followed. Bartholomew Teeling and Matthew Tone (brother of Theobald Wolfe Tone) were among the Irish prisoners who surrendered with Humbert to Lord Cornwallis. They were executed a few days afterward in Dublin.

Close beside the road on a rocky hill they have erected a monument to Teeling. The statue, which is heroic in its expression, looks toward the " Races of Castlebar " and reminds one of that splendid day. One uplifted hand grasps a battle-flag. The face is a poem, grandly eloquent in its chiselling. You think you can catch the thought that was in the sculptor's mind. You can feel that his aim was to represent his hero looking out in fiery appeal and reproach over the sleeping West!

Sligo should by right be a great Irish seaport town, but if it had to live by its shipping interests it would starve in a week. Like Galway, it has had such a dose of British fostering and legislation that it seems to be afraid of ships, and the ships seem to be afraid of it. The city lives independently of its harbour, which it holds in reserve for brighter and greater days. There are, as far as one can judge, three Sligos—the Irish Sligo, the ascendancy Sligo and the Sligo which straddles between ascendancy and nationalism. The Gaelic League is strong in the city, and one of the hardest workers in the West, when I was there, was Father Hynes.

Sligo is very picturesquely situated. Knocknarea guards it on one side and Benbulbin on the other. The hills which face the city to the northward are very beautiful, and beyond and above their fresh verdure are the rocky heights that beat off the keen and angry winds from the Atlantic. You ride down into the streets from a hill which overtops the steeples, and it is only when you come into the suburbs that you can see the bay. Clear and calm it looks from the Ballysodare road, but, alas! not a smoke cloud on the whole of it, not a sail in view, not a masthead over the roofs along the water front. The harbour is not, of course, entirely deserted. A steamer or a sailing ship comes in now and then. The same thing happens in Galway.

But I am not comparing the two cities, because there is no comparison between them. Galway drags on an existence. Sligo is very much alive. Galway went to the bad when its ocean trade was killed. Sligo is able to maintain itself by doing business with the district in which it is situated. Behind Galway there was no populous and fertile land near enough to be a support to business

Behind Sligo are the valleys which support a relatively thriving rural population.

You can spend a very pleasant day in and around Sligo, visiting places of historical interest or picturesque beauty. It was once a war-scourged district, and the scars are still there. The hills around have echoed to a hundred battle cries, some of which were raised for Ireland. At Ballysodare you will find waterfalls that are beautiful even to people who have seen photographs of Niagara and read of cascades in several fashionable countries. There is a ruined castle of the O'Connors, too, which has a history. It was shot to pieces in the days when Connacht was making its last fight for freedom, and it was never rebuilt. It was one of the outposts of Sligo and saw many a bloody fray in its time.

The sea runs in to Ballysodare and makes a bay around which you have to cycle to Knocknarea. Soon after coming to the slope of the hill you meet one of the queerest, wildest and most beautiful of glens. They call it after the mountain.

It is a wondrously romantic freak of nature, planted there in a cleft of the rock and walled off from the world, as if the Great Mother meant to lock it up and hide it away for her own use. It is thickly wooded, narrow and deep. The trees meet over the path in places, and the ferns touch you as you pass. The spirits of Knocknarea must love it. One can fancy how they made it their own centuries ago. A mystic poet might dream his life away in it, holding communion with the hero-dead of Connacht. It would also be a grand place for a botanist, or " a man on his keeping," or an amateur distiller,

When you succeed in driving yourself out of the glen you ought to climb the mountain, on the top of which there is a cairn. There are people who will tell you that Queen Meave was buried there and not at Cruachain. I think they are in error. Perhaps it is one of the earlier kings of pagan Ireland that sleeps on Knocknarea.

Be that as it may, however, the cairn is a resting-place fit for a monarch. It looks down on wide Tir Fiachra, where dwelt "the music-loving hosts of fierce engagements." Away to northward and east-ward and southward are mountain and valley and river and lake and woodland. To the westward rolls the thundering ocean. The mountain has no partner in its glory. It stands proudly over the rocky coast in solitary grandeur. The mourners who erected the burial mound on its stately summit could not have chosen a more royal throne for their kingly dead. They could see the sun-god smiling on it in the morning time before any other peak was crimsoned by his touch, and they caught the last flash of his golden spear upon it as he sank to sleep in the west. The fleecy shreds of vapour which float around it in the Summer time adorn it like some silken scarf of gauze blown against the curls of a woman. The angry clouds of Autumn and Winter cap it. The lightning darts its fiery tongues upon it. The thunder bellows over it. And if the people of Tir Fiachra regarded all these things as being sym-bolic of the sunny or playful or tempestuous moods of their great one, it would only have been quite natural, for they were men and women of epic minds. Their lives were epic. Their fate was epic. Their history is epic.

And about Knocknarea itself there is an epic suggestiveness which you cannot miss if you climb the mountain. You cannot keep your hold upon the present while you are up there. You may smoke twentieth century tobacco and look down on twentieth century towns and railways and roads, but your thoughts are far away.

You can fancy the dead leader from the cairn on the summit gazing prophetically northward across Lough Gill and Brefney and Lough Erne into Ulster, or eastward toward Cruachain and Tara. You wonder is the prophesying all over. Did it all end, was it all fulfilled, in the long ago? Or has a portion of it still to weave itself into form, now that so many bright gleams of the old temperament are kindling in the dreamers of our time?

A bearded stranger found me standing on a bridge in Sligo one morning and proposed to take me up Lough Gill in a boat. I asked him some questions in geography, and found his mind was virgin soil in this respect. All he could tell me was that the water underneath the bridge led to the lake, and that he was a boatman of vast experience and of the strictest honesty.

I asked him some questions in local history, and was informed that the history of Sligo is in books. So he had been told. None of the said history was in his possession, nor had he ever seen it, but he could positively assure me that his personal honesty was above suspicion, and that his boat was comfortable and safe, as the Mayor himself could testify. He offered to take me to Drumahaire and back for six shillings. I said that I preferred to

ride.   This he solemnly told me was impossible
I knew better, for I had ridden it some weeks previously.   But I did not tell this to the champion
boatman of Sligo.   I merely bade him good morning and said that I would mention him to my
friends.   He then offered to take me to Drumahaire
and back for five shillings   I shook my head.
"For four, then," he called after me.   I made no
sign.   "For three," he said, desperately.   He drew
a blank every time.   Then he followed me and
offered to tell me the best road.   I knew it.   Then
in despair he turned away and left me to my fate.

I do not know if there are any other Lough Gill
boatmen in Sligo.   If there are, they do not seem
to be overworked, for you seldom see a boat upon
the lake.   And yet it must be a delightful journey
by water from the city to Drumahaire.   The river
which connects Lough Gill with the sea is short, but
it is very beautiful.   It flows between wooded hills
and past smooth green lawns, and when it opens on
the lake it is a new and abiding delight.

Opposite Drumahaire, which is some distance
away from the water, another river disembogues.
You ascend this stream for about a mile until you
meet a sort of jetty   Here you disembark, for you
are within a few minutes' walk of the Abbey Hotel.
Such is one way to Drumahaire.   The way of the
cyclist is either along the northern or southern
shore, around the lake.   If you start by the northerly
road you return to Sligo by the route which touches
the southern shore of the lake.   If you start by the
southern road you return by the northern.   A day
will take you round Lough Gill comfortably.   It is

a run of about twenty miles—Irish miles, of course.

As you leave Sligo behind you and strike southward in the direction of Boyle the country looks
bleak. It looks bleaker still as you wheel to the
left at a cross-roads outside the city. The land is
poor and the bare rock asserts itself over the clinging heather on the hills near the road. But have a
little patience. Presently you come to a turn and
creep down a steep incline, and then Lough Gill in
all its loveliness and freshness and grandeur bursts
upon your view. The change is so rapid and complete that for the first few moments you are
bewildered.

But for goodness sake let us not hasten to com-
pare it with anything or any place else. Let us take
it on its own merits. The practice of comparing one
beauty spot on this earth with another is hackneyed
and, in the abstract, somewhat sickening. " The
Switzerland of Ireland" is a cry to be abhorred.
So is " How like Geneva ! " So is " How suggestive
of the English lake country ! " And another parrot
cry is " Oh ! dear ! How like the Riviera ! " You
cheapen Irish scenery when you rush into such
comparisons. There is none of it that you can
flatter by calling it German or Italian or French or
English names This land of ours revels in beauty
She is a favoured child of nature; and I pity any
one born of her who would not prefer her loveliness
to that of any other land, for it is second to none.

The change of scenery from the rather wild and
barren country through which you passed after leaving the Boyle road opens full upon your view just
when you have descended into the lake valley

sufficiently to bring you on a level with the tops of the trees that cover the hills around the shore. Above the trees grow the heather and fern, and the weather-stained rocks crown the summits. Below you is the western end of the lake studded with islands, and each island is like a big hillock of verdure, so thickly do the trees grow together. In the Autumn, when the different tints come on the foliage, each islet looks like a big nosegay set in the water, and the heather above the timber belt on the hills is covered with purple bloom.

The surface of the lake is smooth enough to reflect everything—the blue sky and the fleecy clouds and the verdant glory of the trees and ferns and meadows and the royal trappings of the heath, and the browns and greys of the beetling crags. All these tints mingle in the depths, gilded by the glad sunshine that fondly caresses them all. A rivulet murmurs and laughs softly to you as it tumbles down from the rocks under the cool shade of the briars and ferns. There are bird songs in the trees, and a rabbit scuttles swiftly across the road, and you hear the tap, tap, tap of the thrush coming from the forest gloom beyond as he cracks a snail upon a stone and prepares his breakfast. You are alone with nature, and you enjoy it. But do not stop just yet.

Ride down the road to the water and look for a few moments up at the hills and along the lake between the islands. Then follow the road again upward through the woods until you come to a place where a broad pathway leads into the brush under the hazels. Leave your bicycle here—no one will meddle with it, even if they pass the way—and take the path which winds steeply up between the tree trunks at right angles to the road. The hart tongues, and the tall fronds of the wood ferns, and the wild violets and bluebells, brush your insteps; the hazel branches rustle against your head and shoulders, and the dried twigs snap under your feet.

Upward you bend your way across the little patches of light which the sun throws on the ground, as he peeps down through the branches of the oaks and pines, until you come to the level and wooded summit of the hill. You walk out on a rocky terrace and stand right over the lake, hundreds of feet over the pebbly strand which shines below you. This terrace gives you a splendid cross-view of Lough Gill.

The western and south-western creeks and bays are all in sight. You are far over the tree-tops of the islands. You can see the wide lawns of a park sloping downward to the river that flows on to Sligo and the farmsteads of the distant hills beyond which the Atlantic frets and swells. Here, indeed, you may rest and dream, or smoke and think of things. This is beauty undefiled, and you have it all to yourself. No tripper agency has yet discovered it; no railway company has yet fumigated it with coal smoke; no restaurant tout has yet daubed it with advertisements.

But you must not stay here for ever and ever, nor even for hours and hours. You have only just entered the charmed district of Lough Gill as yet, and there are many miles of it still to be seen.

When you have had a good long draught or the loveliness which flows in upon you here, you tear yourself away as best you can from this terrace and go back to your bicycle.

The road now leaves the waterside and goes off round the mountain to Drumahaire. When you leave the wood behind you the country falls into a jumble of hills and valleys and ravines and heathery mountain sides, and racing mountain streamlets which seam the rocks and start from under the ferns here and there, leaping wildly into the radiance of the day. I do not know how many years you could spend going over those roads without tiring of the beauty through which they take you. I have gone over them two or three times. and I want to go back there again.

The hills are of many colours, dark green and bright green with grass or scrub, brown or gray with rocks, or purple with heather. Some of them are thickly wooded, others are bare and grim. You think you are going to get rid of them when you are climbing some steep reach of the smooth road; you fancy that when you have topped the incline in front of you there will be no more of them in your way.

But when you stand panting on the crest you will find another bewildering series of them still before you. Below you is a green valley, and above the fields laughs the gorse that crowns the slope. Beyond the yellow sheen of the blossoms is the dark shadow of another hillside and beyond that again the haze over another valley is purpled by the distance. And, over the valley, the hilltops, one

behind the other—all dim and far away—are peeping at you over each other's shoulders or frowning
at you over each other's heads.

Bagairth a geinn thar dhruim a cheile.

That is exactly how the mountains must have
looked to the poet—nodding their heads one from
behind the other. They were piled up, just as they
are around Lough Gill. They were grimly
humourous in their persistency to hem a mortal in
and plant themselves in his road, turn which way
he would. These are the Leitrim hills. They roll
northward into Donegal, north-westward to Lough
Erne and eastward to Cavan.

Long ago they were called Ui Briuin, Breifni or
Brefney. The territory was so called, says
O'Mahony, from its being possessed by the race of
Ui Briuin. And the learned translator of Keating
goes on to say: " The Ui Briuin race derived their
name from being descendants of Brian, King of
Connacht, in the fourth century." Brian's posterity
possessed the greater part of Connacht, and were
called the Ui Briuin race. Of this race were the
O'Conors, the O'Rourkes, the O'Reillys, MacDer-
motts, etc., etc. And further he says: " The
O'Rourkes and O'Reillys derived their descent from
Aedh Finn or Hugh the Fair, King of Connacht,
who died A.D. 611 * * * O'Rourke's country
was called Brefney O'Rourke and O'Reilly's country
was called Brefney O'Reilly."

There must have been a hardy race bred on those
rugged hills. The mere work of marching over them
would make an athlete of a man or kill him. And
when you come to push a bicycle around in Brefney

you would want the muscle of four gallowglasses
and the lungs of half a clan, and the patience of
Job.   It is a magnificent country.   Its scenery is
splendid in its many sided variety, but it is not as
easy to cycle through it as the Phœnix Park.

"Use makes master," however, and you get used
to Leitrim cycling difficulties.   You accustom yourself to suddenly parting with your wheel and falling
down a mountain with safety.   You may fall
gracefully and you may not, but the main point is
to fall as safely as you can.   If you can manage
to fall into a wood, it is not bad; if into a growth
of ferns, it is nicer, so long as you have a good
distance to roll; it is grand to hear them rustling
and breaking into sweet smelling shreds as you
crash through them.

It is not unpleasant to slip off the road into a big,
bunchy tuft of heather, or into a moss-grown dyke.
But it is unsafe to go headlong into the Atlantic
Ocean or dive into a mountain lake, or take a flight
over a precipice into a heap of rocks three or four
hundred feet below.   After being some years in
journalism a man's hide is fairly hard and thick,
but there are exigencies over which it will not rise
superior.   It has its limits of endurance.   I rode
twice across Leitrim, and, please God, some day or
another I will ride across it again.   It would be
easier and safer work, of course, if your bicycle had
a pair of wings, and if you had fourteen or fifteen
lives; but even with an ordinary wheel and one life
it is grand.

It may be asked, why and how you fall down
a mountain? but no concise or definite reply can be

given.   Ask a great singer how or why he gets such glorious music out of his thro-t, and what can he tell you, only that it comes?   He may be able to give you a few superficial details, but no words of his can reach the kernel of the wonder.   It is a gift. And so with falling down mountains: it is a gift Your wheel slips or slides, or runs away, or you make too sharp a curve, and all the rest is falling, falling, falling, and getting to the bottom.   While you are mending yourself and your bicycle, you may wonder how you did it; but you can never tell exactly.   You can feel it and dream about it after- wards, but never realise it—until it happens again.

Drumahaire was the capital of Brefney O'Rourke. The O'Rourkes had castles at Leitrim, Carrickallen and Castlecar, but Drumahaire was their chief stronghold.   The ruins of their castle stand on the outskirts of the little town, beside a river, overlook- ing a valley.   Both the castle and valley are famed in song and story.   Moore's verses will occur to you as you stand in the ivy-clad ruins.   You remember the lines, of course:

> The valley lay smiling before me
>   Where lately I left her behind,
> Yet I trembled and something hung o'er me,
>   That saddened the joy of my mind.
> I looked for the lamp which she told me
>   Should shine when her pilgrim returned,
> Yet though darkness began to enfold me,
>   No lamp from the battlement burned.

Well, here you have the valley that lay smiling before him.   Here were also the battlements, now no more. They were battered to fragments in the wars of the sixteenth century, but some of the walls remain.

Here Dermod MacMurrough and Dervorgilla, the wife of Tiernan O'Rourke, used to meet. They finally bolted during the absence of O'Rourke, and hence the infamy that has lived on through the ages. When MacMurrough was obliged to fly the country from the vengeance of O'Rourke, he went to England and brought back the Normans. It was a terrible crime, a terrible wrong, a terrible atonement. MacMurrough died, falling to pieces, in the pangs of a loathsome disease, and the evil he did lived after him. I am not concerned about his fate at all. But there is some fiction and wasted sympathy mixed up with this tale of Brefney which should be sorted out, so that history may have fair play. For we can do no good by taking our bitter historical pills coated over with the sugar of romance; better swallow them just as they are compounded for us by cold, stern facts. Thomas Moore was no mean historian, but his poetic fancy got the better of him in Drumahaire. For example, let us take the lines:

There was a time, falsest of women,
    When Brefney's good sword would have sought
That man through a million of foemen
    Who dared but to doubt thee in thought.

Here is a splendid and passionate sorrow grandly expressed, but it existed more in the poetic soul of Thomas than in the fierce heart of Tiernan. For Tiernan O'Rourke was no saint. He was just a predatory mountaineer who had a heart as black as the next man. According to the Four Masters, this Tiernan O'Rourke, who, by the way, was called the One-eyed, led his men in 1136 A.D. across the Shannon, on a certain kind of pilgrimage which was little to his credit.

"They raided and sacked Clonard and behaved in so shameless a manner as to strip O'Daly, then chief poet of Ireland. Among other outrages they sacrilegiously took from the vestry of this abbey a sword which had belonged to St. Finian, the founder." The leader of this raid was the person who was supposed to be returning from some pious journey when he failed to see Dervorgilla's light on the battlements. He was a nice pilgrim!

Dervorgilla was a "false one" when she fled, but there are historians who deny that she was "young." She was about forty years of age, and was old enough to have sense. She seems to have quickly tired of MacMurrough, or he of her. Anyhow she did not remain with him very long; two years would be the very outside of their criminal relationship after the elopement. She either left him or was left by him, or was taken from him, after which she lived with her people, who were chieftains of Meath.

To give her her due, she seems to have reformed her ways. She built some churches and lived a retired life. It was she who built the beautiful twelfth-century church of the nuns at Clonmacnoise. Thirty-four years after Tiernan O'Rourke had sacked Clonard, the abbey was once more looted in a manner that left even the vandalism of the Brefney men in the shade. The raider this time was

O'Rourke's rival, MacMurrough, and he was aided
in his ruffianism by Earl Strongbow and the other
reavers from over the water.

It is sad to think of, but so is nearly every year
of those blood-stained centuries. The ready-
handed chieftains raided each other and finished
nearly everything that the Danes had left, and
it seems we are now beginning to find out that
the Danes left a good deal. The Church was the
most powerful moral influence in the land, but
there was little, if any, real union between it and
the State. The State itself was inchoate. Clontarf
had left it victorious but inorganic. There were
saintly ecclesiastics and there were laymen of statesmanship and patriotism; but neither class had
produced a man to fill the leadership left vacant by
the death of Brian. The Church had neither the
power to protect itself from the blows dealt it by
children of its own, nor influence enough to quell
the wild passions of the times. The State had
neither cohesion nor strength; for the centuries that
had gone by since the cursing of Tara had failed
to evolve a nation self-centred and self-confident
in the practice of well-defined political institutions.
Brian of the Tribute would, in all human probability, have given law and order to the whole of
Ireland had he survived his victory over the Norsemen. But the fates were unkind, and after the
Dane came the Anglo-Norman— and came, alas! to
stay. There was no acknowledged and effective
leader of the Irish race, no central power, no recognised national government to band the clans
together into one solid fighting force and hurl them

with crushing strength upon the foe. The invader came upon us in our weakness and we fell a prey to him. And "through ages of bondage and slaughter" the Church as well as the State was destined to groan beneath the heel of the tyrant, and to look back with futile sorrow to that thrice accursed day when the foundations of centralised civil government were destroyed at Tara by the anger of an all-powerful and over-zealous ecclesiasticism.

And thus it fell out that we passed under the chastening hand of adversity to feel the greatness of our fall, to see the magnitude of our errors, and, in the dark and slow-dragging centuries of oppression and suffering, to steel and temper our souls, that we may be instinct with all godliness and kingliness when we break at last from the house of bondage and march onward once more towards the greatness of our destinies.

Drumahaire is an ideal place to spend a quiet time, far from the roaring crowds of the cities. The railway comes close to the town, but not close enough to be in evidence. It winds in from the Manorhamilton hills and then swings off again across the valleys, and is quickly lost to view. You are within easy reach of busy cities, and yet you seem to be as far away from them as if you were in the heart of a trackless continent. There is no noise, no hurry or worry. No one is interested in your movements. You can stroll along the mountain roads over the hills, and come and go as you wish. No fuss of fashion, no social emulation, no show. Perfect quiet, perfect ease, beautiful scenery, and a hotel—the Abbey Hotel—which is one of the best of its kind in Ireland, and one of the cheapest, although its accommodation is first class. It is called after the old Cistercian abbey which stands beyond the town on the river banks.

The ruined abbey shows many traces of its former magnificence. There are three sides of the cloister arches intact, and the beautiful window tracery of the main aisle, over where the high altar stood, is still flawless. It was a very old religious foundation, and the walls now standing were doubtless built to replace the original monastery.

If you have a week or a fortnight to spare you could make Drumahaire your headquarters, and take a new route each day for a cycling trip of twenty or thirty miles around   You can see new charms in the country on every journey; and if you begin to long for change of scene, pull out for the north, and a day's spin will take you across the Erne into Donegal.

About two miles from Drumahaire, going northward, you skirt a mountain and drop down on the lake shore again. The road runs along the water edge, and over it the scrub-grown hills rise sheer and high into the blue. There are oaks and pines among the hazels, striking their roots as best they can into the clefts of the rocks, and underneath, around the gnarled trunks, the mosses and ferns are year by year making a soil. Here is an object lesson in the uses of afforestation which is of great value. It teaches that most of our waste mountain lands could be made productive, and that many a bare hillside in Ireland could be made beautiful by a wood. In Connaught, Ulster and parts of Munster, aye, even in sylvan Leinster, there is room for hundreds of thousands of acres of forest. Irish Ireland should set about planting them at once. It is work for nation builders.

There is one particular hill close to the eastern end of the lake that you ought to climb. It is a stiff piece of work, but the view from the top will repay you. Leave your bicycle on the side of the road which turns off to the right from the shore, and you will find a sort of path through the scrub which will give you your bearings. You cross a piece of sward where the rabbits' tracks are plentiful, after you have made your way through the hazels on the lower slope, and then you come to the sugar-loaf which tops the hill. This is almost perpendicular, but it is covered with hardy bushes by the branches of which you can pull yourself up step by step over the rocks. In a few minutes you are on the summit, looking down in unfeigned admiration on one of the most magnificent lake scenes in the world. The whole length of Lough Gill spreads out beneath your gaze, and you can see far over the hills and along the valleys which encircle it. The splendid perspective is closed by Knocknarea, with the royal cairn which overlooks the picture—a picture fit for kingly eyes. Grey Benbulben frames it to the right, while to the left the purple ridges and sleeping valleys alternate until the sky drops down upon them beyond the distant headwaters of the Shannon.

Right below you is the valley which, according to Moore, lay smiling before Tiernan O'Rourke. It is smiling now, and is certainly fair. It is one of the many valleys that run down to the shore of Lough Gill, all vying with each other in beauty. The big rugged peaks stand guardians over them, and along their green slopes the white-washed farmsteads are set amid the trees.

Tillage field, and meadow, grove, and haggard, and pasture, alternate along them until the distance blurs the view. When the mists roll upward from them in the morning and when the gold of the dawn flushes the crags and steals down the heather to the corn fields, it would be a callous nature that would not feel moved. No wonder the people love them so. I stood for a long time gazing on them from near the clouds, with one who could feel their beauty more thoroughly than I.

"It must be awful for any one born here to have to go away and never return!" was what we said as we turned to retrace our steps.

Near the eastern extremity of the lake is a mountain called O'Rourke's Table. You remember the old ballad of "O'Rourke's Noble Feast." Well, the top of the mountain yonder is the table on which the feast was set. It is indeed a table fit for such an occasion. It slopes gently from the valley on the far side, but facing the lake it is steep and inaccessible. The solid rock towers aloft on the crest like a huge fortress, and you must, therefore, take it by a flank movement. Unless you care to walk a mile or two round by the chapel, you must climb from near the rocks which front Lough Gill. There is a wood on one side of the mountain, and through this is the safest way. You scramble up through the larches, and then, forcing your way through a dense growth of beautiful ferns, your feet are on the table.

It was a lovely day when two of us stood there, and we shall never forget it. The table is about two miles long and half a mile in width. And such a royal tablecloth! Rich, fragrant, clustering heather! The top of the mountain is covered with peat, and the peat is covered with a growth of heather in which you stand waist high. Rank, sedgy grass and heaps of moss and huge tufts of mountain fern are along the edge near the wood, and right in the centre, where you can look down on the Atlantic and on hundreds of square miles of Ulster and Connacht, as well as Lough Gill, there is moss in which you sink to your knees, and dry clumps of heath in which you could dream your life away. The sedgy beds of broad grass are packed below with dry and withered leaves which yield to your weight as if they were feathers, and crumple as softly under your tread as if they were velvet pile from the old Genoese looms.

You are higher up than the grey peaks of the nearest ranges; you are on a level with the others. You are up in the blue air where only the eagle soars and the skylark sings. The rooks and daws and sea fowl are winging their flight below you over lake and valley and hill. Only the clouds lie here when they are lazy or too full of rain to travel. It is the flower of bogs—the canavaun of the mountain tops of Erin!

Not long ago I was reading one of those whimsical articles on the land question by Standish O'Grady—an article written in that vein of gentle,

kindly raillery for which the gifted author is noted.
He was replying to, or commenting on, some letter
in which a correspondent said that " every man will
have his own bit of land when we get compulsory
purchase." " Then," said the chieftain, " I want to
file my claim to the Rock of Dunamase."

He wanted to own (although he is a kind
Unionist) the rock on which Rory O'Moore's fortress
stood, the stronghold from which the Lion of Leix
so often swept down in anger on the lordlings of the
Pale. Well, there are more people than Standish
O'Grady in Ireland who would like to have the fee-
simple of Dunamase. I am one of them myself.
But I know there are too many prior claims put in,
so I shall not file one. No one has, however, yet
claimed the Table of O'Rourke, so I am first in the
field. It is of little value as an estate. It is only
heather and moss and peat and fern and rock But
I covet it all the same.

CHAPTER III.

*On the Connacht Plains—A Land Laid Desolate—
Rath Croghan of Meave and Dathi—Two Men
Raving on a Wall—The Sheep-crooks—The
Gentry and the People—Sketches of a certain
Regatta.*

If you wish to study the contemporary situation
in Ireland thoroughly, you must make a tour in the
great ranch district beyond the Shannon. My
voyage of discovery was made by wheel, and it
took me over scores and scores of miles of lonely
roads, through dust and sunshine and silence, and
through six long days of a midsummer week.

A deep blue Summer sky, with patches of fleecy
clouds which blotch the bare hillsides with shadows.
Grass lands rolling away in long undulating miles
to the sky rim, crossed here and there by grassy
ridges running from east to west. Along the horizon
low ranges of mountains mingle their deep tints
with the silvery whiteness of the clouds. Slieve
Baun is in the middle distance, to the right, with its
twin summits swelling in purple beauty from the
plain and fronting the hills of Annaly, a proud and
lonely warden of the Shannon.

There are no woodlands, no groves, scarcely any
trees at all. There is no agriculture—the fertile
desert is uncultivated from end to end. Away
from our feet to the crest of the far-off ridges the
public road stretches in a straight line across the
valley, between the stone walls, breast high, which
separate it from the silent fields on either side. On

the broad pastures the flocks and herds are scattered, browsing the rich grass which grows over many a usurped hearth. The thin line you see yonder, like the wavy curves of a white ribbon on the grass, is made up of a few score of wethers wending their way down the slope, along a path, to the little streamlet in the hollow. A few crows and seagulls wing their flight high up in the blue over the lonesome tracts. They are bound Leinsterwards, where the worm-strewn furrows open in the track of the ploughman attending to the green crops. There is no break in the empty silence save the whimper of the winds. Not a bird voice is upon the air. There is no heather in all this fertile desolation from which the larks might rise in song. There are no copses for the throstles and robins to warble in. Nothing but pasture and sheep and stone walls and the western wind and loneliness.

Such is the landscape you meet after passing out into the country through the suburbs of Roscommon; such it is until you reach the environs of Boyle. It is a ride of about twenty miles. You may go eastward from Elphin toward Mayo and ride for a whole day through such a scene. You may strike out in a south-westerly direction into Galway and you will find little variety in the landscape. There are vast and unbroken areas of pasture or grazing lands also in Sligo. They are all more or less the same. The land is more fertile in one locality than in another, but it tells the same story everywhere— the story of a land laid desolate.

There has been a great deal of Irish history made on these Connacht uplands, for even in the earliest times, in common with the other great plains of Ireland, they were of considerable importance in the national economy.

Where the plain of Coman stretches to the dawn-
　　light
Slopes Cruachain to the sky.

And Cruachain, now called Rath Crogan, was a famous place during the heroic cycles of Erin. It is a noble eminence—it can scarcely be called a hill —which crowns a swelling ridge overlooking the plains of Boyle in the centre of the ranch district. Here was situated the ancient capital of Connacht, and here is also the Rellig-na-Riogh or the royal burial ground. It was here they buried Dathi, the last pagan monarch of Ireland when they brought him home dead on his shield from the Alpine frontiers of ancient Rome, whither he had carried his war against Cæsar. His grave is marked by a pillar stone in the cemetery of the kings, around which the bullocks of the ranchers graze in sleek content. Three of the Tuatha de Danaan queens who gave their names to Ireland, Eirie, Fodhla and Banba—were buried at Croghan, together with their husbands. Conn of the Hundred Battles sleeps there, and the cairn of Meave—the beautiful and wayward and astute—is said to be among the royal tombs.

It was by no dictum of blind chance that Rath Croghan was chosen in the olden time to be the

custodian of the throne of Connacht. Neither was
Tara chosen at random, nor Kincora, nor Uisnach,
nor Alleach, nor any other of the high places of
Erin. They were chosen because of the fertility of
the district, the beauty of the scenery and the
strategetic advantages of position. They afforded
splendid pasturage for the royal flocks and herds.
In the forests there was game for royal hawk and
hound. In the noble streams which swept in long
bends through the splendour of the woodlands,
there were fish for the royal table, and cool, retired,
bramble-hidden backwaters where royalty might
bathe. And on the level sward below the palaces,
or in the forest glades, there were fields for athletic
games, and there was room to course the chargers.

To-day Rath Croghan, with its royal raths and
burial mounds, stands on the naked plain, in the
midst of modern grazierdom, and no student of Irish
history who is of the Irish race can look upon it
unmoved. But it is not alone because its ancient
splendour has departed that it makes you sad.
Long centuries have passed indeed since Croghan
was a word to conjure with in Irish affairs. Its
greatness was highest in the pagan times. But all
through the centuries since then, until the accursed
days that saw the chains of the Saxon fastened
upon Ireland, Croghan was the centre of one of the
loveliest and most populous rural districts in the
world. It is for the vanished people that the Irish
heart is sorrowful as well as for the kingdom that
is dead.

Your feelings toward the ancient heroes are mellowed by the glamour of romance. But there is no

softening element in the history of yesterday and to-day as it is written broadly on the landscape. It is for the uptorn homes and the empty fields that you are angry. It is for these things that curses rise to your lips. It is against the infamous law which fomented and sanctioned and authorised the depopulation that you are a rebel to the inmost core of your manhod. And it is for the day that will see English rule swept out of the island, and those plains dotted once more with peaceful, happy, God-fearing, God-serving, patriotic Irish homes—it is for that blessed day of days that you are hopeful with a yearning, hungry hope.

Think of what it would mean to Ireland if such a rich territory, now given over to sheep and cattle, were divided up into farms of forty or fifty acres each with a family of from five to eight children on each farm! Think of that land with its under-lying, health-giving strata of limestone! The lime in the soil is good for the formation of bones—of sound, thick, massive bones upon which you can grow tough and corded muscle. Think of all the big-boned, deep-chested men and women that you could rear for Ireland where horses and sheep are now being prepared for export to the armies and stomachs of foreigners.

The evil of depopulation is a tragic and madden-ing phase of the land question which meets you on nearly every road in Ireland Depopulation of the most fertile land, synchronised with the crowding together of the people upon the bogs and moors and mountain sides. In no country except Ireland would this have been tolerated without a struggle

that would have aroused the world. Blood would
have been shed in torrents over it. Blood has been
shed in Ireland on account of it, but not in torrents—
only in thin driblets. Landlords and their minions
have occasionally fallen under the vengeance of
their victims, and the English Press has shrieked in
Pharasaical horror, calling the Irish peasantry cut-
throats and barbarians. But no country in the
civilised world would have tolerated a worthless
feudalism so long. It would have goaded any other
people into action, tempestuous, and sanguinary, and
devastating. Were it not that the Irish people have
been so obedient to moral restraint, the lives of rack-
renting landlords would not have been worth a
farthing many a time during the nineteenth century.
In other countries famine and despair and exaspera-
tion have waded knee deep in the life blood of
oppression, leaving to the moralists and historians
the task of weighing and fixing responsibility. Our
patience and fortitude in Ireland are glorified as
heroic Christian virtues. And such indeed they are.
But, by Heaven, if there is one thing more than
another a thoughtful Irishman is tempted to regret
when contemplating the tragedy of our history it
is that our capacity for moral endurance was at times
so great and that our spirit of active resistance to
tyranny was not ten thousand times greater!

Some such thought as this must have been in the
minds of two men who sat on a wall by a Connacht
roadside scowling upon a magnificent sweep of
country wherein not a dozen homes were visible in
all the wide miles of luscious grass.

"Do you know what?" said one to the other, waving his hand toward Rath Croghan, which loomed against the cloudless sky in the sunny distance. "I wish I had some of the power that was centred yonder when Ferdiah and his companions went out against the Red Branch."

"What would you do with it?" asked the other. And the first speaker promptly answered.

"To begin with, a man could give grazierdom and its patrons a surprise. It would be worth a year of my life to scoop up all the live stock from these Connacht plains."

"A border raider—a stock lifter! Is that what you would make of yourself?" said the other, shaking his head. "Has history no lesson for you? Did not Meave live to bewail her raid for the Red Bull of Ulster?"

"There is no parallel between my little dream," said the dreamer, "and the old legend which you recall, for I would drive the flocks and herds northward through the Ulster passes to be slaughtered to feed an Irish army that had at last shaken out the war flag. No doubt you will say I am raving, but I am not so bad as that. I am laying down what, under conceivably fortuitous circumstances, might be a practical and attractive military proposition. Do you follow me?"

The other was a man of peace **and** a man of God; but he smote his knee and threw up his head.

"My hand to you!" he cried, in the dear delight of caressing the wild and witching ideal which had burst into his peaceful life. "It would be splendid! To clear out the Connacht plains! It would be a

terrible haul.   Why, listen to me, it would feed
40,000 men for months !   I read somewhere the
other day that there are sheep and cattle enough west
of the Shannon to feed Ireland during a blockade
of years."

"As a matter of authenticated history," remarked
his companion, " there was as much food exported
from Ireland to England during the famine as
would sustain the entire population of the country."

"And we let it go!" commented the other, in a
tone widely at variance with his peaceful calling.
"It is a lesson for the future which Ireland should
remember."

"So you are one of those who have faith in the
future ? " asked the dreamer.

"I am," was the proud reply, " even if the present
were ten times blacker than it is, even if our past
were ten times more tragic.   I look forward to a time
when the rule of the outlander shall be no more in
Ireland, and when the dark shadow cast by his
presence on the land shall have given place to the
sunshine of freedom.   But say, am I raving any way
well ? "

"Splendidly !   Go ahead ! " cried the dreamer,
encouragingly.

"Ah, if all the raving we do were only half a
prophecy ! " he continued with a smile, half sad,
half playful.   "If even our tamest dreams came
true, what a grand thing it would be.   Think of
how joyful it would be, when the fight was ended,
to see the people shifting their homes out of the
bogs and settling down again here on these plains,
where their race has lived for ages.   There would

have to be strict legislation about it, of course, and commissioners to examine and decide regarding claims and all that. And there would be a board to look after afforestation, so that stately groves and woods should in time again beautify the land."

And for half an hour and more the two Irishmen sat there on the wall in the rapture of a proud delirium, weaving patriotic fancies amidst the Connacht desolation.

It is not easy to give an adequate idea of depopulation as it exists. I had no adequate idea of it myself until I saw it. I stood by the pillar stone over King Dathi's grave on Rath Croghan and looked over the grass lands which spread around me for miles. I could see at least three or four leagues in every direction. I can safely affirm that there was not one house to the square mile. I walked hither and thither around the burial mounds, and examined the subjacent plains from various points of view, and at no time could I count a dozen houses.

The richness of the soil was evidenced in many ways. There could be no doubt that the land was some of the best in Europe. It could easily support in decent and prosperous comfort a family to every fifty acres—families that could give higher education to their boys and doweries to their girls. If there were a family to every fifty acres those plains would have a population of thousands and thousands. At present there are tracts of the Pampas more thickly peopled. And there is ample room on the Connacht ranches for all the emigrants that ever left Ireland for the great stock runs of the South.

During my tour I fell in with one of the parish priests of the diocese of Elphin, who said: "I have 110 sheep crooks in my parish," meaning that instead of hundreds of agriculturist families, he had 110 herdsmen. Another sagart with whom I had the pleasure of conversing told me that he had spent all the years of his mission on the Connacht plains. He said that in his own parish at that present moment two-thirds of the congregation were shepherds. The other third consisted of unfortunate people who were living on the skirt of the plains in little holdings which they had themselves reclaimed from the bogs and moors and swamps, and for which they had been rackrented in proportion to the extent of the improvements effected by their own labour.

And let us not forget that the people crowded together on the skirts of the plains—on the bogs and moors and mountains—starved in body and mind, bent by toil and chilled by penury, are the rightful owners of the ranches. They are the descendants of the clansmen who held the land under the chieftains. They are the people who were hounded out of their rights under the laws which English domination imposed upon the country. They are the descendants of the men who were dispossessed so that the soil might be portioned out among the soldiers who had fought for the conquest of the nation. They are the tenants who were evicted by the sheep and cattle breeders.

During my cycling tours through Connacht I have in various places come across the work of the Congested Districts Board. The Board buys any grazing property or other tract of unoccupied land which comes within the possibilities of its financial resources. It then drains, fences, and lays out the land into farms of from twenty to thirty acres each, and the men who are paid for doing this work are from the locality, and are generally the people who will be the new tenants. Comfortable but plain and suitable dwellings are then erected, with outoffices, etc., and the farms are then ready for the occupiers.

The Board is slow in its operations, and it is able to cope with only a very small part of the work to be done. But it is, with all its drawbacks, a move which commends itself to approval and justification by the results already accomplished. And it points the way to the definite solution of the Irish land question. That solution has not been given by the Land Act of 1903. It has merely been played with. The question has been begged, while the price of land has been inflated. The solution of the Irish land question cannot be achieved by half measures. It is a deeply seated evil and needs a drastic remedy. Landlordism will have to go, root and branch, with all its sporting rights and turbary rights and head rents and mining royalties, and every other feudal and archaic absurdity. Compulsory sale, and nothing less, is the only remedy, and come it must soon or late.

I crossed the river Suck south of the little town of Athleague and struck westward into Galway, never halting till I came to Mount Bellew. Here I visited the schools and college established by the Franciscan Brothers many years ago. The institution is now known as the College of St. Francis, and

is one of the foremost educational establishments in
the West. It is, in every sense of the word, an Irish
college, and makes a speciality of the Irish language.

I met the Rev. Brother Superior of the Franciscan
teachers at the College of St. Francis and had the
pleasure of a long conversation with him. When he
spoke of the other houses of the Brothers in Connacht, and of the work still to be done in Ireland
for God and country, you saw at once the fine spirit
of this faithful body of Irishmen—modest, simple,
practical men of the people who have done so much
in the cause of Irish education.

Ah, me! one cannot help wasting thought in poor
Ireland on the Might Have Been! And, while in
the College of Mount Bellew, I could not help
thinking of the fight of stout old John of Tuam
against the denationalising schools of which
Whately was the apostle. If the Lion of St.
Jarlath's had gained his point when the misnamed
national education system was projected, and if
Ireland for the past forty years and more had been
taught by men like the Franciscan Brothers, there
would be little need to-day for the propaganda of
the Gaelic League. Archbishop MacHale stood for
a total rejection of the national schools, and said
that the children of Ireland should be educated on
Irish lines. A temporising policy was substituted
for this wise and manly ideal; and from the day on
which this melancholy error was committed the
Anglicisation of the Irish mind went on apace.

In Connacht, as indeed in the other provinces of
Ireland, speaking generally, the old-time friendly
relations which in many instances existed between

the classes and the masses are passing away. That
those friendly relations have not entirely disappeared is due to the rational and patriotic stand
taken by a few of the gentry who have departed
from the cast-iron traditions of landlordism and
thrown in their lot with the people. It would be
better for their class and for Ireland if their
example were extensively followed; but Ireland and
the Irish people will struggle along without the men
who, after all, are standing more in their own light
than in the light of the nation.

The Land Acts already won by the people, meagre
and shuffling though they are, have still written on
the wall the doom of the landlord oligarchy in
Ireland. Compulsory sale will sound the death
knell of the ascendancy, and after that the fittest
will survive. Any class or clique which persists in
the belief that it has separate interests from the
Irish people will go to the wall. The class known
as the gentry of Ireland—or, to be more accurate,
"the nobility and gentry"—believe they have
separate interests from the people upon whom they
live. Consequently they will not survive. Standish
O'Grady, one of themselves, and one of the best of
them, told them the truth when he said that they
were going, going—"rotting from the land, without
one brave deed, without one brave word." It is a
terrible epitaph to write over the grave of a caste
that might have been the glory and the salvation of
the country. But it is true, and to none is this truth
more sad and appealing than to Standish O'Grady
himself, the knightly Irish gentleman who gave it
utterance.

It was during my cycling tour west of the Shannon that this decay of the Irish gentry was brought most vividly home to me. I think I ought to tell you about it, and in doing so I will ask you to be kind enough to let me unfold the tale in my own way.

I was riding with an Irish Irelander through one of the rare wooded spots in the great ranch district when a few glimpses of the demesne by which we were passing, caught through gaps in the crumbling walls along the wayside, caused me to suggest a halt. On every side were signs of fallen fortunes, of neglect and poverty and ruin. The park was evidently a vast rabbit warren and the sward was overrun with whins. The groves were wide tangles of underbrush. The grand avenue was grass-grown and mossy. The "big house" itself still made a brave show, but the out offices were woefully dilapidated. Under some of the giant elms and beeches to the rere of the mansion the bare gables of a ruined kennel showed where the foxhounds had once fed and yelped and slept. The lodge at the grand gate was untenanted and neglected. The gate itself was rickety, and swung half open on its crazy hinges.

"Who lives here?" I asked, wishing to know the name of the person or persons whose residence had seen better days, and on whose property the symptoms of consumption were so conspicuous and unmistakable.

"A member of the Broken Down," replied my comrade, mentioning a name which there is no need to repeat. "They were great people once, but times have changed for them, and, as you see, they are aground on the shoals of adversity."

" What do they live on ? "

" Rabbits, principally, and three-weeks-old illus-trated papers sent to them more or less irregularly by some wealthy connections who live in London."

" And are the people of their own class in the country round about so unkind as to leave them here in the pangs of genteel famine ? "

" What can be expected of folks who are more or less in the same financial straits themselves ? It's nearly six of one and half a dozen of the other. They are all hard up. If it weren't for their pride and lack of brains they'd be dead long ago. Their pride keeps the best side out, and their lack of brains prevents them from understanding the empti-ness and fatuity of their lives."

" What evil spirit took charge of their destiny, I wonder ? "

" Various evil spirits," explained the Irish Ire-lander. " The evil spirit of denationalisation that led them into a slough of stupid imitation and make-believe in which nothing can thrive; the evil spirit of snobbery which made them live above their means; the evil spirit of pride which would not allow them to throw in their lot with that of the common people; and, besides these evil spirits, there were the devils of drink and gambling and lust. But," and his tone suddenly changed, " what do you say to coming with me and having a good look at these curiosities of gentry ? There is an exhibition of them a few miles away from here at a regatta, and you will find numerous samples amongst the collection worthy of inspection."

"Let us go by all means," I assented very readily, being unwilling to lose any opportunity of learning from any object lesson in Ireland whichsoever the source from whence it might be drawn. So we turned eastward at the next crossroads and shaped our course for the banks of the Shannon.

The regatta had been organised by a few local personages of note, and the people had been offered the privilege of subscribing for prizes and expenses— a privilege which did not appear to have been very highly appreciated. I was unable to ascertain for what precise object the event was intended. It was not for the amusement of the classes, for none of the gentry took part in the competitions, so far as I could observe. It was not for the amusement of the masses; they took but scanty interest in the proceedings, and nobody seemed to encourage them or invite them to do so. No gate-money was taken. There was no charge for admission at all. There were no reserved seats. You came or went just as you pleased.

But it was highly respectable. The committee men wore red badges. There was a patron—some lord or marquis—but I am not certain whether he was alive or dead, present or absent. His name was on the programme, but I forget it. The organising and managing committees were all busy doing nothing in particular, and there was a marquee in which they held consultations and in which they refreshed themselves with whiskey obtained for that special purpose by public subscription. There was a flag staff planted on a hillock, from which floated a Union Jack. Another Union Jack floated from the pole of the marquee. There were four or five yachts in the river and each had a Union Jack Two wheezing steam launches also floated Union Jacks. A sailing boat of a nondescript category was decorated in a similar manner. There were no other flags, except a blue and white signal pennant which was lowered or hoisted as occasion demanded. There were a few jaunting cars, three or four dog-carts, some dozens of bicycles, and one carriage of which you shall hear in due course. There were about a dozen tents for the sale of sugarstick, ginger bread, gooseberries; and there were two or three tents for the sale of drink. Five policemen were on duty. There were, all told, about three hundred people present, including adults and children, classes and masses, committee men and spectators, attendants and competitors.

I had strayed away from my companion and was listening to the remarks of the people around me when I observed several committee men leaving the marquee in a body. Their leader carried a double-barrelled shotgun across his arm. He had a pencil behind his ear and a sheaf of papers protruded from his breast pocket. He marched with a firm tread to where the blue signal flag was flying, hauled it down, and then fired a shot, after which he and his comrades retired for refreshment. The hauling down of the flag and the firing of the shot gave the signal for the departure of the two yachts on a race round the lake. They went away at a spanking pace but their movements excited little interest. After a few careless glances the spectators, gentle and simple, turned their backs upon the race and went on chatting or eating gooseberries, or smoking, or refreshing themselves. The only remarks concerning the contest between the two yachts came from a group of the masses. One of the group who had been standing on a rock to see the start leaped down on the grass and said carelessly to his friends:

"To the dickens with it for a race! Come on, boys, and take something."

The classes had set this spirituous example; for scarcely had the race begun when they invited each other to drink strong waters. It is only the barest truth to say, however, that the masses drank very little, but there was a run upon gingerbread, sugar-stick and fruit. Some of the youngsters played hide and seek, others played leap frog. The elders strolled hither and thither rather aimlessly, or sat on a gentle knoll under the shadow of an old castle chatting pleasantly.

I saw two men who appeared to be well-to-do farmers meet and shake hands.

"Musha, James," said one, "isn't this regatta a mi-adh of a thing with all them English flags and curicaries."

"It is surely," said the other.

"It's dam' tiresome," went on the first speaker.

"It is so," agreed James.

"What the dickens is the likes of us doin' here at all?" was the next remark.

James had no idea. Neither had anyone else. What were the likes of them doing there?

What indeed!

The classes were numerously represented, but they had not left their class pride at home, and hence they were painfully select and exclusive. They held no personal intercourse with the masses, or showed them any personal recognition. So rigid were they in their exclusiveness that if the masses were to have tumbled upon them out of the heavens, they would have disdained to notice the intrusion by any remark addressed to the intruders. And yet they had a thought for the masses, in their own peculiar and exclusive way. I rambled hither and thither amongst them and heard their conversation. One tall lady, dressed in a motor cap, cycling skirt, golf blouse, and walking shoes, said to a girl who was dressed in a yachting cap, tennis shoes, and a man's light waterproof coat (worn over a dainty muslin costume)—said, as they shook hands over an imaginary five-barred gate, in that high-elbowed top-story fashion so much in vogue in high social circles : —

" Lovely day, isn't it ? "

" Chawming," answered the waterproof demoiselle.

" Nice regatta," quoth the tall lady.

" Rather ! " commented the maiden (she pronounced it *rawtha*', this being in accordance with the rubrics of polite society, like that shake hands over the imaginary five-bar gate).

" Have you noticed," went on the taller ornament of the classes, " how little interest the country takes in this thing ? "

" Most extraordinary," replied the other.

It is to be noted that the classes alluded to the masses as " the country." The classes did not regard themselves as being " the country " at all.

Three personages met quite close to me. They shook hands from the regions of the upper air, high over the imaginary five-bar gate, and one of them. a stout, florid-complexioned man, said:

"Lovely day, isn't it?"

"Chawming!" answered the others in chorus. One was a bow-legged cavalier, who wore cycling clothes and a covert coat. The other was a clean-shaven young man wearing a motoring coat and an eyeglass.

"Nice regatta," said the florid-complexioned one.

"Oh, rawtha'!' said the others.

"Queer thing, don't you know," observed the florid personage, "how little interest the country takes in this thing."

"Most extraordinary!" agreed his friends. Then one of them produced a cigarette case and they began to smoke and talk about playing bridge. They were joined presently by a party of ladies, some of whom wore Panama hats, while others carried walking sticks and huge racing glasses. They shook hands over the five-bar gate and fell into conversation.

"Nice day, isn't it?"

"Chawming, oh chawming.   Oh rawtha'!"

"Nice regatta."

"Oh rawtha!   Delightful—Quite too lovely!"

"Most extraordinary how little interest the country takes in it, though?"

"Oh rawtha'—most extraordinary.   Don't you know—quite too queer, don't you know."

Not one of them took the slightest interest in the racing any more than the masses. An unsophisticated person might have pointed this fact out to

'hem. They could also have been told that if they
wished to see the masses take a keen and absorbing
interest in sport they should go to any inter-county
or inter-parish hurling match east or west. But, of
course, they would not have heeded such common
remarks, for they had dropped into a talk about the
game of bridge, and were aristocratically and exclusively happy.

In great weariness of soul I went and sat upon a
rock and observed the classes in perspective, as it
were. They carried their clothes with undeniable
distinction, although a good many of them had
done their best to make themselves freakish. They
were golfish, motorish, jockeyish, stable-boyish, in
dress, but although they had succeeded in making
themselves somewhat ridiculous you could not call
them vulgar. Here and there among them you saw
men and women who looked cloddish despite their
frippery, but, truth to tell, most of them showed
breeding both in feature and carriage. Yet they
saddened me. They impressed me as being hopelessly aloof from their country and their time.
There was nothing about them to show that they
regarded themselves as being Irish people. In dress
and accent and social conventions and amenities
they had fashioned themselves by English models.
Some of them were threadbare in the tarnished glory
of the shabby genteel, but their shabby gentility
was not even Irish: it was English from frayed
gaiter to weather-worn tweed cap, from russet
walking shoe, patched and down-at-heel, to tailor-
made jacket, colourless from brushing and age.
Not one of them sounded a single Irish note. From

father to son, from mother to daughter, generations
of their class had lived by the sweat of the people
without throwing in their fortunes with them,
without a shred of sympathy for the popular aspirations, and without ever having been able to regard
them as men and women of natural rights in any
way equal to their own. Many of them had been
kind to the people in their own way; but in the main
their kindness had little in it that was uplifting—
little that made for a greater self-respect amongst
those towards whom it was shown—little, in the last
analysis, that did not emphasise the difference
between the giver and the receiver, and set upon the
soul of the poor a deeper feeling of inferiority.
And behind this warped and stunted human sympathy of well-meaning but misguided individuals,
there was always the adamantine selfishness of class
which raised no voice of protest, while the homes of
the people were laid desolate, while the coffin ships
were on the seas, while thousands were rotting in
prison or fleeing into exile because they had loved
Ireland with a filial love. The classes of Ireland
looked on with open approval or cynical unconcern
while the masses of the Irish people were made
helots before the law, and while their common
country grew poorer year by year under a foreign
rule that was economically calamitous to both.
They had monopolised for centuries practically all
the opportunities of higher education in Ireland, yet
with a few heroic exceptions they had furnished no
leaders or thinkers or teachers to the people by whose
toil they lived in luxury; and when the economic
developments of misgovernment made it impossible

any longer for the starving peasant to pay a rack-rent, they were shortsighted enough to blame the peasant instead of blaming the causes of his ruin. And now, in the very eleventh hour of their decline, in the poverty-stricken evening of their spendthrift day, there they were still; on view by the Shannon side, as blind as ever to facts—still aloof from the people, still armoured in a rust-eaten plating of exclusiveness, still hopeless—wondering why " the country " took such little interest in Union Jackery and denationalisation—hopeless, hopeless—" rotting from the land, without one brave deed, without one brave word."

I was strolling listlessly through the listless gathering looking for my comrade, when I came upon an outfit which immediately captured my attention. It was an ancient family coach of spacious and imposing dimensions, and of a manifestly stupendous antiquity. It was suspended by straps of leather from ponderous springs, and its make and adornments were reminiscent of an era long gone by. I learned that the family to whom it belonged were of Anglo-Norman stock that had come to Ireland with Strongbow. You could fancy that they had brought that ancient coach with them. It covered an area of many square yards, and it was lofty and rickety and crusted with the rime of the vanished centuries. The ivory handles of its doors were yellowed; the silken blinds were a faded bottle-green; the cushions were worn and moth-eaten. Tottering on its crazy wheels, it loomed upon the landscape an impressive but pathetic ruin. The horses had been unhitched, and were tied behind a merciful briar brake close by which screened them from the eyes of the multitude, where I examined them at my leisure and found them to be in perfect harmony with the coach. They were of a measureless maturity of years, hook-nosed, hatchet-backed, wattle-ribbed spavined, splinted, bow-legged, spring-halted, glandered, blind, and rheumatic. Had they also come over with Strongbow? or had they come from Normandy with William the Conqueror? It was impossible to determine. Their origin, like that of the Round Towers, was veiled in the mists of time.

On the driving seat of the coach sat two old, old men in old, old liveries. They also appeared to be remnants of the advent of Strongbow to the Irish shore. They were shrunken so much from their dimensions of an earlier age that the liveries which had fitted them in the twelfth century were far too big for them in the twentieth. One of those old, old men was asleep, and appeared to have been asleep for two or three hundred years. The other old, old man was partially awake, and was trying to look through a very small and very old pocket telescope at the racing yachts. He was the only human being there who showed any interest in the regatta—probably because his sense of duty and loyalty as a faithful servant obliged him to concern himself about the sport patronized by his masters.

The body of the coach was tenanted by a very old lady, who sat in state in the middle of the back seat and gazed pensively into the distance. She was a mild looking, sweet tempered old lady, but she appeared to have survived all her enthusiasms and all interest in earthly affairs. Her expression had the benign abstraction of one who had long since been divorced from the cares and passions and joys and sorrows of life. Her clothes were modern, but her person and features might have anti-dated the Pyramids of Egypt. The masses came and went, peeped with awe into the coach, or looked with amusement or pity at the two prehistoric men on the driving seat, but she heeded them not. She gazed over their heads in serene obliviousness of their presence, as if her thoughts were with the buried years.

But when a very aged gentleman with white side whiskers, and very thin shins swathed in cycling stockings, approached her, cap in hand, she smiled and held up her fingers for him to shake in the most approved high-toned crook of the present day. Their conversation was also modern and conventional. It ran more or less as follows:

" Nice day, isn't it ? "

" Oh, chawming ! "

" Nice regatta, this."

" Oh, rawtha ! "

" But have you noticed what little interest the country takes in it ? "

" Most extraordinary, don't you know."

Just then there came upon the scene a strenuous female bearing a shooting gallery. She encamped close to the coach, and proceeded to do business with the masses. She issued a verbal prospectus in a strident voice which could be heard at long range, and offered such tempting rewards for excellence in marksmanship that she was quickly surrounded by

eager competitors. The target was a square piece
of pine board, in the middle of which was a small
ring. This ring was the bull's eye. The marksmen
stood some yards away from the target and fired
out of a rusty old spring gun. The projectile was a
kind of awl, and it slammed against the board at
every discharge of the gun with a noise which was
very distressing to the nerves of the classes. And
while the amazonian female reloaded the weapon, or
abstracted the awl from the wood, or took in entrance
fees from new competitors, she kept up a running
fire of criticism and advertisement which smote the
welkin in raucous waves of sound, as if a fog horn
and a saw mill had blended their discordant strains.

"Six shots a penny," she screamed, "and sixpence
if you hit the bull's eye. Now, then, my darlings,
shoot for the honour of your country—six shots a
penny. You didn't hit the centre, my bully boy,
but try again. Fire, you devil, fire!"

The old lady and gentleman were engaged in an
animated conversation across the door of the ancient
carriage, and took no notice of this outbreak in
their neighbourhood; but the aged men on the driving seat showed signs of the utmost indignation and
disgust. The aged man who had been asleep woke
up and croaked sharp reproof to the riflemen and
their leader.

"Go off out of that," he commanded, "take your
thrickery out of this at wanct, woman, do you
hear?"

"Get out, get out, get out!" added his prehistoric
brother of the telescope, "don't you know you
shouldn't be there, so near the quality?"

"Don't mind them, my bully boys," said the strenuous patroness of the spring gun, "go ahead—another champion—here you are, my angel—six for a penny—fire, you devil, fire."

A policeman hove in sight, and to him the prehistoric relics on the coach box made appeal, in this wise :—

"Put her off out of that. This is no place for her. The language of her is shockin'. She's a disgrace, so she is !"

"Musha, will you listen to that ould pair of magpies up there," said the amazon in a tone of withering contempt, "what are they chatterin' about at all, at all ?"

Magpies ! It was a cruelly appropriate figure of speech; for the liveries of the prehistoric servitors were black and drab. Magpies ! It seemed to give articulation to the thought that had been struggling for utterance in many minds. The masses laughed Homerically, and even the constabulary man was forced to smile. But the antideluvian menials were extremely wroth, and the old gentleman who was talking to their mistress was shocked. He was a magistrate, it seems, and he ordered the forces to dislodge the shooting gallery The forces, consisting of the five constabulary men, concentrated upon the rifle range and delivered an ultimatum to the proprietress thereof. She capitulated, and with sundry expressive shrugs, and grimaces and winks, marched away with the moral victory, and set up in business on a hillside beyond the tents.

Then several ladies and gentlemen came and paid their respects to the old lady in the coach, and there was further polite and fashionable conversation.

"Nice day, isn't it?"

"Chawming!"

"Nice regatta."

"Rawtha!"

"Quite too extraordinary the little interest taken in it by the country, though."

"Most awfully queer, don't you know!"

They were beginning to speak about bridge when a friendly voice at my elbow said:

"If you think you can tear yourself away from 'the quality,' I know of a certain house not very far from here where we would find a cup of tea, and maybe a hot cake as well."

"Oh! my blessing upon the music of your voice" I cried in the depth of my relief. "Let us leave this depressing spectacle anyhow. Let us go anywhere away from it."

And with our faces to the west winds, out of the chilly air of the social altitudes, we cycled back into the natural, genial, sunny life of Irish Ireland.

CHAPTER IV

*Through Royal Meath—From Uisnach to Tara—
Poundeth Westmeath Caulcannon—Rochfort-
bridge and the Rochforts—Lough Ennel—
Lonely Dun-na-Sciath—The Irish Rain—The
Drovers—Trim—A Stranger by the Fire—A
few remarks on Grazierdom—Tara rises into
view—The approach—Up the storied hill at last
—Beside the Stone of Destiny.*

I was in a shady valley under Uisnach in Westmeath, vainly studying my road map to find the
road to Tara. The foreigner who had drawn the
map had ignored both Tara and Uisnach. Probably he had rejected them as places unworthy of
notice because he had not been able to connect them
with food or " views " or level roads. My guide-
book, also of foreign manufacture, was equally
useless. It made no mention of either Tara or
Uisnach, probably because its author was ignorant
of their existence. The multitudinous things of
which he showed ignorance regarding the land
through which his book undertook to guide me
would have overflowed a library. With a mental
prayer that some Irish guide book might be written
some time by an Irishman, I folded my useless map
and closed the useless pages which told me of the
" seats " and demesnes of lords and earls and

baronets, and about hotels and repair shops and
level roads, and resolving to puzzle out my way to
Tara unaided, I took my wheel out of the ferns and
made for the eastern slope of Knockastia—the hill
which is one of the most useful landmarks in the
district.   I knew that Tara lay somewhere near
Trim, and that the road to Trim lay through Rochfortbridge. In order to find the direction of Rochfortbridge it would be necessary for me to get sight
of Croghan Hill, in Offaly; and that was why I went
to Knockastia. Leaving my bicycle in the bawn
of a farmhouse by the roadside, I climbed the slopes
of Knockastia until the blue bulk of Croghan rose
twenty miles away to the eastward over the woods of
Tyrrellspass.

I took my bearings a little to the northward of
Croghan, for I knew of old that when you are
standing on the moat of Croghan it seems only a
stonethrow over Ballyfore into Rochfortbridge; and
after a friendly chat with the youngsters in the
bawn, I took to my wheel again and followed the
road to Streamstown railway station, and on eastward still towards Donore, through the country of
the MacGeoghegans. It was a pleasant ride by hill
and dale, along sunny slopes, across shaded hollows,
by laughing streams. The scrub was green on the
ridges that run from Kilbeggan to the Shannon, and
the aftergrass was high and sweet in the meadows.
I remembered that O'Dugan had a verse about it,
and I have rummaged it out as follows : —

> " Precedence be given to the heroic clan,
>   The noble tribe MacGeoghegan,
>   Host of the pleasant verdant lands
>   That rule o'er warlike Kinel Fiacadh."

Kinel Fiacadh comprised the barony of Moy-cashel, with parts of Moycashel, Rathconrath and Fertullagh and the districts about Mullingar. The men of Kinel Fiacadh were truly warlike. They fought it out to a finish. Richard MacGeoghegan, the defender of Dunboy, was one of the blood. They were neighbours of the usurping DeLacys, Petits, Tuites, and other lordlings of the Normans, and they made it hot for them down to the seventeenth century. They are gone now. Here and there you meet the ruins of one of their castles, or a rath of the olden days. Here and there you meet the naked gables and broken arches of some abbey or monastery they endowed. All gone now—castles and churches and lands. Cromwell finished the business.

Croghan Hill rose presently over the scrub, a little to my right—just where I wanted it; and then a turn to the left put me on the straight road for Rochfort-bridge. From there the route was plain. It read off the map as follows:—Killucan, Raharney, Ballivor, Trim, Kilmessan—almost a straight line running N.E. It was more or less the route chosen three thousand years ago by the warriors of Nemedh, the munificent king who made a present of Uisnach to his Archdruid. Croghan had given them their bearings on the Tara road; Knockastia had beckoned them home.

I was thus re-making history, or rather re-conducting bygone pilgrimages, when I met one who knew me. He informed me that there was caul-cannon at his house down the fields to the left, and that I was welcome to a share of it. I said that his words had a wealth of human kindness in them, and that he was to consider me as being completely at orders. I went with him down a shady avenue and came upon the caulcannon, which was only half made. So we were informed by the "girls," my friend's three sisters, who welcomed us, in smart white aprons of Irish linen, and sunny Irish smiles, and a cordial invitation to go to the kitchen and help them with the pounding. We went, the five of us, and pounded. The new potatoes were snowy and delicious, and the caulcannon was a great success. I ate as much of it as was good for me, and then rose to depart. But, God bless you, it was no easy matter to get away from them. "Ah! won't you be time enough to-morrow," said one, and "there will be half a dozen of the right kind of Irish people here by and by, and won't you wait for them," said another. "And one of them is the best singer in the county," said a third. "And it looks like rain!" said the head of the family, with a weather-wise glance at the heavens. That is the way in Westmeath, aye, and through the length and breadth of Ireland. At least that was how this deponent found it—always difficult to get away. It took me over an hour to get free from my friends of the caulcannon. I exhausted all my arguments in favour of continuing my journey, and when no other alternative remained I vaulted through the window, and snatching my wheel from the stand beside the hall door, fled from the delightful place.

Regaining the high road, I raised the dust in a twelve knot spin, and was soon in Rochfortbridge. This village is called after the Rochforts, and the

Rochforts were some Anglo-Norman people who
came to Westmeath seven hundred years ago. They
were a curse to the country. They have rotted root
and branch out of it, but they left terrible traditions
of cruelty and general depravity behind them.
They got a title in course of time, and were called
Lords of Belvedere. They tried to give their name
'ɔ Loch Ennel, but without much success. Some
people call Loch Ennel Lake Belvedere yet. They
think it more genteel; and yet they are naming it
after a monster whose persecution of his wife is a
by-word in the district after more than a century and
a half.

The stories of this Lord Belvedere's eccentricity
and brutality would fill volumes. The people of the
district point to an artificial ruin which he had
erected by an Italian architect in order to shut out
the view of his brother's house, because it seems
this brother had given him some cause to hate him.
From Gaulstown to Rochfortbridge there are
children still hushed to silence by the mention of
his name. The infamy of his life filled the popular
mind for more than a century after his death. Even
to-day more is known in this part of Westmeath of
Rochforts than about those who should be the
heroes of the people. Such are the effects of denationalisation. For years the men of Westmeath
broke one another's heads in Mullingar over the
elections of Whigs or Tories. They thought if they
returned a Magan or a Tuite or some other of the
" gentlemen " to the English Parliament, that Ireland
would be free. Even in the days of '52, the people,
not only of Westmeath, but of the four provinces,

were hypnotised into regarding Westminster as the horizon over which the sun of Irish liberty would rise, "at no far distant date." They are still, to a great extent, keeping their gaze fixed on that murky part of the world. If we Irish could only be induced to turn to Tara for inspiration, what things we might achieve!

On the road from Dunore to Rochfortbridge you catch sight of famed Loch Ennel. You can see it from Knockastia, from Croghan, and I think I could see it from the summit of Uisnach. It is one of the Westmeath lakes, and is peculiarly beautiful. The woods of stately demesnes dip their branches in it, and the rich pastures and meadows slope down to the pebbly beach. Loch Ennel disputes with Loch Owel the honour of having drowned Turgesius, the terrible Danish tyrant who scourged Ireland so cruelly. Keating says that the waters of Loch Ennel did the blessed work, and O'Mahony and others say that he was drowned in Loch Owel. I think that Keating is wrong, for he states that the drowning took place in Loch Aninn, which is now called Loch Ennel. But, as O'Mahony points out, the Irish authorities state that Loch Uair, now Loch Owel, was the lake wherein the fierce despoiler from the North met his fate. After many a successful raid, he was beaten by a chieftain of Meath, taken prisoner and condemned to death by drowning.

"He left us bare here in Connacht. The fellow cleaned us out completely," said Monsignor MacLaughlin to me in his library one evening in Roscommon, alluding to the reaver and his fate, "he made a clear job of it this side of the Shannon;

but I was awful glad to read how a boy of the MacLoughlins caught him, up beyond Mullingar, and threw him into one of the Westmeath lakes. I wasn't ashamed of my namesake at all."

This was the Monsignor's humorous way of modestly clothing his great historical erudition.

" A boy of the MacLoughlins," it was in truth who freed Ireland from the clutches of this predatory outlander. The name of the clan in those days was O'Maeilsechlainn. The O'Maeilsechlainns or MacLoughlins were the heads of the southern race of the O'Neills, and their chief residence was at Dun-na-Sciath, or the fortress of the Shields, on the banks of Loch Ennel. The Maeilsechlainn who defeated Turgesius was afterwards elected Ard-Righ of Eirinn by an admiring people. This was in the ninth century. The Chieftainry was called Clan Coleman, and once carried with it the Kingship of Meath. At the time of the Norman invasion one Murtogh MacLoughlin was King of Meath. Henry the Second gave his lands to Hugh De Lacy, the runaway hero of Horseleap.

The Anglo-Normans were strong in Royal Meath, and the Gaels were crowded out of it. But the MacLoughlins did not go under without a manly fight. They held by their lands to the last, and many a sledge hammer blow they dealt out to their greedy neighbours of the Pale. War and time wore them away at last, and there are none of them left in Meath to claim descent from the chiefs of Clan Coleman.

In the ancient Dun-na-Sciath there is nothing of its former state but the grassy mound on which the rath was situated. The kine and sheep were feeding peacefully on its summit when I saw it. The rabbits burrowed near it. No birds sang in the summer air above it. The ancient home of power and chivalry was lonely—lonely. Lonely Dun-na-Sciath!

.   .   .   .   .   . time's sceptre has swept
O'er the high homes of Erin and conquered them all.

It began to rain when I was about two miles east of Rochfortbridge, and this circumstance caused me to suspend my historical meditations. But do not think I am vexed with the rain. No, no. It has drenched me often and often, but I forgive it. It has spoiled many a lovely day for me, still the memory of it is one that I would not part with for gems and gold.

Irish rain of the summer and autumn is a kind of damp poem. It is humid fragrance, and it has a way of stealing into your life which disarms anger. It is a soft, apologetic, modest kind of rain, as a rule; and even in its wildest moods, it gives you the impression that it is treating you as well as it can under the circumstances. It does not come heralded by dust and thunder and accompanied by lightning, and roaring tempests, like the rain of the tropics. Nor does it wet you to the bones in five minutes. You scarcely know when it begins. It grows on you by degrees. It comes on the scene veiled in soft shadows and hazes, and maybe a silver mist. You think the day is beginning to look like rain, and you are not wrong. But you also think that it may clear off; no doubt, it often thinks so itself.

Nevertheless, it finally decides not to clear off. The shadows deepen. The hazes thicken. And was that a drop you felt? It was—just a drop. Another comes presently, and you feel it on your cheek. Then a few more come. Then the rest of the family encircle you shyly. They are not cold or heavy or splashy. They fall on you as if they were coming from the eyes of many angels weeping for your sins. They caress you rather than pelt you, and they are laden with perfume from the meadow flowers, or the glistening trees, or the sweet, rich earth, or the heathery bogland. But they soak you all the same. In due course you are wet to the skin. They fold you in, do those spells of Irish rain, and make of you a limp, sodden, unsightly thing in their soft embraces. They soak the road and make it slippy, and your bicycle wobbles now and then; and you have to ride it through the mud by the ditch, where the blades of grass and pebbles and leafdrifts give a grip to the tyres.

At first, perhaps, you dread the rain. You regard it as a calamity. The mud on the road is too much for your tyres, and your limited experience, and you have some unpleasant falls. You are spilled into the ditch or over the handle bars, or thrown on your back a helpless case. You would exchange places with the dirtiest tramp you have ever met on a fair day, or with the most extensively married tinker that you have ever met concentrating on Abbeyshrule. But after two or three months you become weather-proof. You get used to the softness of the weather. You acquire such skill in "riding for a fall," that even if you do come down it is only on your feet.

It rained on me the whole way from the Pass of Kilbride. I reached Trim at sundown as wet as a soaked sponge. But I made friends with the people in the kitchen of Connell's hotel, and I had tea and toast and roasted apples, and plenty of jokes as I sat before a roaring fire drying myself. On the homeward run the weather was fine, but the roads were bad until I came to Westmeath. They would have been much better were it not that the Meath ranchmen were trooping their store cattle from the fair of Ballinasloe.

The cattle from the great Connacht fair are railed *via* Athlone to Hill of Down or Enfield stations, and thence trooped along the Trim and Navan roads to the big grazing farms. They leave much puddle behind them, and the men in charge of them are endowed with qualities of mind decidedly tough.

If you want to make the acquaintance of the Irish drovers now is your time. They are lords and masters of the road for the moment, and they know it well. They will not open a way through their troop for you. They will not assist you in any way to get the cattle out of your way. In busy times they are prejudiced against cyclists, more or less, and they are more or less tired, and more or less drunk, and more or less defiant, and more or less blue-moulding for trouble. If you remonstrate with them they will say mordant things to you, and if you retaliate, they will use language most lurid and personal. If you become aggressive you will have to fight, and if you fight, you will have to smite them hip and thigh or be smitten into pulp.

But it would be foolish and fatiguing and exces-
sively risky to commit yourself to a belligerent
policy regarding them; because as there are a great
many troops of cattle on the march, you will have
to fight drovers at every two or three hundred
yards of the road from Kilmessan to Ballivor.

The better course is to use diplomacy. Praise
the cattle, praise the weather if you can, ask them
how prices ruled at the fair, and smile every time
you have to get off your wheel to let them pass.
You will have to get off for every troop, but no
matter, it is better to smile than to fight three reckless characters armed with long ash saplings. I
smiled and was diplomatic, and only fought once or
twice in all the miles of purgatory I experienced.
But I made a vow never to cycle again while the
Meath men are on the trail; and I tried to console
myself with the thought that if I had a few score
of the dusky riders who are often my comrades in a
certain stock country far away, I could clean out
Meath in a week, graziers and drovers and cattle
and all.

You will meet the drovers in other moods than
those of aggression and war. They will often
afford you a chat to relieve the lonesomeness of the
way on a long ride. They can tell you the best
roads and the shortest ones, and when you overtake
them going from fair to fair, looking for work, as
dirty or as splashed as you are yourself, and foot-
sore and tired into the bargain, you can feel for
them. Many of them know as much about land and
stock and pasturage as would make the fortune for
a steady man in another country. Some of them

are sober, and very few of them are dishonest. They earn their wages by hard work, and if they spend their money foolishly when they get it, they never turn to stealing when they are short of cash. They tramp twenty or thirty or fifty miles to the next fair, and there will always be a house here and there along the road where they will not be denied a bit of cold meat or a potato or a crust of bread.

At Killucan railway station I met a man who told me of a short cut to Raharney. He assured me that if I followed his " directions " I could save myself the trouble of riding through the village, and cut at least two miles off my journey.

" Before you go to the town," he said, " turn to your right, and when you go about forty perch you will meet a cross-roads, and there are three roads, but don't take the middle one, turn to your left; and after you pass the schoolhouse about a mile from that, turn to your right, and then, a few perch further on, you will meet a cross-roads, and turn to your left again; and then you have only one more turning, and that is to your ri~ht. You can't miss it."

I am unable to say what he thought I could not miss. But anyhow I missed everything, only the scenery, which was new to me, and the mud which was an old acquaintance. I turned to the right and rode nearly into Kildare. I turned to the left and rode nearly into Cavan. Then I rode back to Killucan and gathered up my bearings again. I picked my course off my road map and got to Raharney. It is a cross-roads accentuated by a publichouse. I think there are other houses also, but I did not slacken speed to make careful observations. A figure in black was standing in front of something white, and I supposed there was a police barrack in the place. What did it matter? I had the trail hot under my wheel now and meant to stick to it. There were over fifty miles of road covered since the start, and it was getting late.

Ballivor is a main street composed of a public-house or two, the Post Office, the police barrack, and some minor buildings. There is a demesne near it, and the woods overhung the road. That meant that the road was still dry, and I tore along it at my best speed until I reached the end of the park, when my old friend, the mud, splashed around my ankles again, and I was forced to modestly and prudently crawl along the narrow and slippery selvage by the ditch.

The first thing I met in Trim was a tall monument of the Duke of Wellington. It seems the Duke was born somewhere in the locality, and there is an inscription on the monument which tells you that it was erected by the "Gentry of Meath."

The next thing I met was a splendid new church which His Eminence Cardinal Logue consecrated in 1902. The third object which called my attention was an old monastic ruin, the history of which goes back a long way. Trim was one of the first ecclesiastical foundations instituted by St. Patrick, and was a renowned centre of piety and learning during the early days of the Irish Church. The fourth object that caused me to raise my eyes from the muddy street was the ruins of one of the old castles of the Pale. Footprints of Patrick! Footprints of the English! Ruins of the Golden Age! Monument to Wellington from the "Gentry of Meath!" Wondrous chapters of our wondrous history might be written under these headings—chapters fraught with the glory and the gloom and the tragedy of the history of our land. I thought of this as I cycled down the slippery street, and somehow it put a chill into the rain.

"It was a softish day for ridin'," said the kindly soul who relieved me of my wheel in the gaslit hall of the hotel. "I suppose you must be wet entirely."

"Entirely, entirely," I replied, "as wet as water."

"An' I suppose as dry as dust, too?" he said slyly.

"Aye, faith," I agreed "as dry as bone dust—and I want fire and moisture all at once, and something to eat."

"Well, then, come in to the fire in the kitchen at once, and we'll do the best we can for you."

That was what they all did—the best they could, and half of it would have been enough to have made a prince feel at home and snug and happy before that glorious fire. As I turned myself round from east to west and back again before the blaze and dried myself they fed me and gave me to drink, and told me stories and wondered what was my errand in this vale of tears.

I resurrected that old legend about the return of the Gaels, and told them I was one of the advance guard. They smiled and said, humouring the fancy of the moment:--

"An' you're welcome; but will they be all as wet and as hungry and as dry as you?"

"And what if they are," I said, "haven't you plenty of turf-banks, and rivers, and cattle in Ireland?"

Then I asked them the road I should take to Tara on the morrow. Everyone of them knew it, mistress, waiters, waitress, boots, and jarvey—and with a readiness of speech, in the tone of which there was a blessing on my journey, they said:—

"Past the Courthouse, to your left, and out by Kilmessan across the Boyne."

Early next morning I was on the road again. Royal Meath was golden-tinted with the bright sunshine and the mellow glory of autumn. The air was clear and fresh and bracing. The sky was blue and cloudless. The weather had got into good humour again, and in good humour it remained until I finished my ride from Trim to Tara, from Tara back to Trim, and thence to the valleys under Ballymore. It was a rush of about seventy miles—a fair spin for one day, when you consider that the roads were heavy, and that the drovers from Ballinasloe and their bullocks and sheep had to be negotiated diplomatically.

I was somewhat disappointed as I rode into the heart of Meath. It was not all that my fancy had painted, but the disappointment was not on the wrong side; it was more agreeable than otherwise. In these modern days writers and speakers describe Meath to us as a grassy desert, a grazier-made wilderness. So it is, but it does not look it. The plain of Meath has nothing of the bleak monotony of the Connacht prairies. As you ride through the trans-Shannon ranches the desolation and utter

emptiness of the land prey upon you, weigh you
down, oppress you.   This emptiness, this woeful
silence and monotony are the first impressions you
are conscious of receiving as your gaze sweeps over
the tenantless expanses of grass. But in Meath all
this is hidden away under the woods and hedges
which grow so thickly on every side you look. The
country is so superbly wooded, that at first sight
you do not miss the population at all. There are
big whitethorn hedges and groves and copses along
the fields, between the farms, fringing the rivers,
connecting one wood with another, stretching from
one demesne to another, from one town to another.
As you look down on it from Tara it is like a great
forest, with clearings in it here and there, extending
on every side to the blue haze and the dim hills on
the skyline.   The road leads you between high
ditches of clay topped with hawthorn and briars
and sloe bushes.   The ash also towers over the
hedgerows, and so do the elm and witch hazel. I
climbed the embankments and, standing knee deep
in the ferns, drew the brambles aside and peered
through the hedges, I could only see grassy fields
bounded by trees or quicks, and beyond that again
other fields and hedges.   The fields were all under
grass—rich, rank, tuffy grass—and no house of any
kind could be seen, but the prospect was charming in
its own way.   Its half sylvan appearance was suggestive of tangled game coverts and cool forest
glades. It resembled parts of Thomond and
Ossory and Leix in all but one thing—the main
thing—population.

It was only when you looked for the houses that you were conscious of a sense of loneliness. In many places you could see clumps of trees which had sheltered farmsteads in the pre-grazier days. But you listened in vain for the homely sounds from the barn door or the bawn. You looked in vain through the branches for the whitewashed walls. No blue wreaths of turf smoke floated over the tree tops. There was no tillage—no ploughman's whistle. In the rich grasses the big dehorned Durham and Polled Angus bullocks fed or lay. There were bird voices in the air, but nothing else rippled on the silence. It was, indeed, a lovely wilderness of grass—a verdant fertile desert from which man had banished himself, and into which he had sent the beasts to take his place!

I learned in Meath that many of the big graziers have gone to the wall. In many instances the herdsmen are now in possession of the farms which their former employers were obliged to surrender owing to financial straits. This is true of other grazing districts in Ireland. In fact, the grazier-ocracy of the country has come down in the world. The cattle of North and South America have horned three-fourths of grazierdom through the bankruptcy courts. The free trade of the beef-eaters on the other side of the Channel has ruined them—that and shoneenism. For the grazierocracy of Ireland was shoneen to the core. There were graziers and there are graziers who were not and who are not shoneens, but they were and are the exceptions. The mass of bullockdom was never simple-minded or natural or Irish. The mass of what is left is also un-Irish.

As it was in the beginning, it is now, and will be to the end.

This bullockdom was always a curse to Ireland, and never was or could be a factor on the side of national prosperity or self-respect. It never gave Ireland any recompense for the Irish homes it swept away, or that were swept away to make room for it. There never was such a nursery of Irish snobbery, and there never will be, please God, for evermore. Amen. It produced the Cawstle Cawtholic, the Shoneen Priest, the Shoneen Magistrate, the Shoneen Prelate, the Shoneen Soldier of England, the Shoneen Foxhunter. The bullockdom of the land has ever furnished raw material to educational centres of denationalisation, where recruiting goes steadily on for the ranks of a materialistic imperialism, and where imitation of an inferior race is a cult.

This bullockdom was known to the world by Irish names, but it never was more Irish than the cottendom of Manchester or the cutlerdom of Sheffield, and never, never for an hour less un-Irish, purse-proud, and arrogant than they. It was a pompous, whiskey-drinking, ignorant gang, upon the whole. It would have trampled Irish nationality into the mud ten times within an hour for the sake of a nod of recognition from the hard-up aristocrats of the County Club. It called many of its daughters Louise, and Charlotte, and Caroline, and Alexandria, and Flossie, and Gertrude, and sent them to English convents to be " finished " (with a vengeance) in snobbery and the English accent. It sent its Clarences and Algernons and Scroops ard FitzHenrys to prepare for the "Awmy" or the "Baw," and then sent them after the hounds—so that they might all the more surely and rapidly ride to the dogs. It lived above its means, did this bullockdom of Ireland; and it made beggared snobs of its Algernons, and powerless goddesses of its Charlottes; and then, when the cattle from over the seas began to low in Birkenhead, this grazierocracy went to flinders, and in flinders it remains.

The Meath land is not only "fattening land," but it is probably the richest land in the world. It is certainly the richest tract of land in Europe. There is "fattening land" in many parts of Ireland, but Meath overtops all their records. In Meath cattle are fat every summer and placed on the market weeks before cattle from other districts. There is no land in Ireland will turn off so many pounds of beef to the acre. There is a good deal of land in Westmeath that would carry a bullock and a wether to the acre and fatten them; but they will not be so bony as a Meath stock, nor will they be ready for market so soon.

Another thing I learned from my roadside chats was, that the Meath men will not stock their land while the spring is raining. The soil is soft and the heavy cattle would cut it up too much. When a man pays from three pounds to five pounds per acre for land, he has to take many things into consideration.

It was on the railroad bridge of Kilmessan that I caught the first view of Tara. There it lay about two miles off, its eastern slope flushed with the morning sunshine. It did not appear to be very

high. In fact it looked small. The country is so
wooded that you can see very little of the lay of the
land, and consequently you do not get as good a
view of the Hill from the distance as you do of
Uisnach or Cruachain. Nor is there much in a
distant view of Tara to call your attention. The
summits of these three hills are flat. Indeed
Cruachain is more of a high tableland than a hill.
The same may be said of Uisnach, more or less, as
you see it from the Hill of Clare, or from over
Ballymore, or from the direction of Loughanavally.
But Tara presents the appearance of a broad, low,
flat-topped hill rising gently upward from the plain.
There is no steepness about it. It does not tower or
loom or throw big masses of rock and shadow
between you and the sky. But it is a big hill all
the same. It is also far bigger than it looks. You
can see little more than the summit of it from Kilmessan. The lower slopes and the base are hidden
by the intervening trees, and the western slope is
concealed by the woods of a demesne. On the
summit you see from the distance what appears to
be a clump of trees. It is in reality the grove which
shelters the Protestant Church of the district.

About two miles beyond Kilmessan, after I had
turned sharply to the left, the road entered a grove
of beeches, and the pedals began to send me
messages to the effect that I was going up hill.
The pedals of a bicycle are very faithful and
accurate topographers in their own way. If there
is a hill to be found on the road at all they will
find it and report it to you at once. They found
the lower slope of Tara before I did and told me

about it. I passed through the grove, and then beyond a turn of the road the pedals became eloquent. It was the same slope, only more accentuated, that rose before me. Further on it was a stiff gradient, and then a long incline, apparently very much disposed to sit up straight and hurl you backward. Then there came a halt. The pedals could not be induced to give another turn, so I dismounted. I had reached the middle slope. There was nearly a mile of the hill behind me. Another mile was before me and above me. I had not yet reached a height from which I could see Kilmessan, and this was how I discovered that you catch sight of little more than the summit of Tara from the distance. After a few minutes' walk the slope sank again, almost to a level, so I pedalled upward and onward until I came to a farmhouse—the only one by the roadside or in view for miles around. Here I left my bicycle and took to the fields. I crossed a stile and found a path which led upward. I followed it through the sappy grasses which overhung it, and which swished big drops of last night's rain upon my insteps. Upward and upward it went through the rich pastures where the cattle were lying in the sunshine, chewing the cud after the morning's feed. It led me over fences, over dykes, over mounds, across hillocks, past circular embankments and other remains of the storied past, and presently I was standing bare-headed beside the Lia Fail on the Croppies' Grave.

Beside the Lia Fail! Beside the Stone of Destiny in the High Place of the Island of Destiny. In the centre of Tara of the Kings. In the spirit

presence of many of the hero-dead of Erin. It was
a wondrous moment, crowded with conflicting
emotions, crowded with intense sorrow, with passionate love and passionate hatred, with shame and
pride, with hope and exaltation.

The past was there around me crudely recon-
structed from the limited materials of an incomplete
historical knowledge and an imperfect historical
sense, yet, in some faint, wild, mysterious way,
realised and felt. The present was tangible and
visible enough—grass and solitude and desolation
and silence, and the Lia Fail worn smooth from the
sides of itchy cattle, and not a stone left upon a
stone of the palaces and halls—a lone hilltop, un-
sheltered and tenantless now as it had been for over
twelve hundred years. And the future? Who
knows? I am not going to inflict a laboured piece
of introspection upon you, nor am I going to analyse
the hope and faith of a patriotism either from the
emotional or materialistic side. Nor am I going to
inquire into the workings of the spirit under the
quickening influences of inspiration derived from a
contemplation of the heroic past. But I am going
to say that it was not a feeling of despondency that
filled my heart as I stood that morning over the
Croppies' Grave, for it is their resting place that the
Stone of Destiny not unworthily marks to-day.
Why could I not feel pessimistic? What reason
has a man to hope for a land that we are told is
bleeding to death? Why are we extant yet in this
world that has so sternly tried to hound us into
eternity? Why are not hope and faith dead and
buried with our heroes? Have we been spared from

extinction merely to be the ill-used playthings of fate to the bitter end? Not so. We have been spared because in the mysterious ways of God He has reserved us for some destiny that is high.

I was sitting on a green hillside over Dublin with two friends not long since, and one of them told how there are people strong in the belief that a child was born in Ireland a few years ago who is to be the deliverer of the land. Did we laugh? Not we. There are many things at which you do not laugh in Eirinn. Many strange and mystic and glorious things are believed in this hopeful land whose story is so old and sad, but whose heart is still so fresh and young.

CHAPTER V.

1ara of the Kings—The Croppies' Grave—The Lia Fail—The Traces of Vanished Greatness—Cormac Mac Art—The Flight of Diarmuid and Grania—The Cursing of Tara—The Royal City as it was.

A broad, uneven hilltop carpeted with luxuriant sward. Mounds and raths and shallow moats, grass grown and trampled, yet still clearly traceable despite the vicissitudes of tne effacing centuries. Green slopes of rich pasturage stretching down to autumn-tinted woodlands. And then a vast plain, extending wide and splendid on every side until it is walled by the far-off mountains, or melts into the hazes of silver grey. Briar and grass and leaflet, wet from the recent rain, glisten and flash in the morning sunshine; and the sweet winds of the south sing gently in the tree-tops over the Chair of the Kings. Such is the picture of Tara that dwells in my memory as I stood beside the Stone of Destiny, alone amidst the desolation of the ages.

There is a statue of St. Patrick close to the rath of King Laoghaire. There is a Protestant Church beside the Druidic altar. There are the footprints of a modern vandal who burrowed for curios in the Rath of the Synods. There is the dust of slaughtered pikemen of '98 under the Lia Fail of the

Tuatha de Danaans. And, knee deep in the juicy grass which covers alike the traces of Druid and Priest, of Pagan and Christian, of ancient hero and of modern patriot and traitor—over the mounds and moats and undulations which mark the sites of throne room, and banquet hall, and bower, and college, and council chamber, the bullocks of depopulaten Meath are fattening for the markets of England. Tara pulls the centuries together, and makes you see them in their nudity and in the cruelty of their tragic co-relation. It is Irish history epitomized, and it gives food for thought. It made me spend an hour and more of the brilliant morning thinking and dreaming before I could bring myself to commence my projected round of the hill.

The Rebellion of '98 added another chapter to the long unopened history of Tara, when four hundred of the patriots assembled to do battle for Ireland around the Chair of the Kings. It was an Irish Catholic nobleman who led the assault against them on behalf of England. His name was Lord Fingal. Most of the yeomen who followed him were Irish Catholics, also, sad to say, who fought to rivet the chains of conquest more securely upon their martyred motherland. They were, unfortunately, well armed, disciplined, and capably officered, and they overcame the patriots, who had neither artillery nor ammunition for their small arms. They were also without a strong and resourceful leader; and after a gallant resistance they were overcome. Their slain were buried on the Hill, and their resting place is known as " The Croppies' Grave." God rest their souls.

> Peace be round the Croppies' Grave,
> Let none approach but Pilgrims brave,
> This sainted hill-side, even yet,
> Should slavery fly with frightened feet.

But not alone because there mingles with the soil
of Tara some of the sacred dust of '98 should slavery
fly the Hill with fright and shame. It is because
Tara stands for the very soul as well as for the body
of the Irish nation that it should be regarded as
thrice-holy ground.

Tara is very old. It is so old that its age is
measureless by the standards of recorded time. It
was old when Christ was born, for it had held the
throne of Ireland from days far back beyond the
morning of our history. It was Ollamh Fodla who
called the first convention of Tara known to authentic records; and this wise king reigned when the
world was very young. And from the days of
Ollamh Fodla to the day when Tara, or Temhair as
it was called, fell under the curses of the saints, it
was one of the world's chief capitals, and a great
centre of political, legislative, and literary activity.
Eocaidh O'Floinn, one of the old bardic chroniclers,
tells us of the Feis of Tara in a historical lay which
has been translated into English.

> Each third year Temhair's Feast was held;
> There righteous laws and rules were made,
> And usage old in force upheld
> By Eri's proud and mighty kings.

The other stanzas tell of the games and revels
which took place during the Feis, and how it was

a crime, punishable by death, for any man to raise
a hand or draw steel in anger while the Convention
was going on. One of the first great troubles in the
life of St. Columcille came to him because he tried
to shield one of his friends who had struck a rival
athlete in a hurling match at the Feis. Some historians appear to think that the war between the
civil and ecclesiastical powers in Ireland began on
that day. But we may doubt it. Later on we shall
glance at a reason or two for thinking that the
trouble was due to other causes more fundamental
and abiding.

The Tuatha De Danaans took Tara from the
Firbolgs, together with nearly everything else they
possessed, and made it the seat of their power. The
Tuatha De Danaans were great politicians, and
knew the arts of heightening a moral effect. It
would be a grand thing for Ireland had the
Milesians been more alive to the value of De
Danaan political methods. It is rather more than
probable that if the Irish people of Celtic days had
been more Tuatha De Danaan in politics, we of the
present might be called anti-idealists, or oppor-
tunists, because it must be confessed there would be
a tincture of the positive and the practical in our
political philosophy. And no doubt, also, we
should find ourselves under the necessity of explain-
ing away to the world our success as a nation. But
the world is always ready to listen to an apology
for success. It is, on the other hand, somewhat
intolerant of failure. People never have a great
deal of patience with a man who has a failure to explain away. They regard him as tiresome and

uninteresting. He failed, and no more about him.
If he desires a favourable hearing from the world
let him first go forth and win his point. Victory is
easy enough to explain—often easy to justify—
Success is a justification of many things; but failure,
no matter how splendid may be the moral victory it
has won, is anathema—especially in politics.   It
may be said, of course, that the Tuatha De Danaans
were failures in the end. All the same, subtlety is
a good thing in politics, on general principles, when
a nation is fighting for its life against heavy odds.
But the subtlety should be shown by the people who
are defending their existence, because if they allow
themselves to be fooled by adversaries who have
them by the throats they are in a hopeless predica-
ment. In such straits a people might well regard
politics not as a standard of human conduct, but
as a series of opportunities to be turned to practical
and useful account.

The Gaels showed good sense, however, in their
attitude towards Tara when they wrenched Ireland
from the Tuatha De Danaans. They occupied the
capital, and when overhauling the institutions of
the conquered people they did not reject the Lia
Fail as an archaic absurdity. They continued the
ancient practices connected with it, and were wise
in their generation. " The Lia Fail was an enchanted stone," says Keating, " for whenever the
men of Ireland were assembled at the great Feis of
Tara to elect a king over them it used to give forth
a loud cry beneath the person whose right it was
to obtain the sovereign power. But it has emitted
no cry since the time of Concobar (Conn of the

Hundred Battles); for when Christ was born all the false idols of the world were struck dumb."

There are antiquarians who say that the Stone of Destiny, or Lia Fail, is not at Tara at all, but that it is under the coronation chair in Westminster Abbey. British and pro-British antiquarians favour this story, because there is an old rann which says that wherever goes the stone there shall also go and abide the sovereignty of the Gael. It is also gravely set down in print that the German royal family, now in possession of the English throne, is descended from Heremon! This, like the West-minster version of the Lia Fail legend is merely fiction, invented for the high political purpose of reconciling the people of Ireland to the blessings of English rule. The stone in Westminster Abbey was brought thither from Scotland by Edward I., and there is a tradition that it had been taken to Scotland from Ireland by Fergus MacErca, an Irish chieftain, who wanted to have himself crowned upon it as King of Scotland. But O'Donovan does not agree with this story, nor does O'Mahony. Petrie also shows that the stone is still at Tara.

Fergus MacErca left Ireland for Scotland in the sixth century; and although Tara was deserted in the same century or very early in the seventh, it is not likely that the Irish kings would allow the stone to be carried away. The Lia Fail had been a cherished object in Tara ever since the days of the Tuatha De Danaans. The Christianising of the land had not wholly weakened the veneration of the people for their ancient traditions; and even if Fergus wished to give his coronation an added solemnity in Scotland by having himself crowned on the Lia Fail, the same veneration for a great tradition which would prompt him to this course of action would also inspire the Irish kings and princes to zealously guard the stone and keep it in the country. The Lia Fail is still at Tara. The fragment of rock under the coronation chair of Westminster Abbey is just a fragment of rock and nothing more. It is the stone that was brought from Scotland without doubt, but the Stone of Destiny is still where it was left by the Tuatha De Danaan kings.

The Hill is more than half a mile in width across the top, and from one verge of this splendid plateau to the other you can, without difficulty, trace the grass grown mounds which overlie the ruins of royal Tara. Here is the rath upon which Patrick preached. You cannot miss it. You can see where the doorway was placed, and, standing there on the threshold, you can look down on a broad demesne such as few kings have ever been able to call their own Well does that magnificent sweep of country deserve the name of " Royal Meath." It was indeed fit for kings to gaze upon; it was worthy of kingly men. A fertile kingdom it was in the fullest sense. Plain and mead and wood and vale all bore witness to the bounty of the soil. On all that magnificent territory there was scarcely a mile of unproductive land. The flocks and herds multiplied upon it, and it furnished meat and corn and milk in teeming plenty for the royal men who ruled it, and for the stalwart warriors who held it, and for the beauteous women who were typical of its loveliness and fecundity.

It was populous, and the sounds of mirth and song came from duns and hamlets and mingled with the bird voices of the woods and groves. The five roads of Erin which ran through it passed many a workshop and cornfield and factory. There was the carol of the maidens and youths in the fields There was the ring of steel on the anvils. There was the open door of the scribe, or the engraver, or the teacher. There were the hoof strokes and the glitter of the squadrons who watched over the peace of the king.

You can picture an Ard-Righ standing there on the threshold of his home, looking proudly down the slope to where the martial Fianna were drilling, or gazing out over that splendid country and feeling every inch a monarch and ruler and lawgiver.

Think of Cormac as he may have paused there for a moment going forth to preside in the Teach Miodhchuarta at the Great Feis. Let us glance at him as it is described to us in the "Book of Ballymote." "Beautiful was the appearance of Cormac. Flowing and slightly curling was his golden hair. A red buckler, with stars and animals of gold and fastenings of silver upon him. A crimson cloak in wide descending folds around him, fastened at his neck with precious stones. A rich torque of gold around his neck. A white shirt with a full collar and intertwined with red gold thread upon him. A girdle of gold inlaid with precious stones was around him. Two wonderful shoes of gold with golden loops upon his feet. Two spears with golden sockets in his hands with many rivets of red bronze. And he was himself besides symmetrical and beautiful of form without blemish or

reproach." There is not an oppressive suggestiveness of red-haired savagery about this kingly Irishman who reigned two hundred years before the
polished and courteous monarch who hearkened to
the message of Patrick.

Here, on the eastern slope of the hill, is a well.
It is the headwaters of a little stream which sings
its way downward into the plain. It was on the
banks of this stream that Cormac erected a mill for
his handmaiden, fair Ciarnaid, so as to lighten her
work of grinding the corn with the quern. This was
the first mill ever erected in Ireland. Above the
well on the hillside were pitched the tents of the
Fianna, and on the other slopes were schools, recreation grounds, workshops, hospices, emporiums, and
all the busy life of a city which grows up around a
royal court.

Come and examine the traces of the Teach
Miodhchuarta, here on the north-western edge of the
plateau, close to the Rath of the Synods. The
building was seven hundred and fifty feet long,
and about ninety feet wide. Two hundred and
fifty yards by thirty yards! That is not by any
means a cramped and meagre extent of floor space.
Cormac MacArt built the hall to accommodate one
thousand persons. It was at once a congress-house,
banqueting salon and hotel. There was a double
row of benches on each side running the entire length
of the hall. Along two sides of the building the
chieftains of Erin sat in the order of their rank,
each beneath his shield. You can trace the hall yet,
from corner to corner. The mounds show where the
foundations were laid. The floor is lower than the

level of the plateau and slopes gently downward from east to west. You can see the trace of the doorways on each side. There were fourteen of them. On this floor, all grass-grown for centuries, were held the sessions of the great triennial conventions. Here is how Keating describes the order in which the Ard Fheis was constituted: —" The King of Ireland sat upon his throne in the centre of the assembly with his face to the west; the King of Munster sat to the south of him, for the ends of the building faced east and west; the King of Leinster sat opposite him, the King of Connacht behind him, and behind the King of Connacht sat the Ollamhs of Ireland. The King of Ulster sat at the King's right hand to the north of him. A number of the real nobility of his own proper (fifth) kingdom sat near each of these princes."

The Rath of the Synods is close to the eastern end of the great hall. This is a comparatively modern name for it. In the days of Cormac MacArt it was called Relta-na-o-filedh (pronounced Railta-na-villah), meaning the Star of the Bards. In it, according to the annalists, the Ollamhs and Bards held their sittings, and here fines and erics were imposed upon those who had violated the laws and customs of the nation.

The other rath was the Palace of the Ladies (Grianan-na-n-inghen). The provincial queens resided in this, each in her own apartment, attended by her ladies, though within the inclosure of the building. In the great assemblies, when the kings and nobles sat in the hall or " Mi-Cuarta," the ladies did not attend. They were feasted in a hall by

themselves. But at some of the great festive gatherings the women mingled with the warriors. They
graced the hall of Cormac on that eventful night
when Grania, the daughter of the High King, first
set eyes upon the dark-haired, red-cheeked youth
who was the darling of the Fianna and one of their
mightiest champions—Diarmuid, grandson of
Duibhne, the friend of Angus Og. The flight of
Diarmuid and Grania is one of the oldest of the
world's love tales, and one of the saddest and most
romantic and touching. The opening chapters of it
were written here at Tara, partly in the Palace of
Cormac and partly in the "Sunny House," or
Grianan of the Ladies.

The love was all on poor Grania's side in the
beginning. Diarmuid was the friend of Finn, and
did not covet the girl upon whom his leader had
set his love. But Grania lost her heart to the
younger warrior, because he had a fatal dowry of
beauty, and it was written that no woman could
look upon his uncovered face without being fascinated. While the feast was at its height in the
royal dun, a fight began outside between the hounds
of King Cormac and the hounds of the Fianna, and
Diarmuid, in running out to quiet them, let fall his
cap in his hurry. Grania was thus enabled to see
the full beauty of his face and gave him her love.
She put love bonds upon him, says the legend, and
made him fly with her from Tara.

"It is bad bonds you are putting on me, Grania,"
warned Diarmuid, and, still loyal to his leader, he
pleaded Finn's cause with the woman. "It is a
wonder you give that love to me," he said, "for

there is not in Ireland a man who is a better lover than Finn.'*

But Grania was obdurate and she insisted. Diarmuid was powerless to resist; yet mark the splendid loyalty of the man to his leader and comrade in arms. When they were about to set forth at last he said to her:

"And if I do bring you with me it is not as a wife I will bring you, but I will keep my faith to Finn. And turn back now to the town," he said, "and Finn will never get any news of what you are after doing."†

It was the very poetry of knightly honour, but it was unavailing. Nothing would turn Grania from her amorous purpose; so forth they went to wander through the years of hardship and danger which culminated in the tragedy of Benbulban. It is a story centred around the idea of Beauty Triumphant. But even so, the surrender of Diarmuid to the witchery of woman is not without its ethical lesson; and the innate chivalry which speaks in his efforts to keep his knightliness unsmirched is one of the finest things in the literature of the world.

It was in the second half of the sixth century that the cursing of Tara took place by St. Ruadhan, an incident of deep and terrible historical importance, to which brief allusion has been made in Chapter I. There are students of Irish history who think that the real reason for the cursing of Tara was not in the uncompromising attitude of King Diarmuid MacCerbhaill regarding the execution of

* "Gods and Fighting Men." By Lady Gregory.
† Ib.

St. Ruadhan's nephew for the murder of a state
official, and the consequent wrath of the saint. That
the murderer was forcibly taken from Lorrha and
executed according to law is not doubted; but there
was more in the uprising of the ecclesiastics against
the civil power than mere indignation at the refusal
of the High King to stay the arm of the law because
the criminal had gained the shelter of a monastery.
It would appear that the Bishops regarded with
apprehension the steady growth of the civil power in
the hands of King Diarmuid. This king must have
been a man of commanding ability and great
strength of purpose. He had evidently set himself
the task of breaking down the system of petty kingdoms and provinces into which Ireland was divided,
and creating a strong and efficient central government at Tara. He had grasped the vital importance
of this policy, and saw that it should be put into
force if the Irish nation were to increase in power
and stability. The ecclesiastics of the day appear to
have taken a more restricted view. They seem to have
considered that, for the spiritual good of the nation,
it would be better to have the civil power as it was—
inchoate, disjointed, and decidedly weak. They
appear to have convinced themselves that with the
rise of the civil government in power and authority
the influence of the Church would decline. Soon after
the advent of Diarmuid to the throne of Ireland
there took place a conference of Bishops at Uisnach,
and there appears to be some ground for the sup-
position that the relations then existing between the
Church and State were discussed with a view to
the adoption of a definite ecclesiastical policy. This

conference was held after the death of St. Ciaran, who was a bosom friend of the High King. Diarmuid, as a fugitive prince, had been with Ciaran at the founding of Clonmacnoise, and had received the saint's blessing on ascending the throne. As the influence of Ciaran was great in the Irish Church, it is supposed that his brother prelates were unwilling to take action hostile to Tara while he lived. Ciaran was beloved by all; and possibly the same feeling which underlay the forbearance of the Bishops during his lifetime may also have prevented Diarmuid from entering into a conflict with the ecclesiastical power. In any case the death of St. Ciaran appears to have precipitated a conflict which had been latent for some time. When such a crisis develops, any incident which, in normal times, might be disposed of amicably, will suffice to start the conflagration. In the case of the murder of a state official by the nephew of St. Ruadhan, King Diarmuid stood rigidly and uncompromisingly by the law. The Bishops stood as rigidly and as uncompromisingly by the interest of the Church as they understood them. And war was the result. St. Ruadhan and his followers amongst the Hierarchy and clergy came to Tara in great numbers and in solemn state; and after an ultimatum to the Ard Righ had met with a negative, delivered with firmness and dignity, the cursing of the royal city began. The terrible ceremony occupied several days. The Bishops fasted, walked in procession round the city, ringing bells and chanting. They prayed that it might be accursed thenceforth, and that no King of Ireland might ever again reign there. When

Diarmuid MacCearbhaill heard of this he said in
the sorrow of his soul : " Alas ! it is not Tara alone
they have cursed, but the whole nation of Erin."
He was right. It was not Tara alone that declined
after the curse was laid upon it. The blight fell
upon civil government as well. The institutional
growth of the nation was blighted, and the seeds
of anarchy were re-sown.

The moral of it is very plain. Woe to the nation
in which one class is at war with the other, in which
one class believes that its interests can only prosper
by the bondage or suppression of another—in which
the State imagines that it can only achieve progress
by the fall of the Church, or in which the Church
believes that it can only hold its own by the fall
or decline of the State. Ireland has had many
centuries of experience—bitter and humiliating too,
God knows—to teach her wisdom in this respect.
There can be no truly powerful Irish Church without
a powerful Irish State. There can be no Irish State
powerful which fears the influence of religion in
moulding the lives of the people. There can be no
national greatness of an abiding nature achieved
that is not founded on a harmonious relationship
between all classes, and this relationship can only
have its origin in Justice and Truth. No matter
what class outsteps its rights, the nation is wronged.
No matter what class nourishes selfish ambitions,
the nation is endangered. And that is some of the
thinking an Irishman is likely to do as he stands
amidst the remains of Tara.

They will tell you in certain circles of Irish
Ireland that there is a living Irish lady who had a

vision of Tara. She saw it as it was during the days of its greatness. That is, indeed, how I would wish to behold it; not fallen and desolate, like now. As I sat on the wall over the Rath of the Synods I thought of Tara as it was when Patrick came. The five roads of Eirinn brought soldiers and bards and Brehons from every corner of the land to take part in the councils of the nation. The plains far down below were covered with tillage and herds. The lilt of song came from glen and vale and field, and the sacred truce of the king allowed it to be heard.

There was passion in love and passion in hate, for the hearts of men and women were strong, and the blood of the Gael was young; but if there was excess there was also vigour; if there was vice, there was also the very rapture of valour in the hearts and in the souls of men. There was no strife that would not have been settled by time; there was no idealism which had not a manly inspiration; there was no law which was based on despotism.

It was not a perfect age, because it was peopled by men and women, and not by angels. It had its failings, because it was human, but it had glories that were bright and great, because it was a verte-brate age—because it bred vertebrate men and women, and because it thought heroic thoughts and did heroic deeds.

"Oh, God of grace! was not life a pleasure
In our green and beautiful Eirinn then!"

It surely was.   But it is a pleasure to live in Eirinn yet   And, although Tara is silent and lonely, there are many people in Ireland whose faces are turned to it not in vain despair but in valiant hope.

CHAPTER VI.

*Into Ulster—The Eastern and Western Routes—
The Irish Railways—Belfast—Nationalism and
Unionism—Religious Intolerance—The Forum
at the Custom House Steps—The Orange Drum
and the Drummers—Belfast's claim to be the
Capital of Ireland—An Inheritance of Spite.*

It had been raining for several days and cycling
had been given up for work, when suddenly the
weather cleared. The roads dried quickly. The
wind blew gently from the South. The glow in the
blue air and the tints on the hills and over the
glens would charm a cyclist out of his grave. And
thus it came to pass that I found myself on the wheel
again, heading Ulsterwards, by what I had come to
call the eastern route. Twice had I tried the route
through northern Connacht, and twice had I completely and disastrously failed. I now chose the
eastern route via Dublin. I skirted the Slieve
Blooms early in the day and reached Portarlington
with an hour to the good on previous records. But
when I reached Monasterevin the weather had
changed. It began to rain, and the Dublin road
refused to tolerate me any longer. It spilled me to
right and left, and became so slippery and uncivil
that I willingly left it for the train.

As a matter of fact, I chose the Dublin route
because it offered the alternative of the railway. I
reached the capital that evening, and early next

day, as I was barely in time to catch the train, I hastily rammed my bicycle into the luggage van and then jumped into a carriage. It was crowded. There were eight full grown men in the compart, ment, and we had no spare room; but, nevertheless, the guard came along presently and thrust a thin, smiling watery-eyed youth into our midst. He sat on somebody's valise and sighed. A passing loco, motive belched several cubic furlongs of smoke into our midst, and it was in the eight or nine hundredth degree abominable. The watery-eyed young man closed the window, and a very stout man sitting beside me opened it again, using several assorted phrases of the language prevailing in the cattle pens at railway stations during the busy hours on fair days. He was a person engaged in the cattle trade, and he was economical in the use of fresh air and soap and the amenities of social life. As I happened to be sitting next the window I promptly raised it, and the aggressive personage asked by what right I had done so. I offered to tell him on condition that he should first inform me by what right he had pulled the window down. He indulged in further assorted language and became much excited. I suggested to him that he should travel in a loose box, or in a waggon with the rest of the live stock, and that a wild bullock was out of place in a carriage even if he was able to enter it on his hind legs. But he was incorrigible. He was taken in hand by one passenger after another, and was more or less ferociously rude to every one of us. He said that he was a well-known "jobber" of cattle, and that in all human probability he had money enough to buy every one of us from the gallows. There are many decent, respectable men in the Irish cattle trade, but this was not one of them. He behaved so scandalously that on arriving at a railway station we tried to have him removed. The stationmaster shook hands with him cordially and told us that if we did not like such company we might leave it. Here was a case in point of the autocracy of Irish railways, and it impressed me very much. Indeed the railway system of Ireland is quite impressive any day in the year, because it is everything that a proper railway system should not be.

In other countries the railways are more or less the servants of the public. In Ireland the railways look upon the public as being subject to them. On some of the main lines there is fairly good accom-modation, and the trains run more or less punctually. But on the branch lines the accommodation ranges from indifferent to infamous, and the time table is smashed into splinters. If you are travelling with ladies you can take chances on a branch line in the third class, unless there is an English garrison at some of the stations, in which case you will do well to leave the third class alone.

In the third class, as in other classes, there are smoking carriages in which you may smoke without seeking anybody's permission, and which are left almost exclusively to men. ᵀ have seen, however, trains on which carriage accommodation was so scan-dalously meagre that ladies were hustled into smoking compartments, in which the smoke had hardened into layers of blue and bluish-yellow.

The railways of Ireland are allowed too free a

hand. They are not entitled to half the privileges
which they enjoy. They should all be expropriated
by the State and then managed subject to popular
control.* In order to make their dividends they
sweat the impoverished country most outrageously,
and are nation-killers, inasmuch as they cripple
industry by preferential tariffs which favour
foreign products coming into Ireland and render
the export of Irish produce, in many cases, impossible. There are railway stations in Ireland
which, in point of filth, are a disgrace to civilisation.
There are civil and obliging railway officials in
Ireland, but there are also railway officials—and not
a few of them, but very many—to whom civility
and courtesy are words without meaning. It would
appear that a railway official in Ireland need not be
civil or obliging unless it is his nature to be so. If
it is his nature to be uncivil and ill-tempered and
arrogant, he may, apparently, be uncivil, ill-
tempered, and arrogant to the public with perfect
impunity.

The most insolent jack-in-office I have ever met
in all my travels, in any country, the most wan-
tonly offensive and unobliging and overbearing, was
a booking clerk in an Ulster town. He was not typical
of the average railway official in Ireland, and it is
only right to say that; but I must also say that the
average conduct of the minor railway official is
seldom conspicuously civil. This is all the more
remarkable because Ireland is pre-eminently a country of spontaneous courtesy. However, let us quit

* This was written in 1902, before the agitation in favour of
expropriating the Irish railways began.

the subject for the present. I want to tell you about Belfast, which city we reached not more than half an hour behind time.

I saw a good deal of Belfast internally. I cycled through it for the greater part of two days and had a good view of its face, as it were. But I did not get over deeply into conversation with it. I had only a few words with it now and then. You can have a broken head after half a dozen words with Belfast, if you go the right way about it, but I did not go there looking for trouble. My visit was a quiet one. I interfered with no wasps' nest. Perhaps this metaphor is too severe. I should possibly have likened the city to a beehive. I meddled not with that beehive in any spirit of aggression or levity. I just walked round it, listened for a moment to the buzz and hum of it, saw the bees at work, and then withdrew out of range. I am now going to set down my impressions of it as best I can give them to you, with diffidence, and only for what they are worth.

Belfast impresses you as being a very rich and a very busy city. But somheow it repelled me. As I stood within it I asked myself was I in Ireland. I thought of Henry Joy MacCracken and of other men and other times, and could find nothing in my surroundings to feed such a train of thought. I saw churches of all denominations, Freemason and Orange lodges, wide streets, towering smokestacks, huge factories, crowded traffic. And out of the water, beyond the Custom House, dimly seen through smoke and mist, rose some huge, shapeless thing which I found to be a shipbuilding yard wherein 10,000 men were hammering iron and steel

into great ocean liners. I saw palatial banks and
insurance offices and counting houses and vast
bazaars or emporiums. I saw thousands of well-
dressed people hurrying to and fro with no flash of
humour in their glances and no bloom of health in
their set and earnest faces. The noise of wheels and
hoofs and cranks and spindles and steam hammers
filled my ears and made my head ache. It was a
hoarse roar, the burden of which was :

> Money, money, money,
> Trade, trade, trade,
> Business, business.

It was overwhelming in a way. I wheeled my
bicycle out of the eddying traffic into a porch and
stood for half an hour looking at the ebb and flow
of city life. Above me, sculptured in solid granite,
was some escutcheon or symbolism which was foreign
in its origin and meaning. In front of where I
stood was a statue raised, at great cost, to a man
who hated his native land, and who did nothing
for his city but fan the flames of sectarian hatred.
No celebrity he—only a notoriety; no patriot—only
a firebrand; no landmark in the national history—
only a freak of parochialism and fanaticism. I went
farther along the resonant thoroughfares and found
other statues erected to the memory of men and
events for which I could find no place in the story
of my country. In the shadow of a great, vibrating,
towering, clanging factory I stood once more and
looked for some signs of Ireland. But the result
was more or less the same. The accent of the people

who passed me on the sidewalk was clear and sharp.
It was of Ulster, and therefore Irish, but the talk
was of un-Irish things. In the distance, seen over
the roofs on the other side of the street, was a
mountain top, gray and cloud-capped. This mountain stands close enough to the city to overlook the
greater part of it. Beyond it are Ulster valleys in
which dwell people who have, I was told, the true
Ulster spirit in them still. But around the mountain
foot, between it and the sea, where is Ulster and
where is Ireland? I asked myself this again and
again, and the clanking machinery on the throbbing
floors above me answered :

> Money, money, money,
> Trade, trade, trade,
> Business, business.

From the mountain came a gentle breeze. It had
swept over the homes of the Kinel-Eoghan and across
the waters of Lough Neagh before it had entered
Belfast. It gently wafted a little yellow leaflet
along the sidewalk and left it curled up between the
spokes of my bicycle. I took up the fugitive piece
of paper and read it. There was not a great deal of
printed matter on it, but every word of it was to
the point. It was an appeal to the people of Belfast
to assemble in their thousands at the Custom House
esplanade to hear " the Word of God " from the
mouth of some wandering creature who had " just
arrived " from Manchester. It was significant
enough. While I was pondering over it the factory
gates swung backward and hundreds of operatives

came into the streets. They were of both sexes, and they hurried on their way in threes and fours, young, cleanly enough, and by no means weakly in look or gait, yet with neither joy in their expression nor buoyancy in their carriage. No merry laughter pealed from them. No witty chaff was interchanged.

A plump, clean-shaven, rubicund man with tight trousers and an enormous scarf pin mingled with them. Some of them regarded him with indifference, others spoke eagerly to him and gave him bits of paper. Others passed him with a scowl. I learned that he was an agent of some gambling concern selling odds on horse racing. The bits of paper handed to him contained money and the names of the events upon which the bets were made. It is illegal for bookmakers to work openly, so they keep within the law by this species of dodgery. The man who explained all this to me said: " Behold how much we are indebted to England. We copy her gambling methods as we copy other things of hers. Then England makes a law against gambling, and forthwith we copy English methods of evading it. Are we not a quick witted people? " He spoke in bitter sarcasm, and one could well understand why. I showed him the piece of paper, and he added : " Aye, that is more of it. England having taught us to sin in her own way sends us over tramp apostles to save our souls ! "

The trade mark of this age of commercialism is stamped upon Belfast. Its physiognomy is eminently matter-of-fact. The city is neat, business-like, roomy. You can feel, before you are half an hour in it, that it looks upon time as money—although it still tolerates horse traction in its tramcars, due, I was told, to some hitch in the contract which prevents the corporation from forcing electric traction on the companies.* Belfast hums with industry and calls itself progressive. And yet, underlying all this commercialism, all this thrift, and all this cult of the main chance, there is a cast iron bigotry—a cruel, corroding, unfathomable, ferocious sectarian rancour.

You feel this, too, before you are long in Belfast. It works its way into most fields of human activity. You see it in the stern features of shopmen, who actually make their business interests subservient to Orangeism. You read it in the Press. At the Custom House esplanade there is a fierce anti-Catholic open air, gutter-orator, propaganda going on nearly every Sunday. The high councils of fanatics and schemers, who direct the No-Popery campaigns, may be said to be in permanent session. Of the ten thousand operatives working in the ship-building yards, I was told that not ten are Catholics. A Catholic's life would not be safe there, according to my informants. The owners of the yards are not bigots by choice. They are the victims of circumstances. If they employ Catholics they would be in hot water the whole year round. To begin with, things would be constantly happening to the Catholics. Bolts and crowbars and hammers and packages of rivets, and sharp heavy pieces of scrap-iron would be falling on their heads, coming, to all seeming and appearance out of the sky. No one could be pointed to as the thrower of such missiles. It would be all put down to accident. There would

* Since this was written, electric traction has been introduced.

be no hostile manifestation of a noisy character
There would be no howling. But, all the same,
Catholic mechanics would be dropping off from day
to day. One would be found lying under a girder
at the bottom of a ship's hold; another would be
found sprawling on a scaffolding with the point of
a three-inch shackel-pin buried in his brains; later on
another would be found under a lift with both legs
broken.

It would all be seeming accident. The employers
might or might not be obliged to pay damages, but,
in any case, they would have no end of legal trouble
on their hands. No one can control scrap-iron in
Belfast when there is sectarian or political trouble in
the wind. Odds and ends of boilers and girders
and other projectiles disappear from the yards and
reappear down town in showers, smashing heads and
windows and the peace of the realm.

The way to look for smoothness in the labour
market, therefore, is to keep the opposing forces
apart. The shipbuilders are not in the business to
corner bigotry. They are merely hard-headed employers, who are wise in their generation. They
know, for instance, that, notwithstanding the honest,
if lamentable, zeal of a few fanatical leaders and
some of their followers, there is another fact—the
fact that Orange hostility to Catholicism is largely
due to sordid political enmity, or, in other words, to
hard cash.

A narrow self-interest is, to a great extent, the
cause of anti-Catholic feeling in Ireland. Broadly
speaking, the Catholicism of Ireland is associated
with Nationalism, simply because Catholicism is the

religion of the majority of the Irish people, who in
one form or another hold Nationalist opinions. The
non-Catholics of Ireland are, to a large extent, un-
Irish, either in antecedents or sympathy. They are
mostly Unionist in politics, not because of their
religion, but because of their pockets. Unionism is
largely a question of business. Thus the politico-
religious war is a struggle between people who
regard Ireland as their country and people who look
upon it as the spoil of conquest.

Let us test the proposition for a moment. When
the non-Catholic becomes a Nationalist no amount
of mere Protestant religious zealousness on his part
will save him from the anathema of the Unionists.
When the Catholic becomes a West Briton, and
throws in his lot with Unionism, he is no longer
submitted to persecution on account of his creed.
Any teaching to the contrary is at variance with fact.
The snob and the turncoat do not win high respect
anywhere, and I am not saying that Catholic political recreants in Ireland are looked on with much
admiration by those to whom they pander. But
they are no longer ostracised; and in this fact, and
in all that it means, lies the force of the argument.
On the other hand, most of the great leaders of
Nationalism whom Ireland has had since the days
of the Volunteers, have been recruited from the
ranks of Protestants and Presbyterians The Volun-
teer movement itself was Protestant. Charlemont,
Grattan, Flood, and the other prominent men of the
Irish constitution of '82 were all non-Catholic. In
'98 Catholic and Protestant were together. Bagnal
Harvey was as much a rebel as Father Murphy.

The United Irishmen were of different creeds, but
they were of one nationality.   From Tone to Parnell
most of our fighting leaders have been non-Catholic.
O'Connell was our biggest Catholic constitutionalist;
but Parnell was a great leader of another creed to
whom, by the way, constitutionalism was more of an
alternative than of a hide-bound policy.   Emmet,
Davis and Mitchel were non-Catholics.   Sadlier
and Keogh were Catholics; and many a scoundrel
like them has been not only Catholic but Ultra-
montane.

There is no need to multiply instances, especially
as the multiplication might confuse the point at
issue, which is not one of creed, but of nationality.
The cry of " No Popery " is simply a shibboleth on
the lips of a party that follows the bread basket.
It means that sectarianism is being used for a political end.   It is foolish, therefore, to say that
Catholics are persecuted in Ireland on account of
their religion.   They are persecuted on account of
their nationality.   No ascendancy door is closed
against the Morris family.   No railway clerkship is
refused to the nominees of men like the Bellews and
O'Connors.   The Castle uses its discretionary powers
not from the standpoint of sectarianism, but from
that of loyalty.   It sends invitations to Catholics
who are professed West Britons.   It sends detectives
after all who are fighting nationalists, whether they
be Catholic or Protestant.

In Ireland true nationality means, among other
things, exclusion from the spoils of office.   Unionism means the majority kept under in the interests
of a minority.   The minority is the ascendancy—the

planted population and its parasites. To the planter, Unionism is daily bread, to the traitor it is his mess of pottage. And there you are.

Ireland must bury the religious hatchet. She only plays the game invented for her by William Pitt when she sets religion and nationhood to fight. Cardinal Logue struck the right note once in Belfast, when he said, in opening a great festival organised by the Gaelic League, that however Irish Catholic and Irish Protestant might differ about religion, they had at least a country in common which they ought to love. This is statesmanship. To a certain extent it was a cry in the wilderness up in Belfast. But what of that? The original cry in the wilderness did not die on the silent air. It has echoed down the ages. It is a far cry from the fierce and withering sectarianism of Orange Belfast to a day of mutual toleration between Catholics and non-Catholics in Ulster and all over Ireland; but it will come.

Belfast is called by its admirers the capital of Ireland, but it is far from having any solid claim to that distinction. It may be very select and may call itself progressive, but it is not an Irish city. Belfast, as we see it now, is simply the creation or the outgrowth of a state of things completely un-Irish. The capital of a country should be a reflex of the national life in all its moods, peculiarities, activities, intellectualities, aspirations, tastes and tendencies. This Belfast certainly is not, and this Dublin to some extent certainly is.

You might drop down into Belfast out of a balloon and fancy yourself in some English or Scotch

city. You could not make such a mistake about
Dublin. I know well that there are in Belfast some
of the most uncompromising Nationalists. But there
are people of that way of thinking even in London.
Belfast, I repeat, did not strike me as being an Irish
city. It seemed to have a foreign complexion. Its
methods, its enthusiasms, its outlook on life, its
idealism seemed to be anything but Irish. The
names of its streets, parks, avenues, docks are un-
Irish. This, unfortunately, is no uncommon thing
in Irish civic nomenclature, but it seems to be a cult
in Belfast.

In other cities of Ireland, even in those of the
Pale, you can read something Irish underneath all
the imported names. But in Belfast not only the
place names, but the names over the shop doors
along the streets are of foreign origin. There are
streets in Liverpool and London in which the sign-
boards are more suggestive of Ireland.

But this is not all. There is no Irish geniality
about Belfast street life. It is cold, austere, rigid,
grim. Even in the very primness and spaciousness
and newness there is something un-Irish. In Dublin
you meet Ireland at every step. It is the tone of the
voices, in the whistle of the street arabs, in the eyes
and features and accents and laughter of the people.
Dublin is brown and weather beaten and old
fashioned, and it looks like a place in which history
has been made for ages. The stamp of the alien
is upon much of its architecture, but undoubtedly
its street statuary has something to tell of a national
past. In its libraries and museums and public
places there is much that is truly metropolitan—much

to convince you that you are in touch with the core of the nation's intellectual life.

In Belfast there is little or nothing of this. Not that Belfast is devoid of books and antiquarian curios and statues and esplanades. It has its share of them, but they are not expressive of anything that is distinctly Irish. Dublin is the metropolis in spite of everything. As it was in the past it is now, and is more than likely to be.

I think James Stephens had a project of making Limerick the capital; but it is questionable if he could have succeeded, even under the most favourable conditions, even if he had been victorious in the field and had been free to shape Irish destinies for a quarter of a century. You can make any village or town or city or field or valley the political capital of a country, but that is very far from being half the battle. You may have supremacy in commerce, trade, finance, aye, even in art and letters; but if you have not tradition you are still out in the cold.

There is, indeed, one spot in Ireland which, under conceivably altered circumstances, might become the political metropolis; but it is not Limerick, much as the Treaty City is favoured geographically, and much as it is a landmark in national history. Tara is the place. Meanwhile, Dublin, not Belfast, is the capital of Ireland.

The Custom House steps in Belfast is a famous place for meetings. Militant Catholics call it an infamous place. Orange apostles of a certain type regard it as sacred ground. The Salvation Army generals look upon it as of primary strategetic value. It is the Sunday forum of the city. It is also the storn. centre of ranting aggressiveness. There is a fine open space in front of the Custom House. Steps lead from this space or square up to the flagged esplanade, which is a few feet over the level of the pavement. Around the esplanade, separating it from the square, is a balustrade. The orators hold forth from the steps, or they lean over the balustrade.

It is an ideal place for open air meetings. The steps and the balustraded esplanade constitute a splendid platform. The space in front affords standing room for thousands of people. The speakers are in full view of their audience, and it is their own fault if they are not heard by a good many hundreds of the crowds who assemble to listen to them.

The Pope is dethroned, scalped, roasted and consigned to eternal perdition every Sunday afternoon during busy times from this platform. Popery with its works and pomps is denounced, menaced, and torn to pieces. Orange demagogues expatiate on the creed and politics of Papists and call forth thunders of applause. All things national and Catholic are thickly coated with mud, and the green flag is flittered into shreds.

Sometimes the oratory is so drastic that the audience becomes infuriated and goes up town on the war trail looking for battle. Perhaps they fall in with a Catholic procession or manifestation, and then there is sure to be trouble. At other times a few hundred or a few thousand disciples of the Custom House prophets, well loaded with whiskey and other fire water, and headed by a brass band, will march up town with colours flying. When they come to a Catholic church they will sing Orange chorus songs and beat the big drum at a pressure of several tons to the square inch. When they burst a drum they get another one. When one drummer drums himself into a fit they get a new man. No procession starts without a good set of drummers. An energetic Orange drummer in Belfast is like the big hundred ton guns—he can only be used a limited number of times. He batters his elbows to pieces and breaks his wind. He lives at high pressure for a season and then succumbs. During his periods of activity, to use a volcanic expression, he knocks the ends out of several drums. After an exciting day it is necessary to take precautions in regard to him, because he is likely to drum in his sleep. I heard of a drummer of Belfast who drummed so terrifically in his dreams that he killed his wife and broke nearly everything in the room that could be broken by a twelve inch shell. If I were a Belfast undertaker I do not think I would be safe in coffining one of those dead drummers without first putting him in handcuffs.

The Salvation Army campaigns in Belfast radiate, so to speak, from the Custom House, or it might be more correct to state that they concentrate there. The generals, colonels, majors and majoresses, and other officers and officeresses do not aim at stirring up the angry passions of the mob. They play concertinas, just as they do elsewhere, and tell how they were saved and speak in the most intimate way about the Deity and the Evil One.

But they are not the only exponents of salvation

for the million in the market. They have colleagues
or rivals. From the opposite corner of the balustrade a man from Clan London is delivering the
message with which he is charged to the multitude.
The message is very unctious, but somewhat ungram-
matical and devoid of accurately located h's. He
has come to save the benighted Hirish from a place
called 'ell—a place so hot that it makes him teem
with perspiration. But he does not call it hot. He
calls it 'ot. He will presently send round his wife
with his hat or 'at to make a collection of what he
terms 'apunce—called half-pence by the benighted
natives. He is a sleek, florid, well fed personage,
and his anti-Catholicism is extremely virulent even
for Belfast.

Religious rancour in Belfast has its humorous
side as well as its tragic aspects. At Ardoyne the
Passionist Fathers started a boys' club—merely a
kind of night shelter for poor urchins, to keep them
off the streets. The boys who frequented the place
were Catholics, and they were militant indeed.
They fought among themselves like dogs and cats,
and you would have required a pole-axe to keep
them in order when they got a bad attack of the
tantrums. They smoked and chewed and drank,
and knew all the wickedness that Belfast could teach
them. They were street boys, through and through,
and to have made them anything else you would
want to have them born over again.

Soon after the club was started, the rector of
Ardoyne was away for a few days on a mission,
and the Fathers who remained at home were busy
with a hundred and one things in connection with

their parish work. The boys' club was somewhat neglected in the meantime. There was no one to pay special and constant nightly attention to it, and the consequence was that the premises and fittings were reduced to ruin. The plaster was knocked off the walls, the windows were smashed, the Indian clubs and other appurtenances of the gymnasium were in splinters.

But you are not to suppose that this wreckage was the result of any hostility to the Fathers or of any tendency to go over to the Orange persuasion. It was simply their playfulness. While they were converting their club into a rubbish heap they were planning a campaign against a colony of Orange street arabs that had appeared in the neighbourhood. They collected an armament of stones and sticks one evening, bore down on the Orange encampment in force, and routed the enemy with terrible slaughter and noise. Nobody slept in the district that night.

A great deal of the so-called religious war in the North is on a par with this battle of the street arabs of Ardoyne. It is not religious zeal. It is merely inherited spite, and that is the biggest factor in the trouble. There are Catholics ready to take their lives in their hands on St. Patrick's Day who may not have complied with their religious duties for years. There are Orangemen ready to cry " To hell with the Pope," who have not been inside of a church since their boyhood. They are born to it, brought up to it. It is an inheritance, this blind, unreasoning hatred. The primary cause of it I have already explained. Constant friction has kept it raw. When

self-interest gets tangled up with human pride and
a tradition of conflict you have an imposing congestion of vexations all knotted together. That is
the case in the North. People have been born into a
fight for over a century. They will have to be born
out of it. Time will heal the evil—time and common
sense and a broader conception of tolerance and
nationhood.

In one way there is too much tolerance in Ireland.
The slavishness of snobbish Catholicism is not true
tolerance; it is the cowardly subservience of degene-
rates. True tolerance is a feeling of charity which
tempers a man's or a woman's righteous fidelity to
principle. It gives that respect to sincerity in others
which it asks for itself. It makes no compromise.
It does not place its hands under the feet of arro-
gance. It does not compound with falsehood. It
preaches dignity and moderation as well as firmness
in maintaining and practising principles. That is
the sort of tolerance to desiderate and teach. It is
quite different from a crawl. There is no cringe in
it. Every bit of it is manly.

Any sentiment of the human heart that has been
tried by the fires of ostracism and persecution has
always the true ring—when it survives. The
Nationalist feeling of the Irish patriots of Belfast
is of this kind. The very intensity of the anti-Irish
feeling which prevails amongst so many of the
people fans the flame of Nationalism in the breasts of
the men and women who hold to the Irish ideal. In
no part of Ireland have Nationalists more to lose, in
a material sense, than in Belfast, yet in no part of
Ireland will you meet Nationalism of a sterner
school, nor of a more daring hopefulness and faith.

CHAPTER VII.

*Derry—A Lumpy City—A City of Contrasts—
Politico-Religious War — Industrial Derry —
Derry of the Sieges--The Walls—Derry of
Columcille—The Saint—The Exile—His Re-
turn—Royal Aileach—The Old Fortress of
Niall the Great—A Superb Picture—The Sleep-
ing Heroes.*

Where Foyle his swelling waters rolls northward to the main,
Here Queen of Erin's Daughters, fair Derry, fixed her reign;
A holy temple crowned her, and commerce graced her street,
A rampart wall was round her, the river at her feet;
And here she sat alone, boys, and, looking from the hill,
Vowed the maiden on her throne, boys, should be a maiden still.

When Charlotte Elizabeth wrote that Orange
ballad (which Nationalists have since made their
own, in part) she achieved a masterpiece. The
"Maiden City" is one of the very finest songs or
ballads in any language. I will say that for it,
although it is an Orange lyric. And what is more,
Derry is worthy of its songstress. I will say that
for Derry, too—although it is one of the strongholds
of Orange works and pomps.

Derry is a lumpy, uneven kind of city, may it
please you; and it is lumpy and uneven from various
points of view. It is hilly to begin with; nay, it
began on a hill—the hill of the oaks, where the
sacred grove was, from which trees the city takes its

name. Derry is a rough, rugged, craggy, precipitous place politically, socially and religiously, as well as physically. It began life, as one might say, under the auspices of a precipitous, lumpy, combative sort of man—St. Columcille. The Apostle of Alba was one of the greatest Irishmen of any time — scholar, poet, artist, and statesman, as well as saint. But in his hot youth he was a man of fiery pride and passion, and during the first years of his priesthood he became the chief firebrand of the sixth century. Derry-Columcille, his own city—for that is the right name of Derry and not Londonderry—took after its founder in one way. It started life with a hot temper and it has never cooled down. It has been something of a storm centre all through the ages. And it is a storm centre to-day. You cannot look upon it without a quickening of the pulses. Something of its rugged history speaks to you out of its quaint old streets. It sits there squarely astride of the Foyle under wild Inishowen, the weather-beaten citadel of the fighting North.

It slopes sheerly down to the river after climbing several hills, which give some of its causeways the appearance of trying to stand on end. During the frosty weather all vehicle traffic ceases in several precipitous thoroughfares, and the popular sport of sliding begins. You may call it tobogganing or sleighing or anything you please. It consists of sitting on a board or in a basket and flying down the slippery gradient at the rate of several miles per minute. There are certain arrangements made by which the sliders shall not be dashed to pieces, or across the river into Tyrconnel; but this is a matter of detail.   With

Bowden brakes you can ride a bicycle down one of those Derry streets; but you would require a ten horse-power engine to work your cranks in the upward direction. If you want to see Derry you must go to work on foot Go over the bridge and climb the hills on the off side of the river when evening comes, and you will appreciate the situation. Tier over tier of lights shine out from the steamers and electric lamps along the water front right up into the sky. Shops, clubs, long lines of factories, depots and private houses—all contribute something to the illumination. They are perched at different altitudes on the slopes of the hills, some of them having their foundations many feet over the level of the tall roofs of others.

Let us now turn to other phases of Derry's lumpiness. Your rambles through the streets reveal them to you. Here is a Catholic seminary; here is a Presbyterian one. Here is the Orange Hall; here is St. Columcille's Hall Here is a street in which live militant Catholics; here alongside, radiating from a common centre, is a street in which live militant Orangemen. Here is a newspaper office from which issue periodical challenges to Croppies; here is another newspaper office from which said challenges are hurled back with interest. Here are the old seventeenth century walls of the city which were manned by Cromwellians in 1648. Here are the historic gates slammed by the 'prentice boys in the face of the Catholic army of James forty years later. Here are the landmarks left by Columcille; here is the trophy statue to the soldier-pastor who made Derry one of the strongholds of Protestantism.

There was a day when this religious feud seemed near its end; and when the Presbyterians of Ulster were tending toward the highest idea of nationhood; but that was before Pitt arose to kindle anew the flames of religious rancour which have burned so banefully through all the nineteenth century, and whose lurid tongues are reddening the sky of the twentieth. It was a sad day for Derry and for Ireland when Irishmen of all classes and creeds forgot that they had a common country to love. Think of all that is implied by such an oversight. Think of all the blood spilled in fratricidal strife over religious rancour, and not a drop for Ireland. Think even of the brave old Protestant Walker and his brave Catholic assailants wasting blood and powder over the Stuarts! Where did Ireland come in? Think of Orange and Green to-day heaving paving-stones and scraps of iron at each other! For what; alas! for what?

The political and social animus arising out of this religious strife is written large all over Derry, as it is over most of Ulster. Near one of the gates in the old walls three or four streets converge. Right in front of the street openings, stands a large shop. When a politico-religious shindy takes place between the opposing factions that inhabit the converging streets, this shop's front is generally mutilated in the most destructive manner. The flying paving stones and other missiles play havoc with windows, and gilding, and signboard, and the furniture on the upper floors. The owner of this shop is a pacific citizen. He has no quarrel, I was told, with anybody. He takes no part with either Orange or

Green. And yet his shop front is periodically wrecked. It is simply because his house is on the battle-ground of the mobs. Ireland is, more or less, in the same position; and if there is a difference at all, it lies in the fact that she pays the piper. The Derry shopman is compensated for his windows. But who or what compensates the nation for the ruinous expenditure of energy on internal strife?

Like Belfast, Derry is a busy industrial centre. There is a good deal of the beehive about it. It has stings, but also honey. It fights, but it makes money. It has some important industries in linen, especially in shirt making, and in materials for the make up of linen shirts. I counted eight or ten factories all working full time, and I could see other smaller establishments also engaged in the linen trade as I looked southward from the heights beyond the Foyle. Along the quays are lines of steamers loading and discharging merchandise, and you may see bales of goods for export marked Buenos Ayres, Rio, Bombay, Melbourne, Valparaiso, Shanghai, etc. The factories give employment to thousands of hands; and after 6 o'clock in the evening the streets are crowded by the spinners and other operatives going home. I did not find out exactly how the manufacturing industry of Derry stands. But I think it as financially sound as it is in any other centre in the three kingdoms. Certainly the mills are all working. There did not seem to be many people out of employment.

The "Walls of Derry" are still to the good. They enclose a diamond-shaped area in which stood Derry of the sieges. The modern city spreads all

round the walls and the walled town, and is to the
Derry of to-day what the New York of 1907 is to
New York of 1860. The population of Derry is
now over 40,000. In the stormy days of the sieges
it was little more than a fortified village. The space
enclosed by the historic walls appears to be smaller
than many a square or plaza in modern cities. The
walls are immense ridges of masonry. Two waggons could meet and pass each other on the top.
They are proportionately wide at the base. Their
height seems to vary, but is in places over thirty feet
above the street. There are parapets, loopholes,
bastions, lookouts and other details of engineering,
all of which had their uses in the days of short-range
artillery and small arms The gateways are arched,
and the principal ones have a due share of architectural ornamentation. I do not know what has
become of the gates which refused to open. I enquired, but discovered no antiquarian in Derry who
could give me the desired information.

The walls were built in 1617-18, at a cost of
£8,500, a sum which represented a great deal more
in those days than it does in ours. They were found
to be impregnable by the Royalists, who besieged
the Cromwellian garrison for four months in 1648.
But the most memorable siege took place in 1688,
when for 105 days it held out against the army of
James II. The beleagured city endured the most
terrible privations, and behaved with a heroism
which Catholic as well as Protestant cannot but admire. The brunt of the fight fell on the 'prentice
boys, and they won. King James was obliged to
raise the siege. His generals may or may not have

been incompetent, and the elements of attack inadequate. Be that as it may, James was worsted.
Derry held her own against him, and he was obliged
to leave her in peace.

> In short, the fact is known, boys, she chased him
>   from the hill,
> For the maiden on her throne, boys, would be a
>   maiden still.

The hero of the defence was the Rev. Mr. Walker.
Derry raised a great monument to his memory on
the walls which he made famous. There it stands
yet, overlooking the city. The sword which the
right hand of the statue held aloft fell with a
mighty crash on the night that Catholic emancipa-
tion for Ireland became law. The prominence given
to this circumstance in Irish history of the nineteenth
century shows that in neither religious camp was it
regarded as a mere coincidence at the time.

On the rampart facing the river are a few ancient
pieces of ordnance presented to Derry by various
guilds of London. Clan London has always been
ready to make presents of anything which would
contribute to the work of keeping the Irishry down
and squelching them, and protecting the warriors
who were doing the trampling down and the squelching. Each gun bears an inscription giving the names
of the donors and the date of its manufacture.
Several of these had pet names in the fighting years.
" Roaring Meg " was one of them. Roaring " was
a favourite adjective used in connection with cannon
in the seventeenth century. And in reality those
" roarers " made more noise than destruction. The

rusted "roarers" on the walls of Derry are kept there now merely as historical landmarks. Like the walls on which they stand, they are useless as elements of defence—a half battery of modern field guns would blow all that stone heap and old iron into ruin in a few hours from any of the hills around the city. But the historic ramparts and ordnance are not there for defence. They are merely symbols speaking from the past.

You cannot mention Derry without dwelling awhile on its great founder, nor yet can you visit the city without meeting his footprints, as it were. Columba, or Columcille, was a Donegal man, but in those days Derry was a part of his native heath, although, perhaps, it might be more accurate to describe it as standing on the borderland between Tir-Eoghan and Tir-Conal. Columcille was of the Hy-Niall race, and according to "The Book of Lismore" might have been high king had he not devoted himself to God. After study under St. Finian and other great teachers, he returned to the North a young priest of twenty-five to found a church in his native territory. That was in A.D. 545. Ainmire, his first cousin, then Prince of Aileach and afterward Ard-Righ of Tara and Eirinn, gave his kinsman Daire-Calgaich, so called from the oaks which clothed the slopes of the hill on which Ainmire's residence was situated. It was from Columba it took the name of Daire-Columcille, or Derry-Columcille. It was from the Sassenach it took the name of Daire-London, or Londonderry. How much of national history you find embodied in the etymology of place names!

And even proper names are also frequently significant. For instance, Columcille means "Colum
of the Church," or, as some call him, "Dove of the
Church." I like "Colum" of the Church better,
for there was not much of the dove about him. He
was an eagle. The blood of the North was strong
and fiery in his veins. The great test of his man-
hood and sanctity was in his power to tame his
haughty spirit. It is because he was so human, so
impetuous, so impatient of restraint, so much of the
warrior, that he got into trouble. And it was by
battling with the salient elements of his nature that
he rose superior to his faults. It is his glory, as Dr.
Healy so well says, that with God's help he conquered himself. We love him because he was a great
saint and a great patriot. He was as great an Irishman
as he was a churchman. His love of God was wedded
to his love of country. It is a pity that this great
Irish Catholic is so little known by the mass of the
people, that the record of his life is so tangled up
with fable and obscured by fiction. The absurd
forgeries which pass current for "Columcille's
Prophecies" are not his. He was a prophet indeed,
but not a mountebank. "Mighty in word and in
work," he was a saint, but not a charlatan. He was
a great teacher—one of the greatest of a nation of
teachers. He founded over thirty educational establishments in Ireland alone. He was a great artist—
probably the greatest colorist and draftsman that
our race has produced. He it was who illuminated
and wrote the Book of Durrow. In the opinion of
some experts he also was the originator of that
peerless masterpiece, "The Book of Kells." In

" Felire of Aengus " we read that he was " a man of
well formed and powerful frame ; his skin was white,
his face was broad and fair and radiant, lit up with
large, gray, luminous eyes; his large and well
shaped head was crowned with close and curling
hair. His voice was clear and resonant, so that he
could be heard at a distance of fifteen hundred paces,
yet sweet with more than the sweetness of the bard."
And he had the true bardic spirit, too, as well as the
genius of oratory, which he showed in the famous
Convention of Drumceat.

It was from Derry Columba set sail for Scotland.
A sad leave-taking that was—sad, yet grand and
beautiful in its consequences. The reason of his
going is one of the most tragic incidents in the
early history of Christian Ireland—known as the
battle of Cull-Dreemimhne, now called Cooladrummon, under the nose of hoary Benbulben, in Sligo.
Two causes are assigned for this terrible engagement,
and both are embodied in legends which have for
one of their central figures another great man, King
Diarmuid, the last King of Tara. This is the king
who tried to consolidate the civil power of Erin,
and evolve a nationhood from the clanships; and
failed because he came into conflict with the Church.

There were great athletic games on the green at
Tara, and hurling—the ancient game of "caman-
acht"—formed part of the programme. In one of
the matches Curnan, a Connacht prince, struck the
high king's steward with his " caman " and killed
him.

Now to raise a hand in anger at the games of Tara
was strictly forbidden by law, and was punishable

by death. Curnan knew this, and flew to Columcille, who was present, for protection. The king
demanded the fugitive. Columcille refused to give
him up. The monarch insisted, and the criminal
was torn from his protector, handed over to justice
and executed. So the saint and the king quarrelled,
and a death feud sprang up between them.

But the ecclesiastic had another grievance against
Diarmuid. Columba had secretly and surrep-
titiously copied a beautiful edition of the psalms
which St. Finian had brought from Rome. St.
Finian set great store by this work of sacred art,
and when he learned that Columba was copying it
he was greatly angered. But he said nothing until
the work was finished, when he laid claim to the
copy as well as to the original Columba refused to
give up the copy, and the matter was referred to the
high king, who decided in favour of St. Finian.
Columba protested against the decision, refused to
abide by it, and appealed to arms. He applied for
aid to the Hy-Niall, his royal kinsmen of the North,
and they took the field in his cause. Aodh of
Connacht, whose son Diarmuid had put to death
for a capital offence against the law, was glad of an
opportunity for revenge, and also joined the revolt.
It was a formidable uprising against the authority
of Tara; but Diarmuid was no chicken-hearted king
who would tamely suffer rebellion. He called his
loyal chieftains to his standard, and at the head of
a large army marched out to meet the insurrectionists.
The forces met near the coast of the Atlantic, north
of Sligo, on the ridge of Cooladrummon. St. Finian
was with the high king and prayed for victory to

the arms of Tara.   St. Columba was with the rebels
and prayed for victory for the rebellion.   The rebels
won.   The high king was badly defeated, and three
thousand of his men slain.   When the bloody fray
was over the conscience of St. Columba smote him,
for he saw the enormity of his transgression.   In
penance for his terrible anger and its calamitous
results to the nation, he was ordered by his confessor
to leave Ireland forever; and he went.   That is why
he made his home in Iona.

History says the fiat decreed that Columba should
never again set foot upon the soil of Erin, but this
sentence was at least in one notable instance set
aside.   And the setting aside of the sentence of
perpetual banishment is part of one of the most
dramatic chapters in the history of Ireland, and one
of the most luminous acts of wisdom in the great
career of the saint himself.   It was all about the
bards of Erin.

Aodh O'Neill of Aileach, Columcille's cousin,
was high king now, and the bards were giving him
great annoyance.   In fact, for some years they had
been going to the bad.   They had surrounded themselves with all the good and bad things of the earth
until their glorious art was degraded.   They had
degenerated to a shocking extent.   They had become corrupt, lazy, avaricious, turbulent—a by-word
and a disgrace.   At last the high king called a great
convention to take the bardic excesses into consideration.   Other high matters of national importance
were set down for discussion, but the chief problem
before the assemblage was: what should be done
with the bards?   Everyone, including the king, was

for abolishing the bardic order. The bards were greatly alarmed at the public indignation which they had aroused, and sent in haste to Columcille, abjectly beseeching him to come to Ireland and save them. He was a bard himself, and his heart went out to his literary brethren, and he came in response to their appeal—back to his beloved city of the Oaks, after an absence of about twelve years. During that period of exile he had become one of the foremost men in Western Europe, and the most influential man of Ireland and Scotland. Churchmen, statesmen, scholars, artists, poets, soldiers and lawgivers had learned to hang upon the words of the recluse whose face they had never seen. From his rocky retreat on the Scottish coast he exercised a moral influence on two nations the potency of which speaks volumes for the masculine immensity of his genius and the wondrous sanctity of his life.

The great convention of Drumceat took place in A.D. 575. It was held at Mullagh, or Daisy Hill, near Limavady, fifteen miles from Derry. King Aodh presided, and was likewise the chief accuser of the bards. "All the princes of the line of Conn were ranged around him," writes Archbishop Healy. "The bards were there, too, with the illustrious chief bard, Dallan Forgaill, at their head. The queen and her ladies were, it is said, also present; and twenty bishops, forty priests, and many clergy of inferior grade were seated near Columcille in this great parliament of the Irish nation. The king brought forward all the charges against the bards—their avarice, their idleness, their exactions, their insolence; and he called upon the

assembly to dissolve the order and take away all
their privileges. Then Columba arose : all that vast
assembly did him reverence. With his clear and
strong melodious voice, which was borne to the
utmost verge of the multitude, he defended the
ancient order of the bards of Erin. He did not
deny the existence of grave abuses—let them be cor-
rected ; and in future let the guilty be severely
punished. But why destroy the order itself ? Who
would then preserve the records of the nation, celebrate the great deeds of the kings and warriors, or
chant a dirge for the noble dead ? His eloquence
carried the assembly with him. The order was preserved from destruction."

Some chroniclers say that while Columcille remained in Ireland on this visit his eyes were bound
in cerecloths, and that there was clay of Iona in
his sandals, so that he might neither see the land of
Erin nor tread upon it. But this seems doubtful, for
we are also told that he visited all the houses which
he had founded—Derry, Durrow, Kells, Swords,
Drumcliff, Screen, Kilglass, Drumcolomb, and about
thirty others. He never visited Ireland again. He
died at Iona in A.D. 597, in the seventy-fourth year
of his age, and the thirty-fourth of his exile. He
was one of the greatest of the great race of Hy-
Niall—aye, or of all the race of Erin—and the
race is proud of him.

As for Derry, she is especially proud of him—
that is to say, Daire-Columcille is : Daire of Clan-
London, or Londonderry, has a hero of its own—
Walker, the fighting Protestant pastor of 1688, who
held the city against James II. Behold, Oh, my

brothers, in this juxtaposition of sects, and cults, and parties, and nomenclatures, the jumbled tragedy of the nation's life!

Three of us started one morning from Derry on foot over the steep and windy mountain roads. We faced westward, leaving the Foyle and the blue peaks of Inishowen to our right. We were bound for the Grianan Hill, on which stands Aileach, the high place of Ulster royalty in the long ago. We had a glorious morning for a walk, and we needed it—not the walk, but the morning. The sun was wintry, but brilliant, and the bracing air was blowing over the uplands of Tir-Eoghan from the south-east. The heather on the peaks bent down before the blast, and the foam from the swollen hill-streams flew away before it like thistledown in Autumn on the pampas.

The road led us down and across deep and shady valleys, and up again into the sunny air, past rushy and sedgy brooks and bare patches of gray rock, through which the water oozed, past tillage fields, in which the ploughs were already at work for the Winter tilling, and from which the sharp " hap " and " get up " of the Ulster ploughman came to remind us that the soft " hup " and " hoe " of the southern furrows are remnants, doubtless, of a mellower Gaelic. After an hour's stiff marching we gained the crest of a ridge, and there before us, in the distance, was the ancient fortress of the O'Neills, the pride of Kniel Owen—Aileach of the Chieftains. The mountain rose, bare and bleak and brown, into the morning sky, and the old stone rath perched upon its summit frowned darkly on hill and vale and stream, as it has frowned for twenty centuries and more. We left the road at the foot of the mountain and took to the fields, and then up over the damp heather and withered ferns and spongy moss and the crumbling rocks. We bent with a will against the wind and the slope until we gained the top, and stood within the storied dun of Niall the Great.

The walls are cyclopean in their massive strength and primitive masonry. The rath is circular in form and built of the same rock which grins through the heather on the mountain The walls are many feet in thickness at the base, and the only entrance is a low, square passage, the roof of which is formed by huge slabs of stone. The outer face of the rath is almost perpendicular and about the same height as a martello tower; but on the inside the wall is graded off into tiers for the purpose of defence. These tiers or circular galleries give the interior something of the appearance of an amphitheatre, to which lead two staircases of stone on the eastern curve of the circle. The topmost tier is little more than a narrow ledge, and the wall rises above it just sufficiently to form a low breastwork. The Grianan of Aileach was partly destroyed centuries ago by one of the O'Briens of Thomond, who was at war with the O'Neills. O'Brien got the upper hand, and he made each soldier of his forces carry away a stone of the fortress as a token of victory.

Time and the vandalism of stormy centuries wrought further havoc on the walls until nothing remained of them but a few feet high of the foun dation. Some years ago, however, Dr. Bernard, of

Derry, happily set about the work of restoration, and it is due to his efforts that Aileach now presents something of the appearance it had in the days of its glory. The work of restoration was carried out in strict accordance with the plans evolved from the most careful and accurate antiquarian research. A mark was painted all round the plinth, showing from what height exactly the walls were rebuilt, and were it not for this it would now be impossible to indicate how much of the work is modern, and how much of it part of the original structure, so per'ectly was the masonry of the olden days imitated.

The south-easter had freshened while we stood on the floor of the rath, and when we ascended the stairs the gale had the strength of a hurricane and the keenness of a razor. But the view which met our gaze as we looked out over the breastworks would have been cheaply purchased by hours spent wrestling with a cyclone, or a day in an Arctic winter. It was beyond description in its stern and rugged magnificence. On one hand lay the Foyle, on the other wild Lough Swilly, the further shores of which were hidden in a silvery mist. The gray ridges of Tir-Eoghan were also draped in haze. But the wild and towering ranges of Tir-Conal were thrown out in bold relief, not a spot of white or streak of gray on their dusky blue and purple. Grand and grim they looked as if they still guarded successfully the homes of O'Donnell and O'Doherty and the other brave septs of Dark Donegal. Down the slopes, to the beach of Lough Swilly, and across the hills to the southward, and far to the westward to the peaks of Derry hills, the bright sunlight flashed on stream and crag and heather; and in the valleys the shadows gathered in blue-black masses, on stubble field and pasture.

There was nothing tame or small about the noble picture. Everything was on a splendid scale. The design was vast and sweeping both in outline and colour. The broad stretches of blue water, the long winding valleys, the deep hues of the mountains, the wide and waving lines of the ridges which rolled southward and eastward—the suggestion of mystic infinity in the hazy distance over the blurred horizon—all, all was superb. And every acre of it was historic. On every hill the ringing cheers of victors had echoed when our race was hot and young. Through every valley marched the hostings of the Red Branch and the warriors of the kings.

Aileach itself was known to Ptolemy, and it witnessed the baptism of the chieftain who knelt to Patrick. It had previously seen the sun-god worshipped on its terraces; and on its coronation stone many a gallant prince had received the wand of chieftaincy. It had seen prisoners brought back from Britain and Gaul, among them being the very Patrick who came in after years to conquer all Ulster and Erin in the name of Christ, and it had seen captive Danes within its halls, as it had seen the hostages of Niall. Out of it came the high kings from whose loins sprang Hugh and Shane-an-Diomais, and Owen. It saw Columba go into exile. It saw the Flight of the Earls. It saw the earliest feats of prowess of the Ulster knights, the daring days of Fianna, and the dark hours when the star of the north went down with the fortunes of the Red Hand.

Gray old Aileach! What joy and sorrow, what triumph and defeat, what pride and ignominy, what hope and despair has it known!

It is under Aileach the knightly sleepers of the Gael are said to be standing beside their steeds, ready for the trumpet sound which shall break the charm that binds them and bring them at a wild gallop back into freedom to win their heritage in Eirin. There are caves under the mountain as there are at Tara and Rath Cruachain. In the latter mentioned, according to the old legends, rest the great ones of the Sidhe, whose mystic power is still known in Eirin. But the tenants of the caves under the Grianan of Aileach are different to the men of Dea who abide under the other enchanted hills within the four seas of Ireland. And the entrance to the caves themselves is known to no living man. Once in the penal days, as they tell, some hunted fugitive strayed by accident into the vaulted chambers of the waiting hosts, and a great leader who stood by his ready steed woke up at the intrusion. But he gave no command. He only shook his head sadly and sternly and said: " Not yet." The time had not come! It is no hunted thing that can bring them forth, the strange tale says, but the summons of Cathleen Ni Houlihan herself. And it is she who is to choose the day and hour. Did I meet a mystic poet up there on Aileach who stuffed me with such conceits? No. But as I stood in the low doorway listening to the roaring of the wind and the notes of the curlews, the old legend which I had read somewhere came back to me, and I fancied if you put yourself to it you might hear the flapping of

banners and the rustle of saffron-kirtles I have
met the legend two or three times in print lately;
and when I attend an Oireachtas or a Feis and hear
the old tongue of the Gael ringing again in song
and oratory, and feel the throbbing of the spirit
which has re-awakened in Eirin, my visit to the
Grianan of Aileach is a vivid memory, and the old
tale of the sleeping riders has a wondrous meaning—a new beauty and power—and a glorious
message for the present and the future.

Oh, Shiela ni Gara, why rouse the stony dead,
Since at your call a living host will circle you
     instead,
Long is our hunger for your voice, the hour is
     drawing near—
Oh, Dark Rose of our Passion—call, and our hearts
     shall hear !

CHAPTER VIII.

Through Tir-Owen — Dungannon — The Kinel-
Conail — Mountcharles — Donegal — The Four
Masters—The Clan Conail—The Humour of
Donegal—A woman who was able to take care
of herself—Ballyshannon—The Royal Irish
Constabulary in action—Belleek—By the shores
of Lough Erne to Enniskillen—Back into
Leinster.

On the road from Belfast to Donegal I made a
short stay in historic Dungannon. This brave old
town is mixed up with a great deal of Irish history.
Tir-Eoghan, of which it is the heart, was a fighting
chieftaincy. Every hill and valley of it saw the Red
Hand waving. It knew Hugh and Shane and Owen.
Benburb is only a few miles from the church in
which took place the famous Convention of the
Volunteers. Frowning over the streets are the ruins
of one of the strongholds of the O'Neills, where
Red Hugh O'Donnell found shelter after making his
escape from Dublin.

I struck Dungannon on a market day. There
was also a wedding. Moreover, I was brought into
communication with a local celebrity, a saddler,
who is the town philosopher. These three circumstances combined to render my short stay unusually
instructive. Dungannon is only half-and-half of
the Black North. The Orange and Green are about
equal, and politics run as smoothly as car be

humanly expected under such untoward conditions.
I am glad that I did not run into an election there.

I saw where the delegates of the Volunteers
assembled, and spent a sad half hour thinking of
the history of a Lost Endeavour. For such is the
history of the Irish Volunteers. The Protestant
patriots who led the great movement of 1782 were
not, unfortunately, able to rise to the level of their
opportunities. Their political thought seems to
have been stopped or blighted in its growth when
it had little more than reached half way towards
the maturity of a generous development. They
were great in their generation, but not great
enough. Some of them were men of genius, but
they lacked either foresight or breadth of mind.
Grattan, who was possibly the broadest visioned
man of them all, was still many degrees too narrow
for the hour. Flood, who had more foresight than
Grattan, as the dark days of 1800 proved beyond a
shadow of a doubt, was still a hopeless bigot. He
did not trust England, but neither would he trust
Catholic Ireland. His ideal of nationhood was an
impossible one—a Protestant oligarchy which would
supplant one Protestant tyranny by another. He
would free Ireland from England, yet under his
dispensation eighty per cent. of the Irish people
would remain practically unfree. He did not grasp
the fact that in a nation a man cannot have freedom
in closed compartments—that while one class is
oppressed, the rights of all are outraged. In his
distrust of England the history of the Union Parliament, to go no further, shows that he was right.
In his religious narrowness of view, as an Irish

Protestant historian has shown, he was tragically and hopelessly in the wrong. Excuse this digression. It is impossible to speak of Dungannon without some word regarding the lesson which is taught us by the collapse of the Volunteers. That lesson is that the Irish nation must not be mutually distrustful and that it must not be sectarian. It must be for all classes and all creeds born within its shores, and who are loyally working for its advancement. Any forward move towards the realization of the national ideal must be made from the broad basis of religious toleration. In nearly every country in the world, citizens of different creeds can contrive to find a common ground for their energies on their love of fatherland. We must do the same in Ireland.

It was night when I reached Mountcharles. Seumas MacManus, who had been waiting for me for weeks, had been obliged to go to Dublin that very day on business. But I was the guest of his parents, and could not have been made more at home in all the length and breadth of Ulster. Mountcharles is a delightfully situated little town. It is perched on a fine slope and overlooks an inlet of Donegal Bay. The broken rollers beat in there from the Atlantic, and the foam of every wave-cap spreads like a trimming of Irish lace around the green mantle of the shore. High ridges hem in the town, except where the land drops down to the water and where the road rounds off to Donegal.

Northward from Mountcharles is The Frossas, a village situated four or five miles inland. It lies near the bottom of a long valley, and is sheltered by the mountains which encircle it. Here in the churchyard, beside the chapel, sleeps her last sleep Mrs. Seumas MacManus, known in literature as Ethna Carbery. Near her bed falls the footsteps of the people whom she loved as they go and come from Mass. The prayers said under the sacred roof pass over her as they go outward and upward on their way to God, holy as her own white soul, sweeter than the breezes which wander in from the hills to croon fondly over her grave. It was to kneel there that I went to The Frossas. I left Mountcharles very early in the morning on my bicycle, and took the road over the hills, in the teeth of the keen "black wind" which the dead singer longed for so often:

Said Shiela ni Gara, 'tis a fond wind and a true,
For it rustled soft through Aileach's halls and
  stirred the hair of Hugh.

It was the wind of Inishowen, sweeping swiftly from the thundering sea over the "hills of her heart." The November dawn was chilly, but as it brightened into day it showed me some of the wild loveliness of Dark Donegal. The sun rose in a faint halo of pink, and flung golden spears from peak to peak across the sleeping shadows of the hills. I passed a little mountain lake, in which every wavelet that rippled the surface seemed to have borrowed its colour from the clear sky over the purple summits of Croachgorm. On every side of me the hills rose far or near, and the valleys were draped in a steel-blue haze, which made them look deep and mystical, and distant, and altogether peculiar and beautiful. The road took a turn to the westward, and I caught glimpses of far-off glens and the sparkle of streams. As I cycled down hill into the valley, a swollen spring by the roadside threw the water on the gravel into which the wheels sank above the rims. And what water it was! I have seen the days under blistering skies when I would have given a horse for a long deep drink of it. Lower still went the road, and presently I was on the valley floor, cycling between yellow stubbled fields and past tidy farmhouses, all closed as yet. I reached The Frossas before any of the villagers were astir, and entered the chapel gates unnoticed. I found the grave without difficulty, as it is marked by a beautiful stone cross of the purest Celtic design, upon which is inscribed an appropriate epitaph in Irish. A rose tree springs from the sod over the heart of the sleeper; and the leaves were green and fresh despite the lateness of the season and the frost in the wind. Hill ferns and mosses grew around the base of the cross, and when the spring comes every year, bright blades of grass will wave above the sod and symbolise the spears of hope which are fencing Irish-Ireland. When Ethna Carbery wrote that strangely pathetic poem, "The Last Sleep of Bridgeen," she seems to have looked unwittingly into the ending of her own bright and beautiful life; and her unconsciously prophetic vision reached beyond the closing hour:

> The purple mountains guard her,
> The valleys fold her in.

You might try for ever and a day, and fail to get a
truer and more beautiful description of the grave at
The Frossas. Nor could the grave itself be more
appropriately located. It is very Irish, like Ethna
Carbery herself. She was a woman whose love for
Ireland was the ruling passion of her life. She
loved the Irish hills and valleys as she could love
no other scenery in the world, but the mountains of
old Tir-Conaill she loved with a special love. They
are the fittest to be custodians of her resting-place.
I thought of this as I stood there in the wintry blast,
and thought of many other things which need not
be recalled. A few days previously I had listened
to Ethna Carbery's mother telling me of the childhood and girlhood of her daughter. All of us who
care for the cause with which the poetess was
identified, must know something of her writings,
and therefore something of her mind and heart.
But I knew as I left her grave in The Frossas, as I
knew before I saw it, that no more beautiful life
has ever been lost to Ireland. No more faithful
and loving and stainless soul looks down with sweet
solicitude on the fortunes of the old, old struggle
from the Courts of God.

It was still early when I left Mountcharles for
Donegal. I took the morning train and got into
chat with a few glenspeople who were going to
market. In Donegal they do not wait for a stranger
to address them. They give you the time of the
day in an off-hand hearty manner, and begin talking
to you as if you were an old acquaintance. In the
train, and afterwards on the roadside during my
journey by wheel to Ballyshannon, I heard plenty

of the Donegal dialect. Perhaps it is scarcely correct to call it a dialect, but it is certainly a way of speaking distinct from the ordinary Beurla of Leinster. The fidelity with which Seumas Mac-Manus reproduces the Beurla of Donegal in his stories struck me as remarkable.

Between Mountcharles and Donegal is the Glen of the Woods. It is a beautiful country. The entire road is one succession of beauty spots; and you get many whiffs of the sea along the way. Donegal is a snug looking town. It is not a very big place, but it is in the midst of big things—big billows, big hills, big associations. It was here the Franciscan monks—the great O'Clerys—wrote most of their "Annals of the Four Masters." They were men of great patriotism, honesty, and industry. When it comes to the writing of history you will find very few men who are equipped for the work, because very few have the necessary knowledge or the knowledge of where to look for their materials; and fewer still have that peculiar balance of mind which enables them to reason mechanically from cause to effect, irrespective of personal likes and dislikes. But the O'Clerys were great historians. They accomplished a monumental work. When the librarian of the Royal Irish Academy showed me the two bound volumes of their original manuscript, he said: "Look with what clearness and method they wrote, yet with what freedom and grace. And the matter is like the penmanship." Down in Boyle they say that some of the Annals were compiled in a monastery on one of the islands of Lough Cey. Probably some of the materials were collected and co-ordinated there. Anyhow the great work was turned out from Donegal Abbey. The Abbey is now a ruin. It went down in the years when Ireland was overrun with war and rapine, because she wanted to be herself, wanted to rule herself, and to worship God in the way that Patrick taught her. The annalists saw that the days were coming when the manuscript materials for a national history would be destroyed or scattered; so they devotedly set themselves the task of compiling a history while there was yet time. That was about A.D. 1632. Some years before that a certain learned and patriotic priest, who was " on his keeping" from the English Conformity Act in the woods of Aherlow, also wrote a history. Geoffrey Keating was his name. All honour to those five priests of Ireland who plucked the annals of their land from the fires of the seventeenth century. They left a noble tradition to their cloth. I often think of them when I hear half-hearted Irishmen saying that they are Catholic first and Irishmen second, just the same as if anybody asked such people to love their country before their God, just the same as if love of country was not, in the last analysis, part of charity, which is love of God! When you hear people making distinctions in Irish affairs between country and religion, you may be pretty certain that you are dealing with persons who are trying to find conscientious excuses for being political humbugs or avowed West-Britons. A man may be as Catholic as St. Laurence O'Toole and be as good an Irishman as Thomas Davis; and St. Laurence was as true a patriot in his own day as Davis was in his, or as the O'Clerys and Keating were in theirs.

Just where the Eske flows into the town stand the ruins of what is called O'Donnell's castle. It occupies the site of the chief stronghold of Tir-Connaill, but dates from a period later than the Flight of the Earls. It was here in historic Donegal that the great Red Hugh held sway when they gave him the wand of chieftaincy. He dismantled his castle in 1601 sooner than let it fall into the hands of the English, and it was granted by the Crown of England to Sir Basil Brook, who built the castle of which the present ruins remain. There is a good deal of architectural sculpture about it; and one chimneypiece in particular is a grand piece of stonework. But it recalls nothing of the O'Donnells only their vanished sway.

The O'Donnells were descended from Conall Gulban. He was brother of Owen, who conquered Tir-Owen, and son of Niall of the Nine Hostages. He established himself in Donegal in the fifth century. From him the country derived the name of Tir-Conaill, and his people after him were called the Kinel Conaill, or the race of Conaill, a name which was also given to the territory. In the twelfth century the O'Donnells became princes of Tir-Conaill. Their tribe name at an early period, according to O'Mahony, was Clan Daligh, from Dalach, one of their chiefs. O'Dugan calls them Clanna na nDonn Sgiath of the Brown Shields. They afterwards took the name of Donnel or O'Domhnaill, from Domnaill, one of their ancient chiefs. The race gave ten High Kings to Ireland, and also Hugh the Red, who was the last great

chieftain of the Kinel Conaill. He sleeps in Valla-
dolid, in Spain. Rory O'Donnell was the last
chieftain of his clan. He is sometimes called
Earl of Tyrconnell. He died in exile, and his estates
were confiscated in the reign of James I. The late
Duke of Tetuan was an O'Donnell of Donegal. The
blood of the Kinel Conaill flowed in his veins. I
saw at Santa Cruz, in the Canary Islands, the house
in which the first Duke of Tetuan was born. His
name was Leopoldo O'Donnell, and he rose to be
Captain-General of the armies of Spain.

It was of Red Hugh I was thinking chiefly,
however, that morning as I sat beside the Eske.
He was just the same personage in every way upon
whom my thoughts ran as I sat one day in the Pass
of the Curlews. He is the same, no matter where
you meet him—a man of elemental greatness, of
stubborn purpose, a born general, a man of truth
and daring, and fine intuition—a man of heroic soul.
But I could appreciate his heroism more fully in
Donegal than on the battlefield of Ballaghboy,
because it was more palpable, more dramatically
apparent, as it were. The general who wins a
signal victory may be a great military commander,
and at the same time one of the meanest and most
selfish of men. I know that the victor of the
Curlews was not mean. But it was not until I had
journeyed for several days through this territory
that I realised how utterly noble was his character.
I had seen the splendid heritage which he could
have retained by temporising. I had travelled
through the glens and over the glorious mountain
sides, and along the valleys, whose lordship this
man refused to accept as the price of treachery to

his country and his race. I had looked upon the beauty of the Kinel Conaill which he left for Ireland's sake to work for her freedom. It is when you measure such a patriot by the immensity of the sacrifices which he made that you realise how terribly contemptible are the creatures who temporised and tortured their flexible consciences for some pious justification of their treachery.

While I was cycling from Donegal to Ballyshannon the wind changed. It had been blowing from the north, and now it came in a half gale from the east. It had been chilly before, but now it was piercing cold. There were some good stiff hills on the road, and I rushed everyone of them, not for the fun or the honour of climbing them at high speed, but merely to keep myself warm. Near Lahy I stopped to talk to a man who was quarrying rocks from off the face of a mountain, high up over the road. He had a poor opinion of the weather. Would it rain, did he think? Aye, then, it might, a wee bit. And also it might "begin till snow at any mennet." Likewise it was "just pelten' black frost." It might also hail or sleet. And, furthermore, he reckoned Ballyshannon to be ten or twelve, or fourteen miles off. And finally, had I a light? I had. Would I mind taking it up to him, or would he just "slidder down till the road for it?" I insisted on climbing. He thanked me for the matches, but sniffed gingerly at my pouch of Murray's Belfast smoking mixture before he would consent to fill his pipe with it.

"And so ye're towerin'?" he asked when he had finished lighting up.

"Yes," I admitted, "I'm doing a little touring. Why?"

"It's a bet late in the year for them things yon," he commented, nodding severely at my bicycle, which lay on the roadside below us. "They don't generally come round on them what-you-callums after September, and it's the middel of November now. Are you goin' far?"

"About seven thousand miles," I replied.

He looked at me narrowly, yet not without a certain solemnity.

"By land and water," I explained.

"On that bike es it?"

"Partly."

"Then," said he, with a twinkle, "God be wi' ye, man. I'm delayen' ye. Don't lose time."

"Maybe you're working by the piece," I said.

"Is it because I go cracken jokes wi' strollers like you?"

"No, but because you are so anxious to work."

"If I could afford it I'd be a towerist m'self, and keep warm by shoven' a pair o' wheels about the world—Good-bye, then, and God speed."

There is a certain village between Donegal and Ballyshannon which has this distinction: you cannot get into it without going down a hill. You cannot get out of it without climbing. It is a reposeful place, and, although the telegraph has tapped the district it has brought little of the bustle of the outside world with it. I entered a shop and said: "God save all here." There was no response, chiefly for two reasons. Firstly, because there was no one in attendance, and secondly, because the person who should have been in attendance was in the kitchen. She was a solidly-constructed matron of middle age, and it turned the cold wind into summer zephyrs to look at her round, smooth, good-natured countenance. She was surrounded by three or four gossips, and they were having a very interesting talk. I was loth to interrupt them, so I waited and occupied myself by making an inventory of the stock-in-trade. I saw spirits, beer, blue, starch, candles, matches, flour, tobacco, candy, cloves, and other goods. When I got tired of the survey I sat on the counter and watched the gossips. One of them saw me after a few minutes, and told the woman of the house about me. Mine hostess looked leisurely round and smiled.

"Fresh day, ma'am," I said.

"Tes that," she replied, rising and coming into the shop. "Why didn't you speak when you came in?"

"So I did, but no one answered."

"Why didn't you go on speaking?"

"Well, four of you were at that, and I thought it might be manners to wait."

"Deed aye? an' now, can we do anything for you?"

"Yes. Please give me a bottle of Apollinaris."

"Bottle o' what!"

"Apollinaris," I replied, suavely. I knew she hadn't it, but I was desirous of levying a kind of tribute for having been kept waiting. She shook her head pensively, and said:

"There isn't any of it here, an', what's more, I don't know what it is."

" A bottle of Krondorf will do as well."

" Never hear of it before."

" Vichy, then."

" Don't keep that either."

" Hops ?"

" Neither."

" Well, then, I think I'll try some lemonade."

" We're out o' 't this three days."

" Ginger ale ——"

" Won't be here till Tuesday."

" Ginger beer, then."

" Haven't any. But would soda water be any use till ye?"

" No, ma'am. It disagrees with me."

" Then I'll tell ye what ye want," she said, beaming at me out of her round, dark eyes.

" What is it, ma'am?"

" The pledge!" she said, tenderly ; that's what you ought to look for."

" But have I asked you for any but temperance drinks?"

" Oh! that's the worse sign at all. You kind o' travellers is always the worst cases."

The gossips freely joined me from the kitchen in the laugh against myself. I surrendered at discretion, and called for a bottle of stout.

" That's a sensible temp'rance drink," she said, as she poured it out. " Why didn't ye ask for that at furst?"

" It was in my mind," I explained, " but you see I had to wait so long that I forgot it."

" It's cruel to think o' you been delayed like that an' ye so busy an' so hurried."

"Aye, indeed, ma'am, and the days so short."

"An' such a pity to think on ye wastin' yer strength over that bicycle," she added, sympathetically. "Couldn't they find somethin' more useful for ye to do?"

"Maybe," I hazarded, insinuatingly, "a man might be on the look out for a chance of settling down."

"Oh, he might, yes."

"And would there be anyone around here to whom you could recommend him?"

"Well," she said, putting her elbows on the counter and throwing down her eyes, "I'll tell ye the trewth. If he were a bashful sort I wouldn't mind putten in a word for him, but if he were a supple-tongued lad like yersel' I'd have to think over it."

"But why?"

"Because the chances are that if he hadn't already coaxed someone into taken him for better or worse, he'd in any case be able to do his own match-maken'."

"Anyhow," I went on, when the laughter had again subsided, "here's every blessing to Donegal," and I raised my glass.

"Slainte and—tuppence," she responded.

I passed over the coppers and took my leave.

"Farewell, O Comely Matron of Donegal Who is Able to Take Care of Herself," I said.

"God speed all bikers," she replied, piously, and give them sense."

I climbed out of Ballintra and struck a fine level road, which took me over a noble stretch of country.

There were wide uplands and woods, and now and then a lough, and in the distance the blue hills were stacked up into the clouds. Cycling from the south, it would be a foretaste of Donegal. Going south- wards from the North as I was, it looked somewhat tame after the country in the basin of the Eske. Still it was very beautiful of its kind—not wild, nor yet tame—about half-way between the two. Indeed, there is little tame beauty in Ulster. Her face is as rugged as her history. It is in Leinster and Northern Munster that Nature has been prodigal to Erin of the beauty called rural.

Ballyshannon is a quiet town. The principal street runs down a steep hill to the bridge over the Erne. I stopped on this thoroughfare, and while I helped myself to a beefsteak I made up my mind as to what I should do next. I had been thinking of taking once more to the railway and making my way home. But although the day was cloudy it was now past noon, and the weather seemed likely to hold good, at least until nightfall. The roads were in perfect condition, and I had still more than three hours of light. I resolved to cycle to Ennis- killen along the southern shore of Lough Erne. I did it, too, but it was a hard pull. The ice-cold east wind was now right in my face and was blowing a gale. At times on the level road I could not make two miles an hour, and I was forced to get down and rest occasionally. I have ridden through two inches of Argentine dust on the soft clay car-track from Moron to Rodriguez against a hot wind, but it was child's play to any of the twenty odd miles between Ballyshannon and Enniskillen. Before I left Ballyshannon I had a talk with two men who stood at the door of a cycle depot, brothers in the craft, who placed their local knowledge at my service. They said that after a few miles the wind would not matter, as the mountains would shelter me. But the mountains left me to my fate. The wind hit me from the lake the whole way. It sprang upon me from the foaming waves and screamed at me, and pushed me back. O Red Wind from the East, if I could have caught you by the wings that wild evening I would have made you redder! And yet I would willingly ride over that road again in the teeth of a hurricane, for it is beautiful with the rich, all-conquering beauty of the lake by the very shore of which it runs nearly all the way.

The Erne was high enough to be at its "highest flood" as it pulled out from Ballyshannon, but I did not "dash across unseen." Two policemen were on the road beyond the bridge, and they eyed me with as much hostility and suspicion as if I were indeed the bearer of tidings to give health and help and hope to Dark Rosaleen. They were not, however, out on my trail, they were merely enjoying a walk, and were well wrapped up—overcoated, gloved, gaitered—all at the expense of our Roisin Dubh. I only mention them because they mixed themselves up with an incident in which I became involved. There was a man with a mule and a crate of turf on the road about a hundred yards away. He was making frantic signs at somebody while he held the mule by the head. That quadruped was decidedly nervous. You could see that half a mile away, for his ears were wagging restlessly hither and thither over the surrounding country, and he was walking backwards towards the roadside, pushing the car with its crate of turf as well as himself into danger, and dragging his master with him.

"What do you suppose is wrong with the mule?" I asked one of the guardians of the peace.

"He's frightened at the bike," said the one who was senior in command.

"Frightened so soon?" I asked in surprise. "He has good sight, then."

"He met an automobile two days ago," explained the Force, "and it unhinged him. He thinks you have another."

"Suppose you men go forward and help the driver to hold him?" I suggested.

"That's not our business," said the Force, "you'd better lay down the bike and stand on one side until he passes."

"It's not my duty," I said; "but I'll do it for the man's sake," and I put the machine into the ditch.

But the mule would not advance. He retreated more and more, his ears swaying wildly.

"He knows it's there still," said the Force from the opposite side of the road.

"I doubt it," said I. "I'm beginning to think that it is you yourselves of whom he is afraid," and with that I lay down by the wayside, behind a shrub, out of sight of the mule, while the Force frowned and flushed.

"You see," I continued, peeping from my ambush, "neither the machine nor its owner is in sight and still he is afraid—can't you get out of the way and not be obstructing the traffic?"

"Take care, now, me playboy," said the Force, "or it might be the worse for you."

"Are you going to stay there," I went on, unheeding the threat, "and look calmly on that mule committing suicide and killing the man? Don't you see he's going to back across that wall and down the slope into the river?"

"Are you lookin' for trouble," asked the Force, turning savagely upon me.

"No," I replied, "I'm seeking how it may be avoided. I am not interfering with you in discharge of your duty, I am only urging you to do it. And, by heavens, if you don't I'll report you."

I said a whole lot more to them, and told them all sorts of mysterious and fanciful things about the influence I had in certain high circles. They marched. They got on the other side of the wall, and I stayed where I was.

I shall never know for certain now what was the real trouble, for when the man was passing me I asked him about it from my grassy couch, and before he could reply something happened. The mule bolted, whether because of the sergeant being plainly visible over the wall, or because of my question, I cannot say. The outfit disappeared over the bridge into the town in a cyclone of kicks and snorts, and curses and dust. I hastened from the tumultuous neighbourhood, and rode off at my best pace towards Belleek. But my best pace was only a poor one, not over three miles an hour. It was rast enough, however, to take me out of danger of pursuit.

Belleek is astride of the Erne, near the western

end of the lake, and seems to be a thriving place. I
had not time to visit the pottery works, as I was
obliged to push on. I was covering the road very
slowly, and the milestones told me that I had still
a long way to go. Soon after passing Belleek I
came in sight of Lough Erne, and presently the road
touched the shore. From there on to Enniskillen I
rode close to the water, and had many splendid
views of the islands, creeks, and headlands. There
was plenty of black frost in the howling wind, and
it was well for me that I had to work so hard or I
should have famished But at times you forgot all
about the cold and the gale and the waning day.
The Fermanagh hills rose to my right, and to the
left rolled the waters of the lake, lashed to foam by
the blustering wind, especially where the reefs
grinned up through the tortured waves. There is
plenty of woodland between the hills and the
southern shore, and the copses and hazel scrubs go
right down to the water from the roadside. The
opposite shore is also dark with woods, and at Tully
Point, about half way to Enniskillen, the wooded
islands thickly stud the noble sheet of water. The
prospect was lovely, even in the wintry blast. How
glorious it must be in the softness and warmth of
the summer. You seldom hear of Fermanagh as
being a picturesque district, and yet you could
linger in it for weeks without tiring of it. In the
shadow of a big mountain that looms over the road
opposite the broadest part of the lake I stopped for
a quarter of an hour and ate cresses from a spring
out of which the icy water rushed in a crystal torrent.
I consulted my road map, but it had very little to

tell me of my whereabouts. The mountain was not even marked upon it. I tried to remember some reference from O'Dugan, but failed. I must have been somewhere in ancient Magheraboy or Clanawley—somewhere in the old chieftainry of the MacGuires, but I am not certain. Anyway it was a place to linger in, and despite the waning light and the wintry blast and the stiff miles still to the eastward, I lingered and enjoyed it. I watched the foam which fringed the big waves rolling in on the shore below me, and the spray which dashed itself in snowy showers on the rocks. I looked at the dark tints creeping down on the woods and the deepening blue of the distant hills. I saw the gulls wheeling and tossing in the air over the thundering surf. I took in every detail of colour, from the sombre grey on the mountain crest to the faded olive on the frostbound sward on which I sat. It was a wild and magnificent picture.

"Aye," I said, " it is winter, but it is superb. You are in a stormy humour now, Lough Erne, but your anger is beautiful. I must come to you once again, when summer has you in its arms and when your mood is one of langour and softness."

A cyclist came whirring along the road from the eastward. The spokes of his machine hummed with speed, yet the rider's feet were nearly idle. The wind, which was against me, was driving him along so fast that he had some difficulty in keeping his wheel from running away. A bag was strapped upon his back, so I expect he was some sort of postman or postal messenger I was thinking of beginning to envy him, not only because the wind

was so much in his favour, but also because his daily
employment brought him into the company of Lough
Erne along that splendid road. His advent, however, reminded me of my journey, still only half
finished; so I rose and went my way. I stopped no
more until I rode into Enniskillen. Darkness was
falling. The street lamps were lighted and the shop
windows were ablaze I went to the first hotel I
met and gave myself up to the waiter. I was cold
and hungry and dead tired. A warm fire was
burning in the diningroom, and a big, deep, easy
chair stood before it. I came to an anchor there and
felt at peace with all the world. That waiter was a
genius. He knew the ailments of a weary cyclist
with all the intimate thoroughness learned from extended experience, and his prescriptions were worthy
of his heart and head.

Next day I pushed on for Cavan, but the weather
broke and I took to the railway. By mid-day I was
back into Leinster. That is to say, I was buying a
few newspapers at the bookstall of Mullingar
station. Then on by Castletown and Streamstown
to Clara, and home, after a fortnight's raid. I left
the Ulster accent behind me at Enniskillen, although
there were a few suggestions of it here and there
along the way until I reached Cavan. The swing
of the porters' tongues at Inny Junction was wholly
Leinster, and the man who sold me the papers in
Mullingar might have been raised in my native
parish.

CHAPTER IX.

*From Dublin to the Slieveblooms—A glance at
"Conciliated" Rathcoole—The Humours of
"Conciliation" — Newbridge College — Irish
Cattle—A Motor Cyclist comes to grief—Irish
Ireland Marching—The Curragh of Kildare—
Knockallen, Finn, and the Fianna—The Gibbet
Rath—Brigid the Great and the Neglected—
A pleasant country side—"More Concilia-
tion"—Monasterevan—An Irish Irelander.*

From Dublin to the basin of the Shannon, seventy
Irish miles—that was to be the day's ride. My
route lay by Naas, across the Pale, and broad Kildare, and the breezy uplands of Leix, through
Monasterevan and Portarlington to Mountmellick,
thence through Clonaslee along the Slieveblooms to
Kinnety, and from Kinnety down the slopes of Ely
O'Carroll into the country of the O'Molloys. It
was the Sunday morning after the Oireachtas, and
the mountains, all radiant in the glory of the sunshine, smiled with the promise of an ideal summer's
day into the city streets. I had passed an exciting
week in the capital, and felt the need of getting
back into myself before sitting down to write about
it for people far away. I had been rubbing elbows
with leaders and poets and orators and militant
writers and epoch-makers of various schools and

grades. I had been at the Ard-Fheis. I had been assisting at the competitions and public perfor- mances at the Rotunda. I had been at the Mansion House. I had been communing with the nocturnal Gaels who foregathered at An Stad. My aching mind was hot from the constant impact of impressions, and I wanted to cool it by a return to the meadows and the woods and the bracken-clad hills and the big windy spaces.

I checked my bearings .n Inchicore by the geo- graphical knowledge of a citizen who was in command of a delivery van, and learned from him that I was to leave one of the historical portals of Dublin yclept the Essex Gate to my left, and go down hill to the Naas road. All this I did, and, in due course, found myself riding into the south wind, with the scenery all to myself. I discovered Rathcoole by the Post Office signboard, and made a brief halt to contemplate some interesting ruins of modern times. Rathcoole consists mainly of roofless houses that were comfortable homes some years ago. The village must have been a thriving place when the benign policy of English pacification and con- ciliation came into play It is well conciliated now. A few years more and it will be pacified down to the Post Office and the police barrack. On the moulder- ing halldoor of a roofless mansion was a placard headed, " Scheme for the raising of live stock." Under the circumstances, it was singularly appro- priate, for there is little or no tillage in the district, since the tillers of the soil, under the blessed influ- ence of pacification and conciliation, moved off te foreign parts or to the graveyard. The rich pastures are occupied by cattle and sheep, and the placard on the pacified hall door of the conciliated homestead was the work of some master mind catering for the pastoral interests. The front of the police barrack was adorned by a few square feet of British humour. On a large advertisement board was a placard, printed in green ink, setting forth some of the poetry of existence which might be enjoyed by any pacified survivor of the conciliated natives eligible for enlistment in "the Irish Guards." There is a fine racy dash of jocularity in conciliating a people down to vanishing point, and then inviting the able-bodied amongst the remnant to participate in the work of fastening the blessings of conciliation upon other nations.

Beyond Rathcoole the land rises gradually, and a few miles takes you to a noble ridge over one of the richest plains of Leinster. To the eastward there is only a grassy slope crested with clustering fern, and beyond that the purple undulations of the far-off mountains, swelling into low-hung flecks of summer cloud. But to the westward sweep the green pastures and meadows and dark welts of timber, with here and there the flash of a river bend, until the wide plain grows dim in the soft haze along the horizon and melts into the sky. A little to the southward, seen over the tall hedges, and through a gap in the wood below you, rises the Hill of Allen, which beckons you to the Curragh of Kildare. Never despise landmarks, whether you are galloping on the pampas or cycling in Eirin. A few good land-marks are better in the daylight than an ordinary road map, once you grasp the general direction of

your route. You can go right across the midlands
from Edenderry to Galway or Sligo by the three
landmarks of Croghan Hill, over Philipstown;
Knockastia, near Uisnach Hill, in Westmeath, and
Slievebawn overlooking the Shannon between
Athlone and Lanesborough. The Hill of Allen was
my landmark for the moment, and I shaped my
course towards it. I lost sight of it in a few minutes
and rode down the country into Naas, thence through
whispering woods and meadows thickly dotted with
haycocks, into Newbridge.

Along this stretch of road there are many associations of the days of '98. There are also many indications of pacification and conciliation. Newbridge
is an outpost of the army of conquest. It is also,
thank God, an outpost of the army of reconquest.
The Dominican College there is doing good work for
Irish-Ireland. It is an educational institution which
does its business on an Irish plan. It is bringing up
Irish youths in the knowledge and love of their
native land. When there are thirty such colleges in
Ireland taking part in the feeding of an Irish university there will be some long steps made in the work
of nation-building. I may remark parenthetically
that while in Dublin I heard a whisper of some
emasculated university, which would place higher
education within the reach of well-to-do Catholics,
and confer degrees on the seoinin without violating
his conscience. Such an institution would be anything but a benefit to Ireland. What is needed
is a Catholic university, broadly National, demo-
cratic, and richly endowed, able to open its doors
to indigent genius as well as to wealthy mediocrity,

and under such control as shall keep its teaching in close accordance and sympathy with the religion of its alumni, and at the same time train them to look upon Ireland as their country, and think and work for its advancement. It is certain that such a university will not be founded without a struggle which will put the spirit and constancy of the leaders of the people to a stern test. But it is equally certain that any watered-down university system, begotten in compromise, nurtured on the philosophy of crawl, and working on a policy of denationalisation, would be a national calamity.

I descended from the altitudes of educational problems to the contemplation of bucolic affairs as I passed a bunch of cattle on the Liffey bank on the outskirts of Newbridge. There were about forty head beside the stream, and they were representative of at least four distinct breeds—Hereford, Shorthorn, Polled Angus, and Holstein. The need of an Irish Government is not more patent in any direction than in all that concerns the live stock industry of the country. Of course it is to be said that Ireland has an over supply of live stock, and that it would be one of the first duties of a National Government to bring back into cultivation many hundreds of thousands of acres now under pasturage. But cattle and sheep in considerable numbers the country should always have; and it should be the duty of the State to interest itself in the selection and improvement of breeds. A well-bred animal will not eat any more than a badly-bred one—and often eats less. Well-bred animals mature sooner, and fetch higher prices; consequently they are more profitable in the end. A well-equipped Department of Agriculture would be able to place the live stock industry on an excellent footing in a few years without any undue expenditure of public money. There is a Department of Agriculture in Ireland at present working under the auspices of Dublin Castle, which looks at Irish rural problems from the English point of view. This Department theorises a good deal, and, I believe, is to some extent troubled by the "writing itch." There seems to be something about it in the nature of the shearing of the goat—great cry and little wool. It would be quite useless, however, to expect any wonder working from such a source. Indeed it would be quite useless to hope that Ireland will ever be well governed in the interests of England, because the interests of the two nations are inimical. The English Department of Agriculture in Ireland does a good deal of pottering and sermonising, and goes through many elaborate experiments to try and overcome the difficulties of fusing oil and water. And periodically it publishes something or says something lamenting that Irish interests are the oil, and sympathising with itself for having failed to reverse the laws of nature. It sends out a lecturer to speak academically about cattle breeding when it should have practical experiments going on before the eyes of the people. It sends out gifted talkers to say learned things about manure, when it should have a model farm in every county to teach in practice what it preaches in theory. "You would get a far more profitable return from your land," said one of these lecturers some time ago to an audience in one of the midland rural districts, " if you would only revolutionise your system of manuring; and I hope you will follow my advice." Whereupon a hard-headed farmer rose and made the following speech : " I'll tell you what, sir : talk is cheap. Will you take ten or twenty acres of land in this parish for a few years, and pay a pound an acre for it, and show us that you can make it pay by your plan for manuring, and all that ? " The lecturer changed the conversation. Once upon a time, a friend of mine, desirous of obtaining information regarding the Brazilian navy, approached a Brazilian admiral whose gala uniform was adding splendour to one of the imperial saloons of the royal palace in Rio de Janeiro, during the time of Dom Pedro. The admiral was very polite and very amiable, but all he had to say was this : " Ah, you, you will excuse me. I know nothing at all about nautical matters, and I have never been to sea. My post is an honorary one, you comprehend. I am a poet myself."

I saw some very fine cattle in Kildare, and some very wretched specimens. The same might be said of every pastoral district in Ireland. The system of buying calves to rear is a good one, but it would be far more lucrative if the calves were more evenly bred. Buying the sucking calves at fair or market is something of a lottery. One calf will turn out a failure, and another will grow splendidly. One will turn out to be an easily fed, well-bred animal, and another will grow into a cross-grained bone-heap, wattle-ribbed and hatchet-backed, capable of carrying the speculative mind back to the kine of the Firbolgs, which were placed under enchantment by

the druids of the Tuatha De Danaan. This is not the
fault of the farmers, and there would be no calves
on sale but well-bred ones if Ireland had a State
Department to interest itself earnestly and wisely in
the rural industries of the country.

Still, notwithstanding the little practical guidance
the farmers of Ireland receive from the State, compared to that which is given to the farmers of other
countries, they are admirably holding their own.
And as for industry and seemly thrift they need
fear comparison with none. The Irish farmer is a
hard worker and a constant one. He is one of the
most truly clean-minded and clean-handed tillers
of the soil in the world to-day   Many another man
would have gone down into utter brutality under the
wrongs he has suffered, under the weight of misery
that has been heaped upon him, and under the sea of
liquor that a pernicious legislation has heaved at his
head. The problems with which he has been surrounded, and the tardy and stinted justice which
has been done to him have not given him much
leisure to think seriously of national issues. The
education which a denationalising Government provided for him, and the narrowness of policy so
lamentably characteristic of most of the leadership
which he has followed of late years have not tended
to foster any passionate conviction in his mind that
he has a country as well as a farm. But if he has
been robbed of his opportunities, he has not been
robbed of his intuitions. And a brighter day is
dawning.

You must excuse my unconventional way of roving
from one subject to another in my rambling in

Eirin. One might as well ramble all he can while he is about it. I shall now ramble back to cycling matters.

I was in the smooth, swift flight of a freewheel jaunt down a long incline between Newbridge and Kildare when a fellow-man streaked past me on a motor cycle. He wore a leather suit of clothes. He wore a leather head-dress, and his countenance was protected by a leather veil furnished with windows. He was vibrating like a tuning fork, and the tail of his leather coat was fluttering boisterously in the wind, which gave him a very tumultuous appearance. His flying tyres licked the dust out of the road with a hiss and scattered in clouds behind him. His motor coughed nefariously and sent forth upon the air certain diabolical fumes, such as Dante must have sampled during his tour through the regions of Woe Eternal. He gave me a careless glance in passing, and then fixed his gaze once more on the infinite distance as if he were bound for Japan or Australia or Mars, or some other destination far, far away beyond the Irish sky. He bore away southward like a comet until he reached a turn in the road, when his programme underwent a change. The motor cycle suddenly slipped on a greasy spot, staggered and fell, and the traveller himself subsided into a brake of briars. On witnessing this performance I recognised the utility of leather clothing in certain contingencies, and I regretted that I was not attired in the same material one evening in the autumn of 1902 when a cycling accident sent me falling down one of the Leitrim mountains through several acres of furze. It did not take me many minutes to reach the spot on which the motor cycle and its rider had parted company, and, observing that their estrangement still existed, I halted in the interests of humanitarianism and scientific research. When the Chilians were thinking of crossing the Andes into the Argentine Republic a few years ago to look for a fight, it became the fashion in Buenos Ayres to learn ambulance work, so I attended several series of lectures on first aid to the wounded. I offered my services now to the man who was enveloped in briars and leather, but as the mantle of oblivion was also about him, he made no reply. It was only when I caught him by the heels and began to tow him out into the sunshine that he woke.

"What are you pulling me all over the country for?" he asked, as he removed his head-dress and the smoked window-glass fittings with which it was trimmed, so as to give vent to his curiosity.

"It is all right," I said, encouragingly, "I am only taking you out here to examine you for breakages. I can give you first aid if you are wounded."

"I'm not wounded," he growled, "I was only a trifle stunned, but would you mind stopping that beastly motor."

I might have mentioned that when I arrived on the scene the motor was desperately busy, and it was still working its heart out. I went as near to it as I deemed safe, and contemplated its sufferings with deep awe. It was in a state of eruption. It was shedding oil and pieces of wire and nuts and screws and other details, and it was snorting and coughing

and shivering and exploding and choking in a manner that was most distressing to witness. It was evidently in a fit. I could not recall anything expounded to us by the ambulance lecturers bearing on a crisis of this nature, so I was forced to admit to the other patient that I could do nothing for his fellow-sufferer.

"All you have to do is to shut it off," he said, getting on his feet and approaching it. "There," he added, stooping over it and doing something to it which silenced it on the moment. He then made a cursory inventory of himself to see if any part of him was missing or damaged, and finding that he was more or less intact, he produced a tool bag and proceeded to overhaul his motor cycle. It was something like dry-docking a torpedo boat for repairs to get that complicated stack of machinery to stand up. I helped him to prop it against a tree close by, and conversed with him while he laid his leathern coat aside and rolled up his shirt sleeves. He informed me that he was bound for Tipperary on commercial business. He was in the dry goods trade, and the keen competition that was abroad obliged him to travel on Sunday by motor cycle as there was no train. He represented a Manchester firm, and was a Lancashire man by birth. In regard to motor cycles in general, he said that the ordinary bicycle was out of date. It was played out. No sensible man would now go creeping around the country at the rate of ten miles an hour when he could do twenty and twenty-five and even thirty miles an hour on a motor cycle. Motor cars were too complicated, but any person could manage such a simple contrivance as a motor cycle. If you rode a motor cycle for one week you would never willingly use an ordinary wheel again. Furthermore, the particular make of motor cycle in his possession was the best in the market for the money. He had special terms to offer to intending buyers from the manufacturers, and it would mean an economy of more than one pound sterling to order through him. I said on my part that I had an Irish wheel which I was trying in vain to wear out, and that in any case I considered a motor cycle too exciting. Moreover, it seemed next to impossible to enjoy scenery through which you were whisked at the rate of over twenty miles an hour. He assured me that the scenery was all rot, whatever that means, and that the only thing of interest in Ireland was to book orders, and obtain inside information about impending race meetings so as to place money on the winning horses. I enquired about the vibration of the motor cycle, and he told me that it was good for the health—a statement to which his extreme thinness and pallor gave a peculiar kind of emphasis. In leaving him to pursue my journey he said he would overtake me before I reached Portarlington. He was as good as his word, but he did not foresee that I was to overtake him again farther on. But enough about motor cycles and motor cyclists for the present. Let us see where we are.

There are not many landmarks to go by now, for the leafy hawthorns, gay with creamy honeysuckle, and the white flowers on the morning-glory creeper, hide the meadow lands on either side of the

road. The brakes are aglow with the fluffy plum-
ages of blossom under which the early blackberries
are ripening. Wherever there is an opening in the
foliage the tall cocksfoot and timothy grasses of
the meadows can be seen waving in the yellow light
through which the cloud shadows are chasing one
another before the playful wind. Then the road
twists itself away from the clinging caresses of the
hedges and runs through hilly pastures where the
cattle are attending to the flies in the shade of
spreading ash or beech, or lying half-hidden in the
bracken, leisurely chewing the cud. On a mossy
bank near a gate four lads are lying on their backs,
with their caps over their eyes. They have been to
Mass, and have done all the morning housework,
no doubt, and are killing time until the mid-day
meal comes round by swallowing long draughts of
the perfumed sunshine. I hail them loudly, and
offer them an apple each for their thoughts. They
roll over quickly on their sides and sit up facing
me, for I have halted and am sitting on the opposite
side of the way. The youngest of them, a bright-
eyed, curly-haired lad, with a saucy smile, asks
me :

" Did you say apples ? "

" Yes," I reply, producing a package of half a
dozen.

" Then hand them over," says the lad beside him.

" And your thoughts ? "

" I wasn't thinking of anything. I was half
asleep."

None of them would give their thoughts away to
a stranger, so I changed my offer.

"I am under a vow not to bestow apples unless for value received," I said, "but I am easily satisfied."

"Do you take rags or bones?" asked the lad with the curly hair.

"No, avic, but can you say 'Good morrow' in Irish?"

He said it—said it in a string of blessings that reached across the road, and drew an apple out of the bag.

"And you," I went on to the next candidate, "can you sing?"

"No, but this fellow can," he said, laying his hand on the instep of the boy beside him, who blushed and shook his head protesting, "No, no, I can't."

"Don't mind him," went on the other, "he can."

"What can he sing?"

"He can sing 'An Paisdin Fionn.'"

It took a great deal of wrangling and contradiction and pressing to get it out of him. But he sang at last. I know nothing about the technicalities of music, nor can I sing, whistle, or play two consecutive bars of any tune that was ever known, but I sat in judgment on that boy's performance with the gravity of a professor, and awarded him a prize. The other two lads did not show indications of possessing much extra talent of any kind, but they could answer questions about St. Brigid and Lord Edward Fitzgerald, and they were awarded prizes for their knowledge.

"Irish-Ireland is marching," I thought as I left them; for I could not help remembering where I was, over the border, so to speak. I was in the heart of the Pale. It was within bugle call of the massed battalions that constitute the main body of the Army of Occupation. Worthy of note in many ways— hopeful, hopeful! With the spread of the national language once more in Ireland will come back the patriotic spirit and the Celtic geniality which declined when the Irish language receded before the long and cruel onslaught of Anglicisation. The future is with us, and our hearts are young.

> Oh! the Judgment hour must first be nigh,
> Ere you can fade, ere you can die,
> My Dark Rosaleen!

A ride through another stretch of pasture land brought me to a wood in which big trees met overhead, and the long aisles, carpeted with violets and thin grass and the fallen leaves of last year, stretched far away to right and left. There seemed to be miles of sylvan shade still before me when an abrupt turn of the road led me out under the naked sky and into the wide plain of the Curragh of Kildare. The contrast between the green gloom under the rustling branches and the rolling expanse of treeless sward is very sharp. But it is also pleasant.

I never see the Curragh without being reminded of the Pampas. It is very like a slice of a camp taken out of Areecifes or San Pedro. The land rises and falls in long and gentle undulations. There are no hills or vales, no hedges or walls— nothing but the shallow depressions and the billowy ridges. There are some clumps of furze here and there to remind you of the "cardo" clumps in the early Summer, standing green and rank in the bare expanse of closely cropped grasses. I ran into a flock of sheep half way across the plain, and this was a further reminder of old times. The flock was small—not over 500—but it was sufficiently large to be suggestive of a corner of the wide sheep runs far away. The flock seemed to be owned by different people, for there were several different brands. There was no one within a mile of me to give me any information about it, so I had to content myself with noting that the sheep were all of the same breed, more or less, that they were in fair condition, and that they were feeding down the wind. I stood and leaned on my bicycle, and thought how closely the scene resembled a certain piece of camp beside the Salto River. It was only when my gaze wandered far afield to the Hill of Allen and the distant mountains and woods that I missed the sense of infinite vastness which is ever present on the Pampas. If you were to gallop across the Curragh in the waning twilight, when the distance would be veiled in darkness, you might fancy yourself away under the skies in which the Southern Cross swings nightly to the pole, and in which Canopus is unrivalled in brilliancy during the months that the Dog Star is absent carrying summer round the rest of the world.

A roll of kettle-drums broke on my ear, and dispelled all thoughts of the sunny days and the starry silences of the Southland beyond the ocean. For the Curragh has certain grim realities to throw at you as you cross it from Newbridge towards Kildare or from Kildare towards Newbridge. There

are huge barracks and acres of white tents to the
eastward where the Army of Occupation is encamped. The green turf by the roadside is webbed
by the tracks of the manœuvring batteries of field
artillery in yesterday's exercises. There are signal
stations, flagstaffs, cavalry pickets, sentinels posted
here and there in heavy marching order, long lines
of stables, band stands, rifle ranges, and all the
many appurtenances of a great military camp. This
camp dominates the Curragh, and, indeed, the rest
of Ireland. It has a parade ground of several
square miles at its door and of thirty-one counties
outside the boundaries of Kildare. It is in existence
mainly because of the sins of omission committed
by the people of Ireland in different epochs, and its
mission is to expound the peaceful lessons of conquest by the moral force of steel and gunpowder.
It is one of the great apostolic centres from which
the blessed message of conciliation has been
preached to Ireland in modern days, and from
which so much gentle persuasion has gone out to the
lamb to induce it to lie down inside the wolf.
Various opinions have at different times been expressed regarding the extent to which its labours
have been fundamentally successful. Thomas
Davis, in his intercourse with the Kildare people,
found reason to doubt that its eloquence had been
entirely convincing, or that it was ever likely to be
so. That was why he wrote:

And still it is the peasants' hope upon the Curragh
     mere,
" They'll live who'll see ten thousand men with good
     Lord Edward here."

So let them dream till brighter days, when not by
    Edward's shade,
But by some leader true as he their lines shall be
    arrayed.

It appears that at the Land Conference of unhappy memory, held in Dublin four years ago, a
different kind of "peasants' hope" was expressed,
which has since been shattered. It was a hope that
conciliation would at long last reign supreme in a
conquered nation, based on the peasant privilege of
acquiring part proprietorship of the land at several
years' purchase more than the whole of its market
value. The conciliated patriotism which dreamt
this vanished dream is now in a position to see how
far astray it was led by the nose. Will it see it?
Will it open its eyes to facts? Will it recognise
that the men who represented the tillers of the soil
at the Land Conference made the mistake of deli-
berately anti-dating, by several centuries at least,
the time for the opportune acceptance of defeat on
behalf of the Irish people?

Knock Allen, which rises, as you might say, from
the western fringe of the plain of Kildare, gives its
name to the bog that extends across the central
counties of Ireland to the Shannon. It is a flat-
topped hill of considerable girth, but of no great
elevation. Its name occurs often in the legends of
heroic cycles. It was one of the favourite camping-
grounds of Finn and his warriors. Finn himself
must have had a special *gradh* for it, because he
was reared in the district, somewhere under the
shadow of the Slieveblooms. One can fancy how

gladly the Fianna obeyed the orders that brought
them back to Knock Allen after their expeditions
south or north. In all Ireland there was in those
days no lovelier place for a hosting. There were
deer in the wild woods around it, and hares on the
plains, and fish in the bright streams, and green
rushes for the tent floors on the moors. It is difficult to imagine that there was ever an army in the
world which enjoyed life as fully as the Fianna
Eirinn. And where shall we look for a great cap-
tain more fortunate than Finn in the singers of his
deeds, from his own son Oisin, the soldier poet,
down to the least gifted of the bards? But, alas!
for the silvery dust on the butterfly wings of
romance. The cold truth of history is that Finn
was not a good Irishman. While the great Cormac
MacArt was on the throne, the leader of the Fianna
was kept within the bounds of loyalty, but when
Cormac was gone, Finn showed himself in his true
colours. He felt himself strong enough to disobey
Cormac's successor, and as a consequence of his dis-
obedience and revolt, the whole nation was convulsed. The bloody battle of Gavra Aichill, in
which the star of the Fianna went down, consumed
national vitalities and resources which were needed
to finish the work of consolidating a central Government. The Fianna, in going to their own undoing,
pulled down the institutions which they had been
organised to uphold. They were brave men,
chivalrous, mighty, splendid men—heroic in their
practice of the natural virtues and in their martial
spirit. But they were led by a man whom ambition
had made drunk, and who forgot or ignored that

the first duty of a soldier is obedience to lawful authority. We should not forget the lesson taught us by Finn. When we come to our own again we should not unduly encourage militarism. Woe to the nation that allows itself to be domineered by any class or caste, but of all domestic tyrants the soldier tyrant is the most dangerous, because his hand is ready armed. There are times, of course, when revolt in a soldier becomes a virtue. There was a day when a little of Finn's insubordination would have been a blessing to Owen Roe in dealing with the talkers of Kilkenny. And it is criminal and cowardly and slavish to disparage the sword as a means to the noble end of freedom, or to cry down the spirit which moves men to fight for liberty. But the main business of a soldier in the actualities of life is war and the preparation for war. Finn was a politician. It is bad for a nation when its army goes into politics; and it is bad for the army. That is the lesson to be learned from the story of the Fianna.

The Gibbet-Rath is another spot of historic interest which comes into view as you cross the Curragh. On the 29th of May, 1798, some hundreds of the patriots were massacred there by the troops of General Duff. They had surrendered, and were about to deliver up their weapons when they were fired upon and Roden's cavalry was let loose amongst them. There were nearly 400 Irishmen conciliated on that occasion. In giving up their arms a musket accidentally went off, and Duff seized on this shot as a pretext for the massacre. The surrender on the Hill of Allen took place on the previous

day; and two days before that, on May 26th, the
Catholic Earl of Fingall proved his loyalty by conciliating 400 insurgents on Tara Hill.   Peace to the
dust in the Croppies' grave.   Peace to the dust in
the Gibbet-Rath.   God's sweet mercy on the souls of
all who went down in the martyrdom of Conciliation !

The Round Tower and the grey walls of the old
cathedral in the town recall the glories of Kildare
under the sway of St. Brigid, and they also cause
the thoughtful mind to dwell on one of the effects
of the Great Conciliation, or, if you wish to put it
in another way, one of the accursed evils which a
partial denationalisation has bred.   Conciliation, or
denationalisation, whichever you like, has parted us
from our past.   We know little or nothing about the
great ones who made fame for our land in the long
ago.   We know most of their names, but there is
little of the magic of inspiration in them for generations reared in pathetic ignorance of Irish history.
Ireland has begun to take herself to task for this,
and to know herself; and none too soon.   Of all
the great figures of the first century of Irish Christianity the greatest, after St. Patrick himself, was
undoubtedly St. Brigid.   She was great in every
way.   She was a great woman as well as a great
saint, and was one of the best organisers and most
capable administrators that Ireland has ever known.
Her labours for the Church were widely extended
and successful everywhere.   All her life was one
long record of sanctity.   The people who called her
" The Mary of Ireland " could find no higher or
more loving word of praise for her holiness and

purity. And yet Kildare has not the grip of the
Catholic mind of Ireland that one might expect,
nor is the name of Brigid held in all the high
veneration to which it is entitled by the Irish people
at home or abroad. Our Catholicism is broad to
the extent of being as much cosmopolitan as national,
and it is doubtful if this is anything to fill us with
rejoicing. When I see the veneration in which Santa
Rosa de Lima is held by the Peruvians, and indeed
by Latin American Catholics in general—for she is
the Patroness of South America—I often think that
if we Irish were more proud of the saints of the
Church who were of our own flesh and blood, we
would be no less consistent in our veneration of the
saints who sprang from other races and who toiled
for God in other nations.

Many people will say that the name of St. Brigid
is greater in Westmeath than in various parts of
Kildare. She spent some time at Uisnach, and
there is a "St. Brigid's Well" near the ruins
of an old convent at Kildare under Uisnach Hill.
I read in John O'Donovan's Manuscript Notes
on the Ordnance Survey that St. Brigid was
professed at Uisnach by Bishop Maccaile of
Croghan, near Philipstown. St. Maccaile's Church
was, according to O'Donovan, situated far up
on the slope of the Hill of Croghan. The ruins
which stand in the field near the road from Tyrrellspass to Edenderry, and close to the battered walls
of O'Connor's Castle, the once proud home of the
chieftains of Offaly, are not the remains of the
edifice in which some of the Croghan people used to
say that St. Brigid was professed. They are the

ruins of an ecclesiastical institution which was of a much later foundation. The name of St. Brigid is specially venerated around Croghan Hill, and also in the district of Ardagh, in County Longford where, according to the learned Dean Monahan, she received the veil. But in both localities the saint is rather a legendary character. I think she is more of an authentic and historical reality around Uisnach Hill than she is in either the country of the O'Connors or in the country of the O'Ferralls. Possibly the reason is that around Uisnach there have been fewer breaks in the continuity of local tradition than in many other places in which St. Brigid founded her convents.

The country to the southward and westward of Kildare is a pleasant one to cycle through. You meet more tillage, more farmhouses, and more people on the road. There is a freshness and wholesomeness about the landscape which cheers you after the ride through pastoral solitudes. The grass lands are beautiful, but there is something depressing in their loneliness. You cannot help sorrowing as you ride through them for the people that have left them. You feel a kind of dumb anger to see the cattle and sheep in possession of the fields, which the hands of happy workers tilled in the long ago. On the other hand, the very look of crops is companionable. There is the track of a human thought in every drill and ridge and furrow. I met families returning from Mass, driving or walking. The blue turf smoke rose from scores of chimneys, and from several open doors the appetising smell of the Sunday dinner came across the neatly clipped hedges.

There is a quality in the fragrance of a roast fowl, or the whiff of frying rashers, or the steam of bacon and cabbage seen floating upward from a kitchen table as you spin past the cheery bawn, which encourages you to be sociable. You are tempted to halt and enter the house, and ask the people for the pleasure of their acquaintance, especially if you have been for some hours on the road pushing a bicycle through a steady head wind.

"Fine smell, that," I said to a grave and reverend senior, who sat with bent head in a shady seat under a laurel hedge, beside the gate of a very comfortable looking farmstead. A newspaper was in his hands, and his straw hat lay at his feet. He made me no reply, so I knew that he was sleeping. The habit of observation impelled me to halt. I dismounted on the soft grass, approached him gently and inspected the soporific literature on his knee. There was a great deal of it, and it lay across the face of nature in kilometric paragraphs, in one of which I saw: "The policy of the Land Conference still holds the field after all . . . a policy of conciliation. . . . The country has been without guidance for nine months." That was all I wanted. I cannot say for certain what it was about; but it was evidently a powerful thing for causing sleep. The sleeper was square of jaw and rugged of brow, and the Sunday shave showed the clear lines of a firm mouth and strong, honest face. It seemed to me as I left him there, deep in the shadows of forgetfulness, that he would not have slept over the study of any manly policy. He appeared to be a man whose eye would have kindled on reading an article advocating the development of national backbone.

I rode into Monasterevan and interviewed a friendly man who sat on a window-sill of his mansion smoking mightily. He directed me to a house wherein travellers are wont to seek hospitality. I went thither and knocked. It was a general grocery, licensed also for the sale of spirits, and, consequently, locked to the public for the day, under the Sunday Closing Act. The door was opened by a matronly woman, who smiled as she noted the dust on my clothing and bicycle, and, in the same breath that she answered my salutation, she asked:

" A traveller ? "

" Yes, ma'am."

" Are you a *bona fide?* "

" I hope so."

" Where have you come from ? "

" From latitude 35 south, longitude— —"

" How many miles, I mean ? "

" About seven thousand."

" But to-day ? "

" From Dublin."

" Then you can come in."

She gave me a whole-souled Sunday dinner, and sent me on my way rejoicing. I had scarcely left her door when I met P. T. MacGinley, one of the men who made Irish-Ireland march. I had already met him in Dublin at the Oireachtas, and had parted from him with a strong desire to see more of him. He took me to his headquarters, and for an hour or more I enjoyed the depth and vigour of his talk. I have never met anyone who more clearly knows

his own mind. He is not one of the echoes, but one
of the men who start them. He is a mortal whom
you might rely on to keep a firm grip of first principles no matter what torrential deluge of sophistry
rolled over the land. He is a sturdily-built figure,
with shoulders broad enough to carry any weight
of individual responsibility, and with wide open
eyes which look through big spectacles into the very
soul of things. I saw him at the Ard-Fheis sitting
quietly for hours at a time, listening to everything
that went on without a single change of countenance,
solemn, silent, but watchful. But any time issues
became confused, or argument showed a tendency to
stray off into unpractical generalities, his massive
head would rise placidly over the surface of discussion, and in slow and deliberate speech of extraordinary lucidity and force he would deliver a few
fundamental truths which focussed thought once
more on the kernel of the question. He impresses
you as being a man for any emergency—resourceful,
clear-sighted, and strong, able to master emotion
and impulse, and to strike with cool ferocity at the
right moment, without a thought of fear, and with
his mind made up to face the consequences, no matter
what they might be.

If there should be a fight by any chance I look
forward to see a burly champion with shining spectacles and a large hat down on his ears descend
gravely from his watch-tower at Monasterevan, and
take part in the slaughtering. That is what I said
to myself as I shook hands with him, and pulled out
on the road for Portarlington.

CHAPTER X.

*Monasterevan—Transit in Ireland—Afforestation—
The motor cyclist again—Mountmellick—The
smiling Midlands—Clonaslee—The motor
cyclist comes to grief and comments on Irish
road-making—The Armed Garrison—Kinnity.*

Out again into the south wind and the sunshine
and into a lovely country over level, well kept roads.
There were eight long hours of daylight still to the
good, and nearly half the journey was over. There
was time to loiter, so I loitered. I loitered by the
Barrow's banks and changed the bait for a lad
who was trying to capture the fancy of a perch with
a two-inch maggot. I loitered in the bawn of a
cottage by the roadside, and obtained topographical
data from an aged woman whom I helped with her
wayward chickens. The chickens were damaging
the kitchen garden, and were disinclined to leave it.
She said that her heart was broken with them, but
she did not show it, and her good humour was
phenomenal for one whose life was overshadowed
by an abiding sorrow. I loitered by the dock of the
Grand Canal and discussed inland navigation and
other topics with three ruddy-complexioned boatmen
who were smoking complacently on the bank, and
keeping the Sabbath day in clean-shaven restfulness.
Something in their careless ease reminded me of a
bivouac of a troop of bullock cart teamsters on a

pampa road. I suppose the men of all nations who
pass most of their lives in the open air, doing more
or less the same kind of work, look with more or
less the same genial indulgence at the world and its
ways. The voyagers at Monasterevan offered me
hare soup, which I was obliged to decline, and they
regaled me with comments on men and things as
seen from the deck of a canal boat. They told me.
in the speech of north Leinster that the nearer you
go to Dublin the more you come into contact with
the economic point of view, which is summed up in
" nothing for nothing." The nearer you go to the
Shannon, the easier it is to snare a hare or trap a
rabbit, or negotiate for newly laid eggs. One of
them gave me some particulars about Monasterevan,
which were not devoid of interest and of a certain
kind of sarcasm.

"Monasterevan is like a beauty of fifty-five," he
said, "her great days is behind her. If you want
a quiet place to sleep, come here and close your
weary eyes, but if you want to live in the whirl of
town excitement, go to sweet Tullamore."

There were three canal boats at the station or
dock, all laden with fine trunks of ash or oak or
beech from the woods of the district. I believe
timber cut from Irish woods, and destined for English sawmills, is at present one of the most important items in the traffic on the Irish canal. Here you
have a twofold object lesson in the crying need that
exists in Ireland for an Irish government to govern
Ireland in the interests of the Irish nation. The
weed-grown and half-idle canal recalled the problem

of cheap transit which meets you everywhere in the country, and the boatloads of timber going seaward recalled the problem of deforestation.

The railways of Ireland now own, wholly or in great part, most of the canals, so that competition between the two means of internal communication is at an end. It is doubtful if there could be found in the wide world a class of economists so unpatriotic, so shortsighted, and so hidebound as the capitalists who own the Irish transit system. Canals are kept practically idle, so that railways may be fed with traffic at blood-sucking rates. The prohibitive tariff of the railways reduce traffic to a minimum, and the only remedy the directors appear to be able to suggest for this is to encourage tourists to come into the country, thus substituting an artificial passenger business for the ordinary carrying trade, which has been killed by extortion.

It actually costs less to send a ton of wheat from Buenos Aires to Belfast than from Athlone to Dublin. It is cheaper for the Dublin merchants to send goods to Sligo *via* Glasgow by steamer than to send them across Ireland by rail. People who live close to the Irish canals are obliged to cart produce and merchandise to and from railway stations several miles distant from them. National wealth is wasted in this manner week by week and year by year. If there were such an institution in existence as an Irish Board of Trade there would be cheap transit. The railways and canals would either be owned by the State or subjected to such laws as would make them serve the economic interests of the people at large. There would be a hundred coasting steamers for every ten that now ply between Irish ports. And there would be a network of canals to carry the bulk of the produce from some of the most important of the agricultural districts.

The problem of deforestation is tragically eloquent of the evils of foreign rule in Ireland. A wise native Government, drawing inspiration from national needs and national interests, would derive from Irish forests a permanent and considerable revenue. Under foreign rule Ireland is being denuded of her beautiful woods. The axe and cross-cut are at work in all directions. A mania for tree slaughter seems to have afflicted the landlords. Hundreds of acres of pine and ash and oak are felled every year, and in very few instances are any trees planted to replace the ones that have been cut down. Twenty years ago one of the landlords of the West was asked why he did not plant trees on his waste lands, and he replied :

" What! Plant trees to give cover to my damned tenantry to fire slugs at me? Not much."

A few days ago I asked a farmer in southern Offaly why he did not plant, and he said :

" Plant, indeed ! Why should I ? Is it to give more cover to the landlord's pheasants and hares ? Besides, he would come down on me some day and claim all my trees as he is doing now."

He was not aware that under one of the Land Acts a tenant can make good his claim to all the trees he plants by merely registering them. The formality is simple, and only costs a fee of half-a-crown. If an Irish Government were in existence it would have a Forestry Department, and there would be expert foresters to teach the people by precept and example that timber is a priceless natural asset. Then the people would know that even in the wooded Midlands there are empty and idle corners, briar-grown ditches, bleak fringes of moor and useless cut-away bogs which might be planted, and thereby converted into sources of wealth. The barrenness of the fertile sheep-runs in Connacht is woeful, awful, terrible. You are saddened to the bottom of your heart as you cycle mile after mile across the treeless ridges and through the hollows where not even a willow stands beside the lonely streams. Down by the skirt of the bog, where the wild wind and the threshing rain have washed away the grass and mould, you may see the stumps of giant pines that gave sylvan beauty to the landscape two hundred years ago. If meteorological data reached back so far we should find that the rainfall in Ireland has increased since the seventeenth century. Even to-day the rainfall is greater in the western than in the eastern districts. I have on several occasions cycled through the rain out of a Connacht county to find the road bone dry in Leinster. The standard of health has fallen, too, in Ireland since her great forests were destroyed. No doubt some of the decline in the general health of the population is due to the drain of emigration, which took away the strongest of the youths and maidens. But a great deal of unhealthiness of the citizens comes from excessive humidity. In the old days this humidity was absorbed by the foliage. It did not rise over thousands of square miles of treeless land in vapour and come back in rain as it does now.

The effects of forests on climate is common knowledge in other countries.   It is Greek to the average
man in rural Ireland.   The reason is plain.   The
people have had no sympathetic and scientific State
guidance as the people who till the soil have had
in other countries, and the infamous legislation
which deprived the tenant of compensation for his
improvements placed a premium on slip-shod
methods.   But now there is a change.   The land
laws are far from being perfect yet, but they give
the tenants a right in their farm.   They can improve
their land now with a reasonable assurance that
their improvements will not be confiscated.   Consequently, they can plant; and everyone who has the
ear of the agrarian and pastoral communities should
make a propaganda in favour of tree planting.   The
Press should team with articles dealing with afforestation.   At present *Sinn Fein* is alone in this
department of journalism, as indeed it is, sad to
say, in too many other works of a constructive
nature.   Every journal in Ireland that honestly
wishes to serve the country should deal earnestly
and luminously with re-afforestation.   If the Public
Boards took the matter up, if the schools and colleges dedicated one day in the year to the planting
of trees—as is done by the educational institutions
of several countries at present—the bleak places
would soon be green with foliage, the climate would
be rendered drier and more salubrious, the beauty
of our land would be enhanced, and a magnificent
source of national wealth would be increasing in
value year by year.

On to Mountmellick through a delightful country, well wooded, well watered, fairly well cultivated. This is a beautiful part of Ireland, and its beauty never saddens you, for it has nothing deserted and lonely about it. The homes of the people are comfortable, near enough to one another for sociability, yet not crowded together. The land is judiciously divided between pasturage and tillage; and there are sheets of bog here and there, with latent energy enough to move the machinery of the world. You can cycle now for miles and miles without meeting startling poverty or any very large extent of fertile solitude. There is neither congestion nor wide depopulation. There are many parks and game preserves, remnants of the broad domains that were robbed from the chieftains of Offaly and Leix after Mullaghmast, and given to the foreigners who fought the Irish for spoil, or the weaklings who sold themselves to the reavers; but there are fine stretches of farm lands on which a Godfearing and industrious population is firmly rooted. You can cycle for many days in this hospitable country. Strike out, let us say, by Geashill to Croghan Hill, through Ballynagar and Philipstown, on to Edenderry. Then back to Tullamore and through Kinnegad into South Westmeath, and still to the southward through Moate, to the Shannon at Athlone; and from Athlone to Ferbane, Cloghan, and Banagher to Birr; and from Birr through northern Tipperary, by Roscrea, across the southern spur of the Slieve Blooms, eastward of Ard-na-h-Eireann, to Dunnamase; and around by Monasterevan back to

Portarlington. It is not a country of lofty crags or rushing torrents, or blue mountain lakes. It is a country of wide valleys and wooded dales and green hills. There is a purple heather along the tops of the Slieve Blooms, but the lower slopes are fertile, and the golden glow of the ripening cornfields, hemmed in by green crops and pastures, and fenced with hawthorn hedges makes the harvest time one long poem of colour. Northward it opens into Annally, southward into the Golden Vale, westward into Hy Many, eastward into Carlow. It touches the storied loughs of Westmeath It is washed by the Shannon, it is blessed by the memories of Durrow, Rahan, Drumcullen, Birr of Brendan and Clonmacnoise of Ciaran. It holds legends of pagan and Christian Uisnach, of Finn, of the Danish invaders, of Margaret O'Carroll, of Ruairi O'More, of the red wars that were fought for freedom, of battles lost and won. I am very fond of it, and fond of praising it. But I fear it is not very actively Irish just now. I fear there are very few branches of the Gaelic League in it or of Cumann na nGaedheal. But many of the children you meet on the roads coming from school are learning Irish and are coming into the knowledge of Irish history. God bless and guide them all. Time is on their side, and time is a wonder worker in many ways. They are on the road to the right kind of knowledge, and when they have learned it there will be a different story to tell. They will feel a noble shame to think that the people of the poverty-ridden mountains and bleak sea coasts have been alone for so many years

in guarding the last distinctive and distinguishing
heritage of the Gael. The old love that has lain
dormant through generations of sordid trial and
denationalisation will stir their hearts again. The
fields and raths and fords will bear messages to
them from the inspiring past, and

> ——many a hill . . . will wake
> The memory of brave days and kindle still
> The fire for Erin's sake.

You turn to the right in Mountmellick by the fine
Celtic cross erected to the memory of the patriots
of '98, and enquire for the road to Clonaslee:
because it is very easily missed. You will know that
you are taking the wrong direction if you find yourselves riding away from the Slieve Blooms, which
stand out in dark purple against the sky. If you are
pressed for time take the high road to Rosenallis.
If not take the lower road, which carries you off
through a maze of woods where the bracing odour
of the pine is fragrant on the mountain air, and
the tall ferns grow rankly by the wayside. This
sheltered run gives you plenty of free wheel,
although it ends in a stiff climb which brings you
into Rosenallis. Quench your thirst at the village
well. It is a spring more refreshing than the
deepest draught of the rarest wine in Europe. I
believe Tullamore takes its water supply from this
neighbourhood, whose wells are fed from the filters
of the mountain rocks.

Up the mountain road now, over the woods and meadows and tillage fields, up into the freer air while the shadows slant and lengthen; up until all the hills of Offaly are flattened into insignificance save one alone—Croghan of the O'Conors and the holy wells and the fleet hares—a sharp cone of blue standing far away to the north-west out of the greyish haze of the plain. Up and up, until you meet the bees flying homeward laden with the honey sucked from the heather on Knocknacara. It is a glorious ride. There is a lower and more direct road, and when I had filled my eyes with a long look into Leix, I came back to it. I had made a round of several miles, but what of that? The climb had yielded two hours of unpurchaseable delight, and the return had been mostly free wheel, unspoiled by hissing brakes.

I halted in a shady hollow under Clonaslee, not to rest or to loiter, but to visit the sick. My motor cyclist was there by the roadside, reclining on the grass, his head-dress lying beside him, his leathern tunic open, his limbs contracted, his face pale and sickly. Both his hands were pressed upon his stomach, and he moaned faintly. The motor cycle stood over him and, as if in sorrow at the contemplation of its work, it was blackening the dust with oily tears.

"Oh, it is nothing at all," he said, peevishly, in reply to my enquiry into the cause of the trouble, "I shall be all right in a few minutes. I met with no accident at all. It was simply those beastly roads. They would sicken a cart horse. They would shake a stone crusher to jelly. Never saw such a beastly shame—all bumps and ruts and holes. I have been suffering from a slight indisposition since my sea-sickness on that beastly passage last night, and this horrible road has finished me. Look at it! Did anyone ever see such a public road in any civilised country! Why it is worse than a blawsted lane. If this is the way your precious Councils do their road-making you ought to hang them."

I disagreed with him on principle, and said that the road was all right. But it was all wrong. I would not admit that for the whole world to the Sassenach, although I had been vainly trying to find a smooth place for the past hour. I had been suffering from the bumps and ruts myself, and had been dimly wondering what might be the sensations of a motor cyclist in negotiating the high road from Rosenallis to Clonaslee. But I stood by the County Council, District Councils, contractors and inspectors. The motor cyclist was disgusted. He drew in his breath hard and asked me painfully:

"Do you mean to say that you have ever cycled over anything like this in all your life?"

I did. For I had cycled along canal banks in Ireland. I had cycled along the bed of a dried-up mountain watercourse. I had cycled from Olivos to Tigre in Buenos Aires. I had cycled from the Once to Lujan on the roadless Pampas. All I said, however, was:

"Yes; I have ridden over far worse roads in my time. The reason you find it so disagreeable is because you are riding a motor cycle. That is one of the disadvantages of these machines—they bump too much. Any little inequality in the road makes them unsteady."

"Oh, I understand," he said, as he caught a more intimate grip of his digestive organs, "you can see nothing wrong with this blawsted road because it's Irish. I noticed that the finger-posts in this country are printed in the Irish language. By Jove, if the language is anything like the road, it must be lovely and smooth!"

"I suppose." said I, severely, "you consider it a dreadful thing to see finger-posts in Irish along an Irish road?"

"Oh, not at all," he replied, "I find it—aw—quite appropriate—far more appropriate than English—for such a road as this."

"Well," I remarked, "you show great courage and self-sacrifice to travel by this road, or to visit this dreadful country at all. Another man in your place would turn back and take the first boat for England, and cut Ireland and Irish roads and Irish finger-posts dead for ever and a day."

I stiffly took my leave of him and I went my way. And as I rode down the next hill I met a series of bumps which smashed one of my saddle springs. While I was repairing the damage, four men in the khaki uniform of the Army of Occupation staggered past me, shouting the chorus of some rank barrack-room song in hoarse and obscene discord. When I resumed my journey I met other parties of khaki-clad warriors. They were from an encampment

established in a field on the verge of Clonaslee.
The encampment was engaged in playing cricket. I
was told that it was established there during the
summer in order to give the men some practice in
mountain campaigning. The heather-clad summits
of the Slieve Blooms which rise over the camp are
used as rifle ranges. The man who told me this
said :

"Every other week fresh soldiers come and some
of the ones that were here march off with themselves.
They go out nearly every day while they remain
and fire at the mountain. Then they march up to
it to see if they hit it."

A few days afterwards I came across another
summer encampment of the Army of Occupation
established at Rosstown, near Uisnach Hill, in
Westmeath. Detachments had been concentrating
there for a fortnight from Athlone, Dublin, and
other centres. They were selling porter, I was told,
at three half-pence per pint, but their canteen was
not popular. If it was on a recruiting excursion they
had gone forth they had signally failed; and for
all such failures let us give thanks to the God of
our fathers.

Once you pass Clonaslee the road is good. Indeed it is only between Rosenallis and Clonaslee that
it is really lumpy. As a rule the roads of Leix are
in good repair. As for the roads through Offaly,
they are, generally speaking, excellent. The road
from Cademstown to Birr through Kinnity affords
an easy run, and takes you through a beautiful
countryside.

I think Kinnity is probably the most beautifully-situated village I have ever seen. It is embowered in the woods, and is a sheltered Eden in the lap of the hills. I wonder if anyone ever tires of it. The mountains, which rise over it, give a fine lesson in afforestation. The woods run up to the very heather, and there is some valuable timber growing on soil that would not support a goat to the acre, not to mention a cow or a sheep, owing to its high elevation. In former years, I believe, those lands used to be top-dressed with lime, after which they grew, for a season or two, clover and several kinds of juicy grass. But once the strengthening effects of the lime ceased, the land fell back again into its wild and unproductive state of hard, thin grass and stunted heather. Then the alternative of planting trees was tried, and gave successful results. There are thousands and thousands of acres along the Slieve Blooms that could be planted in the same way. Kinnity is an Irish-Ireland village, due to the influence of the patriotic priest of the district, and to the teachers in the local school. There is an Irish language class, a needlework class, a hurling club, and a right good Irish atmosphere generally.

An easy spin down to the crossroads, a turn to the right, a race into the valley through which the Kinnity river tumbles past the ruins of old Drum-cullen Monastery, a climb up two or three of the foot hills, and then home. It was just sundown, and the boys were returning from football and hurling. I looked at my cyclometer to find my record of mileage for the day. But it was evidently astray in its registration. It gave a total of 1,554 miles from Dublin, which was manifestly too flatter-ing. The actual distance covered will have been not more than about seventy Irish miles.

CHAPTER XI.

*The valley of the Lower Shannon—From Aughrim
to Limerick—Mountain and lowland children—
The Rim of the World—Nenagh town—Dairy
farming—The unharnessed, idle, beautiful
Shannon—An exclusive Bodach—Upholding
first principles—Killaloe—Ancient Kincora—
Brian and Mahon—Castleconnell Rapids—
Limerick in the gloaming.*

I had cycled from Kilcommedan Hill eastward,
crossing the Shannon at Banagher, and thence
striking southward until I reached a place below
Meelick, near Redwood.   Kilcommedan Hill is
another name for the battle field of Aughrim.   Redwood is the place where Donal O'Sullivan crossed
into Connacht from Munster on his retreat after the
battle of Kinsale.   I had been in the track of De
Ginkell's march to Galway, and had been exploring
the country where St. Ruth elected to make his stand
against the Dutch general.   I had also been picking
up the route of O'Sullivan Beare on the slopes of
Aughrim, where he had fought and routed a jackal
horde that had tried to stop him.   I halted now on
the Munster plain, and considered whether I had
had enough of history for one day, or whether I
should push forward towards Limerick.   My home
under the blue Slieve Blooms lay only about ten
miles to the eastward, and " the City of the Violated
Treaty " lay many miles to the southward.   But the

day was young and the roads were good, and the wind for a wonder came out of the north-east, and would help me on a southerly raid. It was a long ride I mapped out for myself, as I sat on a stone beside a spring which flowed out into the sunlight through the moss-grown roots of a hawthorn and danced and sang over the pebbles, and down hill, falling into silence as it stole out of sight amongst the tempting watercresses. I finished a bunch of the cress, slaked my thirst once more in the laughing shallows, and, after a final look at my road map, concentrated on Borrisokane to begin with. After that my route would bring me into touch with the country of Brian Boru and Sarsfield and Galloping O'Hogan and Garryowen and the Wild Geese.

To the children in the country of the O'Carroll's, north of the Birr, the far-away mountains below Nenagh mark the southern limit of the world. All through my childhood the dim peaks of the Silvermines and the Keepers seemed to be infinitely distant, and when as a boy I learned that there were other countries besides the one which lay between me and the horizon, I often longed to see them, and often wondered if it would ever be my fate to travel in the regions beyond the guardian hills of the homeland. I suppose all this is in the childhood and boyhood of most people born in the valleys. I have never been able to find out what theories of the universe float through the minds of Irish children born on the mountains. I tried to coax this secret out of mountain children here and there through Ireland, but they baffled me. They seemed to have no idea at all that they were of the hills themselves. Any heather-clad peak above them was "the mountain," but the slopes of the range upon which they had been born did not strike them as being big, purple, beautiful mysterious things to the children of the plains and vales.

"What is down there, do you suppose?" I asked a little boy whom I met on a mountain slope over southern Ulster.

"Down where?" he said, with a look which told me he did not understand.

I made a gesture which included most of Cavan and Leitrim.

"Why, that isn't down there," he said, with a smile.

"And what is it?" I asked.

"Oh! it's over there beyont, that's what we say," he replied, and beyond that I could not induce him to go.

But when I fell in with a party of schoolchildren on the road south of Borrisokane, and asked them what lay beyond the Keepers, they could tell me that it was Limerick. And when I asked them, pointing to the north-east, what lay beyond the Slieve Blooms, they could tell me that it was Queen's County. They were children of the plains, and from the time they could walk they had been questioning the mountains.

"I am going to the other side of the Silvermines, and away beyond the Keepers," I said, "and maybe any of you would like to come?"

There was silence for a few seconds, and then a

brown-haired lad asked shyly, as he made crosses with his toes in the road dust:

"Are you goin' as far as Limerick?"

"I am, and much farther," I said—"miles and miles!—going even farther than the coast of Ireland—going over the sea—Will you come?"

He shook his head and smiled. But as I left them there was a wistful light in his eyes and in the eyes of more than one of his companions. And I knew that some Hy-Brazil of their own creation had come into "the long, long thoughts of youth." It was my own boyhood back again. The same dumb questioning—the same inarticulate longings—the same sub-conscious desire to learn what is out there beyond the blue and purple, and to see it, and feel upon your cheek, and hear in your ears the breath and voice of the world.

I found Nenagh very quiet, and left it so. I drank cider, and smoked a pipe, and read the papers, and looked an inquisitive policeman out of countenance. The town appears to be prosperous. There is a fine rich country around it, but not a great deal of agriculture. Dairy farming seems to be the principal industry thereabouts, and also beyond the mountains, on the plains of Limerick. The farms do not, however, run into big acreages. I passed through various districts where a holding of over fifty acres was the exception. The average size of a farm appeared to be somewhere between twenty-five and thirty acres. The land, although under pasture, was not therefore empty of people. Dairy farming requires more hands than grazing. It means that there must be a family at least, or, if

not two or three paid hands to milk the cows, handle
the milk, and feed the calves   Butter making at
home on the farm has become practically a thing of
the past in most dairy farming districts.   The milk
is collected by vans and carried to a local creamery,
where the cream is taken from it by means of
mechanical separators.   Next day the skim-milk is
taken away by the farmers, or sent back to them
The cream is then sent to Limerick, or some other
central place, and made into butter.   There is at
times a good deal of discussion as to the best means
of working a co-operative dairy system.   Opinions
are very much divided at times regarding matters
of detail; but as a rule it is conceded by the farmers
that the general principle of co-operation is fraught
with encouraging possibilities.

Nenagh, like Clonmel, was a more prosperous
town in the great days of the Irish corn trade than
now. I was surprised to find that the impulse of
the Irish-Ireland movement has been felt far less
in Tipperary than in counties which might be supposed to be less Irish.   But a force of the right kind
is working slowly but surely, and a change is
coming.   In the towns of Tipperary, as in the towns
of most of the other Irish counties, there are merchants who regard it as their duty to sell Irish
manufactured goods, and, if necessary, recommend
them to their customers; and in the rural districts
the farmers are waking up to the conviction that
their duties towards the Irish nation did not end,
but in a manner only really began, with the partial
settlement of the land question.   In order to foster
Irish industries some kind of Protection is necessary.

Circumstanced as she is at present—governed as she is by England in the selfish commercial and political interest of England—Ireland is unable to make Protection the law of the land in a legal sense. But she is already beginning to do it in a moral sense. " Burn everything English but English coal," is a saying that was for many years dead in a sleepy and forgetful Ireland. But it has been resuscitated of late, and the fiscal policy of which it is, of course, a picturesque apothegm, coined in the wondrous mind of Swift, is coming into play. The Irish people are learning that every time they buy even a box of matches of Irish manufacture in preference to any other, they are striking a blow for Ireland. It is the policy of moral protection. There is no law of England which obliges Irishmen under penalties and pains to favour English manufactures and boycott their own. And a re-awakening Ireland is taking a firm grasp of this economic fact and of all that it means.

I turned westward in Nenagh, and picked up the Shannon once more at Portroe, where Lough Derg narrows into a long strip of water, not more than a mile in width, bordered on the Clare side by the wooded hills which rise into the Bernagh range. The Tipperary side is relatively flat, but very picturesque; and from this point to Killaloe the Shannon is indeed lordly. But it is, unfortunately, an empty, profitless lordship. It is not the lordship of the Rhine or the Rhone or the Danube. It is devoid of the traffic of commerce. The magnificent river is not a factor in the national economy. Its potentialities are asleep. The Shannon is mighty, but idle.

There is a little island in Lough Derg, opposite
Portroe, which has a very ancient and illustrious
history. It is small in area, not more than two score
acres more or less, but in the early days of the
Church in Ireland it was the site of one of the great
schools of Thomond. The island is called Iniscaltra, and the seat of learning of which it was the
home was one of the greatest schools in Ireland
during the seventh and eighth centuries The school
was founded by St. Columba, of Terryglass. He
died in 552. Another great man, and a more famous
scholar than St. Columba, ruled in Iniscaltra a
hundred years later. His name was Caimin. Iniscaltra is deserted and silent now ; and the tall round
tower merely calls attention to the spot where once
stood the church and schools. There is not a word
of all this in the guide books. Nine out of every
ten tourists who pass it on the Shannon pleasure
steamers give it but a careless glance, and think no
more about it. Only a round tower—another of
them—and a few crumbling walls, and nothing
more but green, green rich grass and Galway cattle.
Yet there was a time when scholars came hither from
many lands. A scion of the Lagenian race and the
descendant of a Leinster King was its rector. He
was the trusted friend of St. Finian of Clonard,
and one whose word went far in the councils of the
sages and scholars of Erin.

The road turns southward, now running close to
the waterside, through scenery which it would be
hard to surpass in beauty even in Ireland. You have
to loiter here and there and fill your eyes with pictures of the blue water and the green fields and the

noble woods—all to be retained in the memory and carried away. There is scarcely a sound, only the soft voice of the wavelets on the shore, and the splash of a fish leaping after a fly, and the low song of the trees But this soft harmony is ripped open by the grating hen-like note of a pheasant in a whin clump under the pines, and through the slit in the pulsating silence come far-off voices over the water, from a sail boat gliding leisurely down stream. I am encamped in a tangle of grass and bracken, with the tuneful woods above me and the Shannon spread out below, and I find it very fresh and sweet and restful. I climbed in here over a wall, swinging myself down from it by the branches of a tree. There was a notice board on the wall prohibiting people from "trespassing," so I supposed I am on somebody's preserves, but the thought does not cause me any uneasiness. I am in possession for the moment, and that is enough. It is all mine for the time being. It is entirely splendid, and I am thinking of going to sleep when I hear a big rustling close at hand in the underbrush. I lean up on my elbow from my recumbent position, and parting the tangle around me with a gentle kick which fills the air with the healthy breath of torn fern stalks, I proceed to reconnoitre the intrusion. It is a man with a fishing rod and a basket, and he walks into the glade with the air of one whose proprietary rights in the soil are unquestionable before the law. He sees me, and a frown gathers upon his face as he comes towards me. He speaks to me in a language almost devoid of " r's," and says, " What awe you doing heawh ? "

I catch my boot toes argumentatively, and regard

him in cold reproof. But the only thing I can bring myself to say to him is:

"Are you accustomed to speak to people before you are introduced to them?"

"I am accustomed to deal legally with trespas-saws, and will now thank you to take youawself out of this."

"And who are you?"

"The ownagh."

"The owner!" and I swept my hand out towards the water and the distant mountains, and backward to indicate the singing of the trees. "You own all this? You? No, *a chara*, you are mistaken. Try again."

"Try again?" he fumed. "I'll teach you who I am——"

"Oh! go away," I said, wearily, turning from him. "Your attitude of mind towards first prin-ciples needs overhauling. I have ridden over fifty miles to-day, and you fatigue me."

I lay back amongst the ferns once more, and closed my eyes to indicate that I considered the interview ended. He stormed round the locality for a few minutes, speaking about law and police and prosecution, and other tiresome subjects. But I took no further notice of him, and he soon grew weary of his own conversation and left me. Then I went back to my wheel, over the wall, and resumed my journey.

A few more miles of the same beautiful scenery. Then a squeezing together of the hedgerows, and the roofs of a township, and the dark grey belfry of a church; a twelve-arch bridge; a few silvery miles of water; a long vista of square fields sloping westward to a wide wild sweep of mountain, and I was riding into ancient Killaloe.

Killaloe is becoming fashionable, and the tourist who fishes and plays golf, and drinks Scotch whiskey, is now an unlovely feature of the land-scape. I believe someone belonging to the royal family of England passed up the Shannon a few years ago, and said that Killaloe was quite a pic-turesque place. Ever since the angling, golfing, whiskeying tourists have patronised the place. You see them trying to catch fish with the wrong fly, and "catching crabs" with right or left oar as they try to row boats along the river. And you hear them at their golf talk as they greet each other at the railway station. But they can only do a little, a very little, to spoil Killaloe. It sees them go and come, and makes a little money out of them, and takes care that they pay cash for all value received. They cannot vulgarise the ancient renown of Kin-cora, or filch a laurel leaf from the wreath of King Brian, or dim the holy lustre that abides round the name of St. Finnan.

Above the bridge, overlooking the river, are the ruins of Kincora. This was the palace of the Kings of the Dalcassian race—the proud descendants of Heber, who won the sovereignty of Erin from the Hy-Niall, and raised Thomond from the position of a third or fourth-rate of chieftainry until it became the hegemony of Ireland. It was to Kincora that a bedraggled horseman galloped with the bloody tidings that Mahon, King of Munster, had been treacherously murdered in the mountains

of Knockinreorin, and when the tale was told in the
halls of the Thomond palace, a prince, the brother
of the murdered king, took down his harp from the
wall, and, in a wild outburst of grief, chanted a
song of lament and of revenge. This prince's name
was Brian, afterwards to be known as Brian Boru,
or Borumha—that is, Brian of the Tribute, High
King of Ireland, lawgiver, statesman, warrior, and
the deliverer of his country.

The death of Mahon is described in the " Wars
of the Gaedhill and the Gall," and is one of the
saddest and most tragic events in the history of the
race of Heber. He was an energetic, hard-hitting,
wise kind of man, and had by his own right hand
won the sovereignty of Munster.   He drove the
Danes out of Thomond, sailed his ships from Lough
Derg to the sea, and was acknowledged as ruler
by all the chieftains of Desmond. Like most men
who fight their way to power, he had made many
enemies, and amongst the most bitter of those who
hated and envied him were the chieftains of the Eog-
hanacht. Donovan MacCathal, of Hy-Fidhgente,
and Molloy, the Chieftain of Desmond, leagued
with the Danish general to bring about the downfall
of the head of the Dalcassians, and between them
they swore that Mahon should die. They invited
him to a friendly conference at Donovan's house, in
order to discuss certain affairs of state. Mahon
accepted the invitation, and set out to keep the
appointment. Some suspicion he must have had, or
some warning he must have received, for he placed
himself under the protection of the clergy, and took
with him, encased in a costly shrine, a copy of the

Gospels, made by the hand of St. Finbar. This sacred treasure was taken from Cork to Mahon specially for the occasion, and the Munster King, once in possession of it, believed himself safe against the machinations of open or secret foes. There seems to have been some difference between Mahon and his tributary chieftains, and that the Bishop of Cork guaranteed that each person assisting at the friendly conference should be under episcopal protection. On his way thither, Mahon was treacherously seized by Donovan, who, in accordance with the agreement entered into with his confederates, sent the royal prisoner to the Chieftain of Desmond. The Bishop of Cork, and Molloy were waiting for Mahon at Sliabh Cacin on one of the slopes of the gorge or gap through which the road passed. The Hy-Fidhgente men and their prisoner were on the opposite slope, and on reaching the spot agreed upon the murderers' steel leaped upon the air. When Mahon saw that his captors were turning their swords against his life, he threw the sacred scroll and the shrine to a priest who accompanied him, so that the blood of a murdered man might not stain it. In a few minutes he was a gory corpse, and his assassins were wiping his heart's blood from their swords. The Bishop of Cork saw the flashing of their steel from his position beside the Desmond Chief on the opposite hill, and hurried to the scene of blood.

"What can I do? Oh, tell me what am I to do?" he said, appealing to Molloy.

" Go and cure the patient; you will find him lying yonder," was the answer given in savage irony.

When the horrified prelate reached the opposite slope of the gap good King Mahon was no more.

Some historians say that Mahon was not taking the sacred book with him for protection, but that he had caused it to be brought to him so that upon it his tributary chieftains might swear their fealty. Others say that when he was attacked he clutched the Gospels to his heart to shield him from the swords of his foes, and that the shrine and its contents were stained with his heart's blood. Mahon was buried where he fell, and it is said that over his grave the Bishop " wept bitterly, and uttered a prophecy concerning the future fate of the murderers," which was fulfilled with a swift and fierce exactness.

In no heart was such sorrow and rage caused by the murder of Mahon as in the heart of Brian. His song of lament has been given an interpretation in English by " The Bard of Thomond," and has often been quoted. A verse or two may, without apology, be inserted here:

> Oh, Mahon, my brother, we've conquered
>   And marched side by side,
> And thou wert to the love of my soul
>   As a beautiful bride;
> In the battle, the banquet, the council,
>   The chase and the throne,
> Our beings were blended—our spirits
>   Were filled with one tone.

Oh, Mahon, my brother, thou'st died
    Like the hind of the wood,
The hands of assassins were red
    With thy pure, noble blood;
And I was not near my beloved
    When thou wast o'erpowered,
To steep in their heart's blood the steel
    Of my blue-beaming sword.

It galled Brian terribly that his brother had been slaughtered unarmed. Had Mahon died fighting against a hundred, Brian would have found some consolation in the proud thought that his brother had fallen like a king. Another fine verse is the following :

Gold, silver, and jewels were only
    As dust in his hand,
But his sword like a lightning-flash blasted
    The foes of the land.

Although his breast was torn with fraternal grief, Brian lost no time in punishing the criminals. He fell upon the Danes, slaying their leader, Ivar, and his son, and many of their followers. The chief of the Hi-Fidhgente was killed in battle, and for many years after his clan suffered for his crime. As for the Chieftain of Desmond, whose sword was the first to enter Mahon's breast, he was hunted like a wolf through the mountains for two years, and finally taken prisoner. He was put to death close to the spot where he had committed his infamous crime, and he was buried on the northern slopes of the pass, where the sun never shines upon his grave.

When Brian ascended the throne he was in his thirty-fifth year. Those who had followed him through a hundred fights against the Danes knew that he was a born soldier. But only one or two of the bards knew that in him Munster and Ireland would find the wise head and the fearless hand and the high and holy purpose of a great and kingly man. The utter defeat of the Danes at Clontarf cannot be thoroughly appreciated as a military achievement unless the student of history learns how Brian organised his victory. His long contest for supremacy with Malachy the Great was part of the work which he had set himself. He was greater than Malachy and he won, and won with honour and profit, for he enrolled his beaten opponent under his own banner, and was able to trust him as an ally. Brian saw that the Danes would rule in Ireland so long as Ireland was divided into petty kingdoms He saw that the evil of provincialism would have to be trampled down if a true national ideal was to prosper, and he trampled down provincialism. It was not for Munster alone that Brian was ambitious, but for the whole of Ireland. Some of the more stubborn northerners held aloof from him, but otherwise it was practically a united nation that he hurled at the Danes on that Good Friday morning of the year 1014. If he had survived the battle, Ireland would have reaped the full harvest of his victory. As it was, however, he showed the way and the only way to every Irish leader who has drawn a sword or lifted a voice for Irish freedom ever since. That lesson is Unity—not the mere unity of the people who think alike, but the unity of the whole people in a national purpose, not mere unity of creed to combat creed, but the unity of men of every creed to combat the common enemy. No Ulster, Munster, Leinster, Connacht, or Meath, no North or South or East or West, no fatuous provincialism, no petty parochialism, but Ireland first and last and always.

That is one of the lessons which may be learned, or rehearsed, or repeated as you sit within the ruins of Kincora. There is another lesson, too, and a very important one. We must not expect that our great ones can be more than human. The man who will do most for Ireland is the man who says little about a thing until it is done. And he must know how to play the game as Brian played it. Ireland must learn to be patient with him—so long as he plays the game for her. An honest man who knows how to play the game, a man deeply and unchangeably Irish in his love and his hate, but a man who will not wear his heart on his sleeve, that is the man who will do mighty things.

I visited St. Finnan's Cathedral, which is a good specimen of Norman ecclesiastical architecture. But St. Finnan's Oratory is a building of quite a different kind. It is a standing proof of the high plane to which art was rapidly rising in Ireland over a thousand years ago. The roof is of stone, and the arched doorway is well constructed. It is not so elaborate as the doorway of the Cathedral of Clonfert, nor so well preserved as the doorway of Devorgilla's Chapel at Clonmacnoise, but it is an excellent specimen of its kind and worthy of study. The Cathedral was erected by King Donald of Thomond before the coming of the Normans.

I tarried for half an hour on the bridge, and watched the shadows lengthen on the water, and on the sunny slopes over the town. The evening gold was deepening along the crests of the hills of Clare as I came within earshot of the rapids of Castleconnell. The Shannon is in a playful mood at this point, and for three or four hundred yards its course leaps and tumbles and breaks into cataracts, and churns itself into foam as white as the bark of the birch trees which look down upon the romping current. And as if the salmon were infected with the boisterous mood of the river, they put their tails in their mouths and leap from the foamy pools underneath the falls into the smooth water above. There is another salmon leap at Meelick, above Lough Derg, and even a better one than at Castleconnell. There is a certain fascination in watching the big fish take the leap and make it. Sometimes a fish will fail once or twice. But another and a stronger effort whirls it like a huge half moon of golden green through the sunshine over the point where the glassy current breaks into a foamy torrent, and throws itself roaring down the fall. It is told in the old Irish legends that long ago there were men upon the world who could leap like a salmon. Cuchulain was one of them. On his great fight at the Ford of the Boyne this " hero leap " of his came frequently into play, and it was one of the means by which he could baffle and defeat his foes.

The red sun was sinking behind the mountains as I took to the wheel again. A few more miles now in the rosy afterglow, a hill or two, a long shaded downward gradient, then a spin along the level. I was on the sidewalk now running smoothly, and wondering if I would reach my journey's end before dark. I did it. A turn in the road brought me within view of the suburbs, and in the dew-laden gloaming I rode into Limerick. The cyclometer registered seventy miles, and I would not sell the tamest of them for a free pass on a railway.

CHAPTER XII.

Limerick the heroic—The city that takes life as it comes—Industrial Limerick—A queerly placed monument on Sarsfield Bridge—The Siege— Sarsfield's raid to Ballyneety—The old walls— "The Black Gate"—Sarsfield's fatal ingenuousness—The O'Connell Monument—George's Street—St. John's—St. Mary's—The founder of Limerick—The Limerick Dogs—Garryowen and " Johnny Collins'—Gerald Griffin—Lord Dunraven and the game of Poker.

After a hungry cyclist's supper at one of the hotels —and Limerick has some good hotels—I strolled through the city by lamplight. Next morning I was astir early and had made a tour of the principal streets before breakfast. I made several other tours during the day, and found much that was interesting at every other turn and crossing. It would have been the same if I had stayed for a week. Limerick is packed with great memories. It breathes history Even its very stone-heaps are eloquent. I crossed the river over and over again, strolled through Garryowen, and through the streets where the great Munster fair is held, out to the reservoir. I prowled around the old parts of the city, and through the more modern streets, visited all that is left of the walls, saw where the fighting was hottest, sat on the wharves of the river, rested beside the Treaty Stone, lounged on the bridges, stood at shop doors and at street corners looking at the faces of the passers-by, and when the time came for me to leave I was sorry. I arrived there prejudiced in its favour. Consequently I liked it to some extent before I saw it. I liked the imperfect view I got of it as I entered it in the gloaming. I liked it ten times better when I saw it in the light of day. I liked it better than ever when I was leaving it, not because I was parting from it, for I have told you I was sorry to go, but just because it had grown upon me.

And yet, as far as appearances go, Limerick is not a show place. It is a quiet old town, a good deal dilapidated here and there, not by any means tidy or methodical, not by any means over-clean, even in the most central streets, grim and grimy and sombre-looking, but very lovable I saw a youth of nineteen or twenty summers working mightily on the quays discharging cargo from a steamer. He was poorly clad; shirt and pants were quilted with patches; yet vigour was in his cheeks and laughter in his eyes; and he seemed ready for the worst that fortune might send him. He struck me as being, in a certain sense, the incarnation of the spirit of his native city. For Limerick, too, works hard, is careless of appearance, is apparently devil-may-care in many things, and defiant of fate Its defiance is not strident or theatrical. There is nothing blatant or melo-dramatic about Limerick at all. It seems to regard destiny with genial mockery, flinging a challenge from out its battered walls amidst a peal of musical laughter.

When you analyse your impressions of places you have seen, you often find them associated with some

particular colour—white or brown, or black, or sky-
blue, or yellow or red. Grey is the colour that rises
before me when I think of Limerick—dark grey,
steel grey, pearl grey, bluish grey. Its walls and
roofs and streets are grey. The morning sky over
it was grey. The wide river was thinly veiled with
greyish mist. There were grey hazes on the
Thomond fields and in the southern distances. But
this greyness is not the fading of age. I cannot
think of Limerick as being stricken in years. You
meet occasionally a man in the world who is independent of circumstances, who is superior to every
depressing and deprecating prank of adversity, who
is independent in thought, untamed in soul, in spite
of everything, who is out-at-elbows but unashamed—
a weather-beaten, healthy, lovable heroic kind of
tatterdemalion. Well, as with men, so with cities.
Each has an individuality. The individuality of
Limerick is that of the man I have described. At
least that is my impression of it. Another man may
go thither and find it a dudish, perfumed, fastidious,
starched, and hot-ironed individuality. I did not.

There is a good deal of industrial enterprise in
Limerick, although, of course, there is room for a
good deal more. There is a flour-milling industry.
The wheat is foreign but the millers are Irish, and
so, I was told, is the market for the output. There
is a thriving bacon-curing industry also carried on,
which gives constant employment to numerous hands.
I know also that there is a tannery. I saw the signboard over a door, and there were unmistakable
odours on the air. I was told that long ago the
Limerick leather trade was more important than at

present. I was sorry to hear this, although, doubt-less, a tannery is not a very fragrant next-door neighbour to have. I met large automobile vans in the suburbs, laden heavily with big cream cans, coming in from the country dairies. There is a big butter-making industry in the city, and it ought to be prosperous considering the constant supplies which it is able to procure under favourable conditions. There was a great lace-making industry long ago in Limerick. It went down in the disastrous industrial decline of Ireland under the Union. But the art of making the beautiful Limerick lace has not been lost, and I noticed a lace school during my rambles. May it succeed. May everything succeed that is honestly trying to create employment in Ireland, thus enab-ling many to make a decent living in their own country who have now to cross the sea to earn a living wage amongst strangers.

The shipping interests of Limerick are far from being what they once were. They are nothing like what they would be if Ireland were governed in the interests of the people of Ireland. When you see the splendid estuary, the wide stream, the spacious quays, the rich country behind the city, and then look at a steamer or two, and half-a-dozen schooners, and a few lighters where there should be scores of sea-going vessels, you realise that Ireland is a cap-tive nation, and that her captors robbed her of trade as well as of everything else but her faith and honour.

When I stood on Sarsfield Bridge first, it was on the night of my arrival. There was but a faint light from the gas lamps, but the partial darkness did not

hide a statue which stands behind the eastern battle-
ment with a cannon on each side of the pedestal.

"It will be the Sarsfield monument," I said in
my own mind, and resolved that I would revisit it
early next morning. The daylight revealed to me
the curious fact that this statue on Sarsfield Bridge
was not erected to Sarsfield or to any other Irish
patriot, but to some hussar officer of the English
army who took part in the charge of Balaclava. It
seemed wonderful just at first. The monument
itself did not impress me greatly as a work of art.
Like the fly in amber,

> It was not that the thing was rich or rare,
> You wondered how the devil it got there.

However, when your second thoughts began to work,
the location of such a monument in such a place was
soon explained. It was there for the same reason
that the monument to Dutch William stands before
the old Parliament House in College Green, Dublin,
for the same reason that a monument to Nelson
stands in O'Connell Street, Dublin. It is all part of
the scheme to Anglicise the Irish mind, to glorify
things English in Ireland, to make English heroes
the heroes of the Irish people, to accustom the Irish
patriot to the constant presence in his native land
of the rule and might and meanness of the Saxon.
This monument on Sarsfield Bridge was erected to
the memory of one Viscount Fitzgibbon, who was
probably some local landlord. In any case he was
certainly a man who never drew a sword for Ireland,
and never was loyal to her. The face, as portrayed

by the sculptor, is rather a weak one. But the brazen lips give an insolent message to Limerick all the same, which may be interpreted as follows :

"You called this bridge after a man who won glory for Limerick and for Ireland, but I am here to remind you of a man who drew the sword for your masters. You celebrate the military and civic fame of your city in the name you give this bridge, but I am here to remind you that neither the valour nor the genius of your sires sufficed to prevail against England. The name of this bridge stands for Ireland; I stand for England. I am here to glorify enlistment. I am a tout for the recruiting-sergeant. I am here because ye are partially tamed. I tell ye to be tamer still. Be peaceful through and through, and thank God ye are slaves. Come to heel, ye helots. Croppies lie down ! "

I found the Sarsfield monument next morning after considerable search. It stands beyond the Catholic Cathedral of St. John in the cathedral grounds upon a site granted to the trustees by the Right Rev. George Butler, Lord Bishop of Limerick. It is not inappropriately located, for it cannot be far from the place where the fighting on the wall was hottest. The monument itself can lay very little claim to be a triumph of art. It is not worthy of Sarsfield at all. But then the hero of Ballyneety needs no bronze or marble to perpetuate his fame. There is a park in Limerick ornamented by a lofty monument to some local magnate who represented the constituency once in the British Parliament. The pedestal upon which his statue is placed is many times higher than the Sarsfield monument. But the

fame of the Irish General will flourish centuries after
the name of the magnate shall have been forgotten.

I crossed the Thomond Bridge to the Clare side
of the river, and located as well as I could the encampment of Sarsfield's cavalry on that memorable
Sunday evening in the August of 1690. I laid my
bicycle against a wall, and leaning against the doorway of a roofless cabin, I called back the past into
the present. It is one of the privileges of rambling.
There are 38,000 English, Dutch, and Anglo-Irish
besiegers on the southern bank of the river, and they
are confident of a speedy victory. Dutch William
himself arrived from Cahirconlish yesterday and
spent the day marking out positions for his siege
artillery. There is a leaden war-cloud over Limerick,
and it appears to be only a question of hours when
the storm will burst upon the beleagured city and
sweep its resistance away. There are scarcely 10,000
men to guard the defences, and a great part of the
war stores, arms, and ammunition have been carted
off to Galway by those carpet soldiers—Tyrconnel
and Lauzun—who left the Irish lines confident that
the walls could be battered down "with roasted
apples." But Sarsfield and Berwick and De Boisseleau
have decided to remain and defend the city, and the
citizens—to their undying glory—have decided to
stand by them, come what may. Even now they are
out in their numbers, men and women of every rank
and age, with their children, helping De Boisseleau's
engineers to strengthen the defences. But there is a
siege train coming to the English from Waterford,
with guns strong enough to lay the city in ruins, and,
worse than all, there is a pontoon bridge coming

which, if placed in position, will allow William's forces to cross the Shannon and take the city in the rear. Guns, caissons, bridges, and stores are all together in the hills to the southward marching steadily to join the besiegers.

It is of this that Sarsfield has been thinking all day and all yesterday, consulting with De Boisse‹ leau, consulting with a few of his officers, consulting also with a certain Rapparee leader who has ridden in from the mountains, keeping his thoughts to himself mostly, this noble Sarsfield, but planning and preparing one of the most effective and splendid cavalry raids recorded in history. He has given certain orders now, and five hundred chosen riders are standing, bridle in hand, awaiting the word to mount. It is dark and late when the Chief swings himself on horseback and sends his commands quietly down the line. There is no bugle call, no roll of drum, no hoarsely shouted order flung from mouth to mouth by the squadron leaders. A half-whispered phrase in Irish—for Sarsfield and his troopers are Irish speakers—a low thunder of hoofs, and then, as silently as may be, they take themselves off into the darkness. They ford the Shannon at Ballvelly, and the dawn of Monday morning finds them on the march through Tipperary. Beside the General rides a guide whose fame is to go down to posterity He is the daring Rapparee horseman, known as " Galloping O'Hogan," who has the secret of every ravine in the Silvermines and every glen of the Keepers, who knows every ford and togher and boreen by heart, and who will conduct the Irish horsemen into the midst of the English convoy before a hoof-stroke is heard and before a blow is struck. Silently as possible out of the mountain passes, where a halt had been made to reconnoitre, silently as possible over the plains, quietly, steadily, surely, by wood and stream and hill, through the soft darkness, the dauntless cavalcade is riding into history. The watchword of the English was learned hours ago as the darkness fell. By a strange coincidence it is "Sarsfield." At three o'clock on Tuesday morning the great deed is done. The drowsy English sentry challenges and demands the countersign from the horsemen advancing over the picket line. It comes in a ringing voice, and accompanied by a sabre cut: "Sarsfield is the word and Sarsfield is the man." Five hundred chargers leap in amongst the sleepers, and five hundred thirsty sabres are at work amongst the panic-stricken soldiery who come hurrying from their tents. Through the camp and back again and once more from end to end sweep the riders of Limerick; and that is enough. The gunners are cut down, or flying, and the siege-train is at Sarsfield's mercy. He has the guns filled with powder and their snouts buried in the ground. The pontoons are heaped upon the overturned carriages and caissons, a train is fired, and the earth and sky for miles around are reddened with the flash with which the mass goes upward in scrap iron The thunder of the explosion bellowed into the English trenches before Limerick and brought William from his slumbers. Too late. The sentry reports that just now the sky was ablaze like the noonday; and William knows that the big guns and bridges, and his tons of powder and ball have oeen scooped up and destroyed. Five hundred men were despatched from William's camp last night to join the convoy; for some rumour that Sarsfield was abroad had been brought in. Two more bodies of horse are now sent forth to cut off the Irish cavalry on its return gallop. But the Rapparees are scouting along the hills, and O'Hogan himself is still with the squadrons of the victors. There are joyous cheers along the Shannon when evening comes, for all Limerick is out to welcome the heroes. The Irish guns beyond the river fronting the English batteries give tongue in a salute, and the very echo in the staunch old city is roused by the cannonade and the cheering as the troopers from Ballyneety come trotting in.

It was a glorious raid. What would you not have given to take part in it!

I went to St. John's Hospital and saw some of the old walls. There are a tower and gateway there which still show marks of the bombardment. There is a stone trough, too, and they call it after Sarsfield. The tower is part of the hospital, and the wall near it serves as part of one of the hospital buildings. Just outside the hospital grounds is another gate. They call it the " Black Battery " and also the " Black Gate." There was terrible fighting about here. On the 27th August ten thousand men were hurled by William at a breach which his cannon had made in the walls. The first onset was partially successful. Battalion after battalion was sent into the breach and the defence was broken down. The assailants poured into the city cheering for victory. But it was only then that their fight was beginning, although they looked upon it as ended. From every street and lane and bridge and passage came men and women, armed with whatever weapons they could find. They faced the cheering enemy, and a terrible street fight began. The blacksmith struck home with his sledge, the butcher with his cleaver, the labourer with his spade, the children threw stones from the windows, the women, armed with broken bottles and knives and staves, fought like furies through the English, down the streets, into the very breach, where they died beside the men. A few squadrons of Sarsfield's horsemen galloped across the bridges from the Clare side of the river and joined in the fray. Blood ran like water, and splashed red in the gutters. The streets were turned into shambles, but the fight went on and on. The English were forced to give way. Foot by foot they were pressed back to the breach and then through it, home to their entrenchments. The Irish pursued them into their very camp; but instead of continuing the slaughter of the routed foe they helped to extinguish the flames which threatened to consume the Williamite hospital. Some of the Irish even helped to remove the wounded from the burning building! Meanwhile the Brandenburghers have effected a kind of flank movement and are swarming over a battery near the breach. But the mine is ready for them and is fired at the right moment. The earth under the battery opens as if hell were bursting through from below, and in a sickening, hollow, deafening roar the ground is ripped to pieces and the storming regiment is hurled skyward, a mass of mangled corpses. Irish and

English stand as if spellbound for some seconds, and then an Irish cheer of triumph rings out along the walls. William cannot induce his soldiers to return to the assault next day, and in disgust goes back to England. The besieging army struck camp during the night and left Limerick in peace.

The victory so splendidly won was unfortunately barren in results. It was the fault of James and of his courtier creatures, Tyrconnel and Lauzun. Had the Galway garrison been ordered to stay, had the truth of the Irish situation been laid before Louis by James, the contemptible runaway from the Boyne, had the fight been for Irish freedom instead of for one of the worthless and faithless Stuarts, had Sarsfield been a negotiator as well as a soldier, then the history of Ireland would have had a different trend, God knows, through the centuries that have come and gone since the accursed Treaty of Limerick was made and broken.

Sarsfield was a soldier, but he was not a diplomat. He was fitted to be an Irish general, although he bore an English-made title, and although he had borne arms for England and had fought her battles. His heart was Irish, and his last words on the field of Landen, far away from Ireland, proved that he loved her well. But the man Ireland wanted then was a Sarsfield who could play the game. One hour of such a man after Limerick would have been worth a hundred of men taking clots of their hearts' blood in their hands on foreign battlefields, to say how much they wished it had been shed for Ireland. All honour to the brave and chivalrous soldier who defended Limerick. But, oh! if he had been

another Shane the Proud! A Shane would have
led a man like St. Ruth by the nose, or mopped his
tent-floor with him. He would also have conducted
the negotiations after the siege of 1691 so that there
would have been a loophole left open by which
advantage could have been taken of the altered
circumstances brought about by the arrival of the
French auxiliary expedition with money, arms, and
provisions.

The Treaty Stone is at the Clare end of Thomond
Bridge. It stands on a granite pedestal now, for
the souvenir-hunters were gradually chipping it
away. When the Treaty was signed on it, however,
it lay on the ground on the river bank, and around
it, on the morning of the 3rd October, Sarsfield and
his lieutenants met De Ginkell and the Lords Jus-
tices, and signed the solemn covenant which was
broken " ere the ink wherewith 'twas writ could dry."

Two days afterwards the Irish army marched out
and signified its choice to cross the seas and fight
under the flag of France. Within a week the French
relieving expedition arrived. But there was no
proviso in the Treaty for such a contingency.
Sarsfield said that even if a hundred thousand
Frenchmen offered to fight for Ireland now there
was nothing for it but to say that the fight could not
be—because the Treaty was signed He would keep
faith with England. So would Shane, but Shane
would have held out for guarantees. Shane would
have negotiated like a man who knew how to play
the game. Of course England never for a moment
meant to keep faith with Sarsfield. If Sarsfield had
been a Shane O'Neill he would have looked upon

this as axiomatic, and would have kept it steadily in view. As it was, he did not take it into account at all—for, alas! he was only a lion-hearted, splendid, chivalrous soldier, and knew nothing about the art of playing the game.

When the Treaty was broken— shamelessly and infamously broken— and when Ireland from end to end groaned, generation after generation, under the Penal Laws, it was only a very poor consolation to the downtrodden people to know that Irish valour was winning victories for other peoples, and that Irish genius was adorning the statesmanship of other nations.

Glory of the Irelands beyond the seas! Glory of the Irish in exile! Glory of the Irish race! Glory of the racial ideal! Of what good is it all to Ireland? The battle for Ireland must be fought in Ireland, by the people of Ireland. Every strong arm and every true heart that leaves Ireland is more or less a loss to Ireland, and this was as true after Limerick as it is to-day.

There is a monument to O'Connell in George's Street, by Hogan. The statue is very gracefully draped, but the treatment of the cloak is not very fortunate. The folds are twisted round the lower part of the figure, hampering the legs and feet. If the statue were draped as a Roman tribune or as a Grecian philosopher, this arrangement of the cloak might not be out of place, but in the broadcloth costume of the early nineteenth century it seems theatrical, exaggerated, and lacking in manly dignity. Foley's manipulation of the cloak is more adequate and convincing. As a matter of fact the monument over O'Connell Bridge is one of the great masterpieces of modern statuary, and does much to redeem the awful decadence of art that fell upon Ireland as one of the curses of her oppression.

I do not know what particular George gave his name to the principal street in Limerick. Probably it was one of the Georges who sat on the throne of England, and who hated Ireland It is a very fine street, this George's Street, and is unspoiled by tramlines. Limerick has yet to adopt the tram-car. Up to the present it has got along very well without it. Most of the big shops are on George's Street, but there are other important business streets. The industrial establishments are along the water front or in the outskirts of the city. The railway station is conveniently situated, being only a few minutes' walk from George's Street.

Speaking about the Georges of Hanover and England recalls another English sovereign in connection with Limerick. King John visited Limerick once upon a time—in the year 1210, to be more exact. He ordered a big castle to be built there, partly to commemorate his visit, and partly to overawe the Thomond people. The castle is still there on the southern bank of the river, looming over Thomond Bridge. It is the most perfect type of Norman military architecture in Ireland. It is in good repair, and is used as a barrack. King John was the only English monarch that ever visited Limerick, and for this small mercy Limerick is duly thankful. William of Orange was in the neighbourhood for a while, as we have seen, trying to gain an entrance into Limerick society, but he was disappointed.

The Catholic Cathedral of St. John's is a beautiful edifice. It is well situated, and its slender spire, which is 280 feet high, can be seen from many parts of the city and within a radius of several miles. The style is Gothic, but not of the flamboyant school, and very chaste and graceful in design. I confess to a feeling of relief whenever I meet a modern Irish church that departs from the stereotyped Gothic style. I was glad to hear of a church of the Irish style of architecture having been commenced in Spiddal, Galway, not long ago, because I regarded it as a straw on the ever-swelling current of Irish thought, as distinguished from English and foreign thought, which has so long held sway in Ireland. When I think of the ruined churches along the Shannon I know that we were on the road to create or evolve a distinctive school of architecture of our own when the calamities of the 12th century fell upon us. This school would not have been Gothic nor Norman nor Romanesque nor Greek. It would have been Irish. It would not have been an original school. Neither is the Gothic. Neither is the Greek. Perhaps the only original things in any architecture are the elemental things, the things suggested by the tent pole, the ridge pole, the doorway and whatever served as a roof. The Irish school of architecture would have been distinctive, inasmuch as it would have reflected the artistic temperament of our forefathers. We know by the relics of art that have come down to us from them that they had a keen sense of beauty. Their achievements in design, so far as they went, were marvellous. Their spirals and interlacings and treatment of colour have won admiration from all impartial critics of modern times. It is certain that they would have developed a wider sense of proportion and arrived at a truer estimate of values. Modern Ireland has done some very fine Gothic work, but the finer the work the more perfect is the imitation, and that is all that can be said for it. Imitation is not always good and is often bad. Gothic is very beautiful, but it would do Ireland no harm if she had less of it and more of her own. Anything, whether in art or industry or letters, that tends to make a nation self-centred is good. Once she is self-centred it is no harm for her to dabble in a little imitation. But self-reliance is never fostered by leaning on other people. The development of native art is an essential part of nation-building, and few arts can be made to have a more noble symbolism and a more fundamental influence upon taste than a native school of architecture.

St. Mary's was the old Catholic Cathedral of Limerick. It was wrested from the Catholics during the great sequestrations, confiscations, annexations, plantations, conciliations, undertakings, or whatever name you choose to give to the big steals and high-way robberies that the English perpetrated in Ireland. I think it was the same King Donald who built the Cathedral of St. Finnan, at Killaloe, that donated St. Mary's to Limerick. His right name was Domnal Mor. He was the last King of Cashel. He was the great-grandson of Tordelbach, King of Ireland, the first man who ever bore the name of O'Brien. Tordelbach O'Brien was the son of Tadg, who was the son of King Brian Borumha. When

Tordelbach called himself Ua-Briain (O'Brien), he meant to have it known that he was the grandson of the hero of Clontarf. Like his great and pious ancestor, the last King of Cashel was a church-builder on a kingly scale. Part of his tomb is still in the Cathedral. Doubtless the whole of it would be there only for the Cromwellian cavalry. Those puritanical vandals stabled their horses in the sacred edifice while they were in Limerick, and greatly defaced the tombs and other monuments with which the place was adorned. There is some fine wood-carving in the choir and nave, and the ruined cloister facing the street shows upon what an elaborate scale the building was originally designed.

It was St. Munchin who founded the first church in Limerick late in the sixth or early in the seventh century. He was named Munchin the Wise, and was of the Dalcassian race, being directly descended from the great Cormac Cas himself. He ruled in Mungret Abbey for many years, and then in his old age retired and built himself an oratory and cell which the people called Cill-Munchin, or the Church of Munchin. It was the beginning of Limerick. The city grew around the cell of the aged saint, as Cork grew around the oratory of St. Finnbar.

I strolled along the southern fringe of the city farthest from the river, struck out from a remnant of the old wall in Clare Street, and headed westward through a labyrinthine jungle of back lanes, alleys, and roofless houses. It appeared to be rather an exclusive quarter in a certain sense, and I doubted, after I had enmeshed myself in its sinuosities, that

the general public patronised it very extensively as
a place of recreation, or exercised the right of way
through it, if such a right existed. It was a bow-
legged dog with a fighting face that fixed this latter
conclusion upon me by coming forward with all his
hair standing and fire in his eyes, barking furiously
He was quickly joined by other dogs of excessive
lung power. They stripped their teeth at me and
advanced inch by inch, whether on a bluff or on real
business, I could not say. To retreat would have
been madness. To advance unarmed would have
been imprudent. To remain inactive would have
been to invite disaster. I therefore, in all modesty,
and on a very small scale, engaged in diplomacy.
In other words, I instigated and fomented a dog
fight. I said: "Catch him, Spot;" "Bite him,
Terry;" "Beat him, Lad;" "Choke him, William
the Third, or whatever your name is" (he was a
hook-nosed, select-looking, taciturn kind of dog
that did most of his vituperation inwardly, as it
were). I addressed the meeting in this strain for a
few seconds, after which the battle began with great
pomp and circumstance. One after another the
dogs went out of commission, howling with pain,
until only two champions were left—Lad and
William the Third. I left them, hoping that
William would get the worst of it. I came upon a
few inhabited houses in an alley farther on, and
asked what part of the city I was in. A woman leant
over a half door and told me kindly that it was
called "English Town." No doubt it was part of
the camp or works that had been occupied by the
English. I pursued my way uphill and made short

cuts over wastes of stone heaps. It was the lone-
liest ramble I have ever taken in any city. I have
prowled in the back streets of La Rochelle, Lisbon,
Funchal, Santa Cruz de Teneriffe, Pernambuco, and
Rio, but never felt so lonely as in " English Town "
in Limerick. It was not that I feared for my personal safety, but chiefly because there was no one
to menace it. I questioned the few people I met
regarding certain ruins which appeared to have been
at one time somewhat pretentious buildings. One
was an old jail, another the house of a former mayor,
another a mansion once inhabited by a local ship-
owner, and so on. They were all roofless, weed-
grown and windowless. Empty fire places and cut
stone lintels stared out upon the grey desolation
around them as if they were left to emphasise the
extent of the ruin which had been wrought. Most
of the roofless gables were of smaller houses. There
seemed to be whole streets of battered down cottages.
Apparently it was a residential quarter of the working classes in former years. It is the home of bats,
cats, and dogs now.

My next inquiry regarding my whereabouts
brought out the information that I stood in Garryowen. I was west of St. John's Cathedral now, and
on sloping ground I caught sight of a piece of green
sward farther away where some boys were playing.
They were doing what is known as a tailors' tumble,
a feat performed by holding your toes and going
head over heels down hill like a wheel. They stood
up at my approach, and replied to my good-morrow
cheerily.

" Where is Johnny Collins ? " I asked them.

They looked at each other, then at me, and then one of them answered :

" He isn't here ! "

" What Johnny Collins do you mean ? " I asked.

" I don't know," was the answer.

" Do you know any Johnny Collins, any of you ? " They shook their heads.

" Never heard of any Johnny Collins?   Come, now, think."

They thought for a while, and then one of them brightened up and said :

" Oh, I know now.   It's the man in the song."

" How does the song go, do you remember ? "

And he quoted instantly the lines referred to from " Garryowen " :

> There's Johnny Collins tall and straight,
>   He'd throw a bar of any weight
> From Garryowen to Thomond Gate
>   For Garryowen and glory.

He tapped his foot on the ground to the beat of the metre, and was doubtless thinking of the tune.

" Correct," I said, as he finished.   " And now, can any of you give me another verse ?   If you can it means gingerbread and apples——"

" I can," they all cried in chorus, interrupting me.

" Good," I said.   " Then this young man with the yellow hair will give me a verse."   And he did.

> Though Garryowen has gone to wrack,
>   We'll win her olden glories back.
> The night, long, starless, cold and black,
>   We'll light with song and story.

We adjourned to a place of their choice where the distribution of prizes took place. Crowning the slope above the field in which I met them was a green mound like a modern fort. They told me it was the reservoir. It used to be the execution ground, and the old gibbet or flogging triangle is there yet.

Gerald Griffin was a Limerickman, and there is a street called after him. I mentioned his name casually to several people. They had all heard about him, but only a few had read him or knew of his work in Anglo-Irish literature. He does not appear to have ever impressed the popular mind. His novels are scarcely read at all now. As for his poetry, outside of a few pieces, little of it is known. He lacked the deep intuition and the passionate love of country which breathe in Kickham's work, and which have made his name a household word in Tipperary.

I chartered a jaunting-car and drove round the city, holding desultory fragments of conversation with the driver, who was so well known in every district that half his time was occupied saying things to his friends. I asked him if there were any special place of interest within convenient reach of the city, and he offered to drive me to Adare on the most reasonable terms. Pretending ignorance, I asked him what was Adare.

" It's the place the pome was made about," he explained, cracking his whip. " Gerald Griffin, the man that one of the streets here is called after, wrote a pome about ' Sweet Adare,' sir, as he called it, and it's a grand place. Lord Dunraven, the man that made the Land Bill, lives there, sir. They call his place Adare Manor. Will we go out to it?"

"I have no time to-day. But, tell me, what kind of a man is Lord Dunraven?"

"Bedad, I don't know much about him, sir, except to see him now and then. He's a thin, spare, long-nosed, sharp-lookin' man. And they say he's fit to mind turkeys at a cross roads. I heard them talkin' about him th' other night in a bar down town, and one fellow—a commercial traveller it was—said that Lord Dunraven was one of the cutest men in Ireland, and that he got the soft side of the Mimbers of Parliament about the Land Bill. A very smart man, sir."

"I'll tell you what an American gentleman said to me a few weeks ago, sir, as I was driving him back from Adare."

"Had he spoken with Lord Dunraven?"

"No, sir, but I was telling him about the lord, and I think he had been readin' about him in the papers."

"And what did he say?"

"'Well,' says he, 'this Lord Dunraven ought to be a great poker player.' Do you know what kind of a game that is, sir?"

"I do," I said. "It is the game of life, in a sense, and, to borrow your own words, my friend, the man who can mind turkeys at a cross road would be just the man to play a good hand at poker. Will you pull up, please, or do you mean to drive me into the water?"

He was laughing so heartily that he took no notice of his horse, although the animal was making a swaying kind of progress along the quay which brought the car alarmingly close to the brink of the river.

I paid him his fare, and then prepared to start. In another hour I was beating to the north-eastward facing homeward through the Golden Vale.

CHAPTER XIII.

*Through Wexford—The Gael and the Gall—
Wexford history as told in the surnames—
Enniscorthy—Vinegar Hill—Forgetful Ireland
—Wexford's Gaelic earnestness—A distinguished
Irishman's position in his own country if he
happens to be a patriot—Labour and education
—The Slaney's sylvan beauty—On to Ferry
Carrick—Two landmarks of our history—Into
Wexford town.*

The more you see of Ireland the more cautious you
become about making any definite statement as to
which part of it is the most beautiful. You
may think Northern Connacht excels until you
have been in Donegal. You may think Donegal
supremely beautiful until you have seen the twilight
fading out of some of the valleys in the Midlands.
You may think the hush of a moonlit night in Westmeath the acme of romantic loveliness until you have
seen the sunrise gilding the Munster side of the
Shannon. You may look down upon the Golden
Vale and think that here at last is the gem of gems
of rural beauty, until you have stood on the Dublin
mountains and watched the morning mists rolling
seaward out of the Vale of Shanganagh. Here,
indeed, you may feel disposed to award the palm
until you have crept into the heart of the Wicklow
ranges.

And when you go into Wexford you have to re-consider the whole question, for Wexford also is beautiful—and not merely beautiful here and there, but beautiful from end to end. There are no wide plains or high mountains or brown boglands in Wexford. A chain of blue peaks wall it off from Munster, and the wooded hills of southern Wicklow divide it from the rest of Leinster.

It is about fifty miles long and twenty-four broad, and the river Slaney runs down the middle of it through wide and fertile valleys. The surface of the land rolls and dips on a generous, graceful scale. There are long and sweeping undulations embracing hundreds of square miles of excellent land, well wooded for the most part, and in the winding hol-lows which seam the country from the mountains to the sea coast the blue smoke hangs lazily over many a pleasant village and hundreds of comfort-able farmsteads. There are a few hills, some of them heather-crested, and some of them crowned with rock, but none of them rise to the height of a thousand feet above the level of the sea.

The land is fairly well divided between pasturage and tillage, although there might be more agricul-ture. Between pasturage and meadowing there is more land under grass than crops, but the difference is not so marked as in the richest districts of the Midlands. I met no Wexford hilltop in my rambles from which I could not see cornfields and wide patches of green crops. I noticed that the harvest appears to be rather earlier than in the Midlands or Ulster. I expect the climate is rather milder than in many parts of Ireland, for the range of mountains along the Barrow shield it from the wet clouds drifting upward from the south-west, while the Wicklow crests break the back of the north winds and catch the snow and rain to feed the silver streams.

Hy-Kinsellagh is one of the names by which Wexford was known in olden days, and the bards had always something pleasant to say of it. O'Heerin and O'Dugan, in their topographical writings, tell of its beauty. Hy-Felimy, on the sea coast, the chieftainry of the O'Murchadas or O'Murphy's, is described as "a delightful district—fair are the lands." You may note, in passing, that Wexford is the ancient centre of the widely-extended family of Murphy, which is a branch of the same race as the MacMurroughs, who were kings of Leinster.

Ferns, one of the Wexford towns, which gives its name to the bishopric, was a royal city, and knew Art MacMurrough O'Cavanagh, the head of his line. The Leinster kings had also a castle at Old Ross. The old topographers also mention the beauty of the country from the Barrow eastward to the Slaney. The barony of Shelburn, " from the dark pool of the fair shrubs," is praised by them. As for the barony of Forth, they lavish eulogies upon it. O'Heerin calls it " Forth of the corn, fair rising ground of strength and beauty. Then came the neighbouring chieftainry of Crioch-na-gCinel, " a delightful district in the land of the fertile soil, a country of the fairest under the sun." This territory lay near that of Fothart or Forth.

Bargy is now the name of the barony next to

Forth, and these two districts had a dialect of their own until comparatively recent years. Many of the people spoke it fifty or sixty years ago. It was neither Irish nor English, but a mixture of Flemish, Gaelic, and Saxon speech. D'Arcy McGee says it was the language in which Chaucer and Spencer wrote, and that the people retained many of the characteristics of their Saxon, Flemish and Cambrian ancestors.

We hear a good deal about Gael and Gall, now-a-days, and probably we hear a good deal too much about them. For my part I like best to hear the name of IRISH given to the children of Ireland, who love her and who give her the service born of love. Has not the gold of Gaelic and Gallic hearts been fused into an IRISH amalgam in the crucible of her woe! Let her sons and daughters, whether of Gaelic or Gallic extraction, have the honour of claiming her glorious name so long as their love is hers. And let the renegades be reviled as renegades, whether their blood be of the Gael or Gall.

Wexford is probably the least Milesian county in Ireland, but does its history teach us to regard it as the least Irish? Were the Wexford men who taxed to its utmost the military power of England in '98 all of Celtic origin? The pikemen of Oulart, and Ross and Vinegar Hill, and Scollagh Gap and of every other blood-stained field of the heroic campaign were for the most part farmers who were descended not from the Gael, but from the Gall. And had the men of the Gaelic counties done their part as the Wexford men did theirs, the end of the insurrection would have been different.

In the map showing the old principalities and
other chief divisions of the nation, as they existed
from the Eleventh to the Seventeenth century, you
will find the following names of the Gall among the
occupiers of Hy-Kinsellagh: Walsh, De Renzy, De
Prendergast, Butler, Talbot, Power, Rossiter, Mas-
terson, Morgan, Meyler, Furlong, Wadding, White,
Comerford, Devereux, Sutton, Stafford, Laffan,
Wyse, Redmond, etc., mixed up with the Milesian
clan names of O'Murphy, O'Doyle, O'Garvey,
O'Cosgrave, O'Dugan, and MacKeogh. Father
Kavanagh, in his "History of '98," gives a footnote
containing a list of the surnames of a Grand Jury
sworn in during the year 1873 in the town of Wex-
ford, as follows: Browne, Devereux, Furlong,
Power, Robinson, Sinnott, Cooney, Meehan, Roche,
Crosbie and Stafford. In the history of the country
you will also meet with such surnames as Cormick,
Godkin, Lambert, White, Codd, and Hervey.
Some of the outland stock came with Strongbow,
some from Flanders, some with Cromwell. But
Wexford assimilated most of them and made them
fiercely Irish.

In the southern baronies they evolved a dialect of
their own, as we have seen, but many of them in
the north and west of the county adopted the Irish
language, and their descendants were not the first
to lose it of the men of Ireland. I heard the other
day in Enniscorthy that there was a good deal of
Irish spoken in Wexford on the battlefields of '98.
And I learned also from my visit that the great-
grandchildren of the farmer patriots are heart and
soul in the Irish-Ireland movement. There are

nearly forty branches of the Gaelic League in Wexford, and most of them are in the farming districts. In no non-Gaelic speaking county, and probably in no county of Gaelic speech, has the language movement been taken up with the earnestness and manliness with which the farmers of Wexford have thrown themselves into the work of de-Anglicising Ireland.

I was glad to visit Enniscorthy for many reasons, and sorry that I had to leave it so soon. It is a pleasant, hospitable, cheerful, thriving town, and sits cosily astride of the Slaney under the sheltering hills. Some of the streets are very steep, and there are some quaint old houses. There is a castle in the centre of the town which is modernised and inhabited by a gentleman who rents it from the lord of the soil.

I have a bad memory for the titles of Clan London, but I think the foreign noble who owns Enniscorthy is called Lord Portsmouth. If that is not his title I give it up. He owns Vinegar Hill also, and I was informed that he had refused permission to the people of Enniscorthy to erect a monument thereon to the memory of the men of '98.

I heard that two influential Irish Members of Parliament were to approach this lord and try to obtain his sanction to the raising of the monument. This news was depressing. It appeared very sad to me that two representative men of Ireland should have to ask permission from an English noble to erect a monument to Irish patriotism upon an Irish battlefield. A grim sarcasm, it seemed, upon a century of conciliation! --an eloquent commentary on a century of Talk!

I heard something also about fifty pounds having been promised to the monument fund on the condition that the monument should be a round tower; and I found myself hoping fervently that Enniscorthy would build something more worthy in memory of the heroes of '98. There is a round tower near Wexford town erected to the memory of English soldiers (Irish by birth, alas!) who fell fighting for England. Why should a replica of this architectural curiosity be raised in honour of Irish soldiers who fell fighting for Ireland? In Glasnevin Cemetery there is a round tower erected to the memory of a man who said that the liberty of Ireland was not worth a drop of blood. Why should a like emblem rear its head to honour the memory of patriots who believed that liberty was worth the best blood in the veins of the people, and who shed it in torrents to show that they inherited the instincts of freemen? The true symbolism of the round tower is difficult, if not impossible, to ascertain, but even if it is to be universally accepted as bearing a religious significance, its place in art is removed from things which appeal to the warrior emotions. The poetry of all symbolism lies in its appropriateness as well as in its truth; and if we misinterpret or misapply the canons of an art, however noble or however lowly, we only achieve its degradation. If, then, the round towers are of Irish Christian origin, their shadows fall like daily blessings across the ruins of the desolated abbeys and convents of Erin, and they appropriately sentinel the places made sacred by the prayers and graves of the saints who filled our land with the love and glory of God before the demons of profanation and rapine came to desecrate and plunder and slay. But Ireland has to honour the martyrs who suffered for fatherland as well as those who were sacrificed for her faith,' and hence it is that Vinegar Hill is worthy of a monument which shall be symbolic of civic heroism, and which shall speak from the past to the present and the future with an eloquence to sustain the courage of the patriot and shame the submission of the slave.

Enniscorthy was one of the storm centres of '98, and paid dearly for that tempestuous distinction. There is a certain sadness always in the thought that you are standing in a street through which rolled the tide of war. You cannot help thinking of the non-combatants, for it is to them more than to the fighters that war is hell. When I recalled the street fighting in Enniscorthy of '98 it brought me back the memory of carnage witnessed in the streets of a distant city of the South during the tragic days of a civil war. I had seen fighting men fall in scores; but they fell with arms in their hands, and their end did not strike you as being so terrible as the deaths of peaceful people who were shot down by accident. The fate of the soldier who falls in battle may be sad, but it is a tragedy that has, in a certain way, been discounted. The soldier goes out to kill or to be killed, and he knows what he has to expect, more or less. He has made his covenant and must abide by it. That is the stern rule of the game of war for the fighting man. It is brutal, terrible, yet not unjust. But the gasp of the stricken woman, or the unarmed man or boy, the pitiful look of pain and amazement, the sickening thud against the cobble-stones as they fell, the choking cough, and the welling blood are things that shriek to Heaven of injustice cruel and awful, and they remain in the memory for ever. They are also in the fortune of war : " Woe to the conquered." Enniscorthy saw its share of such carnage, felt the sting and the flame of such injustice, and the blood of its slaughtered innocents drenched the fire of the Rebellion.

It was after the farmers of Boolavogue and their neighbours from the surrounding districts under " Father John " had drawn first blood in their victory at Oulart that they took Enniscorthy. They marched thither by Carrigrew, and Camolin, and Ferns, and made a rallying halt at Balliorell Hill, where they were joined by Father Michael Murphy with a contingent of stalwarts from the parish of Ballycanew. Enniscorthy was held by several corps of yeomanry, by some of the infamous North Cork Militia, and by a considerable force of armed loyalists. The patriots attacked by the Duffrey Gate, on which three roads converge. The gate was defended by several corps of yeomanry, who occupied a position of exceptional strength. The river Slaney protected them from a flanking movement on one side and the town walls on the other. The insurgents were obliged to make a frontal attack. As they marched up the road towards the gate the cavalry of the defenders swept out upon them, but the riflemen of the storming party split their ranks by leaping into the ditches, out of which they poured a volley into the squadrons of baffled troopers. The main body of the insurgents were a little

to the rear of the riflemen and were waiting for them
to open the gate.   But this was no easy task, for it
was a death-trap, and the only thing the advanced
guard of the insurgents could do was to hold the
defenders at bay and prevent them from sallying
out in force.   It was at this crisis that Father John
Murphy's natural military genius gave a striking and
original proof of its resourcefulness.   He ordered a
round-up of all the cattle in the neighbourhood,
drove the herd into the road before the pikemen and
down at full speed upon the soldiers that guarded
the gate.   The animals were goaded on by the pikemen who followed close behind them, sheltered by
the moving barricade of beef.   The forces of his
Majesty of England fired a volley or two into the
bellowing herd, but the cattle were maddened by
the yells and the pike prods of the men behind, and
dashed forward with irresistible fury, trampling all
before them.   The loyalists fled from the gate and
entered the houses along the street, out of which
they kept up a destructive fire upon their assailants.
But the insurgents were determined to win, so they
attacked the houses one after another, breaking open
the doors and piking the soldiers or putting them to
flight.   At this juncture another insurgent force
appeared beyond the town on Vinegar Hill.   The
suburbs were already in a blaze, the houses having
been fired by the townspeople who were in sympathy
with the insurgents.   The dashing body of men
whom Thomas Sinnot of Kilbride had led across the
Slaney, some miles to the northward, came charging
into the streets, and the men who had rushed the
Duffrey Gate were making headway against all

resistance. The loyalists broke away and ran towards Wexford, burning the homesteads and slaying the defenceless people on their way, as was their inhuman and cowardly custom. The pikemen did not remain long in the town after their victory. When they had secured their spoils of arms and ammunition and liberated their comrades who were in prison, they marched out of the blood-stained streets and smoking suburbs and encamped on Vinegar Hill.

From photographs and maps of Enniscorthy which I had seen, I had come to think that Vinegar Hill lay some distance from the town, but I was mistaken. The summit is within earshot of the suburbs and within rifle reach of the central streets. Vinegar Hill rises from the Slaney's banks, and part of Enniscorthy is built on the lower slope. The crest is flat topped and covered with thin grass, mixed with heather and stunted whins. I plucked some of the heather to send to certain Wexfordmen far away. There is the ruin of an old windmill in the centre of the small plateau which was occupied by the insurgents. On one corner of the crest the rock strata rise slantingly out of the heather and form a little peak, and this is the highest part of the hill. I stood there in the glory of a bright September morning and took a good long look over the wide ridges and rolling plains of Wexford and down the pleasant valley of the Slaney I shall never forget it The sunlight streamed down between scattered patches of cloud and fell upon the masses of vapour which the South wind was rolling from off the fields and streams and woods. Miles and miles of fertile land well streaked with the track of industrious cultivation were visible on every side, thinly veiled, or faintly blurred by the soft transparencies which tinted the fragrant earth with shimmering gamuts of colour, from opal green to amber, from frosted silver to pearl grey, and from chestnut brown to burnished gold.   It was a picture which would have impressed me by its superlative beauty at any time, or seen in any land, but the historical glamour of its " glorious pride and sorrow ' made its natural loveliness doubly fascinating.   The friend who accompanied me knew its story from end to end, and pointed out the direction in which lay each hallowed place.   There were dim shapes looming over the shrouded horizon, or through the far off woods, and there were tracts of smiling country seen through rifts in the shifting haze; and one by one he told me their names—Forth Mountain, Carrickburn, Scollogh Gap, Three Rocks, and Ferry Carrick, and the hills over which tower the spires of Wexford. " Taghmon is nearer to us, to the right of Wexford," he went on, " and Scullabogue is under Carrickburn, and Ross is far off to the West.   Down beyond the Slaney is Killaughran of the woods, and to the east, just beyond the blue ridge of hills, is Oulart, and here to the northward is the road to Tubberneering and Gorey, and to the west of Gorey you have Ballyellis, and northward on the coast is Arklow."   He had the map of Wexford at his fingers' ends, and knew the direction of every battlefield in the county and its history as well.

Looking down from Vinegar Hill on the open country below, you could not help wondering how

the Wexfordmen of '98 kept up the fight so long
There are no natural facilities for guerilla warfare.
The wide valleys and low ridges could be swept by
cavalry, and there is no protection from infantry
or artillery fire. The insurgents were almost desti-
tute of small arms, and although they had an
artillerist of the first rank in Esmond Kyan, he had
no cannon except a few pieces taken from the enemy,
and some old guns of little value to face the powerful batteries opposed to him. Had there been even
a few barrels of gunpowder on Vinegar Hill the
day of the battle, the two thousand rifles of the
Wexfordmen would alone have sufficed, without
artillery, to change the course of history.   Still
it was a wonderful fight.   Over a dozen picked
English generals at the head of 20,000 troops concentrated round the hill with artillery to shell the
farmers from their trenches, infantry to shoot them
at close range, and cavalry to cut off a retreat.   Yet
for hours the pikemen held their ground against the
formidable array, and in the end made good their
retreat towards Wexford with the loss of comparatively few of their number.   There were, indeed,
many Irish people killed on Vinegar Hill and in
the fields below it, but they were non-combatants.
The English soldiery glutted their rage and hate on
the defenceless people and butchered them in hundreds.   It was the old, old story—war on the women
and children and old men—a massacre in one century, farm burnings and concentration camps in
another.   And then, as John Mitchel said, the ear
of the world to explain it all away.

    The non-combatants who were on Vinegar Hill

during the battle should, of course, have been in their houses, and they certainly would have remained at home were it not that they would have been in more danger of destruction therein than in the camps of their armed kinsmen. A long series of burnings and murders and infamies had driven thousands of the defenceless peasantry under the only protection left to them—the army of their people. There is no need to quote a single Irish historian to prove this. Pro-English writers, like Gordon and Hay, place the matter beyond all doubt or question. When the fighting men of Wexford county retreated from Vinegar Hill, after the hard fought day, General Lake gave orders for the insurgent hospital to be burned. His infamous command was infamously obeyed, and the wounded inmates were burned to death. All the wounded picked up on the field and all that were discovered in the houses were slaughtered. The yeomanry were let loose on the non-combatants, who were fleeing in all directions from the hill; and the fields and roads were reddened by the inhuman butchery. It was the old, old trick of "conciliation," the same that was played at Mullagmast, at Drogheda, Wexford, at "the Croppies' Grave," and the Gibbet Rath. A most deadly and effective conciliation! A most wondrous and devilish kind of moral suasion!

Oh, wise apostles of denationalisation that kept the study of Irish history out of the "National Schools!" Well, indeed, may the Plunketts and Dunravens entreat Ireland to forget! And well may the Irish men and women who hate the slavery of their country tell her people that it is right to

remember.   It is because Ireland's memory is so short
that we see Sir Horace Plunkett gracefully waving
his big spoon of political souperism and unctiously
carrying on an insidious loyalist proselytism in the
shape of certain beggarly doles or bribes drawn
from the millions of surplus taxation which are
wrung from the country every year by England.
Ireland has been given every facility for forgetting,
and the only wonder is that she has remembered at
the eleventh hour that she has a soul to lose or save.

I had a card of introduction to Father P. Murphy,
of the House of Missions, in Enniscorthy, but we
had already met in Dublin at the Oireachtas, and
I was right glad to shake hands with him again in
his native county.   The House of Missions, of which
he is a resident priest, was founded many years ago
by a former Bishop of Ferns for the purpose of
maintaining priests of the diocese as missioners.
The priests of the House of Missions are secular
clergymen, living in community, and their principal
work is the giving of missions in their own diocese.
They have chaplaincies in the town of Enniscorthy,
and they also give missions in other dioceses than
their own, but their chief field of action is in their
native county.   They are a most zealous body of
men, and have always been beloved by the people.
Indeed, the main object which their founder had in
view when he instituted them was to make sure that
the diocese should always have a body of missioners,
between whom and the pastors and people there
would be the closest sympathy.

The Gaelic League in Wexford county owes much
to young Father Murphy. He gave great assistance

to Michael O'Sullivan when that unforgetful Irishman raised the standard of Irish Ireland in Enniscorthy a few years ago.   Father Murphy was then
but recently returned from Rome, where he had
studied for ordination.   He has not forgotten the
language of Dante, and during the visit of Cardinal
Vannutelli to Dublin he co-operated with Dr.
Douglas Hyde and Miss Mary E. L. Butler in
writing an address in Italian to the Papal Legate.
It may be remarked, in parenthesis, that you will
meet superior persons, at home and abroad, who tell
you that the Gaelic League is an organisation
governed by a body of narrow-minded cranks, who
are crazy about Irish because it is the only language
they know anything about.   This is worth a smile
any day in the year, for there is a deal of humour
in it.   You can find French, Latin, German, Spanish
and Italian among the men and women who have
made the Gaelic League, and as for the Sacs-beurla,
I doubt that there has been such masculine and
nervous English written in Ireland since the days
of the Young Irelanders as has been used by Irish-
Ireland propagandists.

I had often wished to meet Grattan Flood, whose
name I had seen so frequently mentioned in connection with Irish-Ireland musical and literary work,
and was right glad to have the pleasure of a hand
shake from him in Enniscorthy, where he has his
headquarters.   He is a walking mine of Irish erudition, and is in his element in his library, which is
one of the most extensive of its kind in Ireland.
He is a man whom you cannot meet without learning
something from, yet he carries his erudition easily.

He was busy just then putting the finishing touches to his great history of Irish music, which had occupied him off and on for over twenty years. He has yet to see middle age, so that much valuable literature may yet be expected from him. In a rightly-governed Ireland, such men would be on educational boards or in university chairs, or, under the auspices of the State, sifting out the national history from ancient records and State papers. It is an exasperating thing to think that Ireland is the only nation in Europe, or, for that matter, in the civilised world, in which every one but a patriotic citizen may aspire to the right of a place in the public service which his talents and virtues entitle him to hold. Ireland is the only nation in which the public servant gains preferment by hostility to the people, if he is an alien, and by treason to his country, if he is a native. It is the only nation in which civic courage inspired by love of native land is ostracised from official life, and in which the renegade is at a premium,

Unprized are her sons 'til they've learned to betray,
    Undistinguished they live if they shame not their
        sires,
And the torch that would light them through
        dignity's way
    Must be caught from the pile where their country
        expires.

But after all, Moore, although he was right in the main, slightly overstated a historical truth. For no matter to what extent the men of compromise and

barter may be rewarded or honoured by their pur-
chasers, they have always been reviled by the people
whom they betrayed; and there has always been a
smile of love on the face of our *Roisin Dubh* for the
man without a price.

We cycled to Wexford along the Slaney side, and
it proved to be a most delightful journey. The road
is wide and smooth all the way, and runs through
beautiful scenery. There are some bends of the river
below Enniscorthy, which are particularly fine, and
there is one long reach leading from the turn where
the stream is broad and placid, and fringed with
thick woods which clothe the hills on either bank to
their very summits. It is one of the fairest pictures
I have seen anywhere. A small cargo steamer plies
between Wexford and Enniscorthy, and there are
several lighters. We met a few of them coming
slowly up stream, with big sails flapping in the lazy
wind. We overtook a lighter homeward bound to
Wexford, sliding down the current before the pro-
pulsion of two long poles, which a pair of stalwart
navigators handled in exactly the same way as the
sail boats are driven up or down the streams in the
Delta of the Parana when the wind fails or is un-
favourable. The boatmen stand on the prow, plunge
their poles into the river bed, and then pressing
them with their shoulders, march aft to the very
stern. There was a fire on the afterdeck, and it
threw wreaths of smoke into the air. The cooking
was attended to by a boy who whistled " The Top
of Cork Road " like a prize blackbird, as he raised
the lid of the pot and examined the contents with a
critical eye.

There is a great scarcity of farm labourers in Wexford. The labouring people go in considerable numbers to Wales to the mines. Many girls go to England to look for employment. Others go to the United States. Thus it happens that any farmer who has not help in the members of his own family is handicapped in tilling his land. It will take some time in killing the mania of emigration in the labouring class of Ireland. I mean in that considerable portion of the labouring class that could very well stay at home. A good system of primary education, national in the true sense, and embracing a certain degree of industrial training would do much. But Ireland has no chance of obtaining such a system of education unless she adopts some more strenuous policy than passing resolutions. In the first place, England, even if so inclined, is hardly qualified to give Ireland the education suited to her needs, for the English system is admittedly backward and disjointed. In the next place, even if England were on an educational equality with the most progressive nations, she would not willingly re-model the State schools of Ireland on Irish lines. The system of education which would do most for Irish talent would, in the very nature of things, foster a strong, self-contained, practical national spirit. The growth of this spirit would make the English position in Ireland more difficult day by day, and there is not the slightest doubt that England will cling to that position until she is forced to abandon it. It is, therefore, improbable that she will voluntarily do anything calculated to weaken what she is determined to maintain. We are told, of course, that

Home Rule is coming. We were told it thirty years
ago, and we are told it to-day. And yet it doe
not come. Nor will it come as the result of a worn-
out system of Parliamentary agitation which is at
death's door. It will come when Ireland, by her own
effort, makes England fear her—and not until then.
All the Devolution and Conciliation and " step-by-
step" scheming that could be hatched in a century by
Dublin Castle officials would not be worth one hour
of independent government to Ireland. I was told this
over and over again in Wexford as well as in every
other part of Ireland where I could manage to feel
the pulse of popular opinion. I found no real spirit
of surrender anywhere I found, and it seemed to
me that any impartial observer could find, a national
sentiment amongst the people, passive at times, indeed, but still in existence. It would appear that
the right policy for the men who are entrusted with
the guidance of national opinion should be to rouse
that feeling into a warmer enthusiasm, and not to
chill it by disillusion after disillusion. But even
despite the bad effects of countless disillusions
Ireland is not yet in a mood to accept the role of a
conquered nation. Thus it is that all the drumming
we hear about the statesmanship of accepting a
settlement of our national claims on a basis of
something like sixpence in the pound cannot be
called edifying. If it comes from sincere pessimism
it is still shameful. If it is not the outcome of
honest misjudgment it is knavery, and it may be
both knavish and craven.

I found a very strong Irish-Ireland feeling in
Wexford. I was told that Wexford has over forty

branches of the Gaelic League. Several intelligent
and thoughtful men spoke to me about the Sinn
Fein movement. They were strongly in favour of it.
I may state that it was not in Wexford alone that I
met with this feeling. It is finding favour with
independent thinkers throughout the length and
breadth of Ireland. The policy of refusing to
recognise the Union of 1800 as legal, and of standing firm upon the still extant Constitution of 1783,
is assuredly winning adherents day by day in
Ireland, not, by any means, as the ultimate solution
of the Irish national question, but as the best thing
that can be done under present circumstances.
"What recommends it most to me," said a County
Councillor of the Midlands, when we were discussing it, " is that it would unite in the one organisation
the stalwarts, or, as some call them, the extreme
Nationalists, and the Constitutionalists, and until
we have strong Nationalists with us we will not
count for much."

Some miles below Enniscorthy the road leaves the
Slaney and bends slightly to the east through a fine
expanse of wooded uplands and tidy farms. We
met a farmer's cart on the road bringing home a load
of coal, which is the chief fuel in Wexford. Where
coal is not used the people generally burn wood.
There is scarcely any bog in the county, so that a
turf fire is rare. The coal burned is not Irish. I
understand it is cheaper to bring it over from Wales
by steamer than to bring it a few miles by rail from
Kilkenny. We pass two or three schools along the
road where Wexford children are learning Irish—
healthy, sturdy, red-cheeked bright-eyed children

they are, and full of life. We pass Oylegate and
Kyle, two neat hamlets, with ivy-grown cottages
and shady trees.   There is corn drawing going on in
some townlands and hay drawing in others, and one
early ploughman is finishing a few acres of stubble.
Then a long, easy incline takes us to the top of a
wide hill, from which we come once more into view
of the river.   It has ceased to be a gentle stream,
fringed by tall sedges and rushes, gliding smoothly
through the shady woods.   It is a broad sheet of tossing wavelets now with long welts of cloud shadows
lying on it, and flashing brightly where it catches
the sunbeams.   It widens still more in the distance,
and there are sail boats on it beating up stream.
The southern bank is steep and rocky, but northward
the land slopes gently away into the bluish horizon,
cut by intersecting hedgerows into patches of dotted
cornfields and meadows and pastures.   We spin
down the gradient on an unbraked free-wheel run,
and halt for a few minutes at Ferry Carrick, at
the bridge.   Woods and ivy-clad bluffs overhang
the Slaney here on either bank, and the stream is
wide and strong.   The river is tidal up to this point
and is of considerable depth at high water—although
it shallows greatly round the bend north of the
bridge   The bridge is an old-fashioned structure,
and is probably one of the oldest of its class
in Ireland.   On the southern extremity of it there is
a section which is opened by machinery for the sail
boats and the larger river steam craft.   On the
northern bank, built high up on the rocky bluff,
stands an old Norman castle erected by FitzStephen,
it is said to be the oldest Norman keep in Ireland.

Facing it on the opposite bank, on a high hill, is a
Round Tower erected to the memory of certain Irish-
born soldiers of England who fell in the Crimean
War.   Only the river between them, yet, oh ! the gulf
of time which separates them when you consider them
as landmarks in the accursed history of our sub-
jection.

We crossed the bridge, turned to the left along
the southern bank of the Slaney, and in a few
minutes were in Wexford town.

CHAPTER XIV.

Wexford Town—No Commercial Shoneenism worth noticing in Wexford—The Main Street—Father Kavanagh, the Historian of '98—Industrial Wexford—Doyle's—Pierce's—Back to Enniscorthy and away.

Wexford is a town that works and prospers, and it has the look of a place that enjoys life and minds its business. There is nothing of the sooty workshop in its appearance. The current of its street life runs smoothly. There is no frantic haste and no loitering. The people seem to pay more attention to industry than to fashion, yet they are by no means sour-tempered. There was good humour from end to end of the Main Street, and plenty of business.

I liked the Main Street best. It is not by any means the handsomest street in Wexford, nor the widest, nor the straightest, nor the brightest. It is a very old street—narrow, crooked, and dark. There is an ancient suggestiveness about it which carries the imagination back into far-off centuries and reminds you that Wexford has led the cosmopolitan life of a seaport for many ages. Its shipping has, however, dwindled in modern days. There is a bar at the harbour mouth which shallows the water to a few feet at times, and ocean steamers are therefore precluded from the trade of the port except by means of lighters, and lighterage does not appear to hold out many inducements to Wexford shipping circles. The coasting trade is small and is shrinking. There is a Wexford schooner fleet in existence, but its fortunes are none of the brightest.

Fifty years ago, however, Wexford was a great schooner port. One owner alone had a fleet of ninety-nine sail. He would have had many more were it not that there was some law or some ancient charter which made an owner of a hundred ships liable to certain imposts or services, and, I think, one stipulation was that a man-of-war, fully rigged, had to be given to the English Sovereign. The owner of the ninety-nine schooners was rich enough to make presents of sloops-of-war, but he was a modest man, and never qualified for the honour of building his hundredth schooner. And it is said that his wife was a woman after his own heart, who did not care for titles. He traded with Russia and put his profits into the bank, and died a common person, while ambitious distillers and grocers and fishermen put their thousands into patents of nobility and left their progeny an aristocratic heritage of distinction, which consisted mainly in the gentle art of spending money, unaccompanied by the ability to earn anything but the envy or contempt of mankind You must not think, however, that these ambitious traders who died in the purple were Wexfordians. So far as I could learn the town has never produced a porter earl, or a treacle baronet, or a car grease knight. The names over the shop doors are all plain ones. There is *not* even the stump of a handle to any of them.

"And have you no merchant nobles at all?" asked of the friend who accompanied me as we cycled down the street.

"No," he replied, with the sweetest simplicity, "the merchants of Wexford are of a good average decency."

"And have you no Royal wine merchants by special appointment?"

"None at all."

"Nor any *Honi soit qui mal y pense* bakers?"

"Indeed we haven't."

"Nor any *Ich dien* chandlers."

"Well, no," he replied, with another touch of Wexfordian simplicity. "As a rule commercial shoneenism is far less rampant here than in other places."

And yet Wexford is a thriving town. It is, I consider, the most thriving town of its class in the whole of Ireland, for, although its shipping has decayed, its industries have prospered. There are three important machine factories in the town, all working on Irish capital, and I heard of some minor industries besides.

We passed the old market square in which the Cromwellian butchers massacred 200 Wexford women, and continuing our ride followed the winding streets until we reached a more modern quarter of the town. There are two landmarks of Wexford which are at first a little confusing, and these are the Twin Churches. They stand only a few hundred yards apart and are exactly alike. They are Catholic churches, and are fine specimens of ecclesiastical architecture. They are the principal

Catholic churches of the town, and are conveniently and picturesquely situated. Their spires overtop the ridge which runs along the southern bank of the Slaney from above Ferry Carrick in the direction of the harbour, and are visible for some distance along the Enniscorthy road. From the summit of Vinegar Hill they may be seen on a clear day, and from the heights over the valley of the Slaney they mark the river's mouth.

The Franciscans have a fine monastery in Wexford, a shaded, quiet old place standing back from the street, with a spacious esplanade in front. We called at the monastery for a special purpose; it is the residence of Father Kavanagh, the historian of '98, and I had gone to Wexford to shake hands with him. He was at home, and when he was told we wished to see him, he came to us immediately. He was clad in the brown Franciscan habit which has been worn by many a patriotic Irish monk, and by none more warmly attached to his native land than the one who shook hands with us so cordially and welcomed us to Wexford. He has carried his love for Ireland all round the world—from Wexford to Rome, from Rome to Sydney, and from Sydney back to Wexford, and he will carry it with him to Heaven. The years sit lightly upon him, for his heart is young. Hardy of frame, above the middle height, well knit and with keen eyes and firm mouth, he looks like a man who would glory in combat for the right. There are men who appear to have been destined by nature to be champions of the truth in the field of intellectual conflict and Father Kavanagh is one of them. Before you have been speaking to him many minutes you can see that underneath his natural simplicity and courtesy and kindliness of manner, and the large charity which tempers all his thought, there are an iron strength of character and an invincible courage, and you can realise how it is that the quiet, self-contained, unassuming man before you has said some of the manliest words that have been spoken in Ireland for thirty years. This fact is worthy of notice, because it is a direct negative of the theory we so frequently meet that there is no sanction in theology for anything but the surrender of national principle, so far as the Irish Catholic is concerned Father Kavanagh has preached the doctrine of nationhood, and he has not been brought under ecclesiastical censure for so doing. It is said of him that he has failed to make many friends in high ecclesiastical circles, but this shows, to say the least of it, that he has not escaped censure because of having had friends at court. He has held his own because he spoke the truth and nothing but the truth, and because he uttered it, not in malice or in vanity, but in all charity and singleness of purpose. When he launched the thunderbolt which hindered recruiting for the English army in Ireland in the early days of the Boer War, he took a step which, if it were indefensible on moral grounds, would most assuredly have brought him into trouble.

Although Father Kavanagh is an ardent patriot, he is one of the most devoted of churchmen, and even those who differ most widely from him in secular matters respect him as a zealous and priestly missionary. I am proud to have met him. I had

long regarded him as an ideal type of Irish
ecclesiastic, and I knew as I left him that it is as
such I shall always think of him—an Irish priest
who, no matter in what position he might be placed,
would defend the Church against all enemies, yet
who would at all times be a patriot; and who would
never, under any circumstances, persuade himself or
allow himself to be persuaded, that the high and
permanent interests of the Catholic Church in Ireland could be advanced by disloyalty to the Irish
Nation.

The clang of iron upon iron came from a gateway
opening upon one of the streets through which we
were passing.   It was the entrance to Doyle's
machine factory, and we decided to have a look at
native enterprise in action.   We were soon in the
hands of the manager, who expressed himself quite
pleased at our visit, and kindly accompanied us
through the shops.   We saw mowing machines in
various stages of construction—also turnip cutters,
cake crushers, threshing machines, horse rakes and
plows.   Doyle's mower is akin to the "Walter A.
Wood."   The gearing is the Walter A. Wood patent
modified.   Wood complained that Doyle copied
his American patent, but he in turn copied the Irishman's improvements, so they are about quits.   The
Doyle machine is an excellent cutter, and is of light
draught.   I noticed that the driving wheels were of
different sizes in different machines, and asked what
this meant.   The manager said that it meant only
the difference in the tastes of customers.   The high
driving wheel has no advantage over the low one
The draught is just as heavy or just as light with

one as with the other. The mowing season was over, and consequently the factory was for the time being devoting most of its attention to another class of machinery, viz., the cutters, pulpers, and crushers for the winter hand-feeding of stock. Long rows of these machines were being prepared to send out to the agents, and there were many indications of busy times. Doyle's factory gives employment to upwards of a hundred operatives. There are several Irish speakers in the shop; instead of going to America they went to Wexford. Instead of crossing the sea to work in mines or factories in the United States, they went to work in an Irish factory. If the right proportion of the land of Ireland were under tillage, and if a native government were in existence to foster native industry, there would be room in Ireland for many factories such as Doyle's. The natural overflow of rural population in any well-ordered country finds its way to the industrial centre—that is, to the town. At present America is the town of Ireland. It is on the wrong side of the ocean, and must be brought home. God forbid that we shall ever see the sky of Ireland filled with factory smoke, and the fair face of the land black with factories, as in many parts of England! But Ireland should have factories enough to supply her own wants, and farmers enough to feed the factory hands. At present she has not factories enough to supply her own demand; she is feeding the factory hands of England, and she is exporting factory hands to the United States.

We went to Pierce's works also and found nobody in. It was dinner time, and the workshops and

countinghouse were silent. The hands were absent.
I was sorry for this, not so much on my own account
as theirs. I wanted to show them a Pierce bicycle
that had been through many rough adventures at
home and abroad, and that is still in perfect order.
They missed a great treat, and I sympathised with
them. It was dinner time also at the factory of the
Wexford Engineering Company, and we were,
therefore, unable to see their fine workshops to advantage. It was satisfactory, however, to learn that
all the shops in Wexford are working full time, and
that they have plenty of orders to fill. This is all
the more creditable in view of the keenness of foreign
competition, especially of American manufacturers.
It is quite a common thing, in the spring and summer
months, to see at an Irish fair or market an American
agent with a sample machine and sheaves of pam-
phlets holding forth to all whom it may concern,
with amazing fluency and imagination, concerning
the alleged excellence of his mower or reaper or
horse rake. His splendid pushfulness stops at
nothing. He offers to bet any sum that the machine
which he is selling will, in any given trial on equal
terms, beat any other machine in the market. He
speechifies, he tells wild and wondrous tales, he
has a selected stock of jokes, and draws liberally
upon it as he sheds copies of testimonials by the
thousand, scattering them on all sides until the
circumambient air is aflutter with leaflets, and all
the while he is lynx-eyed for business. Hundreds
of foreign machines are sold in this way, and
against such an active and effective propaganda the
Irish-made machines are left to stand on their merits.

I suppose the Irish manufacturers know their own business best, but to an outsider it certainly looks curious to see them leave the art of advertising so much to their competitors.

We cycled back to Enniscorthy, and next morning I was travelling Dublinwards. I would fain have remained for a week, but I was promise bound and had to go. I went, carrying with me the pleasantest recollections of gallant Wexford and a wish to visit it again. It is an inspiriting corner of Ireland, and as I passed through Gorey, speeding northward, the stirring verses which William Rooney penned to the glory of the battlefields of '98 came to my memory:

These, through a hundred years of gloom and
    doubting,
  Speak trumpet-toned to-day
Above the cry of creed and faction's shouting,
  To tread the olden way.

These, in the hearts of all true men awaken
  The olden fires anew;
These tell of hope unquenched and faith unshaken,
  Of something still to do.

Tell to the nations, though the grass is o'er them
  For many a weary year,
Our father's souls still thrill the land that bore
    them—
  Their spirit still is there.

CHAPTER XV.

In the valley of the Inny—A country that drops into poetry—The idle rivers of Ireland—Baronstown—Abbeyshrule—The Tinker Tribe—A notable discussion upon the dramatic work of Mr. W. B. Yeats—The country of " The Rising of the Moon"—"Leo" Casey's "Singing River"—"Leo's" Songs- By "Derry Heather," and "Leafy Tang."

Both Longford and Westmeath drop into poetry, so to speak, as they slope westward to the shores of storied Lough Ree. Gurteen, where " Leo" Casey's father taught his school, is a quiet townland between Caltragh and Ledwithstown. Auburn, of Goldsmith, is south of the Inny river on the road from Ballymahon to Athlone. From Keenagh, in Longford, to Glassan, in Westmeath, about twelve miles, is the whole length of this poet's country, and you will get the whole breadth of it if you follow the Inny from Pallas, behind Forgny, to its mouth. It is part of the march lands of Royal Meath, and in the old days was under the sway of the chieftains of Rathcline and Shruel—O'Quinns and MacGilligans, and MacGavans, and Dillons of Kilkenny West. The frequency with which *Derry* occurs in the names of places in the district indicates that there were wide oakwoods over the countryside in the ancient time. There is Derrylougher on the road from Lanesborough and Keenagh, and Derry Lough further on to the right of the road to Athlone, and, nearer the Inny still, you have Derrymacar and Derrynagease. The great old forest kings are gone, but the country is well-wooded yet with larch and spruce, and ash, and beech, and elm, and sturdy oaks of later days. Indeed, the Inny's banks are shaded for many a mile, and it is beautiful all the way from its source in Lough Iron to where it disembogues into Lough Ree But its beauty often saddens. The ruined mills which totter over its crystal current tell a woeful tale of our captivity. There was a day when the corn mills of Ballymahon were famous, and when from early morning to late at night, through the winter months, long lines of cars crowded the thoroughfares around it waiting to deliver grain. The rafters are now beginning to peep through the neglected roofs of the towering warehouses; and the basement storey of the mill is used as a porter deposit! The Inny is capable of turning hundreds of mill wheels, but so far as I know the turbine at Ballymulvey is the only one at work. The great mills of MacGann, of Fagan, of Murtagh and others—all busy centres of industry forty years ago—are tenantless, and the owls and bats alone keep guard over the remains of the rust-eaten machinery. The splendid might of the water power is squandered in play amongst lilies and flaggers and sedges. And as the stream courses under the gaunt skeletons of rotted wheels, or flings itself through useless tailraces or over needless dams it sings to the crooning woods. What does it sing, my brothers? Dirges for murdered enterprise? Odes to industrial decay? Hymns to conciliated desolation? Or does it sing now as it sang to our poet in the days of his youth?

> Oh, thank God, there still are beating
> Hearts in manhood's burning noon,
> Who would follow in their footsteps
> At the Rising of the Moon.

That was what "Leo" heard from his "singing river" when it gave him the message of Shaun O'Farrell. That is what he would hear from it if he were alive to-day. It is the burden of every river song of our land. It is the cry of nature, the voice of wisdom. But to most of those who have the ear of the people it carries no inspiration, for, while Ireland has been listening to their promises and platitudes, the fields have been going out of cultivation and the mills out of work, and the young hearts and strong arms have been going away beyond the seas. And all the while we have been talking and talking only —talking at one time in a kind of braggart suppli-cation, at another in a kind of braggart conciliation. Ireland must do more than supplicate—must do more than conciliate. She must fight— if not with arms, then, some other way. Ireland is at last beginning to realise this, and Heaven knows it is time.

But although the gentle Inny has been robbed of its industries, its beauty still remains. I have seen the river many times from Ballycorky Bridge to Murtagh's Mills, and it was lovely always. It was cool and smooth and shady under the wood at

Barronstown, where Malone studied the sonnets of Shakespeare. The Malones were of the old stock, but they were conciliated centuries ago, and the fame won by them in scholarship and law is not Ireland's. Baronstown is a stately place, although its luck is of the worst. It has been burned to the ground twice in recent years. The people of the district have it that some wrong done to the monks of one of the old abbeys near the court has not yet been righted, and, that, although the mills of the Inny are idle, the mills of God are grinding.

The Inny flows through no more fertile and hospitable district than that of Abbeyshrule. The memory of this lovely neighbourhood clings to the exile with a special fondness. Abbeyshrule village is a very interesting place. The abbey, now in ruins, was once a great seat of piety, and was of very ancient origin as a religious centre.

The Royal Canal passes Abbeyshrule, and as I cycled along the banks of this weed-choked and half forgotten waterway, my attention was forcibly drawn to certain remarks made by a man who was sitting beside the towing path, fishing. He was calling upon a boy to bring him another maggot, and the qualifying parts of speech which he applied to the maggot and to the boy were more than vigorous. They were lurid. An aged female, with a rather reckless air of unconventionality, stoo smoking at a door of a hovel near the Canal, and she called to the man who was fishing—called him to come to his tea in terms which were peculiar and drastic and profane. A small boy rode a very hairy donkey along the road. In his small right hand he carried a large club with which he belaboured the donkey, cursing that unhappy quadruped at the same time with a fluency and a vehemence which were shocking.

"Verily," I thought, "it would appear as if the general moral tone of the inhabitants has, in some respects, deteriorated since the olden pious days when the Abbey bells woke the echoes along the Inny's banks."

But in this I was misjudging the good people of Abbeyshrule. I had run into a tinker encampment and had not yet discovered the fact. This part of the Canal bank has been frequented by tinkers from the earliest ages of tinkerdom, and the good people of Abbeyshrule keep clear of it as much as possible.

Meantime the donkey came to a standstill, for doing which the small boy, without ceasing his work with the club, consigned the wretched animal to perdition, even into the hottest flames thereof. I questioned the boy, and from his replies I learned that he was a youthful tinker. Then I remembered having heard many a time and oft of the "Tinkers of Abbeyshrule," and I realised that I had come upon them at last.

When I rated the boy for his cruelty and profanity his frosty little countenance underwent a change, and I laid the flattering unction to my soul that I had set his little conscience to work. I leaned upon my wheel, eyeing him kindly but yet firmly, and waited for results. Suddenly a thought seemed to cross his little mind. He jumped off his ill-used donkey, and holding out his tattered little cap in his knotty little hand, he broke out into a little whine

which had in it all the smoothness of inherited pro-
fessionalism:

"Will you give me a copper, sir, in th' honour of
God, sir, to buy a graineen o' tay—me mother is sick,
sir, and me father is dead, sir; or a bit o' tobacky,
sir, for me—uncle, sir—— ?"

I turned away in the pangs of a bitter disillusion-
ment, but he followed me at a jog trot.

"Do, sir, for the love o' God and His Blessed
Mother, sir, a copper, sir—not a bite or sup I had
to-day, sir——"

I had to pay him to stop, otherwise he would have
followed me half way across Longford. No one
in Abbeyshrule can tell when the Tinkers settled
down there first. They have been there off and on
for ages, and regard the Canal bank below the
Bridge as one of their favourite camping grounds.
They go out from it to fairs and gatherings far and
near, trafficking in tin-ware, mending kettles,
swapping asses, ballad singing occasionally, and
thimble-rigging on racecourses and in other places of
public resort; but, at one season or another of the
year they return to Abbeyshrule and fight out
their battles with soldering irons and other weapons
by the placid waters. They are a puzzling people,
and I have never met anyone who could give a satisfactory account of their origin. They have little in
common with the gypsies, outside the mania for
vagrancy. They have names borrowed from Irish
clans, but they have a hundred characteristics which
differentiate them from the Irish people. Are they
some remnant of the Firbolgs or degenerated Tuatha
de Danann? or are they descendants of some war-

dering tribe that strayed in to Ireland when the land
was empty after one of the great massacres? No
one knows.

Mr. Yeats studied the tinker fraternity in connection with his play, "Where There is Nothing"; but
it appears the harvest of his labours has been publicly repudiated somewhere in the West before a
bench of magistrates, in a crowded court, and in the
hearing of divers reporters of the Press. I did not
know of this until I heard it from a man who was
pitching his tent on the roadside below Ballymahon.
He wore a hairy cap and a black eye, and his
baggage-waggon showed signs of long and dusty
travel. A tired woman lay asleep in the ferns under
the pines, and several children, in various stages of
lawlessness pervaded the highway. He opened the
conversation by asking me for a match as I rode
past. This request brought me to a halt, and having
halted, I thought it might be as well to make myself
acquainted with his views on men and things. He
told me that he had come out of the trans-Shannon
country, and that as it was so late in the afternoon
he thought it best to go into camp for the night.
He would concentrate on Abbeyshrule next morning,
with the help and blessing of God. Further, he
devoutly expressed his gratitude to Divine Providence for having escaped with his life back into
peaceful Longford.

"So you have been in hot water over there?" I
asked, as I complied with his abject request for a
"pincheen" of tobacco.

"In throubles and in melia murdher, sir, indeed
I was, and it all came between me an' another man,

sir, on account of what a pote up in Dublin wrote
about the tinkers, for I'm one of them. No, sir, not
a pote—a tinker. It wasn't a pome that this pote
went and wrote about us, but a play, an' he marrid
a young gentleman be the name of Redledge or
Ledwitch, or somethin' like that, to one of the girls
of the Wards. And, be what I hear, this boy that
marrid the girl in the play was a quare crayther
entirely, who went about the country risin' rucks
with the clargy and the madgisthrates and the
peelers, and fallin' out with everybody, sir. ''Deed,'
says I to the man that towld me about it—a lad
over there in Boyle—''deed,' says I, 'the man who
made up that story isn't much of a pote. For,'
says I, 'the Wards is relations of mine, and I know
them, and I know that none of 'em would marry an
amadan that couldn't earn his bread, and, besides,'
says I, 'the father of the girl isn't a man to let any
pote talk about him, and make a blowin' horn of
his name in print,' says I   'Well,' says he, 'it's all
in the papers, anyhow, and the pote is a gentleman
born and bred in the County Sligo,' says he, 'who
writes songs for the people in Dublin and London
and New York—a very high-up pote that's praised
be your betthers,' says he, 'men,' says he, 'that
knows what they're talkin' about.' ''Deed,' says I,
'you can tell them the story about the marriage is
all in me eye, and that no such boy as this young
Misther Ledwitch, or whatever you call him, ever
joined us, or would be let join us, much less marry
one of us—a good-for-nothin' madman,' says I,
'that couldn't tell a sodherin' iron from a pot stick.'
Well, sir, he stood up for the pote bein' a Sligo man,

and I stood up for our side, and we had words over it, and words led to something worse, and the day was goin' against me entirely, so it was, until Peggy, over there, came to me with the half of th' ass's hames. So when they parted us I had the best of it. And be the same token, as I was comin' through Carrick last night they towld me that Ward himself went up before a lot of madgisthrates and denied the whole story about his girl and young Ledwitch, and said he never gave him lave or licence to make so free with his name, and that he knew nothin' at all about the pote, and never had any thruck with him whatsomever, and that it's damages he'd be claimin' if the story in any way intherfared with his girl gettin' a good match; and all the people that crowded the court to hear the thrial cheered, bedad."

" Then did your friend take an action against the poet for libel ? "

" No, sir, but I believe Ward was summoned for the trespass of his asses upon some man's field of oats, and he brought out all this in his evidence, for he has a wonderful great flow of speech, and always definds his own law cases, whenever he's let."

" But to what particular part of the play did he object ? "

" To the whole of it, sir. 'I disown it all, body and bones,' says he, 'it's all wrong,' says he, 'lock, stock and barrel. Neither that pote nor anybody else who isn't a tinker knows our saycrets,' says he, ' and never will.' "

I happened to pass that way again two hours later. The tent of patched canvas was stretched upon its supporting wattles, and a stick fire was blazing

brightly, over which the supper pot was boiling.
The woman was attending to the cooking and
smoking a rather stylish briar pipe. The children
were deployed along the road, begging. The head
of the family was faintly visible in the gathering
dusk coming out of a field with an armful of fresh
hay for his asses. The evening threatened rain, and
the tent appeared to be leaky, but there was
evidently no thought of seeking the shelter of a roof.
They were more at home camped there by the wayside than any barn or stable could have made them.
Nomads, vagabonds, heirs of generations of
wandering and disrepute, they are still, strange to
say, not at war with society. They merely dwell
apart. I have met several camping grounds of theirs
in my tours, all well chosen, shady places, near
abundance of firewood, and in neighbourhoods
where potatoes and other provisions might be had for
the begging, buying, or borrowing—I have very
seldom heard them accused of theft.

There is a good deal of brown bog on the western
fringe of Longford, but there is also some very good
agricultural and pastoral land. The bogs give fine
straight level roads for cycling, and the uplands are
wooded and pleasant and fertile. It was early
harvest when I was there, and the swish of the scythe
and the snicker of the reaping machine were in the
oats from Corlea to Tang. Four reaping machines
were at work in the fields along the road. Three of
them were of Irish manufacture. The other was a
foreigner and was undergoing repairs, while the
hands were picking blackberries. The Irish
machines are well able to hold their own against

their imported competitors, although some farmers say that they are rather heavy on horses.

A man was binding a ledge of oats in a field overlooking a countryside where the smoke of many homesteads rose upon the air and the face of the land was bright with harvest gold.

"Could you tell me where 'Leo' Casey's school is about here?" I asked.

"Of course, I can," he said cheerily as he twisted a double band and girdled a fat sheaf of the yellow corn. "But it was his father's schoolhouse, you know—not 'Leo's.' You're not far from it now You'll find it up there in Gurteen," and he gave me the fullest particulars of its location.*

"Did you know 'Leo'?' I asked him as I leant against the wall for the chat which I was trying to promote "I went to school with him," he replied, with a smile of humorous reminiscence, but without pausing in his work.

"A cross kind of a man, and a bit queer, was his father. We were shocking frightened of him sometimes. He had a kind of a lock-up or black hole. and he used to shut us into it for punishment. And sometimes we used to set pin traps for him on his chair, and when he sat on a pin he was—well, he was like any other man that sits on a pin."

"Did 'Leo' write many songs in Gurteen, do you know?"

---

*It appears that 'Leo' never taught school in Gurteen, although he may have assisted his father whose school was there. Leo, however, taught at a school in Keenagh, near Gurteen. This, I was told by one who went to the same school—a friend of his, who says he read "The Rising of the Moon" in MS. long before it appeared in print.

"Oh! he was always making songs and writing. I remember when 'The Rising of the Moon' came out, and how everyone was singing it. He used to read the *Nation* sometimes at the schoolhouse of a Sunday evening for the people, and it was grand to hear him. He used to write for the *Nation* himself, you know, and up in Dublin they thought a lot about him. But down here no one passed much remarks on him at all. He was only a bit of a boy at the time—maybe about twenty or twenty-one—and wasn't anything out of the way in his looks. The police used to be after him a good deal, watching him and trying to find out things about him, and he was put into jail at the end, for he was a real Irishman, and wrote songs that would make your head swim to hear them."

"So I believe."

"Aye, indeed. He was terrible fond of Ireland always. He was one of the Fenians; and, sure, them was the boys!"

"And Donal Kenny?"

"Is the playboy that 'Leo' made the song about?"

"Yes."

"I didn't know him very well, for I was young at the time. But he lived over there beyond near that clump of trees. It's many's the time I heard about him though, and he was a gay customer. 'Leo' and himself were great friends, they say."

He told me many other things about "Leo," from most of which I gathered that the poet was dead before the full brightness of his genius broke upon the people who had known the humble, silent, studious boy. Off the high road in Gurteen, and in a field alongside a narrow lane, stands his father's schoolhouse. It was empty and neglected, and seems to be used as a kind of barn or shed. There is a new school near it, built on the side of the high road, with all modern conveniences. It was closed for the vacation.. I went farther on towards the Inny, and met a narrow road turning off to the right, which I followed till it took me to the reed-clumps which fringe Derry Lough. I started water-hens out of the tall flaggers, and a covey of par-tridge flew up from a blackthorn thicket beside the lane. There was haymaking going on in the fields near me and harvesting farther away. The water lay calm and bright in the sunshine, and scarcely a leaf was stirring on the trees. To the left lay a wide sheet of heather, and over it a long ridge of pasturage well stocked with cattle. Southward the green meadows spread out to the glistening Inny, and beyond the broadening river the wooded lawns and sheltered fields of Tang sloped into the sky. It was one of "Leo's" favourite scenes. I looked for features made familiar to me through his lyrics, and fancied I could distinguish them.   Certainly there was no mistaking the local colour in some of the verses :

> In leafy Tang
> The wild birds sang,
>   The dew was bright on Derry heather.

I went and stood knee-deep in the heather, and looked for

The old spot by the river,
Right well known to you and me.

It must have been yonder where the Inny is gleaming amongst the meadows that he pictured the mid-
night drills of the United Irishmen :

There beside the singing river
    That dark mass of men were seen;
Far above their shining weapons
    Hung their own beloved green.

And it must have been down there under the hill
somewhere that the dance was held when Donal
Ruadh was going to America, and where he bade
good-bye to Mary :

A kiss upon her brow of snow,
    A rush across the moonlit meadow,
Whose broom-clad hazels, trembling show
    The mossy boreen wrapped in shadow;
Away o'er Tully's bounding rill,
    And far beyond the Inny river;
One cheer on Carrick's rocky hill,
    And Donal Kenny's gone for ever.

Casey was only twenty-four when death called
him. Had he lived he would now be not much more
than sixty. You cannot help thinking of the noble
work he would have done for Ireland since 1870 in
keeping alive the ideal of nationhood, vigorous and
militant, in the minds of the younger generations.
As I took my way back to the high road the last

stanza of his poem, "The Missioner," came into my mind, and I thought of how appropriately the beautiful lines might be applied to himself :

But ere the reaping, th' Evangelist
From the face of the land he loved was missed,
He trod the path of the yellow stars,
Free from the earth and its slimy wars—
Free! yet his spirit dwelt with those
Who waged the strife with Freedom's foes.
And his voice was heard 'mid the good and true,
"I've shown ye the work for men to do."

CHAPTER XVI.

A beautiful district—A Tower of Mystery—A Jewish Pedlar—A descendant of the Impenitent Thief—Into Goldsmith's Country—"Sweet Auburn"—A Goldsmithian Stone Breaker—A discussion by the roadside about Goldsmith and "Leo" Casey—The Three Jolly Pigeons—On Baskin Hill.

There are some fine hills and ridges in the district of the lower Inny, and although the cyclist will find his progress a more difficult matter than on the straight, level roads between Lanesborough and Derry, he will get good value for his expenditure of energy in climbing when he sees the noble pictures which meet his view from every eminence around. The scenery is varied, and, although the picture which you see from one ridge or hilltop may have certain details of the last left behind, still each has a well marked distinctiveness. Now you see the silver miles of Lough Ree, dotted with many islands, and the plains of Roscommon rising beyond the water. The next hilltop gives you only a corner of the lake, but it allows the eye to roam in free delight over the woods, by Glassan and Ballykeeran, to the roofs and spires of Athlone. Then you will have a section of the woods from your next outlook, but the rest of the panorama is the rolling grass country which stretches far into Westmeath, by Kilininny and Baskin, to where the hazes are gray over Uisnach of the legends. And before you sweep down to the straight descent from Tullywood you can rest to enjoy the splendid expanse of harvest wealth which crowns the tillage fields for miles to the eastward, until the yellow of the oats and barley fades off into the blue and purple of the mountains over Offaly and Kildare.

There is a high hill over Tang, standing some distance back from Lough Ree, on the summit of which is built a tower of considerable height. This tower can be seen for miles around, and excites the curiosity of the stranger. I made various inquiries regarding its origin, uses, significance, and so forth, and obtained the following replies : —

" They say it was built by the soldiers of Athlone, but God only knows."

" They say a rich man, who had a farm in Roscommon, built it and put up a spy-glass there to count his sheep."

" It was a windmill in old times."

" That's one of the Round Towers of Ireland or some ancient building."

" It was built by the Sappers and Miners in the Year of the Big Wind, to hide the mouth of an ancient cave that goes under the cannons of Athlone."

" That's the very middle of Ireland, so it is."

Here is cloth in plenty from which to cut, as the Spaniards say. But to what pattern? Which account of the tower is the true one? I was unable to visit it and put the different versions to the test

There is a tower of a similar kind, apparently, on Knock Allen, in Kildare, and I may mention that my inquiries regarding it at various times have supplied me with the following information:—That it is where Finn MacCool used to pitch his own tent. That it isn't. That it is where Finn MacCool was killed. That it isn't. That it was built to be a watch-tower for the Curragh Camp. That it was no such thing. That George IV. stood there and said that Ireland was a land worth keeping. That he didn't, but that it was Cromwell. When I began to read Mr. Yeats' beautiful preface to "God's and Fighting Men," by Lady Gregory, I hoped to find out something about the tower, for he said he had been to the top of the Hill of Allen. But he makes no mention of that riddle in stone. I suppose I must go up there myself some time and set the matter at rest.

On the Inny Bridge, near the ruins of Murtagh's Mills, I encountered a Jewish pedlar, who was resting himself on the moss-grown parapet. It was a warm day, and a harvest thunderstorm was brewing in the south-west. The pedlar was mopping the perspiration from his forehead with a big red handkerchief, and contemplating the scenery with a languid interest. I seated myself on the opposite wall, for I, too, wanted to look at the scenery, and, moreover, I wanted to have speech of the outland merchant. He smiled an oily, cross-eyed, subtle smile of self-apology and insinuating humility as he met my glance, and said in Hamburg English:

"That vos a warrm day, sar."

"Do you find this country hotter than your part of Germany?" I asked.

"I vos from Dhublin, sar, mineself, und not from Germany."

"You are Irish, then?"

"Irish, yes, from Dublin."

"God help us!   And were you born in Dublin?"

"With der help of Gott, sar."

"Of Jewish parents, I suppose?"

"No sar, Irish."

"An' how did you come by your accent?"

"I vos in America."

I wondered if he was the same Jew who had told the people around Forgny the week before that his name was O'Hara, and that it was a patriotic policy to support Irish trade.   A few days previously in a shop in Ballymahon a Jewish pedlar was offering for sale fountain pens, and rattles, and egg-beaters, and thimbles, and other fancy hardware; and two men of the district, who were of an enquiring turn of mind, were speculating on his ancestry.

"He says he is Irish," remarked the shopkeeper, humorously, "but he must have gone to Germany when he was very young and stayed there for a long time up to his chin in the German language."

"He's descended from Solomon, if you ask me," said the first local personage.

"I don't agree with you," said the other observer. "I don't think this man can trace his descent any farther back than the Impenitent Thief."

The spiritless knave joined with well-feigned heartiness in the laugh against himself, and, with the abject vileness of the renegade who is false to his blood, he tried to heap obloquy upon the Jews and upon the Jewish race, the stamp of which was indelibly set upon his every feature.

I was given to understand while in Longford that these Jewish pedlars are to be met with in many parts of Ireland. I was sorry to hear it. I was told that some of them, out of the profits of their trade, have already established themselves in Dublin and other cities as wholesale merchants and money-lenders. "And," added the Ballymahon man, who gave me the information, "they have two patron saints—Moses and the Duke of Norfolk."

"The Duke of Norfolk?" I asked, in some surprise. "What has he to do with the Hebrew race?"

"Oh! you see," he explained, "the Duke is a soft-hearted man, and his pity always goes out to the landlords and the Jews, and the police and the Lord Lieutenants of Ireland, and all the other poor down-trodden wretches of that class who are victims to the tyranny and injustice of the Irish people. Once upon a time, some cent.-per-cent. money-lending Jews complained in the papers that an Irish priest was nefariously persuading his people to discontinue borrowing cash on such favourable conditions. And when the Duke read about it his great financial heart was troubled for the poor and oppressed usurers, so he wrote an indignant letter about the hateful intolerance shown by his misguided fellow-Catholics in Ireland to his Jewish fellow capitalists; and since then the grateful Sheenies in Ireland swear by him, and bless his name out of the depth of their profitable misery."

I was in Goldsmith's country soon after crossing the Inny. A short ride across a moor took me to the fringe of a fine agricultural district where the harvesting was in full swing. The reapers and hay-

makers were out in every other field, and were not
indisposed at times to exchange pleasantries as well
as cheery greeting with a wayfarer. It was the same
as I rode through western Longford, and at one
place on the road, when the boys and girls invited
me to cross the wall and help them with their binding, I felt tempted for a moment to halt and suspend
all work in the neighbourhood as I had, on another
occasion, suspended all work in a certain townsland
in Westmeath. There was not a house in view but
had sheltered someone who had emigrated to the
Argentine Republic, and I knew it. I had only to
sit on the wall and begin to talk about Buenos Aires
and the Irish of Argentina to gather an audience.
But I saw it would be a shame to make them lose
time in such fine weather, so I held my peace and
went my way.

It was a stone-breaker at work near the cross-roads
under the parish church of Tang who directed me to
Auburn. He was a literary stone-breaker, too, for he
gave his information in poetical language.

"Down that road, sir," he said, nodding in the
direction of Athlone, "and you have only to go a
weeshy bit when you'll come to Sweet Auburn, the
loveliest village of the plain, where health and
plenty cheered the labouring swain, and in a field
convaynent to the road you'll see a bush, and that's
the hawthorn tree, with seats beneath the shade, for
talking age and whispering lovers made. But there's
no village there now, sir, where once the garden
smiled. And the stone of the busy mill is up there
at Misther Nally's door, for it's him that keeps the
'Three Jolly-Pigeons'—the village inn, sir, with the

neatly-sanded floor and the varnished clock that clicked behind the door, where news much older than the ale went round."

He went on in this strain for a good while, smoothly gliding hither and thither through " The Deserted Village " in an even, conversational way, untroubled by quotation marks and unfettered by method. His mellifluent sentences came like shifting winds of summer straying waywardly through the sunshine, greatly to his own enjoyment as well as mine. I thanked him for his kindness, and proceeded to look for the scene of Goldsmith's pastoral, and found it.

There is nothing about Auburn of the " abomination of desolation." Like many another quiet corner of the Irish Midlands, where thriving hamlets once nestled in happy comfort amidst the teeming fields, no evidence remains to show the extent of landlord devastation. There are no bare gables, or crumbling walls, or heaps of briar-grown rubbish to show where stood the homes in which the fires were extinguished and out of which the families were driven into the workhouses or ditches, or into the emigrant ships. Every trace of human habitation has been effaced by the crowbar of the lime-burner or road-maker, and the grass grows luxuriantly where the hearthstones brightened and where the people prayed. I was shown a countryside the other day, in another part of Westmeath, from which scores of families were driven fifty years ago ; and, were it not for the long ridges which seamed the fields from end to end, although low and faintly marked like the graves of forgotten dead, one might have fancied that those spreading pastures had lain untouched by plough or spade and unblessed by the sweat of husbandry since the dawn of time. You might pass Auburn twenty times a week without more than a careless glance if you were not told that it was the place

> Where smiling spring her earliest visits paid,
> And parting summer's lingering bloom delayed.

And yet spring comes no earlier to Auburn in the Westmeath barony of Kilkenny West than it does to any district in the baronies of Fertullach, or Rathconrath, or Moyashil.   We are told that Auburn was "the loveliest village of the plain." Undoubtedly it was, as Goldsmith saw it—not as it existed on the face of nature, but as he pictured it in his own imagination. Auburn was beautified not so much by the dowry of nature as by the magic of creative art.   There were, I am sure, prettier districts in Westmeath, but there was no Goldsmith to change their prettiness into beauty. And yet the beauty of "Sweet Auburn," as Goldsmith interprets it to us, is not Westmeath beauty. If we submit it to the test of historical facts we shall find many inaccuracies in its delineation. It is an Irish picture sketched and painted according to English conventions.   The tragedy of it is indeed characteristic of Irish rural life, but the setting of the tragedy is English. Goldsmith spent part of his boyhood in Pallas, between Ballymahon and Abbeyshrule, in County Longford. Part of his youth was spent in the heart of Roscommon, and part of it in Auburn. The local colouring of his poetry could, therefore, have been derived from various Irish sources; but how much of it is distinctly Irish?

Can the student of Irish history imagine a village like Goldsmith's Auburn in a district wherein every man and woman of forty years of age must have heard the thunder of De Ginkell's artillery at the siege of Athlone? Was the enviable lot of the people who "led up their sports beneath the spreading tree," a typical illustration of social life in an Irish hamlet during the Penal Days? Goldsmith was born in 1728, and died in 1774. Suppose him to have been in his fifteenth year when he took part in the gambols of the young folks under the hawthorn of Auburn, it will connect him with the country life of Ireland in the year 1743. At that time everybody in Westmeath spoke Irish except the descendants of De Lacy's Normans and the occupants of the 58,000 acres of land confiscated upon the men of the county who were concerned in the war of 1688. In Longford and Roscommon Irish was the general language for at least fifty years after Goldsmith's death. Are the characters depicted so lovingly and so beautifully in "The Deserted Village" true to the life of Gaelic Ireland and instinct in all things with the genius of the Gael? Do they strike us at all as being men and women whose religion was banned, whose priests were hiding in caves like hunted wolves, each with a price upon his head, and whose schoolmasters were outlawed? Do they work and play like beings whose lives are overshadowed by that terrible and infamous Penal Code which Goldsmith's friend and contemporary, Edmund Burke, described as "a machine of wise and deliberate contrivance as well fitted for the oppression, impoverishment, and degradation of a people, and the debasement in them of human nature itself, as ever proceeded from the perverted ingenuity of man?" There would be little reason for an Irish-Irelander to trouble himself about the distortion of fact perpetrated by Goldsmith in his fanciful picture of happiness in a Westmeath hamlet one hundred and sixty odd years ago, were it not that many people in the district seem to regard "The Deserted Village" as a beautifully-written chapter of local history. There seems to be no question at all on their part regarding its verisimilitude, for, as far as we can judge, they accept it as absolutely true; and I met several people along the roads who looked upon Goldsmith as a finer type of Irishman than "Leo."

"Don't the grandest of people come here from all parts to look at the place that Goldsmith wrote about!" argued a man who was mending a gate in Auburn. "Don't they come here from England and America and Australia and write about it, and take away branches of the hawthorn tree?"

"Which tree is that?" I asked, inattentively, for my thoughts were on something else.

"Do you see that bush over there?"

I nodded.

"Well, that's the hawthorn tree. Some people that doesn't know the differ will tell you that it is the bush there to the left, farther away; and some visitors believes them and marches off with sprigs of the wrong bush. Aren't you going over to get a sprig?"

"No, but if you could tell me where there is a good straight blackthorn, I would be very thankful to you," I said, for it came to my recollection that in leaving Buenos Aires I had received several pressing requests from friends to procure them genuine blackthorns, and that I had not yet begun work on the collection.

"But there's nothing about blackthorns in Goldsmith," he objected.

"Nor mention of anything Irish, for that matter," I remarked.

"Isn't there, indeed," he replied, with some heat. "Isn't there the whitethorn bush over there, and didn't he write about the dacent church that topped the hill, and about the busy mill, and about the geese on the pool? Go up to 'The Three Jolly Pigeons' and you'll see the very mill-stone that he wrote about on the door-step."

"Yet, but you see there are hawthorn trees in England, too, and busy mills; also decent churches in charge of Protestant clergymen. And as for the geese, my friend, they gabble in many lands!"

"Oh, I suppose a goose can gabble anywhere," he said, with a scornful sniff, "but about the clergy, now, that's the point. How do you know that the village preacher of Auburn was not a priest, and how do you know that the decent church wasn't a chapel? Maybe," and he turned up his nose in an opulent kind of sneer, "maybe you were out in them times yourself, you can tell so much about them?"

"No," I said, ignoring his loud contemptuousness. "I was not abroad then, thank God, but the Penal Laws were, and they were dreadful indeed, so much

so that under them the priests were ' on their keeping'
and the chapels were all closed or pulled down.
Did you never hear about it ? "

" There's not a single word about it in ' The
Deserted Village."

" Well, I said a minute ago that there was no
mention made in it of anything Irish."

" Good heavens ! isn't Auburn mentioned ? ' Sweet
Auburn, the loveliest village of the plain.' "

" Auburn is not an Irish name. It was Goldsmith
invented it, and this place has been called by it ever
since."

" Well, anyhow, Goldsmith holds the sway as an
Irish poet. Anyone will tell you that. I defy you
to name a single one that could put him down."

" I could name dozens of Irish poets who wrote
better than he did for Ireland, and I need go no
farther than the Inny there below to find you one to
put before him."

" Arrah who ? "

" John Keegan Casey."

" Is it ' Leo ? ' " he cried with a laugh of withering
contempt.

" Yes, and it is this way."   I went on as persuasively as I could.   " You see, Casey loved Ireland
better than Goldsmith did, and wrote about Irish
things.   That is why I say he is higher, as an Irish
poet, that Goldsmith.   Of course, he was not a great
genius like Goldsmith, but he was an Irish singer,
and Goldsmith was not.   Goldsmith wrote for the
people in England, mostly about English things,
and Casey wrote for the people in Ireland, mostly
about Irish things   True, Goldsmith's great poem is

about an eviction campaign, and it is some of the
most beautiful poetry that ever was written, but
there is nothing in it to specially mark it as Irish.
And, although there are many people who would tell
you that Casey's poetry is not Irish either, because it
is not written in the Irish language, still it is far
more Irish than Goldsmith's—for 'Leo' sang of
Shaun O'Farrell and the Inny, and Derry, and Tang,
and about Donal Kenny, and fifty other subjects
that are Irish through and through, and that no one
could mistake it for anything else, while 'The
Deserted Village' might be English or Scotch or
Welsh."

The contempt with which he had hailed the name
of "Leo" had died out of his face to give place to
an expression of amusement. When I had finished,
he cleared his throat and delivered himself as follows:

"That's all right enough, bedad, as far as it goes.
But, indeed, it's the first time I ever heard anyone
comparing a stookawn like 'Leo' to a man like Goldsmith. Sure I knew 'Leo'—a half-starved schoolmaster's son down there in Gurteen——"

"As for that part of it," I said, "if you'll pardon
me interrupting you, Goldsmith was a half-starved
schoolmaster, himself, and had to live upon his
friends many a time—a thing that 'Leo' never did."

"Well, last of all, I can't stand some of Casey's
rhymes. I'm not sayin' anything against 'The Risin'
o' the Moon'; that's fair enough, I suppose, and a
few others of his songs isn't bad. But I'm goin' to
tell you that Donal Kenny was no man to write a
song about. Donal Kenny, indeed. Heigh! The

finest scamp in the seven parishes—a fellah that'd
come up to you and give you a skelp of a wattle on
the side of the head just for the fun of seein' you
turn head over heels—a dang rowdy that would have
a shindy ruz while you'd be blessin' yourself.   And
a poocher, too, that wouldn't leave a hare in the
whole country. Heigh! 'Deed, I bet you Goldsmith knew better things than to make rhymes about
a boy like that, so he did—a common go-the-road
that I knew as well as the nose on me face. It was
the blessed day for us all when the same Donal
Kenny went off with himself, so it was—'deed, there
was many a dhry eye afther him as sure as you're
there."

"Still he was evidently a favourite with the
people, for the song says—

> 'Warm blessings flowed from every lip
>   As ceased the dancers' airy motion,
> Oh! Blessed Virgin, guard the ship
>   That takes bold Donal o'er the ocean.'"

"Oh! sure, I know it all. I was there myself,
and it was natcheral for us to pray for him, because
we wanted to get him out of our sight. We were
prayin' sthrong for a long time to be relieved of
him. And as for him givin' his blessin' to Mary and
her boy, 'deed I don't believe a word of it, for it was
only the week before that he done his best to take
Mary from him; but, by herrin's! th' other boy gave
him a fine leatherin', so he did, and more power to
him! Donal Kenny, indeed! Heigh!"

There was a world of scorn and contempt in that

last exclamation, and it bespoke a prejudice invulnerable to argument. I retired, and in the language of the war correspondents, I swung off to the right, towards " The Three Jolly Pigeons," which caravansary I found in due course. Mine host was Goldsmithian to the backbone, but he had a neighbourly regard for " Leo." He said it was simply ridiculous to argue that there was nothing distinctively Irish about " The Deserted Village." He was in a position to settle the question with one word; there, on his threshold, was the identical stone of the " busy mill." The mill-shaft was also to the good, and other relics. I asked for the " twelve good rules," and " the royal game of goose," and " the chest of drawers by day," but they were things of the past. The present inn is not the original " Three Jolly Pigeons," but one that took the name of the old house which stood farther down the road. There is a post-office about a quarter of a mile from the inn, and the name is " The Pigeons." Mine host was most sociable and cheery, especially when he learned that I was from the Argentine Republic. Some near relatives of his are on the Pampas, and many an old schoolmate as well, for in the days when emigration flowed strongly from Longford and Westmeath to Buenos Aires, scores left Tang and the neighbouring parishes on both sides of the Inny. I could give him some account of most of them, and it delighted him. He had no difficulty whatever in accepting my statement that I was from the city by El Rio de La Plata, but he found it impossible to believe that I had any connection with the republic of letters. No wonder; for I had been several days on the march through rain and shine in two provinces and several counties, trying to learn a few things about the history of the present and the past, and feeling, in a way, the pulse of Ireland I had been in Mayo, in Galway, over the Roscommon plains, along the Inny, Shannon and Brosna, through the lake district of Westmeath and into Lower Offaly, and my clothes were in a sad way from dust and oil and mud splashes and rain. But although the man of the house at " The Three Jolly Pigeons " could not admit me into the domain of literature, he did his best to overwhelm me with hospitality. He proposed, seconded, put, and carried unanimously a motion to the effect that I should eat, drink, and sleep under his roof, but I was forced to move an amendment and carry it against all opposition. There was heart-hunger on me for a change of clothing and a wash, and a good rest in a certain valley under Ballymore.

I made a loop round by Baskin Hill just to have the pleasure of looking down for a few minutes on the country between Mount Temple and Knockastia ---one of the choicest gems of rural beauty in the whole of Europe. The cloud shadows lay on the lower hills, but Kilininny was all ablaze in the sunshine, and a big rock in one of the fields near the summit was bright against the sea of green. I never saw the name of this rock in print or in writing, but the old people call it by a name which is pronounced Carrick-an-eagh. There is a legend which tells that in the ancient times a giant in Moyvoughly had a dispute about something with another giant who lived in Killininny, and that, in the heat of discussion, he heaved that rock across the valley at his opponent.

This stone-throwing giant was the Polyphemus of the neighbourhood, and must have exhausted all the available ammunition in his preserves, for there is not a rock in any of the green fields that slope down to the Umma Road.

CHAPTER XVII.

*Through Dublin and Wicklow—A ride to Luggala
—Killiney—The Vale of Shanganagh—The
self-glorification of John Maupas, deceased—
The Scalp—Enniskerry—Glencree—A Moun-
tain Herdsman—A large inheritance—Lough
Bray—The sources of the Liffey—The Sally
Gap — The Glens — Wild Luggala — Back
through the night.*

On a lovely Sunday morning in the early autumn
two of us pulled out along the road to Bray for a
day's cycling in Dublin and Wicklow. We intended
riding to Glendalough and back, but we were
obliged to modify this programme before we reached
Dalkey, owing to a certain pleasant circumstance
which may be termed a morning call. As we were
leaving the suburbs behind us my comrade, who
knows many different types of Irish people, said
casually that there were two men living in a tower
down somewhere to the left who were creating a
sensation in the neighbourhood. They had, he said,
assumed a hostile attitude towards the conventions
of denationalisation, and were, thereby, outraging
the feelings of the *seoinini*. He, therefore, suggested that we should pay them a flying visit.
There was no necessity to repeat the suggestion, so
we turned off to the left at the next crossroads, and
were soon climbing a steep ladder which led to the

door of the tower. We entered, and found some
men of Ireland in possession, with whom we tarried
until far on in the morning. One of them had lately
returned from a canoeing tour of hundreds of miles
through the lakes, rivers, and canals of Ireland,
another was reading for a Trinity College degree,
and assiduously wooing the muses, and another was
a singer of songs which spring from the deepest
currents of life. The returned marine of the canoe
was an Oxford student, whose button-hole was
adorned by the badge of the Gaelic League—a most
strenuous Nationalist he was, with a patriotism,
stronger than circumstances, which moved him to
pour forth fluent Irish upon every Gael he encountered, in accents blent from the characteristic speech
of his *alma mater* and the rolling *blas* of Connacht.
The poet was a wayward kind of genius, who talked
in a captivating manner, with a keen, grim humour,
which cut and pierced through a topic in bright,
strong flashes worthy of the rapier of Swift. The
other poet listened in silence, and when we went on
the roof he disposed himself restfully to drink in
the glory of the morning. It was very pleasant up
there in the glad sunshine and the sweet breath of
the sea. We looked out across the bay to Ben Edair
of the heroic legends, now called Howth, and wondered how many of the dwellers in the " Sunnyview
Lodges " and " Elmgrove Villas," and other respectable homes along the hillside knew aught of Finn
and Oisin and Oscar. We looked northward to
where the lazy smoke lay on the Liffey's banks, and
southward, over the roofs and gardens and parks
to the grey peak of Killiney, and then westward and

inland to the blue mountains. We stayed far longer
than we had intended, and talked of many things,
regardless of the hour, until it was too late to think
of going to Glendalough. One of the chief difficulties about cycling in Ireland is the start. When the
morning is bright, and the roads dry, and a light
wind straying idly over the fields, you prepare for
a long ride with the pleasantest anticipations; but
when you are ready to set out some inducement to
delay your departure will present itself, and time
will steal away from you until nearly half the day
is gone. The shadows were shortening for noonday,
when at last we got away from the tower, so we
decided to go no further than Luggala. It is some
miles nearer to Dublin than Glendalough, and, like
the storied glen of St. Kevin, is one of the treasures
guarded by the Wicklow mountains.

"By Bray, through the Scalp, to Enniskerry,"
said my friend, mapping out the road, "and from
Enniskerry to Glencree. From Glencree, by Lough
Bray, to the Sally Gap, and on to Luggala. Then
back by Sliabh Cualann to Bray, and home by
Dunleary to Dublin."

We skirted Dalkey and ran up against a formidable hill which bulged skyward so aggressively that
the road had to stand on its hind legs, so to speak,
in order to look over the top. We humbly dismounted and commenced to laboriously negotiate it,
and as we pushed our wheels upward, my comrade
encouragingly informed me that it was merely as
the moon to the sun compared with the mountains
and peaks with which he promised to make me
acquainted during the day. When we reached the

bottom of the opposite slope we found ourselves on
the shore of the Bay, near Killiney, and the road
led us under the plantations that clothe the lower
slopes of the Peak. This is an earthly paradise
superimposed on a foundation of magnificent
granite. Killiney Hill is an immense heap of this
valuable rock. The road is repaired from granite
quarries. Every stone that peeps out of the clay
is granite. There must be enough granite there to
build a wall round Europe, yet it appears that some
of the granite recently used in Dublin architecture
was imported by certain outland builders. If you
loosened the boulders from the side of the Peak they
would scarcely stop rolling until they reached
O'Connell Bridge. But even if they rolled to the
very scaffolding, dressed and ready for the masons,
there are anti-Irish foreigners in Dublin who would
scruple to use them. We left the high road and
took a winding footpath through the trees. After
a steep walk of nearly half-a-mile we reached the
summit of the Peak overlooking Dublin City and
Bay and the lovely Vale of Shanganagh. It will
always be a glad memory to me that I saw Shanganagh at its best. At least I fancy it was at its
best that morning, for I cannot fancy it looking
more beautiful. There were thin transparent screens
of haze floating in mid-air, and through them, as if
seen at the bottom of a vast lake of the clearest
water, smooth lawns and pastures and meadows
showed along the valley in fifty different shades of
softened emerald, until the grass melted into the
heather on the engirdling hills. And out to the rim
of the eastern sky lay the sparkling sea, laughing

into the cloudless blue from a million flaming wavelets, and with a faintly marked bordering of foam along the shelving strand.

But all is not lovely on Killiney Hill. A monument stands there which is an architectural monstrosity and a vainglorious abomination. It bears an inscription which I copied as a curiosity, but, unfortunately, I have lost it. This inscription states that in a certain year, far back in the eighteenth century, one John Maupas, seeing that there was a famine in the country, and that it would be "hard with the poor," gave employment by having built at his own expense the walls enclosing the hill, "and this, etc." It will be noticed that the guileless John makes a little joke of an unconscious kind at the end of his pharisaical self-glorification. He calls his monument "this etc." He can find no word to describe the hideous thing he has built, so he calls it—"this etc." It is a very suggestive name. The etcetera stands for any qualifying term which posterity may wish to apply to the stony gift presented by John to a starving people. You change "this etc." to "this freak," or "this nightmare," or "this horror," or "this phenomenal heap of ugliness." The model chosen by the designer seems to have been the sawed-off stump of a candlestick surmounted by an extinguisher. Its ugliness is outlandish as well as intense, and it seems to have inflected the nomenclature of the beautiful residences all around Killiney. There is nothing Irish in the names which you read on the gate piers of the stylish villas on every road leading to or from the Peak. Nor is there any truth or appropriateness in them either. You meet a "Hollybrook" where there is neither a brook nor holly, and a "Mossfield" where there is neither a field nor moss, and an "Elmgrove" where no grove ever grew and where no elm has been known to lift its head in all the ages of recorded ime.

A false social standard is a great affliction to a country. It makes people grow ashamed of everything they should proudly cherish. It is a false social standard which we may debit with our Sackville Streets and our "Devonside villas," and our Algernons, our Lydias and our Stellas, and all the other fancy but unchristian and un-Irish names which doting *seoinini* have culled for their offspring from the serial stories in the pages of the *Young Ladies' Journal* and *Bow Bells*. Thank God that an Irish social standard is again set up in our social life! It came none too soon.

We went southward trom Killiney across the mouth of Shanganagh Valley toward Bray along a perfect road. We did not pass through Bray, but turned to our right some distance from the town, ind laid our course for The Scalp. When the world was young some growing pain convulsed one of the Dublin hills and burst it in twain from base to summit The cleft thus made is called "The Scalp." It is V-shaped, just wide enough to leave ample room for a road at the bottom. The slope facing the south is wooded in places, but the rocks on the other side are bare. It is one of the portals of Wicklow, and probably there has been a road through it from the time when men first trod Irish soil.

The beetling crags which frown hundreds of feet above the road on either hand must have witnessed many strange sights in the forgotten mutations of the earlier races of Erin. The defile leads from one land of song and glory to another, and has seen much history made from the days when the Druidic fires blazed on the Dublin mountains to the days when the Wicklow glens re-echoed to the cheers and musketry of Michael Dwyer and his guerilleros.

Enniskerry is a near little town wedged into a hollow. You almost tumble head over heels into it before you see it, and it has the name of being quite Swiss in its appearance. It is overshadowed by high hills and by Lord Powerscourt. The hills rise outside its backyards, and Lord Powerscourt rises from his demesne, which lies along the hills. Pictures of the Dargle and of Lord Powerscourt are plentiful in Enniskerry. The Powerscourt Waterfall is also a great inspiration to local art. The Dargle is famous for its beauty, and the Powerscourt demesne is a show place; and, furthermore, Enniskerry is on the road to Glendalough. Consequently the town is a tourist resort.

We turned to the right outside of Enniskerry, and, crossing the Dargle River, went off westward through a maze of woods, climbing long slants of forest road, which made heavy demands on lungs and sinews. It was strenuous work, but the enjoyment it brought was worth it all. The woods were just turning with the first mellow hues of the autumn, and the air was laden with the bracing fragrance of the pines. A ride of about half an hour brought us out on a mountain side, from which we looked across a deep valley into a series of hills darkened with spruce and larch or with tangled heather.

We met the mountain breezes now, and they challenged us to a tussle with them, which we accepted with a will. Conversation dropped suddenly, for there is no breath to spend in words when a Wicklow road takes you on a long excursion cloudward against the wind which whimpers down the hills. The woods fell away from us now, and soon there was not even a sheltering hedge by the wayside. We were up among the rocks and the fading bracken and the spongy beds of moss. Upward still through the wide miles of heather, with an occasional rest which we took by walking. We had a deep cool drink from one of the many streams which trickle down the slopes to feed the rivers in the valleys far below, and then another long climb, until on looking backward the faint blue of the ocean showed over the distant peaks.

We met a few score of mountain sheep browsing among the green tufts of shrub, and farther on we came upon the shepherd sitting chin deep in the scented heather smoking a new clay pipe and looking dreamily into the wild waste of peaks which overlook the valley of Glencree. We hailed him as we passed, and he greeted us right cheerily in reply. What a large inheritance he was enjoying there! If he had only the gift of articulation, which would enable him to share his untroubled reverie with the world, what freshness he would bring to the jaded and aching souls whose emotions are dried and withered by the red flame of fevered life!

We left him near the head of Glencree, in the solitary enjoyment of one of the fairest scenes in Ireland.   For although the Vale of Glencree is unknown to the professional photographers, and although you seldom, if ever, see it mentioned in guide books, it is of a wondrous beauty.   It begins under some of the highest of the Dublin Mountains and slopes down towards the coast between two lofty ranges. A river winds through it which flashes here and there as it catches a sunbeam, and finally melts into the deepening shadows.   The sharp peak of the Sugarloaf sentinels it far to the southward, and over the purple gloom of the woods near Enniskerry shines a bright streak of Irish Sea, filling the space between the jagged crestline of the hills and the blurred horizon. From the base of the Sugarloaf to the base of the Glendoo is eight good miles, and that is the length of Glencree. It is about two miles wide.   In some place the beauty is quietly pastoral, where green stretches of sheep-runs slope gently to the heather on either side of the valley, dotted by occasional clumps of trees.   In other places it takes its beauty from the thick mantle of woods which cover the mountain sides and which spread across the valley until their shadows mingle in the river.   Then again, it is beautiful higher up, with a wild rugged beauty of grayish peaks and heathery slopes.   It is beautiful from end to end, and it has not yet been profaned and vulgarized by cheap trippers.   None but the toughest cyclists penetrate its recesses, and only to them and to the tireless pedestrian tourist will it show the wonders of its loveliness.

We turned sharply eastward once more near the old barracks of Glencree, which is at present used as a reformatory. The wind favoured us now, and we climbed blithely through a mountain turbary district until we reached lower Lough Bray. Here we tarried for a few minutes to see the lough, which is only a few acres in extent, but of fathomless depth. The mountain hares go hither to nibble the soft grass which grows along the level shore, and from the rocky side of Kippure mountain, which towers over its gloomy waters, no echo comes save the call of the grouse on the wing. It is very lonely up there, and very wild and impressive. You might sit under Kippure and look out on brown wastes of heather and grey pinnacles of rock and fancy that all living things had left the world but yourself, and that the windy solitudes were moaning under the weight of your unwelcome presence. There is a cottage under the crags, on the eastern side of the lough, hidden by a bend of the shore and by a fir plantation. My comrade told me that a British Lord Lieutenant of Ireland was once cured of something by somebody, and that through gratitude he built the cottage and made a present of it to his healer. Some people might think that it was a peculiar way of thanking a man for a great favour to send him to live in that lonely place on the roof of the world. But tastes differ. There are people who think it a grand thing to be able to get away out of the whirlwind of human affairs now and then, and who would prize such a gift. And for my part I think they are wise.

We pursued our way further up the mountains,

and soon passed Upper Lough Bray.   There is only
a short distance between the two loughs, yet they
appear to be unconnected one with the other.   The
overflow of each falls by a separate stream into
Glencree river, which is an affluent of the Dargle.
A little beyond Upper Lough Bray we came to a
bridge, and my mentor informed me that we were
at the source of the Liffey.   There was a thin trickle
of bog-water glistening under the rank heather by
the roadside, and a few paces further up there were
a few scattered tufts of rushes growing out of wet
moss.   It was, indeed, the beginning of the Liffey.
The ooze and trickle become a rivulet under the
bridge, and the rivulet is swelled by many springs
as it sings its way down the slopes out of Wicklow
into the plains of Kildare.   It enters County Dublin
near Leixlip, after a wayward and joyous ramble
through some of the most beautiful scenery in the
world.   From its source to its mouth as the bird
flies is scarcely twelve miles, but the entire length
of its course is, perhaps, over seventy.

From the source of the Liffey to the Sally Gap is
a splendid ride.   You have reached the level mountain-top at last and the wild wastes of heather swell
and roll away to the horizon on every side.   The
strain on the pedals has ceased and the slightest
effort sends you skimming along the smooth road.
Few carts or waggons ever pass this way, so that
there are no ruts.   The surface is well sanded and
the thin spokes hum as the wheels fly over it with
increasing speed.   Faster still and faster.   We have
topped the last undulation of the crest line, and the
pedals stop of their own accord under the sagging

chains, for the free wheel has felt the downward
gradient and the universe is slipping behind you so
swiftly that you instinctively handle your brakes.
The road is grass-grown now and the only smooth
running is found where the wheels of other cyclists
and of a few light vehicles, or perchance of an occasional automobile, have kept the gravel bare. The
sun is low and the sky is clear, and a fresh wind
laden with unpurchasable fragrance of the wilderness comes in long deep breathings out of the bosom
of Wicklow. A hare springs out of the rushes and
streaks along the road. He is a playful fellow, for
his ears are laid back and his shoulders are hoisted
in the big chuckle which he is having all to himself
at our expense. We throw a few pedal strokes into
the snoring speed of the free wheel and shout as
we gain upon him. He shakes some creases out of
himself at this, becomes serious, erects his ears,
leaps from the highway into the bog and is off to
tear a hole in the horizon, leaving us the moral victory. Then we start a grouse and he is indignant.
He flings himself like an arrow down the wind,
shouting "Hur-r-r go back! go back! go back!"
He has friends and relations all over the heather
kingdom and his clatter gets upon their nerves.
From far and near comes their echoing vociferation
"Go back! go back! go back!" We go on and on,
and presently a bend in the road shows us a change
of scene. The mountain falls away to our right,
and from many crests in front of us and to the
southward the heather ridges dip and dip until there
is a wild glen below us, gloomy with the shadows
of the peaks, and winding away into weird darkness

far to the southward. Down yonder behind the
shadows and along the distant ridges, which the
low sunbeams are flooding with golden light, were
the strongholds of Fiach MacHugh and the terri-
tories of the fighting O'Byrnes. Down yonder also
are Imaal of Dwyer and the wild glens where the
echoes know the name of Holt, and where freedom
died hard and bravely. Hosts of stirring memories
crowd upon you, and as the darkening slopes shut
in the lonely glens from your view there is a prayer
in your heart and on your lips that the peace of God
may be with the warrior souls of the men who died
for Ireland's sake.

From the Sally Gap we bore to the left and met
some awful hills, which we flew down at reckless
speed, scattering flocks of mountain sheep to left
and right, and stopping for nothing in our haste to
reach Luggala before the twilight died. The sun
had already sunk behind the crests, and we were
flying through the afterglow at a breakneck pace.
We had been obliged to lose time over a puncture,
and we were straining every nerve to recover the
loss. It was a very close race, but we won it. We
reached Luggala just at dusk, and had one good
look from the cliffs over Lough Tay, along the glen,
to Lough Dan, and farther still to the peaks over
Glendalough. It surpassed in wild beauty anything
that we had seen during our long and beautiful ride.
My friend was sorry for me. He said that if I had
seen Luggala under the glory of the mid-day, I
would have enjoyed its loveliness ten times more;
or if we had arrived even an hour earlier to watch
the radiance paling before the rising shadows, I

would have seen it to far more advantage than in the gathering dusk. But I was well content to see it just as it was at that moment. There was a mystic splendour over it which the sunlight might have dispelled. No human dwelling, no trace of human life is anywhere visible. The peaks and ridges are above the grassy altitudes, and only the heather clothes the brown peat. Where the grey rocks stand out of the mountain, gaunt and bare, in the gloom, they add to the untamed ruggedness of the perspective. No plough has ever furrowed those virgin hills, no spade has ever turned a sod along them. The heather and the blue water and the moss-grown rocks looked just as they do now when a human eye first beheld them; and long before a human foot intruded on the solitude of the glen they had been the same. Far off beyond Lough Dan, where the heather meets the sky, there is a weird light caught from the west which holds the eye and fancy. It seems to lead you out of the present and take you back to the ages when the Druids wove their spells, and when the Men of Dea were mighty in the land. The wind is singing in the pines far below us on the shore of the lough, and the waves are splashing softly on the strand These are the only sounds, and they have a slowly swinging, solemn rhythm which seems to bear some message from the elder time. How is it that so many of the high places of Erin change so greatly in their potentiality of appeal to you after the sun has set? When the twilight or the moonlight falls upon them all the resources of word-painting fail before their powers, because as you look upon them your thoughts are mostly subjective, and you are searching your inmost soul in vain for the sweet, evasive, half-sad, half-joyful emotion that has quickened it so strangely.

It was dark when we left Luggala, and we felt our way cautiously on foot down to Luggala Gate. The hills were the steepest we had yet encountered, and we agreed that the safest way to negotiate it in the darkness was on foot. This precaution is necessary at any time, for the descent is very steep and the road surface loose and dangerous. When at last we had made our way down to the main track, my comrade made scientific preparations to light his acetylene lamp. I despised the use of a headlight, and suggested that we should not trouble ourselves about such a detail. He said nothing, but went on quietly fixing his lamp, and when he had it ready he started an illumination that lit up the night like a bonfire. Down and down and down we rode on our homeward journey, until we met the hedgerows again, and the trees loomed through the darkness. We passed Sliabh Cualann, between the mountain-side and a precipice, and rode down into Bray, then through Little Bray, and on towards Shankill. There were newly-made patches of quarried stones on the road, and in riding over one of them I punctured a tyre. We found the puncture by the lamp-light, and as I patched it, the following remark fell upon me out of the darkness:

"You see, after all, a lamp-light has its uses now and then."

I received the gentle proposition in a spirit of meekness, and humbly rode behind the man who had made it, until we passed Dunleary. At times in the black darkness under the trees I thought how much like a huge fly he looked silhouetted against the blaze of lamp-light. But I kept the remark to myself. There were loose stones still on the road, and I feared another puncture. It was very late when we parted in Eccles Street, and our cyclometers marked seventy-three miles for the day. We had spent as much energy on some of those miles as would have taken us many leagues on the level. But now that the ride was over, I knew I should always think of it with unclouded pleasure. We are to make a more extended raid into Wicklow some other time if all is well. That was the last thing we settled before we said *beannacht leat*.

CHAPTER XVIII.

Through Ossory, to the County of Kickham—Beside the infant Nore—The Motor Cyclist once more appears—An excursion into polemics—A historic district—Aghaboe of Virgilius—Dunamase of Rory O'Moore—Durrow—In the District of " Knocknagow" Kickham in poetry and prose— One of the Homes of Tipperary.

I lay resting beside the infant Nore, in a valley of Upper Ossory, after a stiff ride over the mountains from my native place. A wood skirted the road, and shut out the view of the great wastes of heather through which I had come. From the time I had left the Gap of Glendyne until I had reached my halting-place, the road had been very lumpy, and I had been expending plenty of energy on the work of cycling up long and slippery gradients in the teeth of the wind. While I was discussing lazily with myself whether I should set forth again or spend another half-hour on the golden moss under the hedge-row, listening to the singing pines, I heard the clatter and thump and sneeze and sputter of a motor cycle, and looking down the road I saw one of these machines with a cyclist attachment coming towards me at a speed of about thirty miles an hour. On seeing me, the cyclist attachment turned sundry handles and worked divers levers, and brought the

perspiring machine to a halt. A voice then addressed
me from out a suit of leather clothes and from
behind a leather mask ornamented by two smoked
glass windows. And it said :

" Hello, is it you ? "

" It is," I answered.

" How have you been since we met last ? "

" When was that ? "

" Do you not remember me, then ? "

" Not at present. It is about as difficult to identify
you as if you were a diver rising out of the sea, for
during business hours one diver resembles another,
and the same may be said of motor-cyclists. But if
I could get a look at you I might possibly be able to
place you."

" Oh, of course—I forgot," and he removed his
head-piece. " I suppose you can locate me now ? "

With his features stripped of leather, there was no
delay whatever in recalling him to mind. You
may remember how I told you something about
extracting a motor-cyclist from a briar-brake beside
the Dublin road on a certain Sunday morning. This
was the same patient. He said he was glad to meet
me again, and that in case I had changed my mind
about motor cycles, he could now offer me a splendid
machine, almost as good as new, not more than three
weeks out of the factory, a very little more than half-
price. When he learned that I was still unwilling to
resign my individuality, or merge it in a stack of
machinery, or give it in charge to a petrol motor, he
produced his road map and proceeded to consult me
regarding a route to Galway. He wanted the flattest,
shortest and smoothest road. Scenery was no concern

his. He said that he would not go a quarter of a
mile out of his way to look at the most beautiful
landscape in the world, unless there was a business
possibility in so doing. When he had dried up my
fountains of information he said :

"Do you know, I have had wretched luck. I have
not booked thirty pounds' worth of orders in three
weeks."

"I am very glad to hear it," I remarked, "because
I met an Irish commercial traveller yesterday, who is
travelling for Irish-made goods, and he told me that
trade was brisk. It is encouraging to see Irish-made
goods in demand, and English-made goods at a
discount. It means that Ireland is trying to protect
her own industries against foreign competition. She
cannot do it by law, more's the pity, but she can do
it by closing her purse to English sellers."

This led us into a deep and turgid discussion on
nationality, political economy, free trade, rebellion,
coercion, the British Empire, treason, the shooting of
landlords, the late Queen Victoria, the growth of
Irish-Ireland opinion, the land problem, the Union,
Henry VIII., Queen Elizabeth, Cromwell, Castle-
reagh, Edward VII., Lynchehaun, the Stage-Irishman,
and a long array of other themes, regarding which
we were unable to unburthen our souls during our
other interviews.

"Oh, well," he said at length, "business is business, you know, and I must be away. He resumed
his leathern things and started. The motor coughed,
shivered, sneezed, and scattered the fumes of petrol
over the mountains. Then it dashed up the hill with
its patient and was gone out of sight in a few

minutes. I lifted my silent Pierce out of the ferns and resumed my way. I decided to ride down through Ossory as far as the Kilkenny border, and then map out the rest of my tour according to the state of the roads.

I was in the country of St. Fintan, one of the contemporaries of St. Columcille. He was of the race of Eochaidh, brother of Con of the Hundred Battles. Clonenagh, where Fintan's great school was founded, lay a little to the northward. It is nearly fourteen centuries since Clonenagh knew him in the flesh, but the fame of his sanctity has not died. He has been compared by ecclesiastical historians to the great St. Benedict, the founder of western monasticism. Fintan of Clonenagh was the first of the Irish monks. Clonenagh was a great school in its day, and flourished until it was sacked by the Danes. In the 12th century it had become a mere parish church. It is now only a green mound and a great name.

There is scarcely a hillside in this country through which I am riding that is not associated with some saintly name which carries the mind back to the splendid youth of the Irish Church. This morning I passed near Saigher, or Ser-Ciaran, in the territory of Ely, where Ciaran, the Elder, lived. From a hill not far from Ciaran's cell I could see the smoke of the town of St. Brendan. Yesterday, in the parish next to my own, I sat amidst the ruins of the old monastery at Drumcullen, visited by St. Cartbach the Younger on his way to Lismore, after being expelled from Rahan. Here on the eastern slope of the mountain I came to Aghaboe, the old abbey of

St. Canice. And besides there are Kyle and Mona-hincha, and Disartbeagh and Coolbanagh.

Aghaboe was once ruled by an Abbot, who was the greatest scientist of his age. His name was O'Far-rell. He is known in history as Fergil the Geometer, and as Virgilius, Bishop of Salzburg. He left Ireland for the Continent in April, 745. The Mayor of the Palace of the Court of France at that time was Pepin, afterwards king. Fergil of Aghaboe and this monarch were the closet friends, and Fergil lived with him for two years. He taught in the great schools, and his teaching marks an epoch in the history of science. It was he who first expounded publicly the fact that the earth is round. This was a proposition far in advance of the times, for it was advanced, of course, long before the system of Copernicus was known to the scientists of Europe. Bishop O'Farrell was also one of the great theologians of his age, and his exposition regarding the doctrine and ritual of baptism is well known to students of ecclesiastical history.

These names of saints and scholars and teachers and schools are reminiscent of peace and piety and learning, and the great happiness of a nation opening its heart to the gladness of grace—exalted, enraptured by the ecstacy of Faith. But there is the name of a place a few miles to our left that is suggestive of the slogan and the battle. It is the Rock of Dunamase, the fortress of Ruairi O'Moore. Here dwelt one of the stoutest hearts and one of the swiftest-striking men that ever withstood the English power in Ireland. O'Moore was the kind of Irish-

man that Gavan Duffy had in his mind when he
wrote :

Oh ! to have been an Irish chief
   When hearts were fresh and true,
And a manly thought, like a pealing bell,
   Would quicken them through and through,
And the seed of a generous hope right soon
   To a generous action grew;
And men would have scorned to talk and talk
   And never a deed to do.

The one consolation—a red-eyed, fierce one it was,
too—for the calamity which befell Leix and Offaly
at the hands of the English, in the awful perfidy
of Mullaghmast, was the high flame of vengeance
which blazed from the sword of O'Moore until the
Pale was scorched by its searching fire. One night
in 1577, Francis Cosby, the district commander of
the forces of Queen Elizabeth, held high festival at
Mullaghmast, one of the ancient raths of Leinster,
near Athy, in Kildare. He had been negotiating
and playing with the Irish for some months, and was
now determined to pacify them in a permanent and
radical manner. Hundreds of the O'Moore's,
O'Kellys, Lalors, and other Irish clans accepted his
invitation. Cosby had around him a chosen band
of English adventurers who had already received
grants of land in the district, or who were waiting to
obtain share of the plunder. They were there for
the fell purpose of murder, and as the Irish guests
entered the rath in twos and threes, they were set
upon and butchered before they could raise a sword

in self-defence. The butchery was carried on silently, so that the unfortunate people who were approaching the rath in parties and groups, had no suspicion of foul play.

> False Sydney! Knighthood's stain,
> The trusting brave—in vain
> Thy guests—ride o'er the plain
>   To thy dark coward snare.
> Flower of Offaly and Leix
> They have come thy board to grace—
> Fools! to meet a faithless race,
>   Save with true swords bare.

Four hundred of the Irish had fallen when one of the Lalors, who was riding up to the rath at the head of his people, became suddenly suspicious, and halting his troop entered the shambles alone. For a moment he was blinded by the horror of the sight which met his gaze. Then his sword was out, and he was hewing a path through the butchers, fighting his way back to his friends. They escaped and warned the others.

Next day Ruairi Og O'Moore, the chieftain of his clan, rode out from Dunamase to inflict his first series of punishments on the English. Ever after, until his death in the following year, he kept the foe on the run. He raided Naas, Athy, and Leighlin, struck apparently simultaneous blows in Kildare, Carlow, and Kilkenny, and each day that passed brought tidings of some daring deed of vengeance that gladdened the hearts of the Irish and struck terror in their oppressors and despoilers. It was a pity he was so rash. He was run through the body in an unguarded moment by a common English soldier, and died of his wound. Cosby, the arch-assassin, lived to meet the undeserved death of a soldier, when the flag of England went down in the defeat of Glenmalure. And Owney O'Moore, son of Ruairi Og, finished off the Cosby brood nineteen years later at the battle of Stradbally Bridge, when the son and grandson of Cosby of Mullaghmast were numbered among the slain.

Forty years later another Ruairi O'Moore of Leix appears in history as the chief of the Insurrection of 1641. He had been brought up at the Spanish Court with the young O'Neills. He began his work of organising the Irish Chieftains in 1640, and in a short time he had Maguire, O'Reilly, MacMahon, Tirlogh O'Neill, Phelim O'Neill, and many other men of influence in line for Ireland. It was he who prepared the way for Owen Roe O'Neill.

I have made many enjoyable cycling runs in Ireland, but none more so than my flight through Ossory. It was still early in the day when I swung out of the woods at Leap Castle and went away at a fine pace into the valleys below the southern spurs of the Slieve Blooms, on to Borris-in-Ossory, Abbey-leix, Ballinakill and into Durrow. This territory is now part of what is known as Queen's County. It was called by this name in honour of Mary Tudor, wife of Philip II. of Spain. Ui Falghi or Offaly was named King's County at the same time in honour of Mary's husband, and Dangan, near where the chief stronghold of the O'Connors Falghi was situated, had its name changed to Philipstown. Ancient Ossory extended from the Nore to the Suir and was separated from Leinster at the beginning of the Christian era and added to Munster. But it was divided up afterward. The chieftain of Ossory at the time of the Norman invasion was MacGillpatrick. He made a tenacious stand against Strongbow and gave him several hotly contested batttes. O'Heerin's mention of Ossory is as follows:

We journey across the Berba of ancient streams,
And treating of the heroes of Leinster.
To the level plain of the land of my heart,
To the noble hosts of Ossory.

To MacGillpatrick of the fine fortress,
The land of Ossory is by law ordained,
From Bladhma southward to the sea;
Brave are his battalions in the battles.

The town of Durrow is never mentioned in the guide books, yet its situation is very charming and the country around it is one of the gems of the basin of the Nore. A high range of wooded hills runs from east to west behind the town. This boldly sloping woodland is part of the Ashbrooke demesne, the entrance to which is located in the town itself.

And not only are the environs of Durrow very picturesque, but for many miles in every direction you may revel in many beautiful kinds of scenery. Go eastward, and you will cross Carlow and ride straight into the lone fastnesses of the Wicklow ranges. Go southward, and you will follow the windings of the beautiful Nore. Northward, you

have what O'Heerin called "the land of my heart."
And eastward you have the road that leads you to
Thurles and into a country that I want you to see.

In the square or green of Durrow we are at the
parting of the ways and a choice has to be made. It
would be grand if we went on down the Nore to its
confluence with the Barrow at New Ross. It would
be a pleasure full as great to strike eastward into
Wicklow. And as for the northward road, you can
guess whether it would be pleasant travelling to me
when I tell you it would lead me to my native place.

But none of these three roads are we going to take
now. We are off to the country of Kickham. We
are going to ramble for a while in the district of
vanished "Knocknagow." We are going to see the
Anner, and Slievenamon, and the Galtees, and the
hills and fields from which material was drawn to
write some of the most touching and noble literature that has ever come out of Ireland.

"Don't forget to go down Mullinahone way,"
wrote a friend to me from New York in the beginning of the summer. "Give us something about
Kickham's place."

"And if you are in Munster at all," said a Tipperary man to me in Buenos Aires before I sailed,
"be sure and take a run along the foot of the
Galtees and past Slievenamon, to Kickham's grave
at Mullinahone."

"You could not do better," said a Dublin friend
to me one morning when I told him that my next
cycling raid was planned out so as to include the
country out of which grew "The Homes of Tipperary." "You are up against a great literary

figure when you come to Kickham," he went on with
enthusiasm. "I say that of him although I am not
a Tipperary man, and although I never heard of
'Knocknagow' without sorrowing in my heart that
such a book was not written in Irish. If you want
to move Tipperary as nothing else can move it you
must strike a Kickham note. It is wonderful the
influence his writings have amongst the people. And
here in Dublin it is just the same. I know scores
of Tipperary men and women to whom Kickham is
a cherished and venerated friend. His works are as
familiar to them as the fields amidst which they
were reared. They are always quoting him.
'Knocknagow' is their favourite book amongst all
the volumes that have ever been published descriptive of Irish life. From its pages they take standards of conduct and criterions of life. You will
hear them give the names of Kickham's characters
to people of their acquaintance. You will hear
them call one man 'Mat the Thresher,' and another
'Phil Lahy,' and another 'Barney,' and they will call
one girl 'Grace Keily,' and another 'Mary Kearney,'
and another 'Bessy Morris,' and another 'Miss
Lloyd.'"

Mullinahone, where Kickham was born in 1825,
is a quiet little town near the Anner River. It lies
under the mountains, about half way between the
Nore and Suir, in South Tipperary, and in what
might be termed a fighting district. Ballingarry is
only a few miles to the north of it, and Slievenamon
rises in majesty right out of the valley of the Anner.
One of the few and isolated armed protests against

the rule of England in Ireland in the 19th century was made in this district. It was also a storm centre in '98. And it has been legendary for ages.

Slievenamon is one of the enchanted mountains of Erin When the Tuatha de Danaan were defeated by the Gaels they went into the heart of the hills to dwell in peace under the bracken and heather. So we read in our legends, which contain one of the most romantic and splendid of the world's mythologies. Slievenamon was one of the hills chosen by the sidhe as their dwelling-places. From their halls near the summit they could ride down on the moonbeams into vales and dells, and sail homeward over the morning mists, and waft messages by the night winds across the dewy distances to Pallas Green in Limerick, and to Carrig-Clena below Mallow, where the great queen of all the Munster fairies dwelt amidst the rocks.

Legends of the Munster Fianna were told around Kickham's cradle. Legends of the great days when Cormac ruled in Cashel were also to be heard in Mullinahone. And you may be sure there were legends of '98 and Rory of the Hill. Then, besides, kind nature that has been so lavish in her generosity to Ireland, threw her riches broadcast over this storied countryside. The valleys are shady and fertile, and the bright streams that wander through them dance and flash in the sunlight as if revelling in the glad anticipation of throwing themselves into the embraces of the Suir. A hundred knolls all gay with cowslips ; a hundred lanes all golden with the primrose; a hundred copses all white with the fragrant spume of the hawthorn; a hundred

thatched roofs over which the turf-smoke rose in
tiny clouds of softest blue; a hundred tillage-fields
where the whistle of the ploughman was heard, and
over which floated the songs of the maidens milking
in the early morning, or in the sunset splendour—
all this Kickham saw around him as a child. And
over the smiling fields and heathery boglands and
flashing streams rose the sheltering mountains,
gray in the dawn, rosy in the flush of the sunrise,
blue at noon, purple in the evening time, dark and
grim when the twilight faded, silvery and beautiful
and mystic when the moon climbed over them to
light up the sleeping world; and always, always
ordly and impressive and potent to quicken thought.
And then what love and laughter in the lives of the
people!—the kindly prayerful salutations as they
met each other; the pious congregations at Mass
or Rosary; the happy gatherings at crossroad dance
or inter-parish hurling match; and the helpful, unselfish, unclouded charity and friendship that
blessed their cleanly lives! It was into this am-
bient of poetry and romance and happiness that
Kickham was born. God endowed him with a mind
powerful to see and capacious to retain many of
the wondrous things that are in the Irish heart, and
his environment and up-bringing did the rest.

I was thinking of all this as I stood by his grave
in Mullinahone churchyard, and as I sat on the bank
of the Anner. And I wondered why he did not
write more poetry. For the poetic faculty he had
without a doubt, and had it in a large and masculine sense. Do you remember when you were
learning by heart the verses which tell the story of

" that rake up near the rafters," for, of course, you will have committed some or most of them, if not them all, to memory at some time in your life. Do you remember how your breath came quicker, and how the lines became blurred when you read:

> She looked into her husband's eyes,
>   While light her own did fill,
> " You'll shortly know the reason why,"
>   Said Rory of the Hill.

I was a boy of twelve when I first read this stirring poem, and I shall never forget how it fascinated me. I supposed it was because it gave voice to intuition and set free some of the deep, dumb things of the soul that were planted there before life began. The first stanza of the piece that was caught by my memory was the one which tells of Rory's moonlight journey to the rendezvous of the patriot leaders:

> The midnight moon is lighting up,
>   The slopes of Slievenamon,
> What foot affrights the startled hare
>   So long before the dawn?
> He walked up where the Anner stream
>   Winds up the woods anear,
> Then whistled low and looked around
>   To see the coast was clear.
> A shieling door flew open,
>   In he stepped with right goodwill.
> " God save all here and bless your work,"
>   Said Rory of the Hill.

The movement of the lines is firm and martial, and there is music in the sound of them which has a charm of its own. But the real power of the stanza lies deeper than words or cadence or measure—deeper than the clear picture that is given of the frightened hare streaking across the moonlit pasture from the path of the belated wayfarer. It lies in the thoughts which it awakens—the thought of the man with a price on his head, stealing through the country like a hunted animal, the thought of the men assembled in the sheiling to confer with him, each one of whom has taken his life in his hand, the thought of the old, proud, undying, unconquerable ideal that is the bond between them, and the thought of the noble self-sacrifice they made for its sweet and holy sake:

> They sat around the humble board
>   Till the dawning of the day,
> And yet no song, no shout was heard,
>   No revellers were they.
> Some cheeks flushed red with gladness,
>   While some were grimly pale,
> But pale or red from out those eyes
>   Flashed souls that never quail.
> " And tell us now about the vow
>   They swore for to fulfil,"
> " You'll read it yet in history,"
>   Said Rory of the Hill.

What a fine sequence there is in the taking down of the ashen handle next day, when " the toothed rake full scornfully into the fire he flung," and sub-

stituted for it a gleaming pikehead.   And oh! wives
of '98—oh women of Ireland!—what a verse is the
one that follows:

> She looked at him with woman's pride.
>   With pride and woman's fears;
> She flew to him, she clung to him,
>   And wiped away her tears.
> He feels her pulse beat truly,
>   While her arms around him twine,
> " Now God be praised for your stout heart
>   Brave little wife of mine!"
> He swung his first-born in the air,
>   While joy his heart did fill,
> " You'll be a freeman yet, my boy,"
>   Said Rory of the Hill.

A hundred years before that, the same spirit was
shown when the women of Limerick stood dry-eyed
in the breach fighting and falling beside their husbands and children and lovers.   It was the thought
that was in Ethna Carbery's mind a hundred years
later, when she wrote:

> Mine own is mine, and at Erin's need
>   I would send him forth at her side to stand,
> Blessing the day, and blessing the deed,
>   With the steel in his strong right hand.

It is this passion for the olden cause which must
burn again in the breasts of the women as well as
of the men of Ireland.   There is now a hope of
kindling it since Irish-Ireland has taken to planting

its foot upon the evil denationalising convent education, and patiently yet sternly inculcating the doctrine that only a generation of worthy Irish mothers
can suckle sons worthy to bear the Irish name.
It is only from Irish breasts aglow with the flame
of patriotism that Irish children are to draw the
yearning to see, and the courage and constancy to
fight for and win, the freedom of their land.

There are only two other poetical compositions
by Kickham that have taken hold of the popular
mind, of the very few pieces he published. One is
" Patrick Sheehan," and the other—a beautiful
ballad of its kind—" The Widow's Brown-haired
Daughter." Why is it that a poet of such feeling
and fancy left so little poetry behind him. I suppose the reason was that he sacrificed his own
inclination to the needs of the time in which he
lived. The crowding and tragic problems that
developed in Ireland after '48 left no poetic leisure
to Kickham, for he was one of the men who
took up the task of preparing Ireland to fight for
her liberty. Instead of wooing the muse he threw
himself into journalism with John O'Leary and
others, and, together, each in his own honest and
utterly unselfish way, they tried to show Ireland
the path of duty. There is no time for writing
poetry in the fettered life of a militant journalist;
nor are the conditions by which he is surrounded
favourable to the preservation of that contempla-
tive mood and detachment of mind in which poetic
thought is matured and out of which it finds its
most perfect expression. Kickham's journalistic
work brought him into contact with the harsh actu-

alities of intellectual combat, wherein there is no emotion untroubled. He was obliged to exercise constant vigilance, to decide swiftly, and to hit accurately and heavily. He wrote with fire and force, but it was in prose, on current political topics, and to meet the exigency of the moment. This was no environment for a bard. Davis wrote propagandist verse which was so good that it remains as literature. But Davis was not chained to the " Nation," as Kickham was to the " Irish People." And, besides all this, Kickham was misunderstood, just as his friend and comrade, John O'Leary, was misunderstood. This was inevitable. Most of the 19th century in Irish political life was a great misunderstanding, sometimes showy, sometimes squalid, but always more or less windy, unreasoning, and intolerant. Kickham was one of the men who saw through the misunderstanding, and who braved contumely and enmity in order to right it.

The remnant are right, when the masses are led
    like sheep to the pen.

And he was one of the remnant. He was one of the first to be sent out of the way to prison when the '67 trouble was maturing. England paid him the compliment of rightly estimating his worth; and she locked him up.

I was told by one who knew him that the statue erected to his memory in Tipperary is a very good likeness of Kickham. The figure is seated, pen in hand, smiling serenely. There is no passion in the lovable, kindly features, no rancour, nothing small.

There is plenty of humour in the smile, but it is playful, healthy, clean. It is an open, honest, handsome face, very intellectual and very brave. He was not of a very strong constitution, although a rather tall and loose-limbed man, and there appear to be indications of physical suffering on the brow.

I was thinking of him and of "Knocknagow" as I rode through the parish, and I spoke of him to all the country people I met on the road within miles of his burial-place. Not one of them but could tell me something about him.

"Do you think was ' Knocknagow " a true story?" I asked a man near Fethard, " or was it only a story that Kickham invented?"

"Of course it was true," he answered in a tone which showed that there could be no question about it ; " he changed the names of the people, but that was all. Me father knew Mat the Thresher and sure it was only last year that a grandson of Tommy Lahy's came here from New York in his automobile carriage to see if the beech tree was standin' and to see where his grandfather was born."

But the beech tree, in the branches of which Tommy Lahy learned the art of climbing, is there no more. They showed me the place where it is said to have stood. But not even a stone heap remains of the hamlet, and the well down the road is weed-grown.

The village that Kickham had in his mind when he wrote of " The Homes of Tipperary " is gone. But the book remains ; and will always be a classic.

I do not say this because "Knocknagow" has always been my favourite novel, and I expect always will be. My reason for saying that it maintains the place it has taken as a classic tale of Irish life is that it is such a faithful and beautiful study of Irish character. It is not a faultless work; nor are some of its blemishes of the most trivial nature; but take it on its merits and submit it to the most searching literary and historical test, and it will come through the ordeal with its fame as a masterpiece undimmed. "Knocknagow" should be in every Irish household. It is one of the first books that Irish boys and girls should read in English. It should be read in the same year as John Mitchel's "Jail Journal," A. M. Sullivan's "Story of Ireland," and the poems and essays of Thomas Davis. There are, perhaps, novels descriptive of Irish life more brilliantly written than "Knocknagow," but I do not know of any tale that shows such insight into the Irish heart. There is scarcely a chapter in which you do not find some fine intuition, or some exquisitely subtle touch, or some pregnant truth brought home to the understanding of the simplest person.

"Well, indeed, it's too late for you to think of going to Tipperary to-night," said a hospitable farmer with whom I had been talking Kickham for an hour and more. I had met him near his snug home, in the twilight, and we had fallen into conversation, in the course of which he had quietly taken me by the arm, saying:

"Sure the tea is ready, and you're not goin' to pass the house. 'Twouldn't be right to go without bit or sup out of this part of the country after you comin' so far to see it. Why, Kickham would turn in his grave if he knew it. Come in."

In I went and was presented to Herself and the family as one who had ridden ever so far to see Knocknagow. There were some hot griddle cakes on the table, brown on the crust, and white as driven snow inside until the yellow butter melted on them under the hospitable efforts of one of the girls, while the mother cooked rashers and eggs. I was, in real truth, homerically hungry, and I did homeric justice to the feast. We talked about the men and women of " Knocknagow " and " Sally Cavanagh," and of the wild times of '67, during which Himself had spent a week on the hills half-buried in snow. He had known Kickham in his prime, and had seen him in his evening of life. He had been out with Smith O'Brien and had seen many a head that was brown and black turn grey from the hardships of the prison, and the heartache of failure, and the sullen rage against fate. But he was not a pessimist, for in his heart was the song of undying hope.

There was no getting away from him that night, and despite my most vehement protests I was put up in the best bed. And God knows it felt cosy and comfortable and grand; and I went to sleep feeling very proud of having been welcomed, for Kickham's sake, in one of " The Homes of Tipperary."

CHAPTER XIX.

Cork—The Valley of the Lee—A tolerably old city—Its Patron Saint—Finn Barr the Holy—Gougane Barra — Mediæval Cork — Patrick Street—The Covered Car—On Patrick's Bridge —The Irish Dress—Father Mathew—Industry and Education—"The Bells of Shandon"— "Father Prout"—"Paddy's Market"—The Cove of Cork.

A wide, beautiful valley, running from east to west, sheltered between lofty and grassy hills, along the crests of which are the groves and terraces of many pleasant villas; a silvery stream winding through the fields, now shadowed by the overhanging woods, and now emerging into the sunlight between sloping lawns and meadows; and, far down in the valley, tall spires and long tiers of grey houses on the shelving hillside—such was the first view I caught of Cork the beautiful. I had been rambling through the mountains for a few days above the Nore and Suir and Blackwater, up in cloudland, above the heather, in the free winds which sang to me the songs of the Comeraghs and Knockmealdowns and Galtees. It was pleasant to come down into the world again, and find myself for the first time amidst the undulating fields and green pastures of northern Muskerry It was grand to pass through the fertile districts where the fat of the land is converted into golden coloured butter through the agency of hundreds of dairies. When I entered the valley of the Lee, miles below the place where it flashes out of the Kerry hills, it was still more enjoyable. And it was an unpurchasable delight to follow " the pleasant waters " into Cork.

I have read somewhere that Cork has been called the Irish Venice, and also the Irish Amsterdam. The patronising writers who paid this left-handed compliment to Cork were foreigners, of course, who desired to tell the public in the first place that they had been in Italy and Holland, and in the next place qualify their praise of an Irish city by implying that it reminded them of some more beautiful place in foreign parts, of which, in a sense, it was an imitation or an understudy. As a matter of fact, Cork is sufficiently beautiful to stand alone amongst the cities by the sea and claim the admiration of travellers on its own merits. Nor is there anything foreign in its appearance. It is no more foreign-looking than Dublin, or Derry, or Limerick. It shelters some people who look upon England as their country, and upon everything English as godly, and who regard London as the political and social capital of Ireland. But for all that, Cork is an Irish city. Its heart was troubled when I was there because of the debauchery of national sentiment effected by an International Exhibition and the baronetting of its Mayor, and certain royal and naval visits and other sorrowful manifestations of slavishness. Nevertheless, its instincts are manly, and the bulk of the people are on the side of Ireland.

It is a tolerably old place this beautiful capital of of Munster, and dates, as a city, from the beginning of the seventh century. It is peculiarly situated. Before reaching the city the river Lee branches into two main channels, which meet again further on, thus forming an island. It was on this island that Cork was founded, and it is here that the heart of the city is still. Besides the protection of the encircling streams, the island was girdled by walls during the middle ages. But, in modern times, Cork has stepped across both streams and spread itself along the outer shores and back into the valley and up the slopes of the hills. Six bridges link the island with the mainland, and there are various excellent lines of electric tramways.

Cork derives its name from Corcagh, the Irish word for a marshy place. It is a marshy place no longer; but, in the long ago, when the mountains sent their torrents rolling down the Lee during rainy weather, the right bank overflowed and the waters covered the land for miles, forming a great lake, which was called Loch Irce. This lake gave greater security to Cork, or, as the old Irish writers called it, "the great Corcagh of Munster," and made it a most desirable place of residence in the early days of Christianity in Eirinn. It was, doubtless, because of its isolation that Corcagh was chosen by St. Finbar as a place upon which to build a monastery. This happened early in the seventh century, and from the advent of the founder of the great school of Cork may be dated the rise of the city into religious and intellectual importance after centuries of uneventful history.

"Who is the patron saint of Cork?" I asked a party of boys whom I met on their homeward way from the fine schools of the Christian Brothers. They were Cork lads to the marrow, and the one who replied to my question had a wealth of Munster fun in his big, blue eyes, and the Munster music in his soft and mellow speech.

"St. Finbar is the patron saint of the Irish part of Cork," he said, "but the King of England is the patron saint of the shoneens."

I hailed the statement as a sign that Cork is still "rebel" and that the memory of the saint is still green by the Lee. It is so over most of Southern Munster. The chief reason of this is that in South Munster the people are still in touch with the past. The survival of the Irish language has kept alive the ancient history of the land, and hence the names of the men who made that history have a meaning and force for posterity.

St. Finbar was born in Muskerry, and there is a strange legend connected with his birth. His father was an ostracised scion of the Hy-Briuin Ratha of Western Connacht, who strayed into the territory of Hy-Liathain in Cork. He was a skilful artificer, and he was employed by the chieftain of the country to execute various works. In the dun of this chieftain dwelt a lovely maiden, his ward, whom her guardian had forbidden to marry. All the men of the chieftain's household were forbidden to speak to her of love, and this prohibition extended to the artificer from Connacht, who was plying his craft at the palace, fashioning spear heads and sword hilts, and incidentally bestowing his heart's fondest affection upon the forbidden maiden. She returned his love, and they were secretly married. When the chieftain discovered what they had done, he ordered the lovers to be thrown into a lighted limekiln. But a great thunderstorm came down from the mountains, and the rain, which fell in torrents, quenched the fire. The people then cried out that this was the work of God, and that the parents had been saved by Divine intervention, so that their child might be a servant of the Most High When the infant was born it was christened Lochan, but, as the lad grew up, they called him "Find-barr," from his fair, flowing hair. From this term of endearment come all the names by which the saint is known—Barra, Bairee, Barry, Barre, and "St. Barry."

Find-barr was trained for the religious life from his earliest youth. He spent some time in Rome, and was a disciple of St. Gregory the Great. He founded various monasteries before he came to Cork. One of them was at Gougane Barra. This monastery was built on the isle which Callanan has handed down to fame in his undying verse:

Oh, where is the dwelling in valley or highland
So meet for a bard as this lone little island?

It is indeed a scene of wild and romantic beauty. The towering mountains sentinel the lake, and are reflected in its depths. The island is near the south-eastern shore, and is like a rare and brilliant emerald placed on the face of a mirror—that is, when the lake is calm. When "the waters rush down 'mid the thunder's deep rattle," it is like an emerald on frosted silver. When the moonbeams kiss the water and gild the hill-crests, the island is still like an emerald thrown on dark velvet in a darkened room. It is emerald always—a rich, lovely unconquerable green —amidst the grey desolation of lightning-blasted peaks and brown, heathery mountain sides. It is belted by trees, under which the wavelets murmur on the shore. Out of the dark waters near the island sallies a flashing streamlet, which tumbles down a glen in white foam from rock to rock. It is the Lee starting on its course to the parent ocean.

A place where dreams might come of a deep and mystic kind. A dwelling " meet for a bard," as the poet said of it. And meet for a saint as well, as Finbar showed—meet because so lone and solemn and grand—because in it the soul could lift itself over the world by high and holy contemplation, and feel itself in the presence of God. The Saint spent several years here, meditating, planning, preparing himself for the work before him. Then he went down to Corcagh, and founded his school, to which students flocked from far and near, and around which a city soon began to rise. The church-monastery and schools were founded on the south-west corner of Corcagh. The ancient buildings have long since disappeared, and the site is now occupied by the Protestant cathedral. The Protestant cathedral is named after St. Finbar, in accordance, no doubt, with the fashion set by the pious reavers of the Tudors and Stuarts and Cromwell, who were most careful to steal the names of the Irish saints as well as the church lands and the churches. The School of Cork, founded by St. Finbar, was, during its day, the most famous scholastic centre in Munster. Many of the most eminent teachers of the seventh and eighth centuries were its alumni.

Cork was a walled city in the Middle Ages. There is a map extant of Cork in the year 1600. The walls were still intact, and were strengthened by various towers. The English had made it one of their military bases for the conquest of Ireland, and it played an important part in the great war of the Ulster Confederacy, which ended with the flight of the Earls. In 1601 all Ireland was ablaze, and the fight for freedom was going bravely on West and East, and South and North. The Spanish fleet, under Don Juan del Aguila, had sailed from the Tagus, and was daily expected to arrive in some of the Munster ports, probably in the Geraldine country. It was some days after the middle of September when a rider of the English dashed out from Cork with fateful tidings. The Spaniards were making for the coast. On the 23rd of that month Mountjoy was in Kilkenny; and around him assembled in council were Carew, Ormond, Marshal Wingfield and others. They were discussing the military situation and the chances of success against the Irish forces, when the messenger from Cork, all splashed and weary, arrived with the news that the invaders were entering Kinsale. There was saddling in hot haste then in the Marble City. Riders were sent out on every side to order a concentration of the available English forces of Southern Munster. In Cork the guards were doubled on the walls, and the troops in charge of the arsenal were called to arms and maintained on duty, in expectation of an attack. The English generals were in hourly anticipation of defeat, and despatches were sent to London begging for reinforcements. On the other

hand, the Irish, who were loyal to Ireland in Cork
and Munster, and in all Ireland from North to
South, were cheered by a mighty hope. But alas!
it was too late. Of the 6,000 Spaniards that had
left the Tagus, only 3,400 arrived at Kinsale. The
port of debarkation was the wrong one under the
circumstances, and, sad to say, there were Irish
chieftains who had lost the sacred passion for freedom. The strong hand of O'Neill had banded them
together, but the craft of Carew had undone that
work of leadership. Some had grown indifferent,
others had been led away by personal ambition. Others by treachery. The "Sugan" Earl
and Florence MacCarthy were prisoners in London. Brave Feach MacHugh had been murdered
at Ballincor. O'Neill and O'Donnell were fronting the enemy in the North. And of all the
Irish chivalry of the South, only noble O'Sullivan Beare and O'Driscoll and O'Connor of
Kerry drew steel for Ireland. Meanwhile the
English forces began to concentrate on Kinsale;
5,000 fresh troops soon arrived in Cork from England. 16,000 more marched in from Desmond and
Thomond and Leix. By the 17th October there
were 25,000 English and Anglo-Irish troops facing
the Spaniards. The Ulster chieftains pressed
southward with the utmost speed, and O'Donnell's
night march over the crests of Slieve Felim has won
plaudits from military critics ever since. But valour
could not achieve the impossible. The Spaniards
were disillusiond, disgusted, and disheartened.
The failure of the attempt to relieve the town
decided Don Juan del Aguila to give up the struggle.
He surrendered on January 12th, 1602, and agreed

to give up at the same time as Kinsale, the fortresses
of Dunboy, Baltimore, and Castlehaven. "Speak
for yourself, Don Juan," cried stalwart Richard
MacGeoghegan, when the news of the Spanish
surrender was brought to him in Dunboy. "No
enemy enters here while an Irish arm is within the
walls to strike him down." The defence of Dunboy
is a page of glory in the record of that disastrous
epoch. The march of O'Sullivan Beare to Breffni is
another. The rest of the fateful story is some of
the saddest reading in the history of the world
O'Donnell was poisoned by the hirelings of England
on his way to the Spanish court. O'Neill made submission at Mellifont. Then came the culminating
sorrow for our land when the Chieftain Tir-Eoghan
and his family and the family of the murdered
Chieftain of Kinel-Conaill were obliged to fly the
country, leaving Ulster and Eire without a leader.
It was the last of the ancient Irish nation—for the
time being.

All this comes into your memory as you journey
through Munster or come within the sound of the
billows breaking along the southern coast of Ireland.
You cannot escape it. The pleasure you derive from
climbing the heath-clad mountains or roaming
through beautiful valleys, or sweeping at full speed
over grassy upland or down the slopes of fertile
hills, is clouded by the ever-present thought the
shadow of foreign rule is over it all, and that the
sunlight of freedom has still to shine on the land
and make its loveliness perfect.

Well, I am going to tell you now about Patrick
Street in Cork. I found it to be one of the plea-

santest streets in Ireland.   It is a fine, airy, spacious, well-proportioned thoroughfare, and your eye can travel along it without feeling cramped.   By well-proportioned I mean that the houses are not too high for the street, nor is the street too broad for the houses.   The sidewalks are wide and smooth and there is plenty of light both by   night   and   day. Patrick's Bridge, which spans one of the branches of the Lee, contributes much to the splendid appearance of the street.   And, moreover, from the sidewalks in certain places you see the slopes of the hills beyond the city clothed with thickly-foliaged trees. A double electric tramcar line runs along the middle of the street, and the posts which carry the overhead wires have large arc lamps.   The tramcars are well-managed, and are extensively used.   I counted seven other kinds of vehicles for the transport of passengers, to wit, the ubiquitous automobile, the jaunting car, the landau, the brougham, the inside car,' the hansom cab, and last, but not least, the " covered car."

In no other city or town have I seen the covered car during my rambles, and when I asked a Cork jarvey if it could be found in any other part of the visible universe he answered me a " No " which struck echoes out of the arches of Patrick's Bridge. I suppose the " covered car " of Cork is a survival. It was once common to the whole of Ireland.   It is an inside car with a roof and sides and ends to it— a kind of covered coach on two wheels.   There is a box seat in front for the driver, and the conveyance is entered by a door at the rere.   It is an excellent institution for wet or cold weather—at least, it is excellent for the passenger. I do not know that it is excellent for the horse that has to furnish the motive power. There are many " covered cars " in Cork for hire. I made a trip in one of them and held converse with the driver through the front window. It was not a very convenient way of carrying on a conversation, but when you are out after information you have to moderate your standards of comfort and make them suitable to circumstances.

" It must be very hard on a poor horse to pull this car," I remarked through the window, addressing myself to the small section of the driver's side face which was visible on the limited horizon. He raised his whip hand and looked downward in my direction under his raised elbow as a bird looks under its wing.

" Would you mind sitting a little more behind, sir," he said persuasively; " we're too heavy on the poor horse's back."

I meekly took the gentle hint and sat more towards the door. But I still managed to keep my face near the window so as to be within speaking distance.

" Don't you think," I asked, " that a jaunting-car is much better than a walled-in, loose box like this. Don't you think an outside car would be lighter on the horse and airier for the passenger ? "

" Them's all things that the jaunting-car jarveys puts into people's heads, sir," he explained in a more or less affable shout so as to be heard over the rattle of the vehicle and adown the altitude which separated us. " You take my word for it there's

nothing like a covered car. Supposin' now, sir, you
were a girl comin' home from a ball an' it rainin'
cats and dogs, where would you be on a jaunting-
car? But get into your covered car and you're as
snug and dry as a moushyeen in a hayrick. Or suppose you's a lady goin out to see your friends in the
wet, what would become of your hat on a jaunting-
car? Wouldn't it be like a dishclout by the time
you get down town? But get into your nice
covered car and you're as spic and span as if you
came out of a bandbox. And, suppose, sir, you're
a thrifle tight goin' home afther a little flare-up,
aren't you safer in a yoke like this, that you can't
fall out of, do your best, than sittin' on the side of a
jaunting-car with somebody holding you on, and
the driver afraid of his life that your neck 'll be
broke, and that not a penny of his fare he'll get if
you're killed. And besides, if you're goin' anywhere
that you don't want the people to know, how are you
goin' to keep it quiet stuck on a jaunting-car? Sure
you might as well be Father Mathew there standing
upon his pillar [we were passing the Father Mathew
monument at the time]—the whole world'll see you.
But get into your covered car and shut the windows
and the door and pull down the blinds and not a
man, woman or child will know anything about you."

" I didn't notice any covered cars in Dublin," I
remarked next.

" There isn't any in Dublin, he said.   " And, anyhow, sure Dublin was never to be compared to Cork."

" No covered cars in Dublin?" I said in an in-
credulous tone, not that I doubted his word, but
merely because I wished to draw him out.

"No," he replied decisively, "nor anywhere else. Cork is th' only city that you can drive in in your covered car."

"Do you mean that there is no covered car to be found but in the city of Cork?"

"I do, indeed."

"No covered cars in any other part of the world at all?"

"No place at all," he shouted politely. "There may be cabs and carriages and all kinds of yokes on two and four wheels, but there isn't any covered cars anywhere except here in Cork."

That disposed of the subject.

I stood for half-an-hour on Patrick's Bridge, and watched the people passing to and fro. They were well-dressed, as a rule, both men and women, and right gracefully they carried themselves I had often heard that there were no eyes in Ireland so bewitching as the eyes of the Corkonian damsels. Before deciding on this point you would require to see a large congregation leaving St. Mary's, say after ten o'clock Mass on a fine Sunday morning, and I had not this opportunity. There were many handsome women in the streets, but I have to say that there were more handsome men. I saw scores of fine, slim, sinewy athletes under thirty years of age. And I liked their dress, nearly all of home manufacture, and simply yet elegantly made. Most of them wore the knee-breeches, which is coming back into favour in Ireland. I do not mean the riding-breeches which the bank clerk affects, nor yet the baggy, shapeless cycling knickerbocker upon the manufacture of which some misguided foreigners

waste useful cloth.   I mean the graceful garment
that is neatly buttoned below the knee, where the
knitted worsted stocking is gartered over it.   This
costume is winning its way in Dublin also, but then
Dublin has remembered of late years that it is the
capital of Ireland, and that, consequently, it is its
duty to be an Irish city in spirit as well as in name.

"It will be hard to make fellows with pipe-stem
shanks take kindly to the knee-breehes," said a friend
to me in Dublin at the Oireachtas. "The pantaloon
is merciful."

It certainly is, but there would be less deformity
in ankles and insteps if the foot were not half
covered by the unsightly pantaloon.   Two or three
generations of the Irish costume would correct the
faulty lines which now shrink from view.   There is
an impulse in nature to seek perfection of form.   It
is only when nature is trammelled and cheated that
she is unlovely.   She is a great reformer, remodeller,
and rebuilder when she gets a chance to work her
wondrous will.   She will quicken a sense, change a
cast of feature, make the voice more musical and the
limbs more shapely once the impulse towards perfection is unshackled.   Encase the foot and ankle in
clothing that will not hide their ungraceful outlines,
and the impulse of nature to seek perfection of form
will at once awake and go to work.   Take horses,
soft of hoof and thick of fetlock off the grassy
pampas, and drive them away into the Andine
regions.   In five years their hoofs will have become
pointed, hard, and narrow.   The first horses foaled
in that region will have hoofs like mules, and shins
like racers.   Why?   Just because the impulse to-

wards perfection has been set to work. In this case
the impulse has been awakened by a physical necessity. In the case of a man the impulse is more
complex. There is the desire of the conscious being
to obtain greater physical perfection, and there is
the unfettered natural tendency of the limb itself
towards symmetry of form. There was a member of
the Royal Irish Constabulary standing on the
bridge, who evidently considered himself to be a
very fine-looking fellow. So he was in a general
way, but he failed to impress you favourably, in
detail. He was five-feet-ten in his boots, and his
feet were number elevens. In his semi-German
uniform-cap and great coat he looked well enough.
But if he had been dressed in shoes and knee-
breeches he would have been conscious of his bulky
ankles and flat insteps. It was because he had never
had any active consciousness of them that they had
assumed such proportions. They were still growing.
So was his head. It appeared to be already a size
too small for his cap. I do not say this because he
looked at me most suspiciously and walked all
round me, inspecting me from various points of
view. It is the truth, and it has occurred to me to
state it—as an after-thought and nothing more.

The Father Mathew monument near St. Patrick's
Bridge is one of Foley's best works. The figure is
draped in the graceful cloak which has, unfortunately, gone out of fashion in Ireland. The pose is
very appropriate—firm, dignified, alert. The face
and head are splendidly modelled. The right hand
is slightly extended. The left gathers some folds
of the cloak to the breast. The expression is a

triumph of art, and does justice to one of the greatest
of Munstermen, and one of the greatest of the Irish
race. Strength—calm, self-contained, mighty strength
—is on the brow; and the eye has the fulness of
genius. The chin is massive, determined, eloquent
of will power. The lips are beautiful, with an infinite gentleness. It is a magnificent face, regular,
even handsome in outline, and illumined by the
inspiration of a noble and undying purpose, and
with a charity sweet as the love of angels and wide
as humanity. The attitude is that of a man of
action—a man who would do things and get other
men to do them—a man of tireless physical and
mental energy, yet thoroughly self-contained—the
attitude of a great leader and teacher.

And a great leader and teacher Father Mathew
was. He had the simplicity of genius and the constancy of all virtue that is heroic. In no place is his
memory held dearer than in Cork City. His grave
is in St. Joseph's Cemetery, but the good he did is
not buried with him. As I gazed on the sculptured
features of the face overlooking Patrick's Bridge, I
could not help thinking of the other statue by the
same artist—the statue of O'Connell overlooking the
Liffey. You will seldom see it stated that much of
the might of the O'Connell movement was due to
Father Mathew. Yet such is the clear historical
truth. The temperance which the Cork priest
preached and fostered bred moral strength and self-
respect, and when the clarion voice of O'Connell
sounded the rally of the men of Ireland, they
hastened to him in millions—millions of temperate,
vertebrate, manly men. And, alas! when the

supreme moment came, those millions of men were told that liberty was not worth a drop of blood.

Ah, well, there are men and women working again in Eirinn to foster national self-respect and national manliness of purpose—to organise and discipline our forces and hold them in readiness for the day when our next great leader shall arise. Pray God that his vision may be high and unclouded, and that his heart may be infinitely strong and true.

I crossed the twin streams several times, took passages on various lines of tramway, went to Lough Mahon, Sunday's Well, and Blackpool, and explored the suburbs and outlying wards. It was pleasant work. There are at least a dozen points of vantage in Cork from any of which you can obtain an excellent view of the city, and every view you obtain is picturesque. I will also say that upon the whole every view is encouraging. There is the appearance of industry about Cork without being in any way suggestive of a vast, grimy, sweltering, clanging workshop; and Heaven forbid that any Irish city should ever become such an earthly hell. There is room, and plenty of room in Cork for more work-shops and factories yet. But meanwhile it is gratifying to note so many thriving industries, and to think that each industry gives its share of employment to the working classes. The Cork Industrial Association has shown Ireland what can be done in the way of promoting home manufactures. This Association has acted as the pioneer of national self-protection. The idea of the Irish Trade Mark is entirely good. It appeals to every manufacturer of Irish goods in Ireland. It is one of the finest pieces of constructive policy that has come out of the intellectual awakening in Ireland. I visited the Mardyke, the South Mall, the Queen's College, Parnell Bridge, and all the churches. The Mardyke is a beautiful promenade. If you had a cent for every vow of love that has been spoken there you would be fabulously rich. The South Mall is a kind of financial quarter. It has a monopoly of banks and such offices. The Queen's College is a teaching institution, to a large extent, without pupils It is a fine building—quite as fine as the Queen's College of Galway, and fully as useless. It is an outrageous thing to see the mind of Ireland handicapped in this enlightened age by the want of a National University, while there are thousands and thousands of pounds of Irish taxation applied for the upkeep of universities that have never had the confidence of the Irish people. If there were a constituent college of a National University in Cork it would have an attendance of hundreds of Munster students. The Queen's College has scarcely enough of students to form a football match, unless it commandeered the College authorities and made them goal-keepers.

There is a quaint old church tower of a style of architecture something akin to the Spanish, which has been misleading me for some hours. I thought at first that there were two towers in the city of the same pattern, but of different colours. I now find as I stand close to it, that it is one and the same. It is quadrilateral, and while the southern and western sides are faced with white limestone, the northern and eastern sides are of red sandstone The upper part of the main body of the tower is ℴccupied by a clock, and over the clock in their snug belfry are

> The bells of Shandon
> That sound so grand on
> The pleasant waters
> Of the River Lee.

This is the Shandon Church and in the church-yard is the grave of the Rev. Francis O'Mahony, known in literature by the name of Father Prout. Cork is very proud of him and there are only a very few Corkonians who will tell you that he and his writings were and are a dead loss to Ireland. I do not entirely agree with the few, but I think their view is the right one. I say this although I am a lover of the Prout Papers and have always admired them for their scholarly playfulness, their classic raillery and their refined humour. But what are they after all but a valuable and exquisite contri-bution to English literature? Moore's lyrical and historical work entitles us to regard him as being, in a sense, more Irish than Father Prout, but when all is said, the "Melodies" are not Irish literature. Not all that Father Prout has left behind him is, when considered as Irish literature, worth a single page of Father Peter O'Leary's inimitable Irish prose. Father Peter knows and loves the Irish people and writes for them and of them, not in Eng-lish, but in the living, flexible, idiomatic Irish lan-guage—the language that was spoken in Ireland for centuries and centuries before the English of the Anglo-Normans was spoken anywhere. The difference between the Irish and English language as means of expressing the Irish mind is the difference between the absolute and the relative. At his best, therefore, Father Prout could only do in a relative sense what Father O'Leary is doing in an absolute sense. But it was not always that Father Prout essayed the task of expressing the Irish mind, while " Father Peter " has never essayed anything else. It is a hard thought to think that while so many gifted minds were writing prose and verse, of and for Ireland, during the past two centuries, they were only writing, in a literary sense, contributions, more or less durable or evanescent, to English literature, simply because they wrote in English. A bush story is Australian, a veldt story is African, Kerry story is Irish, a Kentucky story is American, a St. Lawrence story is Canadian. But so long as these stories are written in English what are they in a literary sense but pieces of English literature? It is hard to think that " Davis's Essays " and Mitchel's " Jail Journal " and Kickham's novels are things which enrich English literature. It is hard to think that when those gifted writers were dealing their mightest blows at England they were still, in a literary sense, adorning English letters

I paid a flying visit to Paddy's Market, and now I am going to tell you something about it. There is another name for it, but it does not appear to be often used. It is at times called the " Coal Quay Market." It is situated off the Coal Quay near the Opera House. There is a very elaborate kind of market on the Grand Parade called, I think, " The English Market," probably to distinguish it from the Irish market, which is an open-air institution. The retailers in the Irish market dispose of their wares along the streets, and although there are some shops, they are establishments catering more for the market as a whole. You can obtain an infinite variety of things in Paddy's Market—old books, old furniture, new and old clothes, fruit, vegetables, baskets, cradles, crutches, pots and pans and tinware, stockings, sweets, cakes, blackthorns, lace, rosaries, pictures, tubs, and a-hundred-and-one things that you would never think of.

"A most wonderful and interesting place is Paddy's Market. That's the solemn fact, if you ask me," said an exiled Corkonian once, over a boulevard coffee table under the shade of tropical vegetation in a city far away. We were talking about the wonders of Cork and we had come to the subject of the commercial importance of the permanent fair held near the Coal Quay. "Yes," he went on, with a very solemn and judicial tone, "that market is unique. It is the only place that I know of in the world where your handkerchief can be stolen from you as you pass in on one gate, and sold back to you as you pass out on the other."

"You should leave to those who are not born in Cork the sorry pleasure of flouting your native city," I remarked.

"It would not be healthy for them—at least, in my presence," he replied; "for although a Corkman may permit himself the luxury of a little joke about the city, it would not do to allow outsiders to share in that privilege; and if ever you write anything about Paddy's Market bear my words in mind."

I promised to do so, and I have done it—even to the extent of giving his words verbatim.

The selling in Paddy's Market is mostly done by women, and anything that one of those Cork women will fail to sell may be sent to the scrap-heap as a hopeless case. I saw a group of them eyeing me over their knitting and making humorous remarks about me parenthetically between their intoned advertisements of their respective goods. They chanted the praises of their socks and cradles and onions and fruit in the pleasant rhythm of Corkonian speech, and occasionally, out of the corners of their mouths, they made a joke at the expense of the man who had apparently lost himself.

"Wisha, is it looking for a four-leaved shamrock you are, sir, or don't you want to buy nothin' at all?" asked a cross shawled, bare-headed, brown-haired, dark-eyed matron to me, while her face broke into a sunburst of a smile.

"I'm admiring you all," I said gallantly. "It is all I can do for the present, as I do not see for sale here the article I wanted to buy."

"And what was it?" they asked one and all.

"One of the big old-fashioned rosaries that you see still here and there with the old people. I wanted it for a friend far away."

"Is it one of them big long ones, with the big brown stones?" they asked.

"The same," I replied, "and I was told up in Tipperary that I would find one in Paddy's Market."

This was the simple truth, and somehow the statement of it wrought a great change in the manner of the marketwomen. There seemed to be a friendlier and more serious note in the voice of the woman who replied. She said that those " big, brown beadses " were no longer made ; and that the young people of to-day like handier rosaries than their mothers carried. I changed the conversation round to lighter topics presently, and when I left they shot darts of genial wit after me, all of which were well aimed. But there was no unkindness in any of them. Still I would be very slow to provoke them.

The Lee from St. Patrick's Bridge to the Cove of Cork is singularly beautiful. The stream spreads itself out into broad lakes and narrows again into passages that leave no more than convenient room for navigation. There are bays and inlets and rounded headlands and islands. The shores are fringed with shady trees which grow down to the water's edge, and the low hills are a maze of woodlands, amidst which are set many beautiful country homes. The sky was free from clouds when I saw the Lee at Passage, but a silvery haze was in the air which made the opposite shores of the loch seem dim and far away. It softened the light on the water, and deepened the shadows of the trees, and blurred the outline of the hills. There was a dead calm, and the waters were ruffled only where the steamers tossed them aside on the up or down stream course. It was restful, silent, and lovely, with a sweet and tender loveliness unutterable.

The Cove of Cork had its name officially changed to Queenstown when the late Queen of England landed there. She never did anything for Ireland but preside over more than three-score years of its most disastrous history. She never expressed a kindly thought for the Irish or did a single kindly, womanly, act for their sake. She regarded them with cold and stolid dislike, and was known to be their political enemy. Yet an Irish town must needs be named after her!

And when you turn the matter over in your mind for a while you may come to the conclusion that the name of Queenstown has at least one element of appropriateness. It is the port from which the stream of emigration flowed during the long and bitter years that Ireland languished under the blight of the Victorian Era. During the reign of the late Queen of England the population of Ireland dwindled from 8,000,000 to nearly 4,000,000. It was during her reign that the coffin-ships were on the sea. It was during her reign that the greatest exodus that has ever taken place from Ireland went on and on. Most of the stream of emigration passed through the Cove of Cork—where the English Queen landed to visit the land that was perishing under her rule.

Queenstown is a beautifully situated place. But it saddened me greatly. The islands in the harbour are covered with military barracks. The English convict prison of Spike Island has been converted into an English naval depot. Rocky Island has an English powder magazine. At Roche's Point are two powerful English forts guarding the harbour entrance. In the harbour itself are English men-of-war—battleships, cruisers, and torpedo boats; and on one of the islands are English dry docks and all the other appurtenances of a minor naval base.

There is a beautiful, although partially unfinished, Catholic Gothic Cathedral dedicated to St. Colman. It crowns the lower hill over the port, and from its spacious esplanade you obtain a magnificent view of the town and its environs.   But the trail of the serpent is over it all, hill and town and haven—the serpent of foreign rule.

On the streets in the evening time and at night hundreds of English soldiers promenade.

Once a week, all through the year, the landing-stage is crowded with people running away out of Ireland.   The tide of emigration still flows on. The stout arms are going.   The ruddy-cheeked girls are going.   The Irish race is going through this town into exile, between lines of English barracks, between lines of English warships, between grinning ranks of foul-mouthed English soldiers, between towering English forts—going, going, going, out and away, generally for ever.

Queenstown? Aye, faith! There is a certain ironical appositeness in the name of this lovely but depressing Irish harbour.

But Ireland is not dead yet for all that. And the mills of God are grinding.

CHAPTER XX.

*Over the Galtees—From Tipperary to Mitchelstown
—A select driver—Up the hills—The golden
vale—Cashel of Cormac—A mountain ravine—
The Glen of Aherlow—The select driver's authority is set at nought—Through Aherlow—A
climb to the top of Galtymore—An intoxicating
moment—Mitchelstown—Fermoy—Mallow   of
Davis.*

The morning was raw and cloudy as I took my
place on the jaunting car which awaited me at the
door of the hotel in Tipperary where I had passed
the night.   The driver of the car, a very select
person, was demanding more rugs from the porter,
and demanding them in tones of high and haughty
authority. The porter was diplomatically insinuating that it might be as well for the driver to mind
his own business.

"What do we want more rugs for, anyhow?" I
asked.

"You don't want them at all, sir," replied the
porter.

"Of course we want them for the fogs," said the
driver, "there's fogs and mists and cold up the
mountains, sir, and you want to be prepared for
them."

"One rug is enough," I decided, "so let us lose
no more time over the point. "Are you ready to
start?"

" Yes, sir, but——"

" Start, then—forward—march," and I lay back against the middle of the car and leisurely contemplated the town of Tipperary.   The driver exchanged a defiant glance with the porter who was calmly smiling at the door of the hotel, and with another glance in my direction, which was one of " proud subordination " and pity we set out.

You will gather from this that for the time being I had forsaken my wheel.   It was late in the year and the roads all over the country were undergoing repairs, so that, on account of the large patches of broken stones, there would have been punctures and delays and bitterness of spirit.   I had, therefore, decided to negotiate the Galtees with the aid of a jaunting car.   The driver considered it his duty to take charge of me, and I saw that from the first moment of our acquaintance.   It was quite evident that he regarded himself as the leader of the expedition, and I left him under that illusion for the time being.   I retired into the seclusion of my upturned coat collar and bided my time.

As we drove through the town I asked this individualist of a driver several questions regarding markets, fairs, and local industries.   He could answer none of them.   But when we were passing the military barracks he was brimful of information. He drew my attention to this building with much satisfaction, and asked me what I thought of it.   I shocked his feelings greatly by asking him if it were the workhouse.   To me it might have been one institution or the other.   The dwelling places of the Army of Occupation resemble very much the pauper houses made and cherished by the sway of its bayonets. Both are fitting monuments to English dominion erected on Irish soil. The resemblance between the home of the soldier and the pauper is appropriate, for both the military occupation of the country and the English-made pauperism are means towards the infamous end of the enslavement and demoralisation of the people.

Needless to say, I did not allow such thoughts to intrude on the respectable attention of the important man upon the other side of the car. It would have been taken in very bad part.

"The workhouse, sir? Not at all—not at all—not at all, sir!" he said in his superior way. "That's the barracks, sir—the military barracks. It can hold 1,200 men without being crowded. It is one of the finest barracks in Ireland, and a great help to the town."

"In what way does it help the town?"

"Why in every way, sir. It gives the publicans lots of custom, and brings a stir in the place."

"Indeed? I think I read in a paper at the hotel that the troops quartered here are fed with frozen meat imported from abroad."

"Yes, sir, a big railway waggon full of foreign beef comes down twice a week. and sometimes three."

"And do the Tipperary butchers think that this helps the town?"

"Well, I couldn't tell you that, sir, but I know there's publichouses in the town would have to close if the barracks was shut up."

"Very probably, indeed."

"Fact, sir. And that range of buildin's you see

there apart, them's the officers' quarters. It is given up to them, sir, to be the best officers' quarters in Ireland. The mess room is splendid. And as for the smoking room and billiard rooms, there's nothing to be compared to them on the Curragh of Kildare."

"You seem to know a great deal about military affairs."

"Well, I ought, sir, I was an officer's servant for six years, and I drive the officers nearly every time they hire a car; I drive them to shootin' parties and balls and all that."

"I understand."

"Yes, sir, the officers won't have any one to drive them but me if——"

"What hills are those?" I said by way of gaining some information, in which I was interested, and by way of drying up his flow of military talk, which was becoming tiresome.

"Them hills, is it, sir? Well, I call them Clonbeg. That's what I call them. Other people calls them by other names."

We were going down hill from the town at the time into a deep valley, on the other side of which rose the range under discussion. Upon one of the highest parts of the crest line stood a plain cross, tall, and graceful and clearly outlined against the sky. The driver told me that it had been placed there by the late Count Moore when he was elected Member of Parliament for Tipperary. He also told me that part of the mountain belongs to Count Moore's family, and the rest of it to Lord Barrymore. There were big larch plantations high up on the slopes, and higher still the dark tops of firs stood out against the brown background of the heather. The trees seemed to be small, but when we crossed the valley and began the ascent of the hill, the tops of the tapering larches waved full forty feet above the road. The driver could not tell me how long they were planted, but thought it might be " ten or fifteen years." It certainly could not have been more, and the fine growth to which they had attained in that time was remarkable. The high ground on which they were growing was rocky and broken. It would have been utterly useless for any purpose but that of afforestation. In its natural state it would not have been worth a shilling an acre. Before the children who go bird-nesting there now are men and women of middle age, those larch plantations will be worth thousands and thousands of pounds. It is a good sign to see so many thinking Irishmen interesting themselves now in afforestation as a means of increasing the national wealth.

The road through the larch plantations was quite steep, and it took us some time to climb it. At first it ran in a westward direction, but farther up the slope it turned sharply to the southward. The larches were not thriving so well up here, probably because the soil was lighter, but the firs were doing well, and the fresh wind came through them like the roar of a far-off waterfall. The road spewed reddish ooze from the iron in the rocks; and the grey masses of protruding strata drove their points through the scanty heather Another quarter of a mile and the mountain is but scantily covered by firs of stunted growth. The sun flashes out now, and through openings in the trees I catch glimpses of the

woods below and of the wide plains veiled in mists
of pearl grey. I call a halt, but the driver demurs.

" There's no use in stopping here, sir," he says,
authoritatively.

I do not argue the point with him, but reaching
my right hand across the car I seize the reins and pull
up. He is indignant and tells me it is the first time
that any gentleman he has ever driven in the whole
course of his life laid a hand on the reins. I have no
remark to make in connection with this statement,
and I heave a sigh of content as I divest myself of
my overcoat and muffler and throw them on the
cushions. As I catch a festoon of the over-hanging
heather and am pulling myself up off the road, he
asks me where am I going. But I have nothing on
my mind to tell him in this connection, so I make
him no answer.

" And where'll I wait for you ? " he asks, as I gain
the top of the cutting.

" Where you are," I reply.

" And when'll you be back ? "

" I have no idea."

" But how long am I expected to wait, then."

" Oh, if you are there any longer than a week or a
fortnight, go home if you like. And if you return
without me don't forget to mention where you saw
me last."

With that I scramble over a pile of rocks and take
my way up the slope, leaving him to the contemplation of his grievances. The wind is sharp, and the
way is steep and rough, but it is bracing work and
it is grand to escape even for a short time from the
depressing company of that select driver who has

been for six years an officer's servant, and who is in such high favour with the military.

After a climb of about twenty minutes I reached the uppermost verge of the firs, and had an uninterrupted bird's-eye view of the country to the northward. The valley across which we had approached the mountains had risen into the general flatness of the plain, and the hill upon which Tipperary seemed to stand two hours ago had disappeared. The town lay below me on the verge of a vast plain which extended as far as the eye could reach to the eastward, northward, and westward. I was looking down into the far-famed Golden Vale; and it must have been on some mountain near where I stood that Cromwell said "This is a land worth fighting for." The air was not very clear although the sun was bright. The hazes were impenetrable in some places, while in other directions they showed dim areas of verdure shading off into palest olive and losing itself in the silvery vapour.

Far away to the northeastward a great grey mass caught the sunlight, and looking more intently I could make out the roofs and walls of a town. It was ancient Cashel. The grey mass which had caught my eye was the famous Rock crowned with King Cormac's Chapel. The Rock of Cashel is a name known to Irish people all the world over. Its greatest day was when it was the seat of the Munster kings, especially during the reign of the illustrious and munificent Cormac. And if the court of the prelate-king was splendid and brilliant, the kingdom over which Cormac held sway was worthy of such a capital and such a monarch. It was rich and fertile and beautiful beyond all power of expression. It teemed with plenty—its resources were inexhaustible. From one blue mountain range to another it was a garden and a cornfield and a school all in one. There must have been great happiness all over the Golden Vale then, for the chroniclers tell us that the kingdom "was filled with divine grace and worldly prosperity . . . the cattle needed no cowherd and the flocks no shepherd so long as he was king . . . and many books were written and many schools were opened by him." A great man, but he had his weak side. He could be led into devious ways. He was led into the war against Leinster for tribute which ended in his defeat and death. He made the fatal mistake of putting Cashel before Ireland. He had to learn that Ireland is greater than its greatest city, or its greatest province, or its greatest men, aye, and greater than them all together. The difference between the kingcraft of Cormac and Brian lay in their attitude towards Ireland. Cormac wanted Ireland for Cashel: Brian wanted Ulster, Munster and Connacht for Ireland.

I returned to my car and found my select driver smoking meditatively. He told me, as he put his pipe in his pocket, that I was a great climber. I nodded. I did not believe he was sincere in his praise, but this was a question apart. Neither did I believe that I had climbed enough since leaving him to merit his eulogy. I meant to do some more climbing before the drive ended. But this was also a question apart, and I kept it to myself. I resumed my over coat and muffler and told him to go ahead. We traversed a wind-swept space where nothing grew but the heather, and then we came to more firs. We were descending the southern slope of the hill now and were soon in the shelter of a forest. The road zig-zagged into a wood of lofty oaks which covered the slope above us and extended down into a steep ravine out of which came the laughter of a racing watercourse. The trunks and even the upper forks of the oaks were green with tufts of beautiful fern. Another variety of fern covered most of the ground between the trees, and a third variety clustered in the crevices of the rocks. We jogged leisurely through this delightful tangle of verdure, and when the road turned again, long slanting rays of light flooded the forest aisles. The canopy of branches parted, and over the bank on the offside of the way, my gaze wandered straight out into empty space, then turned downward and found itself soaring as if in mid-air over a world that was as lovely as dreamland. A mesh of tangled forest rippled down the precipitous mountainside beneath my feet and along the lower slopes far away. Below and beyond the woods lay a wide ten-mile belt of the brightest green, dotted with trees and crossed with hedgerows. And another turn in the road showed me a blue mountainside, apparently almost within a stone's throw, towering into the sky. It was only for a moment, however, that it appeared to be so near. A second glance and the illusion was gone, and I knew that its blue tinting came from the miles of clear air across which I viewed it. The enchanting picture came so suddenly into view that for a moment I was lost in amazement, forgetting that I had been vaguely expecting something of the kind.

Then thought flowed on again and I knew that I was looking down on the Glen of Aherlow and that the big mountain before me was the monarch of the Galtees.

The Glen of Aherlow runs from west to east, and is probably more than ten miles in length. It is two or three in width. A branch of the Suir winds down it from end to end. The Galtee mountains wall it in to the southward, and the mountains that overlook the town of Tipperary guard it on the north. Viewed from the place from which I first saw it, the brightness and freshness of its beauty are entrancing. It is the same when you see it from the summit of Galtymore, the same when you look up along it from the valley of the Suir, the same when you look down it from the foothills under Galbally. It is not densely populated, but neither is it a big grazing ranch. The farms are of a fair average area, and the white-walled farmhouses which stand out so pleasantly against the vivid green, are comfortable and neat. When you travel through it you may find yourself regretting that the hedgerows are not thicker, and that there are not more trees around the houses. It would be more homely-looking, perhaps, if it were more sylvan, but it would be difficult to enhance its present loveliness. Those green, swelling, smiling fields, that silver stream, the heather-clad slopes of the Galtees, and the thick woods along the northern hills are glorious.

Aherlow was, however, densely wooded in other days, and for centuries it was a wild and lonely fastness resorted to by many a fugitive from English law. Le Fanu instinctively turned to this retreat under the Galtees as an asylum for his hero, Seamus O'Brien, after the escape from the gallows:

" To-night he'll be sleeping in Aherlow Glen
And the devil's in the dice if you catch him again.

It is probable, however, that the balladist was alluding to the traditional fame of Aherlow as a hiding-place rather than to the security it could offer in the end of the eighteenth century. For by that time most of the ancient forests had disappeared. O'Sullivan Beare sought the protection of the glen on his march from Glengariff to Leitrim and gained it, but not until he had fought his way through the foes who threw themselves across his path at Bellaghy Ford. The war-worn heroes of Beare slept in Aherlow that night, and in the morning breakfasted upon its herbs and water, then on to fight for eight hours before the sun went down, and win the day. It was in the woods of Aherlow that Dr. Geoffrey Keating fled when the bloodhounds were on his track three hundred years ago, and it was here he wrote his great historical work, " Foras Feasa ar Eirinn." How he remained in this wild retreat is not known, but there is every reason to believe, according to the most reliable authorities, that the greater part, if not the whole, of his monumental history was written there. Not a trace of his hiding-place remains. But his name, and the fame of his work, and the tradition of how loyally the Glen's people guarded the secret of his abode, are justly cherished yet as glories of Aherlow.

As we descended the road leading into the glen, the driver called my attention to an opening in the wood and a briar-grown track which ran steeply upward into the gloom of the firs. It was a bit of the old coach road, and a glance at it revealed to the imagination something of the excitement of travelling on the Bianconi mail cars. Certainly a driver in those days must have had enough on his hands without assuming or trying to assume control of the passengers. This was what my driver was doing now. He was making another attempt to assert himself over me, and regain command of the outfit. He proposed to drive through some man's demesne on the northern side of the glen, and when I told him that I care more about mountains and valleys and natural beauty of all kinds than the umbrageous monotony of demesne drives, he tossed his head and said that all the gentlemen that ever he had taken out, including the officers, of course, had preferred the demesne drive to the road through the glen. We were at the cross-road by this time, and he was turning towards the demesne when I quietly pulled the reins out of his hands and kept the horse on the straight road.

"I am going through the glen," I explained, "and I am taking the horse and car with me. I suppose you are coming, too?"

"I am, sir, of course, but you see ——"

"Well, if you are coming you may as well drive." And I handed him back the reins. He took them in silence and in silence we entered the glen, crossed the river, and came to the feet of Galtymore. Then I called a halt. He obeyed, but when he saw me taking off my overcoat and muffler he once more fell into the speech of a man who is accustomed to meddling with other people's business. He asked if I were thinking of "going up," and when I told him that I was going to do some more mountaineering, he asked me if I would take a fool's advice, and I said "certainly not" and left him, telling him to wait for me. I crossed a few sloping pastures, leaped a brawling hill-stream, and then entered a dreary belt of moorland, waterlogged and ankle-deep from the mountain ooze. No doubt that select driver rejoiced greatly on seeing me pause and study the scenery. But if he hoped to see me return, he was disappointed. A high ditch of peaty sods ran up into the heather, and along this causeway I passed triumphantly, dry-footed, over the morass. Then up and up, over rocks and peat-beds and moss-grown crags, and boulders, catching a tuft of heather now and a bunch of dwarf-rushes the next moment, and for the rest trusting a good deal to luck. It was stiff and stiffening work, and there was a great deal of it. When I had been at it for half an hour, I calculated that I had climbed a mile or two, and looked down to see if I had not done three or four. I was saddened to find that I had apparently not climbed more than forty or fifty yards. I looked upward, and the cold summit seemed to be sailing through the air ten or fifteen miles away. I paused for breath and to remove a few furze-thorns that had stuck in my hands. When I was able to whistle the nearest attempt I am capable of making to the opening bars of the Shaskin Reel, I made another start, and climbed until my temples throbbed. When I looked down now I was pleased to see that the horizon had widened, and when I looked upward the mountain-top was within stone-throw. Another scramble over smooth-faced rock, in the shallow indents of which scraps of peat were clinging like clay in the eyes of a huge potato. Up through a tiny cloud that half-floated in the cool air and half-rested on the slanting crag. Up into the clear blue above the world, on the rounded crest; then a gasp of relief and restful loll, face skyward, to get back my breath.

It would take me a week to tell you half the splendour of it. The hills on the other side of the glen were dwarfed, and over their crest-line rose the wide plains that stretch northward to the Midlands. Aherlow itself was even more beautiful than when I had seen it first from that lofty terrace on the wooded slope beyond the river; and out of the opal haze down below Bansha, a flash from the Suir's bright current leaped into the face of the sun. There were clouds in the western spurs of the range which I bestrode, but all was clear to the southward and eastward and northward, and for one intoxicating half-hour I stood amidst the giants, and my enraptured gaze roamed from one to the other, round and round, and back again—now resting on the Knockmealdowns, now on the Comeraghs, now on the Nagles, now on the peaks of the Silvermines, now on the top of Slievenamon; and then it would try to pierce the distant hazes and reach out beyond the horizon and away, away, away. Behind a ridge of the Comeraghs there was a wide patch of

faintly luminous blue.   It might have been the sky,
and it might have been the ocean.   But it added to
the sense of immensity which filled the mind.   I do
not know how many counties I could see.   Nor did
I count the valleys and woods and streams, nor yet
the iridescent hillsides where the sunlight sported
with the vapour.   You could not take account of
these things.   Your mind was trying so hard to
expand and encompass the infinite grandeur around
you that it lost its grip of details.   And when you
saw how inadequate were thought and sense to
measure themselves against the immeasurable, you
were dazed and saddened, and there were moments
when your tortured emotion was so sweet and painful and exalted and despondent that you could have
thrown yourself on your face and sobbed.

It was only by a determined effort that I con-
trived to " keep my stirrups," as the horsemen of
the pampas say in their expressive Spanish, when
they wish to picture equanimity of spirit under difficulties.   I remembered that I had still to drive
round the Galtees.   I returned to the car with
aching limbs and quivering sinews.   But I was content.   I felt at peace with the world.   And when
that select driver asked me with a patient meekness,
which was too elaborate to be genuine, if he might
make another start for our destination, I said, as I
tucked the rug around me and buttoned my overcoat :—

" Yes, as soon as you like, to anywhere you like,
by any road you like.   It is all the same now."   And
I looked farewell to Galtymore.

I parted from the select driver at Mitchelstown.

where I took the train. As we steamed out of the station I saw him enthroned on his car, holding vehemently forth to the policeman, the postman, a station-porter, and a few others. His whip-hand was raised over his head, pointing skyward. I suppose he was telling them of the irregular, disrespectful and high-handed manner in which I had sought the altitudes while under his guidance, and how glad he was to be rid of me.

On to Fermoy, which sits on the Blackwater, in a beautiful valley under the Nagle mountains. Fermoy is a new town. It grew up round the English military barracks, which was established there in the last century. It is overshadowed by the barracks yet, and labours under all the moral and political disadvantages peculiar to garrison towns in our poor, garrison-ridden country. But even here under the barrack walls, and within arm's reach of the rifles and bayonets, the idea that is making New Ireland powerful has stricken its roots deep into the soil. There is a very strong and active branch of the Gaelic League in Fermoy, and one of the best of the Munster feiseanna is held in the town. I sought out the moving spirit of the work and found him in a law-office—a tall, dark, brown-eyed, soft-voiced but inflexible man, who has done ten men's work for the cause of Ireland. Padraic MacSweeney is his name. I had met him at the Ard-Fheis in August, and had been impressed with his forcefulness. He took me to see the Diocesan College on the heights over the southern bank of the Blackwater. We were most kindly received by the learned and reverend President, and shown over the institution. I was greatly delighted with the library. In it are many valuable Irish manuscripts in modern binding. The college treasures them carefully and is laudably proud of them. They have accumulated there little by little. Most of them have come to the library from the bookcases of deceased priests of the diocese. Some of them were in the handwriting of one of the O'Longans, the famous Munster scribes. All of them were in excellent condition, and will last for centuries yet. In turning them over you could well explain why it is that Munster Gaels are so proud of their Irish. They have a great literary tradition behind them—the greatest by far of any section of Gaeldom. They are not always very meek about it either, but I doubt if I would be over-meek myself if I were from Munster. It seems to me that I would be continually congratulating myself that some of my forefathers heard Geoffrey Keating say Mass. And speaking about Irish literature reminds me that another great literary figure of the present movement lives near Fermoy. Father Peter O'Leary's parish is only three or four miles from the town. Padraic MacSweeney offered to take me to "Father Peter," and God knows it was not my heartfelt inclinations that prevented me having that great pleasure. But, please God, it was only a happiness deferred.

I went on to Mallow, dear to every Irish heart which beats warmly for the memory of Thomas Davis. Mallow was his birthplace, and truly that beautiful country of fertile valleys, forest shade, and mountain grandeur was a fitting cradle for one of the noblest Irishmen of the nineteenth or any other century. Mallow itself is in a deep hollow, but the country all round it rises gradually to the foot hills of the distant ranges. As you stand on any eminence near the town you scarcely know what to look at, so perfectly lovely is the scenery on every side. No wonder Davis loved it.

But there was one thing he loved better than his beautiful Mallow—dearer than life itself—and that was Ireland. If he had taught us no finer lesson than anti-parochialism, he would not have lived in vain.

CHAPTER XXI.

*North-Western Leinster—By Cloghan and Ballyna-
houn to Athlone—On the Bridge of Athlone—
Moate—The stranger stops the work of a whole
district—The rural beauty of Westmeath—
Uisnach Hill — Horseleap — Ballymore — The
Inny River—Into Annaly—The delirium of
speed—Back through Offaly—A Post Car Ride.*

Out into the summer sunshine, along the dry
bright roads—out into the beautiful Midlands for
a run of two or three days, by Cloghan, across
Delvinara, to Athlone; thence to Moate and Ballymore and beyond the Inny, through Annaly to Longford and Granard; thence back to Offaly, by the
Westmeath lakes and Mullingar, to the confines of
Birr of St. Brendan. The tour is not in any guide
book. No scion of Royalty has made it by the aid
of the reporters. It is just the ramble of a world-
tired exile home for a rest, and careless of the beaten
track.

The soft winds from the blossoming heather of
the Bog of Allen were fragrant with honey and
adrone with working bees; and silver showers of
melody fell out of the blue above from the carolling
larks. The distances on every side were dimmed by
a hundred shades of golden haze, as if the dust from
the wings of countless myriads of butterflies

thickened the perfumed air.   The mountains had doffed their kingly purple for the day and lay along the horizon, filmed in shimmering lilac against the brilliant sky.   It was perfect weather, and it seemed ever and ever so grand a thing to be alive with nothing particular to do but just loiter through the wondrous land.

The lark song grows clearer, louder, gladder— rings and trills and swells in the rapture of its freedom and joy.   I loiter and listen.   I am never tired of it.   I looked forward to it before my return, and ever since I have been ready to revel in its wild and luxuriant sweetness.   It was a longing to hear the lark sing again that drew me out of bed into the dawn one morning very soon after my home-coming. Ten or twelve of the songsters were on the wing over a piece of moorland, when I found them, singing their loudest.   There never was such a concert as they gave me.   No wonder the poets are fond of the lark.   He is one of the poets himself, and he sings as every poet should, out of holy love of song.   He is the hardiest and homeliest, and sweetest of all the songsters.   Up in the woods you have the throstles and blackbirds.   In the haggards and in the hedge rows are the robbins and finches.   But the lark, like the canavaun flower and the heather bloom, loves the moor and the bog and the bleak mountain side.   No sylvan scene in all the wide world is made so melodious as he makes the wastes where the coarse grass withers beside the reeds or sedge, or where the *froghans* ripen in the bogs.   Up he soars at dawn over the clear pools of water, or over the heather or tussocks: and the glad notes fall from him like

pearls upon alabaster. He whistles and chirps and
gurgles and trills and warbles until his throat swells
under the strain of the gushing torrent of music. I
sat down on a rock that morning and listened to the
wondrous notes. I watched the singers as they zig-
zagged upwards in little jerky flutterings, their out-
spreading wings drooped, and their throats opened
to the sky. Up and up they sang into the blue until
you could scarcely see them. But no matter how
high they went, you could always hear them, and the
farther they went away the wilder and clearer and
more joyous seemed their singing. The sky lark is
unchanged at any rate. He sings to me here by the
roadside as he sang to the first man who walked on
the soil of Ireland He sings now, as he has sung
all through the ages, to the lowliest as well as to the
highest in the land.   There is nothing snobbish
about him.   He is the least foppish of birds, but
there is beauty in every part of him. Look at him
in a cage and your heart goes out to him.   You
cannot help feeling that he is out of place there. He
seems to long for the brown " cush " or the "curragh"
or the wind-swept mountain crest. The grey solitude of the wilderness and the callow and the marsh
seems to speak to you out of his clear eyes, and it
seems to be reflected in the drab of his plumage.
Not a bright or gaudy feather is in his coat. There
is nothing perky or saucy about him. He is to the
linnet or the canary what the born hill man is to the
music hall singer. He looks the part which nature
has assigned him. The rôle suits him. He is to the
manner born. He is the fairy singer of desert places
who makes the desert lovely by his voice alone. He

is the only bird that never fails to give the wanderer a welcome home. Go out to hear the thrush or blackbird or any of the others and you may listen in vain : they are not in the humour for singing or they are nesting, or hunting snails or grubs or flies. But the lark never disappoints you. And you would be tempted to imagine that he knows you are listening to him, and that he is making a special effort to please you.

Loitering, I came to Cloghan. It was an important place in the old days before the Grand Canal " fly boats " took the Dublin passenger traffic from the mail coaches. In the pre-Union times it was a stopping place on one of the Dublin roads. Dennis Bowes Daly had a house in it, I think. At least such is the local tradition. Bowes Daly was the heir of Mac Coughlan, the last chieftain of Delvinara. In Cloghan still there are legends of Mac Coughlan, or as they called him " the Maw." Of course, this term is a corruption of the Irish affix " Mac." It was a vulgarized abbreviation of " The Mac Coughlan." Cloghan was a strenuous town up to twenty-five years ago. It was a very lurid storm centre in the Land League days. There were people in the village and district who had exuberant vitality, and their vigour forced itself into many impressive outlets. For example, there was a travelling showman, once upon a time, who visited Cloghan fair and gave a performance, to his great and abiding grief. Next morning, his establishment was found upon the roadside many miles away, in a depressed condition. The showman himself was bandaged. His acrobatic daughter was in tears. His musical and vocal wife was in hysterics. His van showed signs of having been visited by a ten-inch shell. The horse was exhausted.

"We were in Cloghan last night," began the showman, in a weary effort to explain the nature of his calamity. But the listening neighbours interrupted him quickly.

"Oh, you were in Cloghan!" they exclaimed. "That is enough. We understand the rest."

Some of the Cloghan boys had put two round stones under the ladder leading to the door of the van in which the performance was given. The stones were placed in position after the commencement of the play, when the audience had assembled. When the Cloghan people were leaving the theatre after the fall of the curtain the ladder travelled smoothly on its ball bearings and came down into the black night. So did the audience. By the time their feelings were relieved the theatre was verging on dissolution.

On to Ballinahoun through the summer woods, a delightful journey. Ballinahoun was also noted for the great vitality of its people. Its youths were practical exponents of a strenuous trend of life. It is on record that when the spirit of unrest quickened the minds of the young men of Ballinahoun, the local Constabulary force made urgent appeals for reinforcements, and wrote farewell letters to their relatives. But, like Cloghan, Ballinahoun is quiet enough now—too quiet, perhaps. Its turbulent spirit has been quieted in the tenements of New York and in the factories of Connecticut. Emigration has drained the young people in their hundreds from the fields and homes.   The O'Malones were the chieftains of Ballinahoun when the chieftains held sway in Eirinn.   There is a strain of the family yet extant.   But they have dropped the O—with all things else that made them Irish, except the land. They were conciliated centuries ago.

Knockanee, near Athlone, is an uncompromising lung-trying hill.   But the view from it is fine.   It shows you miles of meadow and woodland and tillage, and the wide swinging curves in which Leinster rolls down to the Shannon.   But it does not show you the Shannon itself.   It is only when you reach the outskirts of Athlone that you can see the storied river from the Leinster side.

Athlone is an important town.   It is something of a railway centre, has a flourishing woollen industry, a good market, and it is held in force by the Army of Occupation.   From the legendary cycles to our own times it has been one of the strategic fords of the Shannon, and its value in a military sense is frequently thrown into grim relief in the history of Ireland.   It sustained two memorable sieges in the days when Ireland was wasting energy in fighting the battles of one English king against another—fighting heroically, but unwisely and vainly, for James II. William sent General Douglas with 12,000 men and fourteen guns against Athlone.   Douglas bombarded the fortress for a week and then raised the siege.   His powder had run out and he had learned that Sarsfield was coming up with the Irish Horse from Limerick.   The defender of Athlone on this occasion was Richard Grace, colonel in the Jacobite army.   Douglas withdrew to Mullingar, where he reorganised his forces and then marched on Limerick to join William, ravaging Leinster on the way and shooting as a rapparee every Irish person he met.

In the following year, 1691, Athlone was again besieged. The Baron de Ginkell was now the commander of the Williamite army. He besieged Ballymore Castle on the 7th of June, and, despite the heroic resistance of Colonel Ulick Bourke, he captured it and sat down before Athlone on the 19th of the same month at the head of 18,000 men. The Irish fell back from the Leinster side of the town across the Shannon, destroying two arches of the bridge on the Connacht side as they went. The English tried to throw planking over the broken arches, but eight or ten Irish soldiers ran forward and tore down the planks and beams. They lost their lives, but they saved the day, and their heroism will live on in history to gild their self-sacrifice with imperishable honour. They fought for a monarch who was not deserving of such intrepid valor; but they thought they were fighting for fatherland, and if they died for the Stuart, they also died for dear Ireland's sake. Ginkell could not cross the Shannon by the bridge, but he discovered a ford lower down, and d'Usson, the defender, was not equal to the occasion. The fortress which, although reduced to a heap of rubbish, was still impregnable by virtue of Irish valour, fell by a surprise assault.

Half an hour I sat on the battlements of the bridge and ruminated. There were many passers-by and the road was spotted by red-coats. The iron that has entered into the soul of Ireland chilled the air for a while and depression fell upon me. But pessimism stayed away, and while I was looking down on the current lapping the arches I felt the sunshine warm in my heart again. For the song of the river was that the patriots whom it folded to their hero sleep did not die in vain, and that as the Shannon itself flows on, and ever and ever on, so shall the blood of the Irish race forever flow through life and time in Eirinn. We shall come to our own again! Hurrah for the men who died on the bloody bridge! Their glory is ours, and the strutting foul-tongued soldiers in Khaki and scarlet cannot rob us of its inspiration.

Back through the quaint streets, up the Leinster slopes again, into the woods, by breezy moor, and waving cornfields, on by hill and vale to Moate in fair Westmeath.

The full name of Moate is Moate a Grenogue; that is how it is called in Sacs-beurla. The name comes from a large Moat or burial mound outside the town. It is the grave of a princess whose name was Young Grania or Grania Og. When the mass of unedited Irish literature that is now entombed on the shelves of so many famous libraries in Gaelic manuscript is given to the world the early history of the district around Moate will "astonish the natives." They will rub their eyes and ask themselves can it be true that they and their ancestors, for so many generations, never suspected that their lot was cast in one of the most storied corners of Europe. At present the Moate people have no traditions older than Hempenstall, the infamous hangman and agent provocateur of the English Government in the awful days before '08. Beyond that period local history is a closed book. It was closed when the Irish language was banished from West-meath.

I did not delay long in the town, but I heard that the great April cattle fair has declined; and that foreign mutton is sold in Mullingar. " There is one of the triumphs of free trade for you ! " said the sardonic person who told me this. " First we were manufacturers and our manufacturing industry was squelched to enable the suffering English to live upon us. Then we became agriculturists and we were made free traders so that our produce might reach the English Markets on terms favourable to the toilers in English factories. Now, when so many of us are qualifying for out-door relief, the benevolence of free trade comes to offer us a cheap mutton chop which we are unable to buy. But there are always two consolations: One is that we have relations in America; and the other is that we are a quick-witted people ! "

After that I struck out into the heart of West-meath. The afternoon was splendid and so was the country. Two or three miles took me into the turf belt. It was turf-cutting time, and when I came upon a whole colony of turf cutters I stopped to watch the work. The turf banks were over a stone's throw distant, and the workers—wheelers and cutters—were strung out for hundreds of yards on the bog, a line of picturesque figures thrown into pleasant relief against the brown background of peat.

" Why do you stand there like a crane ? " asked a female voice with an open, silvery laugh in it.

I turned and found three girls close to the road

amidst the drying turf, laughing merrily at me or at themselves, I could not tell which.

"God bless the work," I said.

"You, too," answered one of them, "but won't you tell us what you're standin' there for?"

"Well, *a chailin dhas*," I said, "suppose I put it, that I was wondering whether I should go or stay?"

"And are you afraid of the girls?" asked another, as she put the finishing touch to a little pyramid of sods.

"No, then, I'm not—but——"

"But what, then? Why not come out and help?"

"I was going to say that I was afraid of something else."

"Arrah, of what?"

"Why, that I might stop all the work on this bog."

"Then you must be smarter than you look," said the maiden who had not yet spoken.

"Take not the book by its cover, honey," I replied. "And now that I am here I think I will just call a halt, and give you all a rest."

They looked at me, shading their eyes with their hands, and then they looked at one another inquiringly and not altogether unconcernedly. "What ails him?" was their unspoken question.

"Yes," I continued suavely, "I am going to suspend all work in this electoral division, or precinct, or department. I am under bonds to tell you of your cousins, brothers, sweethearts, uncles and aunts in South America. I was told by a truthful man up the road that one could not see a soul in this part of the country who has not a relation in Argentina—so I am at your orders."

" And are you from there ? "

" Sure."

" Go on now ! "

" Positive fact, *a cailin dhilis.*

" Mike ! Here, Mike ! " they shouted.   " Come over here quick.   He's after coming from Buenos Aires," and they pointed three round bare arms at me, while their eyes danced.

" What's that you were sayin', girls ? " inquired Mike, as he stepped across the drain and clambered up the roadside, bringing a sweet whiff of the turf bank with him.

" He's home from Buenos Aires," they cried.

" For God's sake ? " he exclaimed, turning to me.

" All the way," I replied, nodding amiably.

" Musha, whoever you are," he said, " put it there," and he held out his hand

I shook it, turf and all, and asked :

" Who is this you want to hear about ? "

Who didn't he want to hear about ? And who didn't everyone of them want to hear about ? For, of course, all the others came along too, down from the houses and the fields—from everywhere.   And they sent for more.

" Run over beyond," commanded Mike to one of his sons, " and tell Jim to come.   And here, gossoons : run over, one of you, to Larry and give him word; and tell Tomeen and Pat, on the way back; and if your Aunt Mary's at home tell her to come, too. This is powerful ! "

That describes it more or less.   It was just power-ful.   They came and came !   In a quarter of an hour I had half a congregation; and fresh contin-gents were arriving at every moment.

⌐ stayed with them for more than two hours   A few of them remembered their Spanish and plied me with it.   There were brothers and sisters of men I had met on the pampas, and nieces and nephews and even parents as well.   I gave a good account of everybody.   Some of them didn't deserve it, maybe, but no matter.   I sounded all their praises.

When I rose to go, the trouble began.   Wouldn't I stay the night?   What hurry was I in?

"Ah, take that bicycle from him and hold on to him until we get him home."

"Don't be talkin' about goin', man alive : stay here for a few days."

"Come home with me, and I'll show you how I haven't forgot to cook a puchero."

"Come with me, and put up your old bike.   I'll leave you wherever you want to go on a car—and not have you wearin' out them legs of yours pushin' this danged thing through the country."

"'Deed, now, it's us that has the best right to him. We brought the whole of you here."

"Don't mind them; come to my house."

"But last of all, you can't leave here without taking a sup of something from somebody."

I had, indeed, a difficult task to get away.   It was almost impossible.   I left a piece of my coat and some of my bicycle behind me in the scuffle.

It was better to have rushed away from their kindness than from their displeasure.   But either would not have been child's play.   Their hospitality would have been, in a way, as terrible as their anger.

"And besides," I said, "what would happen if I couldn't see the rest of Westmeath, not to speak at

all of Longford?" I knew if they got me to stay
that my bones would be likely to remain among
them. I could see it in their eyes. I could read
there that they were bent on stuffing food down my
neck and giving me sups of one thing or another
until death should us part.

Far up the road, under the trees, a man stood looking intently in the direction whence I came.

"Good evening," I said.

"Good evening to you," he answered heartily, "and
would you mind telling me what is that crowd at
below on the bog?"

"Oh!" I said lightly, "I don't think it's of any
account, what is going on. Some fellow just home
from South America was gabbling to them, and they
were all about him like flies on sugar, listening to his
yarns—that's all."

His face lighted up, and he asked me hurriedly:

"From South America, did you say? A fellow
home from South America?"

"Why, yes—from Buenos Aires, or some such
place."

"By the holy farmer!" he exclaimed, and put his
best foot foremost down the hill to join the others.

For my part, I made myself scarce at a fearful
pace. Like a comet, I swept down under the trees
of Moyvoughly, past the schoolhouse and the cross-
roads. The children were leaving school and they
shouted playfully to me as I tore by them. A Moyvoughly chicken narrowly escaped being crushed to
death under my wheels. The Moyvoughly school-
mistress was startled and seemed to be in dread of
many things as she closed the school door. A Moy-

voughly boy who sat on a stile jumped down and in the fulness of his little heart let a stone fly at me. It was all charming. Fain would I have stayed to revel in it, but self-preservation is the first law of nature. So I waved my hand and gave them my blessing, and fled.

I want to tell you of a picture I saw next morning as I lay in the sunshine on a hilltop over Ballacurra. It is one of the fairest and freshest and sweetest pictures I saw in Ireland. The chapel of Ballymore rose over the trees to the northward, and beyond the trees the land sloped downward to the woods about Ballymahon. In front of me rose Knockastia Hill, with the golden gorse on its summit, and the snug farmsteads at its base, sheltered by elms and white-thorns. To my left was the Hill of Clare, green as an emerald, with the stock kneedeep in the Summer grass which clothed it like a meadow. To my right was the Hill of Cruchan Ruadh, and beyond it the fine rolling land that sweeps from behind Moyvoughly to the banks of the Inny. The little Ballacurra River, winding round the base of Ballinlug and Clareen Hill, caught the sunlight on one of the bends beyond Calthragh, and shone bravely over its trout and pike before it buried itself in the wide grass lands farther away. And filling in the noble perspective in the opposite direction lay the hill of Uisnach, or Usnagh, as they call it now — famous since the far-off days of Nemedh in the history of our land.

I wish I could make all this appear before you as I saw it that morning. I wish I was able to make every exile who knows it close his eyes and conjure it

up in all its beauty and magnificence—aye, ano
pathos, too. I wish I could show them every cornfield and meadow and pasture, every hill and stream
and wood, every sunlit slope and shady hollow,
every homestead and hedgerow and winding country
road, and the soft blue sky above, and God's own
smile on the flower-strewn verdure. And I wish I
had time to write its wondrous story. For every hill
and vale between us and the horizon is historic
ground. There is scarcely a townland that does not
recall some great fact in the annals of Ireland.
There are memories of the druids and of the high
kings, memories of Padraic and Brigid, memories of
battles won and lost, tales of the Penal Days, and
there are legends of the fairy folk hanging around
the names of a hundred raths and forts.

In a valley under Ballymore, there took place a
great slaughter during "the wars of Ireland." That
is the local tradition. I saw the place, and questioned the people; but there was nothing definite to
learn from them. Some of them had heard that
Cromwell fought there against Owen Roe. There
is a hill over the battlefield called Cruachain Ruadh.
Whether the Ruadh or Roe is a qualifying term
derived from the tint of the hill itself in the eyes of
those who named it in the long ago, or whether it
comes from the Ruadh of O'Neill is uncertain. In
the fields below this hill the grandfathers of
the present generation ploughed up heaps of
human bones which whitened on the clay after a
spring shower as if light snow had fallen. The
account of the battle which lives on amongst
the people says that Owen Roe retired from his

trenches on Cruachain Ruadh after nightfall, leaving his camp fires lighted. He had received the news from his scouts that the English general meant to rush the camp by night, and that was why the retreat was made. A counter surprise was planned. The English stormed the Irish trenches in the darkness, but found them empty. Then came the counter stroke planned by Owen. The retreat of the stormers was cut off by the road along which they had come, and in their panic under the onslaught of the Irish they fled towards the river in the valley, hoping to find a ford. But the river was in flood and they were unable to effect a crossing. They were slaughtered in hundreds and the next day's sun rose on a heap of slain. No official account of this battle has been published in any history, so far as I know. I have never seen it mentioned anywhere.*

Uisnach Hill was half hidden under summer haze as I swept over the road towards Longford, raising Westmeath County Council dust, and keeping my bearings on the woods of Annaly. It is not a remarkable looking hill, this storied Uisnach. Yet it is not an easy hill to climb, and it is higher than it looks. It is flat-topped like Tara and Rath Croghan,

---

*There is an account given in the " Aphorismical Discovery," and also in the journal of Colonel Henry O'Neill—one of Owen Roe's officers—of a battle which took place in Ballymore during the autumn of 1648. I am indebted to Mr. James Woods, of Ballymore, the historian of Westmeath County, for this valuable reference. The battle was fought between Owen Roe and Lords Dillon and Taaffe. There are a few particulars in which both accounts referred to agree with local tradition, but in the main the divergence is very great. As, however, the continuity of oral tradition was broken in the district by the loss of the Irish language, it is very probable that the original version of the battle current in the district differed greatly from that which is now in existence.

and some of the land around it is extremely fertile.
The hill is all under pasturage now, but in the olden
days a great city crowned it. There is more Irish
history connected with Uisnach than you could put
into a big book. It was here that blazed the first
fire lighted in Eirinn to the pagan gods. Here fell
Lugaidh Lamfada, one of the greatest of Irish kings.
Here Eri, one of the queens of the Tuatha-de-
Dananns encountered Amirghin, son of Mildeh of
Spain, and when he asked her for her name her
answer was " Eri is my name and from me this land
is called Erin." Here, on a large stone, was the
point where the ancient divisions of Erin or Eri met.
Here was held the great fair the like of which was
unknown in all the world at the time. St. Patrick
stayed here for several months, and here also St.
Brigid founded a convent.

Beyond Uisnach to the eastward, where the woods
are darkening the hills, is a famous village. They
call it Horseleap now : and Horseleap has been its
name for centuries. The leap of the horse was made
over a chasm in a kind of causeway which runs along
the heights over the village. " The tracks are there
yet," I was told. I looked and saw them, or what
are said to be the marks of the horse's hoofs,
carefully preserved from generation to generation.
When the Normans came to Ireland, Hugh de Lacy
was sent to smash the Gaels of Westmeath, and was
granted most of their lands in advance. In trying
to get possession of his baronies he met with considerable opposition. Once while he was out demanding possession from some of the MacGeoghegan
chieftains they fell upon him and put himself and

nis knights to flight. Not only that. They followed him in deadly anger—being stubborn Irishmen who believed in fighting for home and freedom —and chased him to the very drawbridge of his castle. It was in his feverish hurry to get away from the clansmen that he leaped his charger over that yawning abyss. De Lacy's ride took place towards the close of the twelfth century, and his desperate feat of horsemanship has lived on in tradition ever since.

But Horseleap has another and a greater tradition, and one which recalls the old Irish name of the place. This old name is Baile-atha-an-Urchair. In other histories it is called Ardnucher, the ford of the east. According to O'Clery's calendar it was here that Conor MacNessa received the wound of the brain ball at the hands of Cead Magach, a chieftain of Connacht. Cead had raided Ulster and was on his way home when Conor MacNessa overtook him. In the battle which ensued Cead wounded the Ulster King with the brain ball which contained the brains of Mesgechild, a Leinster chieftain. The legend is that Conor's life was saved by allowing the brain ball to remain in his skull. But his physician cautioned him to guard against excitement less the ball might leave its place and re-open the wound. It was when Conor's druid told him about the death of Our Lord on Calvary that the wound re-opened. The king rushed into the woods and began hacking at the trees with his sword, showing what treatment he would mete out were he among the slaves for having crucified the Son of God. The fury of his passion started the ball from where it was wedged into the bone; the wound re-opened, and his brains rushed through it.

This is said by some historians to have happened on Good Friday, the day of Calvary. But Keating points out that the Redeemer was not born for a long time after Conor. He says it was in Lamrigh wood that the ball flew out, but he does not mention the place where the battle was fought in which the wound was received. It is Michael O'Clery who says it was at Ath-an-Urchair which he identifies with Horseleap in Westmeath.

I crossed the Inny at Forigny and rested under the shady woods. I am near Forigny and Pallas, where some of Goldsmith's youth was passed. But it is not Goldsmith's poetry that is in my memory now. I am thinking about William MacGeoghegan and " Leo " Casey. Both of them write of the Inny. Goldsmith never did. I remember one of MacGeoghegan's verses : —

> Green grows the turf by Inny's side,
>   And white the daisies spring.
> When April cometh forth a bride
>   To hear the brown thrush sing,
> And peeps my bonny gem of blue,
>   Sweet, pure, forget-me-not,
> The sheltering rushes slyly through,
>   And by that favoured spot
> The proud swan sails with open wing,
>   The water lilies wait
> Till Summer's sun to them shall bring
>   The white robes of their state.

And here is another : —

> In Inny's banks, by Inny's stream
>   In Ballymulvey's grove,
> I dreamed my earliest, tenderest dream
>   Of never-ending love.

Ballymulvey lies below the bend to our right.   It is just the place for such dreams as the singer brings into his song.

The river is fringed with giant trees, and flows over pebbly shallows, and leaves back waters here and there, in which the trout and salmon are to be found.   The groves along the banks do not always hide the lovely country behind them.   There are breaks in the bosky splendour which reveal wide lawns, and smiling uplands and dales and glades all carpeted with moss or fern.

On past Ballymahon to Longford, but not too easily.   It is a hilly country, and the hills are not mere lumps in the road.   They are tough and sheer, and they have to be approached in a business-like frame of mind.

At times you have to dismount and walk.   It is a rest for you, in any case, and you benefit by it. Besides which, the toil of climbing up one side is rewarded by the pleasure of flying down the other. And when the other side is a long, smooth incline, and when you fly down it with the brakes lifted and feel the old earth slipping behind you at the rate of many miles an hour, you enjoy some of the splendid, ineffable exhilaration of rapid motion—the queer, elemental, reckless intoxication which high speed puts into the blood, urging you to force the pace, faster

still and faster.   All the tame fibres of your being go
to sleep and the other ones wake up, and take charge.
Something of that nature happens to most people
who are going half-a-mile a minute.   It happened to
me.   As I flew down the third or fourth hill I fell
off, as I might say, and another being took my place
—a dusty, muddy, perspiring wretch who waved his
cap over his dishevelled head, and cheered for the
warrior memories of Longford.   The pace and history
had got into his brain; and he was cycling through
other centuries.   He recalled, no doubt, that there
was little room for quiet folks in those parts
during the splendid days gone by when there
was battle in the wind.   From every ridge and
dale and glen which alternated between him and
Westmeath, from every slope and moor and wood to
his left, away to the purple hills that loomed beyond
the Shannon, there had swarmed in other days, in
defence of home and hearth, and altar, strong fighting men of Ireland, with the bright steel bare.

> MacGeoghegan's flag is on the hills,
>   O'Reilly's up at Fore,
> And all the chiefs have flown to arms
>   From Allen to Donore.
> And, as I rode by Granard's moat,
>   Right plainly might I see
> O'Ferrall's clans were sweeping down
>   From distant Annalee.

It was through Annalee, or Annaly, that the
deranged person on the bicycle was now sweeping.

Two constables out on duty met him half way down the gradient. They were shocked and indignant at his appearance and conduct, but they sprang into the ditch, leaving him the whole of the road. They made signs to him to stop, and shouted menaces to him as he hummed past them in a dusty streak, but he heeded them not. He swooped forward towards Longford, shedding the mud of three counties and leaving the echoes of "treason" floating on the air

On to Granard next day. More hills, more woods, more pleasure. I met William Ganly, of Irish Ireland fame, and passed a night under his hospitable roof at Creevy House. Longford is delightful—homely, friendly, hospitable. I skirted Lough Sheelin, from Creevy, then on to Mullingar, and Tullamore, through the country of the lakes—Derevaragh, Owel, Ennel, and the others—by Multyfarnham and Clonhugh, Dysart, Kilbeggan and the woods of Offaly. Still homeward through the Charleville forests, by Muckla, to Kilcormack, where I met with a mishap—ran into another cyclist and was obliged to adjourn for repairs. I was still a few miles from home, so I hired a post-car. There had been a run on post-cars in Kilcormack that day, owing to a fair having been held in a neighbouring town, so the only available horse belonged to what might be termed the reserve. He was lame and lazy and blind. But it was late at night and the charitable darkness hid us. The driver was a boy, and he talked to the horse the whole time. He spoke in a threatening undertone, as if he intended his remarks for the private ear of the hobbling quadruped between the shafts. His innate courtesy forbade him to intrude the unpleasantness upon my attention, so he carried it on in a minor key of suppressed but concentrated fury.

"Gwan out o' that, you old cripple—gwan now! Bobbin' that head of yours up and down like a lame dog. Gwan, I tell you, or I'll murdher you. Hee-up! Do you hear? 'Deed, when I get you home, you'll see what I'll do to you, so you will! Bad luck from you, gwan!—gwan!—gwan!"

I was tired, and it lulled me to sleep.

CHAPTER XXII.

*Clonmacnoise—" Pattern" Day—The Ancient Home
of St. Ciaran—The Whispering Arch—The
Cross of Clonmacnoise—Spanning the Cross—
St. Ciaran's Oratory—Other Ruins—The Round
Towers far older than the Churches—Story of
St. Ciaran—King Diarmuid and the Saint—Love
making amidst the Ruins—The Blind Piper—
Home through the evening glory.*

On all the roads between Banagher and Athlone
there are troops of people facing westward. They
are on vehicles of every kind, from the dashing
excursion brake to the humble donkey cart, and
every kind of bicycle procurable is also in evidence.
Hundreds of people are tramping the roads in the
dust; hundreds are footing it over the fields and
hills; and there are many boats on the Shannon, all
laden to the very gunwales with people from Connacht. And whether the crowds come out of
Westmeath or Western Offaly, or from Galway or
Roscommon, they are all converging in a common
destination; they are all on the way to Clonmacnoise
of the Seven Churches. For this is the Sunday
morning nearest to the 9th of September, the feast
of St. Ciaran (or Kieran). It is " pattern " or patron
day—a day of prayer, or penance, and cheery festi-
vity, too, and courtship and laughter and dancing—a

day made up of Irish faith and Irish history,
revealed in the softer lights of Irish character. I
am going to the "pattern" myself, and I am taking
the reader with me, if there is no objection.

Two round towers, a wilderness of crumbling
walls and naked gables, a forest of tombstones, and
the wide river flowing peacefully through the callows
which are studded with haycocks up to the very
boundary of the cemetery. That is Clonmacnoise
as we first catch sight of it from the Cloghan road.

There is a long, low range of grassy hills between
the bog and the river, and on the western slope of
this ridge, just where the Shannon makes one of its
magnificent loops, St. Ciaran founded his little
oratory on the 23rd of January, A.D. 544. Ciaran
died in a few months afterward, but his oratory—
the Eclais Beg—developed into a great seat of piety
and learning, was surrounded in course of time by
a populous city, and its name spread throughout
Europe, from nearly every country of which scholars
flocked to its schools and university.

This holy place which we are approaching by the
hilly roads that wind past the farmsteads of Clon-
fanlough is in ruins, for it has seen stormy times
and it is very old. It was old before the Saracens
were smashed at Tours, before Norman William
landed at Hastings, before the Crusades were
preached or fought. It was old before many of the
present great universities of Christendom were
founded, and before any of the present royal
families of Europe were heard of in authentic history. It was old when the Danes raided its cloisters.
It had celebrated the eleven hundredth anniversary

of its foundation before the sacrilegious soldiery of Elizabeth reduced it to ruin. It flourished in the golden age of Christian Erin, and it received and holds the mortal remains of the last of the Irish Kings. All this is down in history; and it is written on the gray walls and tombs and monuments of the Seven Churches here beside the Shannon.

Let us enter the ruins. Tread lightly on the graves which crowd the sward, for some of the noblest and loveliest and purest and greatest that Ireland has seen are sleeping here. This thought is assuredly present in the minds of those men and women who are praying in groups here and there. See, they have taken off their boots and stockings, and are going barefoot over the holy ground. They go round the graves of the saints on their knees. They kiss the floors of the churches. They tell their beads below the great sculptured cross in front of the Dananlaig or Tempull McDermott. They go bareheaded along the causeway to the old nunnery of Devorgilla. They cross themselves before drinking from the blessed wells. They whisper pious invocations as they drop hairpins or buttons or matches or pebbles into the niches and cavities where teethaches, headaches, warts and other ills are left behind.

Here you have a husband and wife from beyond the Shannon who have come fasting for miles to " do the stations " and perform all the traditional devotions of the day. They are bareheaded, and their feet are bare and red from the scratches of briars and the stings of nettles. They are kneeling on the damp grass in front of the small cross now, and

the man is giving out the Lord's Prayer in Irish.
The woman gives the responses in the Irish also. How
soft and sweet the words are! What piety and
supplication are in the cadences! How appropriate
is the old language on their lips in prayer this day
and in this place! It is not only an echo of the
past. It is the continuity of tradition. It is the
tongue that was on Ciaran's lips when he preached
and taught and prayed. It is the tongue in which
the sages of Clonmacnoise lectured and wrote. It is
the soul's voice of Holy Ireland—the treasure house
in which her heart is guarded from the pollution of
the rotting world.

Here at the entrance to Tempull McDermott is
the Whispering Arch. The mouldings of the arch
are so deep and well preserved that they carry a
whisper from one side of the doorway to the other.
There is a youth from near Shannonbridge standing
on one side of the door with his mouth close to the
mouldings. On the other side, with her back turned
towards him, is a maiden from near Banagher,
blushing at the amorous nonsense which the swain
from Shannonbridge is whispering.

It is a dalliance like unto that which is carried on
by conversation lozenges. Two of the girl's friends
draw near and put their ears to the moulding. They
giggle and blush and say "Oh, d'ye hear that?"
and they say things back to the youth from Shannonbridge, who opens his face in a festive grin or
looks sheepish, according as the message received is
sympathetic or caustic. He is joined by two other
youths of the party, and they guffaw and punch one
another in the ribs and whisper more or less pro-

foundly original inanities into the hard worked old arch which a forbearing Providence keeps from falling down and crushing them. This whispering has been going on for generations—aye, for ages. In the graveyard is the dust of men and women who made love there at the doorway, as these youngsters are now doing; and the young people of the future will do the same no doubt.

The Whispering Arch is not as old as the church. It dates from the fourteenth or fifteenth century. The church was repaired or rebuilt by Tomaltach McDermott, Chieftain of Moylurg, some time about 1320 or 1330. Hence the church is called Tempull McDermott. It was originally built in A.D. 909 by Flann, King of Ireland, and by Colman, Abbot of Clonmacnoise.

It was to commemorate the building of the church, and also to mark the grave of King Flann that the great cross was erected. This is Petrie's opinion, an opinion shared by Bishop Healy and also by Dean Monahan, the learned author of the "Records of Clonmacnoise." The Great Cross of Clonmacnoise is hewn from the solid limestone in the Celtic style of panelled statues and interlaced tracery.

On every "pattern" day it is the centre of a crowd of visitors. Not only do many of the pilgrims pray around it, but many of the men try to span its shaft with their arms. Any one who is able to meet the tips of his fingers around the shaft is believed to have certain powers conferred upon him by virtue of which he is enabled to save human life in certain given circumstances. Hence it is that so many men of all classes and ages are anxious to span the cross;

and hence it is also that their friends are anxious
for them to succeed.   There goes a young husband
to span it, but the tips of his fingers are still a good
half inch apart.   There are two sturdy pilgrims
praying at the base of the cross and to them the
wife appeals: "Give him a hand to span it, and
God bless you," she says.   They are on their feet in
a twinkling of your eye, and one of them climbs up
on the base of the cross in front, and the other climbs
up behind.   The one in front catches the husband's
fingers and pulls the man's arms further round the
shaft.   The one behind shoves the candidate between
the shoulders and crushes his breast.   Thus aided
and stretched and tortured, the young husband's
fingers meet around the shaft, and with arms
benumbed and a bruised and aching breastbone, he
thanks the pilgrims and returns to his wife, who is
smiling with pride and happiness.   Nothing can
terrify her now.   Her life is safe.   Her husband
has spanned the big cross of the Seven Churches!
She says "God bless you" again to the obliging
pilgrims, but they have resumed their prayers, and
another man is already throwing his arms around the
sculptured panels of the Cros na Scraeptra, as the
cross is sometimes called.

He is a low sized man—this new competitor for
the honour—and he would need two or three inches
more on each arm before he could even hope for
success.   But he is so desperately in earnest, and
so persevering, and his inability to span the shaft
so manifest that the crowd laughs heartily.   He
strains and stretches and gets red in the face, and
asks for help; and this provokes more laughter.   If

he is to span that shaft he will have to be pulled to
pieces first and made into a rope. At length he
gives in, and very crestfallen descends to earth
again, quivering from muscular exertion and excitement and bathed in perspiration.

Another takes his place, a young giant, lean of
chest and long of arm. Without aid from anyone
and without making any extraordinary effort he
meets his hands round the shaft and the crowd
applauds. Then there is a long chorus of inquiries.

Whence this man? Who is he that has spanned
the cross? Where does he live? He is a man of
mark now. Some Winter's night, months hence, he
may be called out of his warm bed and requested
for God and Mary's sake to go off miles and miles,
through the frost and bitter wind, in order to span
a sufferer who is in danger of death. It is to find
out his name and address that so many people are
enquiring about him now; and he, the hero of the
hour, blushes and smiles modestly as he retires;
for he is a mere youth and a stranger here,
and it is only now that he has been told all that
spanning the Cros na Scraeptra involves. Others
take his place on the stone plinth, and the spanning
trials go on and on as they have done on every
" pattern day " for centuries.

In the middle of the grounds is the little oratory
of St. Ciaran—the Eclais Beg. In the long ago it
was, as it is now, the " centre of the holiness of Clonmacnoise." But it is not the oratory that Ciaran
built. The original structure must have been of
wood or wattle and clay. But the present ruin
occupies the exact site of the cell of St. Ciaran.

The saint's grave is supposed to be beside it. Other saints are buried within. The general voice of local tradition says that St. Ciaran's grave is outside the walls of the Eclais Beg—on the side near the Shannon. But many people are uncertain about this point.

Do you see these men and women who are scooping up handfuls of clay from under the stones? They are going to take that clay home with them— and they are going to take it with a simple unshaken and unshakable faith which surprises what people call philosophy in this sceptical age. What are they going to do with it? Ask them. To banish red worms that eat the oats. To sprinkle on grass land that has been pested by disease. To scatter on the floors of houses where sickness abides. There are scores of people here who will tell you of rescued crops and resweetened pastures and banished infection due to this miracle working clay gathered by the graveside of St. Ciaran.

And at the saint's well beside the Shannonbridge road, down the fields yonder, you will find people taking away bottles of water to cure aches and pains. You will find others drinking, for a like purpose, from St. Finian's well, beside the Shannon, as you go to the old nunnery.

On the western boundary of the churchyard is Tempull Finian, which was built probably in the ninth century and dedicated to St. Finian, the great prelate of Clonard. The chancel arch of this church is considered to be one of the finest specimens extant of Celtic Romanesque. There is a round tower attached to this church which is complete and perfect. It is a small tower, being only fifty-six feet high.

Tempull Connor was founded by Cathal, son of Conchobar. But it does not seem likely that King Rodrick was buried in this church. His grave, according to the antiquarians and local tradition, is beside the high altar of the great church of Tempull McDermott. Some of the MacCoughlans, chief of Delvin Ara, are buried in the same place, I think.

Near the Eclais Beg is Tempull Kelly, built by Connor O'Kelly, one of the Chiefs of Hy-Many. On the other side of the great church is Tempull Righ—the King's church, built by the southern branch of the Hy-Niall in memory of King Diarmuid. Tempull Hurpan, in front of which stands the smaller cross, stands to the right of Tempull McDermott. O'Rourke's round tower stands at the north-western corner of the cemetery. The " Registry of Clonmacnoise " says it was built by Fergal O'Rourke of Brefney, King of Connacht, toward the middle of the tenth century. O'Rourke, we are told, built this tower, and kept the churches of Clonmacnoise in repair during his life, for his soul's sake, and as the price of his family sepulchre in the holy ground of Ciaran. But is this account of the building correct? It may well be doubted.

These towers seem to have nothing in common with the other pieces of masonry. The very materials are different. The tower, which stands on the corner of the ruined church of St. Finian, was certainly not built at the same time as the church. Its side was grooved in a slanting direction to admit the roof of the building.

When Ireland has schooled herself to go back to the honouring of mere Irish saints the name of Ciaran will stand out as one of the greatest in the history of the Church. In Irish hagiology he is usually called Ciaran Mac-in-Tsair—the son of the carpenter—and sometimes Ciaran the younger, to distinguish him from St. Ciaran, of Saigher, the patron of Ossory. His father, although a tradesman, was of noble lineage. They claim his birthplace for Roscommon, and also for Westmeath. He was baptised in A.D. 512, doubtless the year of his birth. He received his education at Clonard, and there made the acquaintance of the holy men who were afterwards known as the Twelve Apostles of Erin. St. Finian was his master.

When he left Clonard he went to Aran, where he worked with St. Euda. Then he was on Scattery Island in the Lower Shannon for a time. From there he went to Hare Island, in Lough Ree, where he founded an oratory, the ruins of which are still to be seen. He also founded an oratory at Athlone. From Hare Island he went further down the Shannon and founded another oratory; but the land around it was too fertile for a man who had made a vow of holy poverty, and so he went on to Ard Tipratt—the Hill or Height of the Spring, afterward called Clonmacnoise.

The word Clonmacnoise, according to John O'Mahony's note on page 94 of his translation of Keating, comes from Cluain-MacNois, signifying "the retreat of the sons of the noble," either from the great numbers of the sons of the Irish nobility who resorted to its college for education, or from many of the Irish princes having burial places in its cemetery. Joyce says it means "the meadow of the Son of Nos." The Four Masters call it by this same name practically. St. Ciaran took only four months to build his Eclais Beg. The following legend regarding the founding of Clonmacnoise is told in the "Chronicon Scotrum," and also in the "Leabhar Buidhe Lecain."

When Ciaran was planting the first post to mark out the ground at Clonmacnoise, Diarmuid MacCearbhaill, a young prince who was a fugitive in the district, helped the Saint with his own hands to drive the pole into the ground. "Though your companions to-day are few," said Ciaran, "to-morrow thou shalt be High King of Erin." One of Diarmuid's companions was Maelmor, his foster brother, and, hearing the prophecy, this man went and slew King Tauthal Maelgarbh, great grandson of Niall the Great, who had set a price on Diarmuid's head. The men from Tara and Meath then sought out Diarmuid, who was the true heir to the Ardrighship, and proclaimed him High King of Erin. On the Great Cross in front of Tempull McDermott the saint and the King are represented on one of the sculptured panels with their hands on a pole in commemoration of the founding of Clonmacnoise.

Diarmuid ascended the throne of Tara in A.D. 544. It was during his reign that Tara was cursed by St. Ruadhan of Lorrha. Soon after the curse was pronounced Tara was deserted.*

St. Ciaran lived only four months after founding his monastery. He died at the sacred age of thirty-

---

* One of the deepest students of Irish history in our day wrote to me as follows: "I do not believe a word about the cursing of Tara. It is an invention of the century."

three in his Eclais Beg, and near the very spot where his ashes are said to rest. His bosom friend, St. Kevin, of Glendalough, was with him to the end. His death was a tremendous loss to Ireland. Had he lived, the influence which he exercised in the councils of the Church would have kept the other Bishops of Ireland from making war upon Tara. Thus, King Diarmuid would have been free to en¬ force the laws, to quell the wild insubordination of the petty kings, and to lay securely and broadly the foundations of the State. Had this been done the Norsemen would have found Ireland a strong and united nation. And as for the Anglo-Normans, they would never have dreamt of attacking a people whose institutions of civil government had been sufficiently developed to place the combined and ordered force of the nation at the service of the nation's need.

Here is the ruin known as " Devorgilla's Nunnery." She was the wife of Tiernan O'Rourke, of Breffney, who eloped with MacMorrough. She repented of her sin and separated from her paramour after two years, as we have seen in another chapter, to spend the rest of her life doing good works. This is one of the convents she built. The doorway of the chapel is still beautiful. It was repaired some years ago. It is of the flat-arched Norman school, which would in time have developed into a style distinctly Irish. Even as it is there is a distinctiveness about it which is worthy of close study. It marks undoubtedly the beginning of a school of architectural design which had many splendid possibilities.

Have you noticed how Clonmacnoise brackets two Irish names fraught with tragic significance—Diarmuid and Devorgilla? Diarmuid lived centuries before Devorgilla, and was of a character quite different to that of the faithless wife of Drumahaire But connected with each of their names, although for widely different reasons, there is a chapter of history crowded with the ruin of Ireland.

At the Nunnery ruins there is laughter and some quiet match-making. Under the twelfth century arches there are flirtations going on, for it is now late in the afternoon. At 4 o'clock this morning, when the sky was barely grey over the Shannon, pilgrims crept under those very arches on bare knees. Peradventure some of those same pilgrims are here now on another quest. It is quite possible. There is all that and something more in this Irish nature of ours.

Beside the ancient causeway which leads from the Nunnery to the church there are many luncheon and tea parties; and they are all gay. Chickens, ducks, sandwiches, bread and butter, and bottled stout are in great plenty, and in great demand. And you hear the popping of lemonade and soda water corks, and the rattle of teacups, and the laughter which rises above the animated talk.

Here is a man with a cornet, which he can play splendidly. Listen! there goes the "Coulin," played exquisitely. He is a character is this strolling musician, and he is utterly forgetful of the dancers who pound the green sward with the weight of solid flesh and bone and shoe leather, manufactured, let us hope, in Ireland.

Here are two pairs of lovers seated on a mossy bank beside the silent river, and it is evident that Cupid has his hands full They are sitting on ground over which hundreds of people are coming and going, but they have eyes and ears only for each other. The folk who have kindness in their hearts for everything that is human, regard them with a passing smile of comprehension and tolerant benevolence But the majority of the pilgrims look upon them with calm amusement. No one wonders at them. No one questions their right to be there. No one is shocked or scandalised. One buxom matron with the red petticoat and dark cape and snow-white cap of the trans-Shannon women nods her head approvingly at them and gives them a friendly word in Irish, which a man beside me translated as: " Bless you, my children four." And let us say amen to that by all means, and hope that they may live happy forever after. See in each idyll around us, my brothers, the triumph of life and love over death. In the graveyard—even over the bones of the dead—even where death may lay claim to a victory—Love laughs and takes his own—takes it smilingly, and joyously holds out his hands to the future—proudly conscious that nothing avails against his sway over the continuity of life.

There are tents beside the narrow road leading from the cemetery to the highway. There are apple carts, ginger bread carts, shooting galleries, and other enterprises, sporting and commercial. We make our way through them and gain the open fields beside the Shannon. The day has flown quickly, and the feast is over now. The rest is soon told.

A snack of cold fowl, a smoke, a pleasant chat in the shadow of the old castle built by John de Gray at some distance from the churches. A stroll back to the cars. A glorious drive along the hill rests in the sunset splendour. Then the fading of the shadows and the brightening of the moon and the cool sweetness of the twilight. Miles of level road through meadows and under autumn woods and past fields where the yellow corn drank the falling dew. Through the villages where the windows flashed bravely, and where the kitchen fires gleamed over the neat half-doors. Bowling home with the hoof strokes ringing on the gravel, and the wheels flinging back the moonbeams. Oh, it was grand—grand—grand!

CHAPTER XXIII.

L'ENVOI.

The Winter—A Farewell Ride over Frozen Roads--
The Silences of Erin—The Mountain Sheep—
Sliding—An affair of a Lasso—Coursing—
" Come Back Again."

It was mid-winter, and as it had been freezing
for a day or two the land was frost-bound. The
roads were hard. The sunshine was inviting. The
air was bracing. Several weeks spent indoors, hard
at work, had created a longing for the open country
again. And so it came to pass that I went forth
for a farewell ride.

Northward into Westmeath again to bid good-bye
to friends, and also for the keen pleasure of racing
through the crisp wind. There was frost everywhere, and it flashed ever so bravely. Everything
flashed. The sunshine danced on frost crystals on
grass and thorn, and the clear air was ablaze with
winter radiance. There was ice on the road, on the
water under the hawthorns by the wayside, on the
pools in the fields, on bawn and haggard, on bog
and pasture—white and chippy, where it lay on a
spring ooze which crossed the road in zig-zags down
a slope; blue black where it lay on deep water; pearl
grey where the Winter flood had shrunk from

beneath it; thin and clear as the finest glass where it crusted a running stream; tinted with brown or red where it hung from eves or branches—flashing all night long and all day long, crunching under passing wheels, drumming faintly under cautious footsteps, and hoof strokes, mirroring the cold beauty of earth and sky, multiplying the moon by ten thousand, duplicating all the constellations over and over until each star in the heavens had myriads of twin brothers on the world below.

And the silence! The silence which falls amidst an Irish Winter is a poem in itself. The voice travels far through the elastic atmosphere and is mellowed by the distance. The sounds which come from the farmyards are no longer smothered by the foliage of hedgerow or woodland. They travel on the thin clear air between the bare branches and make long excursions in quest of echoes. But now and then a silver silence will fall which is ravishing in its perfection. It is not like the silence of Autumn. It does not breathe. It is frozen stillness. Interstellar space seems to be drawing you toward it, so pulseless is the dead cold quiet around. But suddenly the calm is shivered into vibrating atoms by a rooster crowing to keep his throat in practice. He is a mile off. A blackbird flies across a meadow near you, laughing all the way. The cries of half a dozen urchins sliding on the pond near the forge, or the schoolhouse peal across the valley. And a robin begins to sing from the ivy. The old world has shaken off its lethargy and is awake once more.

There were guns in the woods below Ferbane, and the frightened pheasants were on the wing

The grouse were noisy on the bog lands beyond Moate. The rabbits stirred in the bracken near the roadside in the moors of Longford. The mountain sheep were on the march across the uplands of Ardagh, drifting westward, in their peculiar way, towards the heathery altitudes of Iar Connacht. Mountain sheep in the Midlands? Yes, thousands of them. They have made some history, too, and history not devoid of humour. There was a time, and it lasted until recent years, when the only sheep in the Midlands were crosses of Cheviots or Roscommons or Lincolns. But these breeds ceased to thrive, and no amount of new blood sufficed to strengthen their hold upon the market. There was something in the land, or in the grasses, which proved fatal to them. Then an experiment was made with the mountain sheep of Connacht, and it proved to be a success. It also proved to be a fertile source of wonder, of occupation, and of fury to many people in the district.

The new sheep came into the green pastures east of the Shannon with their horny heads in the air— defiant of boundary fences and drains, contemptuous of walls, scornful of shady valleys and tender grasses. A man near my native place put a batch of them into a pleasant field near the woods of Bal Ivor They left it in disgust, and established themselves in a cornfield in the next parish. A bill for damages was presented in due course, and had to be paid according to law. The sheep were brought back prisoners, and a boy was put to mind them. He attended conscientiously to his duty, and it reduced his weight by several pounds per day, for he was constantly on the trot. His flock took morning exercise by scampering in Indian file along the top of a high wall near their pasture. When he went home to his first meal they struck camp and drifted into the middle of the Bog of Allan, and from that they marched in the direction of Ferbane, across ancient Delvinara, browsing leisurely in cabbage gardens and turnip fields, until they came to the Grand Canal. They were brought back again, and a closer watch was kept on them, but they were still restless. On the Sunday morning following, the weary shepherd limped into headquarters and reported a new escapade.

"Some of them is on top of our house," he said tearfully, "and some of them is on the top of me uncle's barn, and one of them is knockin' down the Widow Mack's turf-clamp, an'—an'—bad luck from them, me heart is broke with them."

It took several months to reconcile them to their new surroundings, and a whole year to reconcile their owner to the privilege of owning them. He would have sold them at a discount only he could get no one to buy them. But when the lambing time came they gave a fine return. Nearly every one of them had twins, and the lambs fattened quickly, and were sold at a good price. This encouraged others to invest in the breed, and next spring several people went to the fair of Clifden and made purchases.

Then the land groaned under the depredations of the strangers. They floated over the north of Leinster in predatory batches of ten and twenty and thirty, ravaging kitchen gardens, and laying bare every cabbage-stalk that grew in their line of march, which was as uncertain as the progress of a thunderstorm. A few of them would encamp near a garden for a week, and move on only when the last onion or cabbage head or leaf of rhubarb had, in spite of every effort of the hapless growers, disappeared down their throats. Then they would settle down near the garden of the next house and proceed to clean it out.

There was no hurry in their movements. They marched with a deliberation and with a sordid and felonious purpose which filled the country with dismay. Their general direction was westward— concentrating on the fords of the Shannon. They were seeking the West, sad at heart for the high places of Connacht, homesick and dejected, but ever voracious and predatory. They occasionally amused themselves by jumping to and fro over a wall or across a river, and even climbed on to the roof of a parish chapel in the barony of Garrycastle.

But this intermittent sportiveness only increased the sorrow and the longing which drove them ever westward. They yearned for the rugged crests and the strong grass, and the heather and the windy brightness of their native mountains. But they were too closely pursued to escape.

Only a few of them succeeded in crossing into Connacht. The others were captured and driven back to their new pastures, where their progeny still remains. Time has brought them some consolation. They no longer try to break away out of Leinster, and they have adapted themselves fairly well to the altered circumstance of existence. But in the lambing time, nature asserts itself again, and the ewes will go off into the woods or the bogs so as to have their offspring all to themselves. The frost, too, makes them restless at times, and they march over the frozen hills until the Shannon or their pursuing owners stop them. When I reached Ardagh I met a man who asked me for information regarding horny sheep. He gave me their number and colour, and I sent him after them rejoicing.

I dined at a snug fireside in a valley under Edgeworthstown, then on to Carrickedmond, to have an hour's instructive chat with the learned Dean Monahan, at that time the Parish Priest, who is the historian of his diocese. Next I bore back into Westmeath, halting occasionally to join the lads who were sliding. I slided in twenty-five parishes, in three counties. Skating is all right, and I say nothing against it I was a skater once myself But sliding is a dearer, gladder memory, and it brought back some of the fun of other days.

Near Mullingar I had another pleasant reminiscence. It was a case of lassoing a dog. The dog had escaped from durance, and a boy was after him with a rope to bring him back to discipline. I halted and gave the boy my assistance. The dog was conscience-stricken and half inclined to obey the repeated calls of " Here Shep—come here ! " But he kept out of range. The boy had a nine-inch noose on the rope to slip over the dog's neck when the delinquent might see fit to offer his head in meek submission to the bonds. I took the rope, made a four foot loop, and, by a lucky throw, secured the culprit. Then I handed the rope-end to the boy.

ınd rode off into the future. He gazed at me in silent wonder. He was too much amazed to say anything or to offer any sympathy to the dog. And the dog wanted a few kindly words to soothe him, for he was howling vigorously in wrath and terror and scattering hair upon the wind and cutting the most painful and intricate capers at the end of the rope. A man with a grievance depicted on his face hailed me from his frozen bawn as I got under way and asked me what the something or other, which is of no special account now, had I done to the dog.

"It is a professional secret," I replied, "and I wouldn't tell you for the whole world."

He shouted something after me which I did not hear, and even had I heard it I should probably desire to hide it in forgetfulness. He was in no mood for word-choosing. He had evidently vested interests in the boy, the rope, and the dog, and was excited about the rights of property.

* * * * * * * * *

The weather broke, and with the thaw came a certain coursing match. The basis of the sport was the boxed hare, and I was disgusted. I forget how many hares were sent out to the slaughter, but they were gobbled up after a few turns at short range— all but one, and he was a marvel. Boxed hares are a sorry substitute for the swift ones of the moors that are free from the stiffening imprisonment of a wooden crate. But this hare was an exception. He led the dogs for nearly a mile down the callows on which the coursing match was held—led them by twenty yards at least—then crossed the river at a bound, took to the ploughed fields on the opposite slope, came back again, took a wide turn around the course, climbed the hill where the spectators were massed and ran through them, men, women and children cheering him to the echo. The two hounds were close to him. One, a big brindled dog, would lay his long snout on the hare's quarter, but had no strength to do more. The other was a few feet behind running his heart out. The hare was just able to keep ahead. Its ears were laid on its neck, the eyes were wide open, with the hunted, backward look in them of the wild thing, no matter what it may be, that is being chased for its life. And yet it looked droll. It seemed to snigger as it swayed from side to side out of the very teeth of the panting greyhound. Its draggled fur was close to the skin, and the long legs on that account appeared longer than ever. A prize-winning, athletic, experienced hare, it appeared to be, racing with head as well as feet—a cool, desperate, persevering character that would run to the last inch, the last breath, and die squealing. Was there no one there to throw a stone or stick at it? you might ask, if you did not know more or less what might happen in case there was foul play shown. Whoever threw anything at that hare would have thereby endangered his personal safety to no slight extent. A fair average punishment for him would have been a broken head, torn clothes and a dirty name that would have stuck to him for the next ten years.

And the hare was worthy of being protected by people who, although few of them may have been aware of it, inherited the traditions of epic sport. It led the way to a formidable hawthorn quick under which ran a wide dyke. It cleared the dyke at a bound, scrambled through the quick and went clean away. The dogs were too tired to follow it. The last card was that jump, and it had won. The crowds cheered again and again. Some men slapped each other on the back. Every one seemed delighted that the hare got away, except one man with a red face, who owned one of the dogs. When the people cheered he took a flask from the breast pocket and poured some brandy into the hound, and also into himself.

There were bookmakers yelling bets against the next event, but I withdrew out of earshot of their clamour. I was thinking of a summer morning's coursing in the long ago. I am thinking of it now, too. It is early, so early that not a bird but the lark is astir. The sweet dew is falling in showers around your ankles at every stride, and pink drifts of the daisy petals are swimming on your insteps.

" After him, ' Brian ! ' Catch him, ' Galway ! ' "

Twenty voices—all lusty with the strength of youth—shout to the hounds to encourage them as they fly after the hare that has been roused from a tuft of bracken. A fine, graceful hare it is, too, and as supple and swift as you can find in the length and breadth of Offaly.

How soft and glossy the fur is on him as he stiffens his neck and flings himself over the field with the speed of the wind! The fur is as white as snow under the tail, shading off into russet brown between the shoulder blades, and as clean as if he had spent hours and hours upon his toilet. It will be muddy and soaked enough presently. The hounds are close to him now, and ho! for the breed of the Ballyboys! "Galway" wins the first point. The chase is over wide fields, through gaps in stone walls, round patches of whin and bracken, under towering ash trees, past the blackthorn brakes where the sloes are beginning to ripen, down the gravel of the river bank, splashing through the stream and into the sedge beyond, out of the moor and out to the edge of the purple heather of the bog! "Brian" takes his turn now—a lead-up or a go-bye or a half moon or a wrench. I forget exactly what. Then "Galway" shoots ahead and evens the score. "Good dog, 'Brian!'" "More power to you, 'Galway!'" "That's me darlint, 'Brineen!'" Stick to him, 'Galway!'"

Oh! a grand, grand chase! out of the grey dimness through the silvery half-light, into the gold of the dawn, into the glory of the day! Dead at last in a moreland hollow, fringed on one side by clustering ferns, and on the other by a froughan bank— dead after a run that has tried the mettle of the two best dogs in the barony! And which won? That is the point we cannot decide. We puzzle over it and wrangle about it as we go home, but we cannot come to an agreement. It is still an open question, after all the years. It has been discussed in two hemispheres, and in four different countries by those who took part in it, and the only thing ever settled upon was that they all wished it could be run over again.

Over again? Ah if it could be done! But who

could bring back the men from over the seas, or their youth, or all the fresh sweet joy in life that swells in the hearts of boys?

*   •   *   *   *   *   *   *   *

Over the sodden roads, homewards from the last ride of a seven months' holiday that can never die in my memory. The bare branches werc dripping and the dead leaves were slippery, and the patches of broken stone were bristling with trouble for long-suffering tyres. The white mists were rising off the valleys. The whistle of the curlew came down the chilly wind. The call of the wild geese came over the hills. It was very lonely, yet there was sadness unutterable in the thought that it was soon to be left behind.

"Good-bye, good-bye, and come back again— Come back again!" Each landmark that rose to view seemed to have some kind of message like that. From every one of them some pleasant memory was appealing— calling, calling.

"Come back again—Come back to us, scmetime— won't you?" Oh the heart-cry of the Gael! It is heard so often in Eirinn that the very echoes of the land have learned it.

THE END.

INDEX

Page

Abbeyshrule 81, 293
Adare 255
Afforestation 40, 205
Aghaboe 341
Agriculture, Dept. of 180
Aguila, Don John del 365
Aherlow 393
Aileach, Grianan of 147
Ainmere, Prince of Aileach ...140
Allen, Hill of 177
"Annals of the Four Masters"
                                              159
Annally 417, 422
Anner, The 350
Aodh Guaire 7
Ardagh 197, 445
Ard-na-hEiraun 8
Ard Feis at Tara, Keating's
  Description of 105
Ardoyne, Passionist Fathers
  at 130
Arrough, Lough 21
Athleague 55
Athlone 18, 407
  ,,   The Fight at the Bridge 408
Auburn 290, 310

Ballacurra 415
Ballaghboy 20, 162
Ballinafad 21
Ballinahoun 406
Balliuamuck 23
Ballingarry 348
Ballivor 85
Ballybrit 17
Ballylea 5
Ballymahon 415, 421
Ballymore 320, 416
  ,,   Battle at 416
Ballymulvey 291

Page

Ballyshannon 168
Ballysodare 25
Banagher 425
Banba 47
"Bard of Thomond," The 228
Bargy, Co. Wexford 260
Baskin Hill 320
Belfast 117
Bellaghy Ford 394
Belvidere, Lord 177
Belleek 171
Benbulfin 21, 41
Bernard, Dr. 148
Birr 17, 207
  to Portumna Railway 6
Blake, Mary E. 3
Bog of Allen 401
"Book of Durrow" 141
"Book of Dimma" 8
"Book of Kells" 141
Borrisokane 217
Boyle 29
Bray 321, 336
Breffney 33
Brendan, St. 341
Brian Boru 38, 217, 226
Brigid, St. 195, 416, 418
Brosna River 5
Buenos Aires 184, 211
Bullockdom 90
Butler, Miss Mary 273
Burke, Edmund 313

Cademstown to Birr road 213
Caimin (of Iniscaltra) 222
Canice, St. 347
Carbery, Ethna 156, 353
Cashel, The Rock of 390
Casey, "Leo" 292, 300, 316
"Castlebar, Races of" 23

Page

Castleconnell 232
Cattle Drovers, and their
  ways 82
Cattle in Kildare 179, 181
Cathleen-ni-Houlihan 151
Church and State 38, 108, 110
Ciarnaid 104
Ciaran, St. 109, 425
Ciaran, St., of Saigher 431
Clara and Banagher Railway ...7
Clan Coleman 79
Cloghan 405
Clonard 37, 432
Clonaslee 209, 213
Clonenagh 341
Clonmel 220
Clonmacnoise 109, 425
Clontarf, Battle of 38, 230
Collooney 22
     „   Battle of 23
Columba of Ferry Glass 222
Columcille, St. 99, 134, 140
     „   Prophecies of 141
Concubar 100, 433
Congested Districts Board 54
Connacht Plains, The 45
Conn of the Hundred Battles 47
Cork 359
Cormac Mac Art 103, 193, 390
Cosby, Francis 343
Coursing Match, A 446
Cove of Cork, The 381
Covered Car, The 368
Creamery System 220
Croghan Hill 74, 210
Cromwell 364, 390
Cronan, St. 8
Cruachain 19, 26, 47
Cruachain Ruadh 416
Cuchulain 232
Cull-Dreemimhne 142
Curlew Mountains 20
Curnan, Prince of Connacht...142
Curragh, The 189

Dairy Farming 219
Dalkey 323
Dallan Forgail 145
Daly, Bowes 405

Page

Dargle, The 323
Davis, Thomas 355, 357, 400
Dathi, King 47
   „   Grave of 53
Deforestation 204
De Boisscleau 214
De Ginkell 240, 313, 408
De Lacy, Hugh 418
Depopulation, Evils of 49
Derry 133
Devorgilla 36, 427, 437
Diarmuid, King 144, 436
"Deserted Village, The" 311
Diarmuid and Grania 145
Dimma, Book of 8
Domnal Mor 250
Donegal 74, 158
Donore 78
Drumahaire 28, 35, 39
Drumceat, Convention of..142, 145
Drumcullen Monastery......214, 341
Douglas, General 407
Dublin 126, 372
   „   Contrasted with Belfast
                                 126
   „   Bay 2
   „   to the Shannon, Route 174
Duff, General 194
Duffy, Gavan, quoted 343
Dunamase 43, 342
Dunboy 75, 367
Dungannon 153
Dun-na-Sciath 79
Dunraven, Lord 255
Durrow 346
Durrow, Book of 141
Dwyer, Michael 328

Eccl. and Civil Power 109
Education System 276
Eirie 47
Elphin 46
Elizabeth, Charlotte 133
Ely O'Carroll 17, 175
Eunel, Loch 77, 78
Enniskerry 328
Enniskillen 172, 174
Enniscorthy 263

Page

Enniscorthy in '98 265
     „   House of Missions 272
Eocaidh O'Floinn 98
Eri, and Aerghin 418
Euda, St. 434

Farmer, The Irish 182
Fergil the Geometer 342
Fergus Mac Erca 101
Fermoy 399
     „   St. Colman's College 399
Ferns 260
Ferry Carrick 279
Finbar, St. 361
Firian, St. 37, 143, 222, 432
Finn and the Fianna 106, 192
Finnan's, St., Oratory 231
Firbolgs, The 99
Fintan, St. 341
Flann, King of Ireland 429
Flood 154
Flood, W. H. Grattan 273
Fodhla 47
Foley's Statue of Fr. Mathew 373
     „   „   O'Connell 374
Folliat Estate, The 21
Forigny 420
Forth, Barony of 260
Frossass, The 155

Gaelic League, The ...24, 208, 273,
                              275, 399
Galtees, The 393
Galway 24
Galtymore 393
     „   View from 397
Ganly, William 423
Garryowen 254
Gavra Aichill, Battle of 193
Geashill to Croghan Hill 207
Gibbet Rath 194
Glencree, Vale of 330
Glendalough 334
Glendoo 330
Golden Vale, The 257, 390
Goldsmith 312, 316
Goldsmith's County, In 309
     Gougane Barra 363

Page

"Gods and Fighting Men" ...337
Gorey 295
Grace, Richard 407
Granard 423
Grania ....'06
Grattan 154
Gregory, Lady 307
Griffin, Gerald 255
Gulban, Conall 161
Gurteen 290, 300

Haymaking 15
Healy, Archbishop 143, 147, 429
Holt, General 334
Horseleap 418
Howth 323
Humbert 23
Hyde, Dr. Douglas 273
Hy-Kinsellagh 260
Hynes, Father 24

Inchicore 176
Inishowen 147
Iniscaltra 222
Inny, The 129, 292, 305, 420
Iona 144, 146

"Jail Journal," The 357, 375
James II. 138, 245, 40
Jewish Pedlar, A 30

Kavanagh, Father 284, 287
Keating, Geoffrey 100, 160, 394
Kevin, St. 436
Keepers, The 8 217
"Kells, The Book of" 141
Kilbride, Pass of 82
Kickham 348
     „   The Country of...347
Kilcommedan Hill 216
Kilcormac 423
Kildare 195
Killaloe 221 225
Killiney Hill 325
Killininny 306
Kilmessan 91
Kincora 225
King, John 248

Page

Kinnity 214
Kinel Conaill ....
Kinel Fiacadh 75
Kippure Mountain 331
Knockallen 192, 307
Knockastia 74
Knocknacara 210
" Knocknagow " 348, 356
      „   The District of 347
Knocknarea 21, 25, 41
Knockshigowna 12
Kyan, Esmond 270

Lake, General ....
Landen 245
Lark, The 403
Laoghaire 96
Lauzun 240
Lee, Valley of the 359
Leitrim Hills 33
Leix 210
Lia Fail, The 93, 101
Liffey, Source of the 332
Limerick 216, 233
      „   Siege of 240
Loch Ennel 78
      „   Owel 78
Lough Arrough 21
      „   Bray 331
      „   Dan 334
      „   Derg 221
      „   Erne 33, 173
      „   Gill 26, 31
      „   Key 20
      „   Ree 18, 305
      „   Tay 334
      „   Swilly 149
Logue, Cardinal 85, 125
Longford 417, 421
Lorrha 7
Lugaidh Lamfada 418
Luggala 334

Maccaile's, St., Church 196
MacCathal, Donovan 226
MacCerbhaill, Diarmuid 7, 107, 435
MacGeoghegan, Abbe 12
      „   Country, The 74

Page

MacGeoghegan, Richard 361
      „   William 420
MacDermott, Tomaltach 429
MacErca, Fergus......................101
MacGillpatrick 346
MacGinley, P. T. 199
MacHale, Archbishop 56
MacHugh, Fiach 366
MacLaughlin Monsignor 78
MacManus, Seumas 155
MacMurrough, Dermod 36
MacSweeney, Padraic..............399
MacNessa, King Conor 418
Magach, Cead 418
Mahon, King of Munster 225
      „   Murder of 226
Malachy the Great 226, 230
Mallow 400
Mathew, Father   374
Meath, The Plain of 87
Meave, Queen 26
Meelick 212, 216
Mitchelstown 398
Moate 419
Molloy, Chieftain of Desmond 226
Monahan, Dean 177, 429, 445
Moore, Thomas 35, 260, 274, 377
Moore, Count 8, 387
Monasterevan 113, 199, 202
Motor Cyclist, The 183, 210, 338
Mountmellick 207
Mount Bellew............................55
      „   Franciscan College 55
Mountcharles 155
Mullaghmast 257, 343
Mount Melleray 9, 11
Moyvoughly 414
Mullagh 145
Mullinahone 348
Mullingar 174
Munchin, St. 251
Murphy, Family, The 260, 377
      „   Father John 266
      „   Father Michael 266
      „   Father P. 272

Naas 178
Nenagh 219

Page

Newbridge 178
   ,,   College 178

O'Brien, Smith 358
   ,,   of Thomond 148
O'Cavanagh, McMurrough 260
O'Clerys, The 159
O'Clery, Michael 420
O'Donnell, Duke of Tetuan ...162
   ,,   Red Hugh ...20, 153, 161
   ,,   Rory 162
O'Donnells, The 161
O'Donovan, John 101, 196
O'Faly 345
   ,,   Roads 213
O'Grady, Standish 43, 57
O'Hogan, Galloping............217, 240
Oilfinn, Danish Chief 12
Oireachtas, The 199
Oisin 193
O'Kelly, Conor 433
O'Leary, Father Peter 377, 400
O'Leary, John 354
Ollamh Fodhla 98
O'Moore, Owney 345
   ,,   Ruairi 208, 342, 345
O'Neill, Aodh 144
   ,,   Owen Roe 194, 345, 416
   ,,   Sir Phelim 345
   ,,   Shane 246
O'Rourke of Brefney 433
   ,,   Tiernan 36
O'Rourke's Table 42
O'Rourke, The 35
Ossory, Through 345
O'Sullivan, Beare 215, 367, 394
   ,,   Donal 216
   ,,   Michael 273
Owel, Loch 78

Paddy's Market, Cork 378
Pampas, The 189
Patrick Street 85, 96, 150, 418
Patrick Street ...85, 96, 150, 195, 418
Plunkett, Sir Horace 272
Portarlington 113, 208
Portroe 221
Protection of Irish Industries 220

Page

Protestant Leaders of
    Nationalism 124
Prout, Father 377
Ptolemy 150

Queenstown 382

Raharney 84
Rain, The Irish 80
Rathcabban 5
Rathcoole 176
Railways in Ireland 115
Ranch District, A 45
Rath Croghan 47
Redwood 216
Regatta, A Shannon 60
Rellig-na-Riogh 47
Rochfortbridge 74, 76
Rochfort Family, The 77
Rooney, Wm., quoted 289
" Rory of the Hill " 351
Roscrea, Battle of 12
   ,,   Monastery of 8
Round Towers, The 264
Roscommon 46
Rosenallis 209, 213
Ruadhan, St. 109, 435
   ,,   Abbey of 7

Saigher 341
" Sally Cavanagh " 358
Sallygap 332
Santa Rosa de Lima 196
Sarsfield 217, 240, 407
Scalp, The 327
Scenery of Ireland 258
Shandon Church 377
Shane the Proud 246
Shanganagh, Vale of 325
Shannon, The 18, 221, 232, 432
Sheep, Connacht 442
Silvermines 217
Sinn Fein 206
Sinn Fein Movement, The 278
Sinnot, Thomas 267
Slaney, The 259, 275, 278
Sliabh Cualann 336

	Page
Slieveanierin	21
Slieve Bann	45
Slieve Blooms, The	115, 209, 216
Slievenamon	348
Sligo	23
„ Route to from Dublin	18
Spaniards at Kinsale, The	365
Spiddal Church	249
Stad, An, Dublin	176
Stephens, James	127
St. Ruth	216
Strongbow	38
"Story of Ireland, The"	357
Streamstown	74
Sugar Loaf, The	330

	Page
Tang	299
Tara	7, 91, 96
„ Croppies' Grave, The	93, 97
„ Cursing of, The	107
„ Grianan-na-n-inghen	105
„ Lia Fail, The	93, 101
„ Relta-na-o-filedh	105
„ Teach Miodhchuarta	103
„ When St. Patrick Came	111
Feeling	23
Tinkers of Abbeyshrule, The	294
Tipperary	355, 384
„ Driver, A	384
Tone	23
Fordelbach	250
Tramp's Meal, A	13

	Page
Transit System, Irish	203
Trespassing Case, A	223
Trim	82, 85
„ to Tara	87
Tuatha de Danaans	47, 99, 349, 418
Tullamore	209
Turf-cutting in Westmeath	419
Turgesius	78
Tyrconnell	243, 245

	Page
Ui Briuin	33
Uisnach Hill	73, 415, 417
University, The Needed	178

	Page
Vereker, Col.	23
Virgilius, Bishop of Salzburg	342
Vinegar Hill	267
„ View from	268
Volunteers, The	154

	Page
Walker (of Derry)	136, 139
"Wars of the Gaedhill and the Gall"	226
Westmeath Lake District	78
Wexford	259, 281
„ Family Names	262
"Where there is Nothing"	296
Wicklow	333
William III	240, 407
"Willy Reilly"	21
Woods, Mr. James	417
Yeats, Mr. W. B.	296, 367